THE UNIVERSITY CRISIS READER

VOLUME II

Confrontation and Counterattack

Edited by

IMMANUEL WALLERSTEIN

and PAUL STARR

Published in the United States by Random House, Inc., New York, and simultaneously in Canada by Random House of Canada Limited, Toronto.

ISBN: 0–394–46263–7

Library of Congress Catalog Card Number: 71–140736

Manufactured in the United States of America by The Colonial Press Inc., Clinton, Mass.

2 3 4 5 6 7 8 9

FIRST EDITION

Acknowledgment is gratefully extended to the following for permission to reprint from copyrighted works:

Look Magazine: "Columbia: To Be a Revolutionary or Not To Be," by Jerry Avorn, May 13, 1969. Copyright © 1969 by Cowles Communications, Inc.

James Brown Associates, Inc.: "We Needed a Revolution," by Leo Litwak. Copyright © 1969 by Leo Litwak.

Ramparts: "Two, Three, Many Columbias," by Tom Hayden, June 15, 1968. Copyright © 1968 by Ramparts Magazine, Inc.

Peoples Press: "Columbia," by Mark Rudd. The article first appeared in the March, 1969 issue of *The Movement*.

Young Socialist Alliance: From "The Student Revolt: An Analysis," by Tony Thomas in the *Young Socialist* magazine, June, 1969. Copyright © 1969 by Young Socialist Alliance.

Doubleday & Company, Inc. From *Committed Spending,* edited by Robert Theobald. Copyright © 1968 by Doubleday & Company, Inc.

Daedalus, Journal of the American Academy of Arts and Sciences, Boston, Mass.: From a statement by Prof. Walter Metzger in "Dialogue on Governance of the Universities," Vol. 98. No. 4, Fall, 1969.

The New York Review of Books: An exchange between Marshall Windmiller and John Gerassi. Copyright © 1968 by The New York Review.

Random House, Inc. From *Crisis at Columbia: Cox Commission Report.* Copyright © 1968 by Random House, Inc.

The New York Times: From articles by Kenneth Keniston, Tom Wicker, Robert Paul Wolff, John R. Searle and Milton Konvitz. Copyright © 1968, 1969 by the New York Times Company.

Peninsula Observer: "Behind the Free University Crisis," by Jo Anne Wallace. The *Peninsula Observer* existed from June 1967 to September 1969, Palo Alto, California. All rights reserved. This statement does not necessarily represent the position of the current membership of Students for a Democratic Society.

Columbia Daily Spectator: For the editorial "The University Politicized" and "Orwell! Thou Shoulds't be Living at this Hour," by Allan Silver. Copyright © 1969 by the Columbia Daily Spectator, Inc.

Educational Record: Excerpts from "The Trojan Horse in American Higher Education," by Sidney Hook. Copyright © 1969 by Sidney Hook.

Dedicated to the memory of C. Wright Mills

Acknowledgments

This book originated out of our involvement in the intellectual debates at Columbia and our awareness of the vast flow of interesting documents that emerged from those debates. We could not, however, have put together this book had not many persons throughout the United States made available to us their own collections of material and in some instances assisted us in tracking down elusive documents.

We collected so much material that we could only use a fraction of it and some very interesting cases had to be omitted altogether. We apologize both to those who helped acquire the unused material and to the readers who will not see it. We can only say that the university crisis has surely been a prodigiously verbal one.

We offer especial thanks to Harry Alderman, James Bowen, D. Michael Collins, David Elesh, William H. Friedland, Nathan Glazer, Ruth Goldman, Richard M. Gummere, Jr., Richard Hill, Milton Himmelfarb, Serge Lang, Otto McClarrin, John Meyer, Chandler Morse, Rae A. Moses, Leslie Rubin, Edward E. Sampson, Howard Schless, Jay Schulman, Richard D. Schwartz, William Scott, Philip Shapiro, Richard Sklar, Richard Strassberg, Judith Wallerstein, Robert S. Wallerstein, David Wiley, M. Crawford Young, Aristide Zolberg.

Summary of Contents

VOLUME I: THE LIBERAL UNIVERSITY UNDER ATTACK

Prologue

I. The Educational Role of the University

II. The University as a Firm

III. The University, the Government, and the War

IV. Racism and the University

V. University Governance

VI. The Educational Process

VOLUME II: CONFRONTATION AND COUNTERATTACK

I. Procedures of Change: What Means Are Legitimate?

II. SDS and the Left: How to Build a Movement?

III. The Role of the Faculty

IV. The Establishment: How to Respond to Turmoil?

V. The Counterattack Against the Student Movement

Concluding Essays

Appendices

Contents

Introduction xix

PART I: PROCEDURES OF CHANGE: WHAT MEANS ARE LEGITIMATE? 1

Chapter 1. *The legitimacy of mass obstruction* 3

What we want, Columbia Students for a Democratic Society and Students' Afro-American Society 4

On violence, San Francisco State protesters 7

The allowable limits of civil disobedience, thirty-five Columbia law professors 9

Strike for the eight demands, Harvard strikers 10

Resolution on disruption, Stanford Board of Trustees 11

The necessity for discipline, Harvard Committee of Fifteen 12
More frightening than militant tactics, Benjamin R. Barber 16
To be a revolutionary or not to be, Jerry L. Avorn 17
Campus disorders, American Civil Liberties Union 21
Academic freedom and the first amendment, Staughton Lynd 24

Chapter 2. *The anatomy of confrontation politics* 30
A foolproof scenario for student revolts, John R. Searle 31
Not foolproof, but foolish, Jeff Lustig 41

Chapter 3. *Disruption as a tactic* 51
Work! study! get ahead! kill! the story of the indelicate dinner, ten members of University of Chicago SDS 52
A dialogue on classroom disruption, Columbia students 57
The university as a sanctuary of academic freedom, 800 Columbia faculty members 61
Whose academic freedom? Douglas Dowd 63

Chapter 4. *Politicizing the universities* 66

San Francisco State

Costs of the politicized college, John H. Bunzel 67
We needed a revolution, Leo Litwak 76

Columbia

The university politicized 81

Columbia Daily Spectator
Orwell, thou should'st be living at this hour! Allan Silver 85

PART II: SDS AND THE LEFT: HOW TO BUILD A MOVEMENT 93

Chapter 5. *Organizing students on campus* 97
Toward a student syndicalist movement, or university reform revisited, Carl Davidson 98
The praxis of student power: strategy and tactics, Carl Davidson 108

Chapter 6. *"From protest to resistance"* 125
Resistance and the movement, Todd Gitlin 127
Toward institutional resistance, Carl Davidson 129
Program for a spring offensive, SDS National Council 138
"Base-building," a counterproposal 140
Potentialities and limitations of the student movement: 1967–68, three Princeton SDS members 142
Appraisal and perspectives, Eric Mann 148

Chapter 7. *The Columbia revolt: the tension of alliances* 160
Two, three, many Columbias, Tom Hayden 162
Remaking a community, John Thoms 165
The strike: a critical reappraisal, Rusti Eisenberg 167
Columbia, Mark Rudd 177

How the anarchists destroyed the Columbia strike, Columbia Labor Committee 194

Chapter 8. *Beyond the university* 198

What is to be done? Mark Rudd, *et al.* 201

The student revolt: an analysis, Tony Thomas 205

Shut down the universities, Les Coleman 208

The critical university, Carl Davidson 211

Beginning to bring the war home, John Jacobs 213

Toward a revolutionary youth movement, Mike Klonsky 216

Fight racism; build a worker-student alliance; smash imperialism, SDS National Council 221

Repudiation of "Fight racism," SDS National Council 226

Factionalism, Staughton Lynd 228

Parasites of the youth revolution, David Doggett 230

Chapter 9. *A cultural revolution?* 232

Restructuring the universities, Don Benson 233

Behind the Free University crisis, Jo Anne Wallace 235

The Berkeley Liberation Program: whom does it speak *for?* whom does it speak *to?* Bob Kaufman 242

A left wing alternative, Greg Calvert 247

Chapter 10. *The splintering of SDS* 257
You don't need a weatherman to know which way the wind blows, Karin Ashley, Bill Ayers, Bernardine Dohrn, *et al.* 260
Adventurism, Carl Davidson 293
Build the campus student-worker alliance, Fred Gordon 296
Provocateurs, Worker-Student Alliance SDS 299
Notes on a decade ready for the dustbin, Carl Oglesby 300
PART III: THE ROLE OF THE FACULTY 321
Chapter 11. *Faculty as mediators* 323
Harvard: the voice of a non-striker, J. C. Helms 324
The confrontation crisis, Independent Faculty Group 328
Authority at Columbia, Walter P. Metzger 329
Chapter 12. *Professional responsibility* 341
Trouble at San Francisco State: an exchange, Marshall Windmiller vs. John Gerassi 341
PART IV: THE ESTABLISHMENT: HOW TO RESPOND TO TURMOIL 371
Chapter 13. *Official responses* 373
Interim statement on campus disorder, National Commission on the Causes and Prevention of Violence 374
Separate statement, Leon Jaworski 384

Crisis at Columbia, the Cox Commission 386
Chapter 14. *Hard-liners vs. soft-liners* 396
The Trojan horse in American higher education, Sidney Hook 398
Segregation and the abuse of due process on the American campus: whose law and order? William M. Birenbaum 404
Cornell
Pledge, faculty members 410
Why one professor changed his vote, Milton R. Konvitz 411
Humanity vs. principle at Cornell, Tom Wicker 416
Reply, Allan P. Sindler 418
PART V: THE COUNTERATTACK AGAINST THE STUDENT MOVEMENT 421
Chapter 15. *The underpinnings of protest: generation gap or social conflict?* 423
The umpirage of reason, Grayson Kirk 424
No wonder the gap exists, Harold Taylor 427
Reply to Uncle Grayson, Mark Rudd 428
Nihilism, a product of the liberal system, M. Stanton Evans 430
Chapter 16. *The culture of irrationality* 436
The agony of the campus, Irving Howe 437
Student revolt: the hard core, Bruno Bettelheim 438
Alienation is being taught by professors, S. I. Hayakawa 439

Reason and the left, Robert Paul Wolff 441

Chapter 17. *The student revolt: is it historically irrelevant?* 446

Revolution and counterrevolution (but not necessarily about Columbia!), Zbigniew Brzezinski 447

You have to grow up in Scarsdale to know how bad things really are, Kenneth Keniston 453

CONCLUDING ESSAYS 469

Radical intellectuals in a liberal society, Immanuel Wallerstein 471

Moving on, Paul Starr 478

APPENDIX A: THE DEMANDS 483

Howard University 485

Columbia University 486

Northwestern University 486

Stanford University 488

San Francisco State College 489

University of California, Berkeley 491

University of Chicago 492

City College of New York 493

Harvard University 493

National Student Strike 1970 494

APPENDIX B: REPORT OF THE PRESIDENT'S COMMISSION ON CAMPUS UNREST 495

Introduction

The documents in the first volume of this anthology dealt with the major substantive issues under debate in American universities. Sections focused on such topics as Black Studies, ROTC, military research, student power, university discipline, and admissions policy. The subject of the second volume is not the university so much as the political conflict that has taken place there. This is a book about politics, but a very special kind: the politics of confrontation.

Direct action, of course, has a long history in America, and the student protests of the late sixties are often seen as successors to the civil rights demonstrations earlier in the decade. The dynamics of confrontation politics, however, are significantly different from those of civil rights protests. During the civil rights struggle, radicals aimed at calling attention to an issue—focusing the nation's eyes upon some injustice—in the expectation that support from the national press and liberal politicians would follow. Protests were essentially means of arousing indignation, bringing to bear the pressure of public opinion and inspiring federal legislation. In confrontation politics, there is almost no effort to awake latent support in the press and government, since it is clear that little will be forthcoming. The demonstrations are rather intended to have their primary impact within the local community (the university), through the radicalization of large numbers of students and changes in institutional policy. Confrontations attract public attention, but not sympathy. If the federal government acts at all, it is clear that it will act against the protesters, not in their behalf.

As in the first volume, most of the material we have selected is polemical. When it was written, it was meant to persuade—or to dissuade. From various campuses across the country we have taken mimeographed pamphlets, speeches, reports, radio transcripts, editorials and columns, and arranged them into a series of debates.

The book is divided into five major parts. The first deals with the basic question, what tactics are legitimate in the university? The argument here is basically between radicals, on the one hand, and liberals and conservatives on the other.

In the following three sections, the scope of debate narrows. Within each of the major factions in the university crisis—the radical movement, the faculty, and the establishment—there have been significant disagreements, both over ultimate goals and strategy. No side in the conflict has been thoroughly united.

Since the disagreements among radicals have changed over the years, their internal discussions are presented as they evolved historically. We move from the period in 1966 when many members of Students for a Democratic Society were still concerned with changing dormitory regulations to the period three or four years later where some were advocating terrorist attacks on the police. This section is the longest part of the book and it virtually constitutes a documentary history of SDS in the late sixties.

The next section deals with disagreements among the faculty. For a while it seemed as though the faculty might become a mediating force between students and the administration. The major debate among professors was the wisdom of intervention. But when the campus situation polarized, the faculty became less capable of acting as a third force, and their disagreements became essentially the same as those within the establishment.

The problem facing university administrators, government officials, and most professors was how to respond to the student revolt. The different tendencies—hard-line versus soft-line—are explored in the fourth section of the volume.

The fifth section contains the counterattack against the student movement which the latter's attack on the liberal university evoked. The counterattack came from those within the university whose function it was to protect its integrity (the administration and trustees), from those in the society whose function it was to protect the society's integrity (the political leadership), and finally from those whose role was most profoundly called into question—the liberal faculty.

Much of the material in this volume (about one quarter) comes from Columbia University—partly because the sequence of confrontation and counterattack was particularly strong there, partly because we experienced the Columbia events first-hand. Perhaps we are betraying a certain institutional chauvinism in choosing so many documents from the same campus. Nevertheless, the issues at Columbia were typical of those at other universities, and it is unlikely that the political picture would change greatly if the geographical origins of the documentary material were more varied.

I.W.
P.S.

New York City

PART I

PROCEDURES OF CHANGE: WHAT MEANS ARE LEGITIMATE?

To the public, what seemed dramatically new about the student revolt and what commanded immediate and sustained attention were its militant tactics: sit-ins, disruptions of public events, seizures of university buildings, clashes with the police, mass strikes. Newspaper and television accounts focused on these tactics, especially on violent encounters, often ignoring the students' demands or trivializing them. On the campuses, too, protest tactics were as much in dispute as university policy.

In the eyes of their critics, radicals failed to use legitimate channels for seeking change, trampled on civil liberties and academic freedom, sought to impose their will on the majority through intimidation and coercion, and threatened the democratic process. The faculty accused protesters of trying to subordinate the intellectual aims of the university to political ends, and argued that politicization would destroy the university without advancing the radicals' own cause.

The student left responded that the "legitimate channels" did not work and that they had no alternative but to resort to obstructive tactics. They contended that civil liberties, academic freedom and the democratic process were hollow concepts, part of a deceptive ideology that obscured the reality of oppression. The university, they said, was already subordinated to political ends, and it was their intention to substitute good ends for bad ones.

Those are the broad outlines of the debate on the tactics of the student movement. Within the debate there were several distinct issues:

—the legitimacy of obstructive action by large numbers of students.

—the role of "manipulation" in what came to be called "confrontation politics."

—the disruption of meetings and classrooms by small numbers of students.

—the politicization of the university.

Each of these is treated separately in the following pages.

CHAPTER 1

The Legitimacy of Mass Obstruction

Two leaflets justifying obstructive protest open this section. Issued in the heat of campus strikes at Columbia and San Francisco State, they were written by demonstrators specifically to convince other students to join them. In "What we want," SDS and the Students' Afro-American Society (SAS) claim that peaceful tactics, such as petition, brought no response from the Columbia administration. Moreover, the strikers insist that they did not initiate the use of force, but that the university had employed force and coercion all along—for example, against campus employees and tenants in university-owned apartment houses. This idea is developed more explicitly in the flier from San Francisco State, "On violence." A third document appealing for support, a strike poster from Harvard, conveys a sense of the urgency and personal significance that protest had for students.

Three condemnations of strike tactics follow: a statement by thirty-five law professors at Columbia, a resolution passed by Stanford's Board of Trustees, and a report of a Harvard disciplinary committee. The points stressed in the documents vary. The law professors see the use of force by the students as a transgression of the allowable limits of civil disobedience and as a negation of reason. The trustees, in addition, deplore interference with university operations and the waste of "priceless intelligence which should be contributing to a solution of the world's problems." The disciplinary committee responds to a whole range of arguments in favor of obstruction, denying that ordinary channels of redress had failed at Harvard.

This kind of liberal response to protest upset some people—also liberals—who considered it both inconsistent and hypocritical. In the next two pieces, Benjamin Barber and Jerry Avorn do not endorse obstructive protest enthusiastically, but consider it understandable in view of the rigidity of universities. For them, obstruction is the lesser of two evils. Avorn's comment is illustrative: "I'm more worried about the kind of damage done to a university by trustees who involve it institutionally in war research than I am about the damage done to it by students who take over its buildings for several days."

The relationship of obstructive demonstrations to civil liberties and academic freedom is explored in the final two documents. The American Civil Liberties Union takes the position that obstructive tactics "violate and subvert the basic principles of freedom of expression and academic freedom." The radical historian Staughton Lynd maintains that, on the contrary, obstructive action is still within the framework of civil liberty and academic freedom. So long as it is non-violent, Lynd says, obstructive protest belongs to "the twilight zone between reform and revolution" and remains compatible with the rule of law.

Leaflet distributed by SDS and SAS (Students' Afro-American Society) on the Columbia University campus, April 24, 1968.

What We Want

Many students who did not attend SDS/SAS's noon rally Tuesday may not understand why we and hundreds of our fellow students took the actions we did: tearing down part of the fence at the Columbia construction site in Morningside Park and, after one of our brothers was arrested there, occupying Hamilton Hall and not permitting Columbia College Dean Coleman to leave his office. What, people ask (spurred on by the administration and the Conservative Union), what do they want? Do we see here at Columbia that evil Lyndon Johnson so abhors in Vietnam—"random, irrational violence"?

Our actions cannot be viewed in isolation: they were, in fact, a *reaction* to University actions, the culmination of months and years of demands by different groups of black and white students and affected community people that Columbia account for and justify its actions and policies. Just recently SAS has demanded that Columbia honor Martin Luther King with actions, not words, against racism; SDS has demonstrated and presented a petition (signed by 1500 people) against the Institute for Defense Analysis; both groups, and many other people, have demanded an open hearing on the issues involved in the discipline of the IDA six. There has been no response. Instead, the Columbia administration every day holds violent demonstrations disruptive of people's lives—in Morningside Park, in the Institute for Defense Analysis headquarters in Washington, in the cafeteria kitchen (I refer chiefly to the working conditions and wage scales, not cockroaches), in every building on Morningside Heights (except, of course, Riverside Drive), and many buildings in Harlem and the West Side.

But what do we mean by "liberal racism" and "institutional racism"? How can Administrators Grayson Kirk and David Truman, upstanding liberals who are against the war, for civil rights, who would go so far as to hold a memorial service and even cancel school for a day to honor Martin Luther King—how can they be racists? It is actually very simple. Like all other institutions in this society, when it is in the administration's economic interest to exploit and oppress people, they try to pick on downtrodden people who will have no support. They need cafeteria (and other) workers who will take execrable working conditions and salaries like $65 a week—so they hire black and Spanish-speaking people. But if these people had a union, they would have the strength to resist Columbia and wrest improvements from it—the administration fights unions tooth and nail (since 1928) through intimidation, scabs and firing workers. They want land to put their buildings on (or to build housing projects—contractor at guaranteed profit rate Percy Uris, Trustee, Columbia University). Where will they get the land? By throwing black and Spanish-speaking and poor white working people out of their homes BY FORCE AND

VIOLENCE. (How would you like the heat turned off on *your* family in mid-winter?)

And they want to build a gym. They want to put it in a park. Whose park do they pick? Do they pick a recreation area in Riverside Park across from upper middle class, white Riverside Drive? No, indeed. They take more land from a park they've been eating away at for years; a park used by black people and their children, in a black community. Who cares? The city government will never do anything for them. Neither will anyone else.

And when black and other oppressed people get tired of being screwed by Columbia and every other American institution—Columbia has to defend itself. The administration doesn't worry then about violence—it calls up all the violence it can get, from city cops to the army, using weapons and tactics developed by Columbia-sponsored IDA research. (IDA invented Mace, the newest form of nonviolent chemical warfare for use in ghettos.) At the same time, it runs pacification programs for its local ghetto.

So when the administration says "Let poor Dean Coleman go; don't hold him prisoner by force," we say, "Let Fred Wilson (the arrested demonstrator) go; he's held prisoner in *prison;* and don't hold half the SDS steering committee hostage with expulsion, the draft, etc., hanging over their heads." And when Dean Truman says, "Stop your actions, and we'll talk to you," our logical response is to say, "Stop *your* actions. Get out of IDA. Stop building the gym. Remove your threats of discipline. Then we'll talk to you." However, we are moderate: we only say, "Stop threatening us (the demonstrators) and we'll talk to you." That is why only our first demand is not negotiable; we will discuss with the administration the means by which (as a eulogy of Dr. King?) it will terminate its racist policies.

Here are our demands:

1. All disciplinary probation against the six originally charged must be lifted, and no reprisals taken against anyone in this demonstration.
2. All construction of the Columbia gym must stop NOW.
3. The University must use its good offices to see that all charges against persons arrested at the gym site be dropped.
4. All relations with IDA must be severed, including President Kirk and Trustee William Burden's membership.

5. President Kirk's edict on indoor demonstrations must be dropped.
6. All judicial decisions should be made in an open hearing with due process judged by a tripartite committee of students, faculty, and administrators.

At the present time, in response to the University's seizure and barricade of Morningside Park, SAS is barricaded in Hamilton Hall, and SDS is barricaded in Low Library to enforce the above demands on the College and University administrations.

SUPPORT THOSE IN HAMILTON AND LOW—
SUPPORT OUR DEMANDS
COME TO THE SUNDIAL
COME *NOW!*

Endorsed by the School of Architecture, SAS and SDS.

Leaflet by protesters distributed during the student strike at San Francisco State College, ca. October–November 1968.

On Violence

I. Violence in perspective

During the course of the strike at State, acts of "violence" occurred. Hearing "violence" many students recoil in horror, for it is their belief that violence, regardless of why it was committed, is a reprehensible thing. Since many of us operate under this assumption, let's check it out.

When Patrick Henry said "Give me liberty or give me death," he wasn't talking about a sit-in, a picket line or a petition—he was talking about an armed revolt. And yet, how many of us would consider what Patrick Henry said "reprehensible"? Probably very few! Why? Because people realize that when their freedom is taken away, whether it be by COVERT or OVERT force, they have the right to regain their freedom, by any means necessary.

II. Organized violence of the system

When people are being oppressed, when their freedom is being denied, a very real form of violence is being employed. The source of this violence is the system itself. This system uses organized force to maintain itself. The Army, the National Guard and the Police are its instruments and are used by those who run this country to maintain a system where poverty, unemployment and oppression among nonwhite people are deeply imbedded. This organized violence surrounds us every day, although we rarely question its legitimacy. The more subtle forms of violence—the violence of hungry children in the richest country in the world; the violence of minority unemployment (25% of all Black ghetto youth) in the most advanced economy in history; the violence of housing unfit for human beings in a country of skyscrapers and townhouses—SHOULD make us recoil in horror. Rather than condemning the violence of a broken window or a disrupted class, we must condemn and act against the oppressive nature of the system.

III. The university as an instrument of the system

We have seen examples of this "legitimate" violence at State—the firing of George Murray, the failure to establish a Black Studies Department, and a withering of the program for minority admissions. Our education system is filled with examples: over 50% of those in public schools in California are minority students, yet there are less than 5% minority students in our colleges. Why this covert violence?

Our schools and universities are an integral part of this system, and as such they function in the interests of those in power. The demands of the B.S.U. are an attempt to make the University serve the masses of people rather than IBM, United Fruit, etc. Therefore, the corporations (through the trustees and the administration) will actively oppose these demands and will not meet them without a fight.

IV. The struggle on campus

This strike is a struggle against the covert violence of the corporate control of our Universities. Whatever violence may be initiated is not intended against the students, but rather against the state and college administration. However, those students who break the strike by attending class are objectively playing the same role as the state and administration, whose objective is to break the strike. Any "violence" on the part of the striking students must be seen as part and parcel of the struggle to turn the University into an institution that serves the students and the community rather than the corporations.

From a Declaration of Confidence in Columbia's Future *by thirty-five law school professors and administrators, Columbia Law School, May 16, 1968.*

The Allowable Limits of Civil Disobedience

Like the rest of Columbia University, the Faculty of Law has suffered grave disruption during the past several weeks. We believe that the suffering was needless. Because disorderliness threatens to become respectable among some students, we who are teachers or administrators in Columbia Law School join now in declaring our confidence in the orderly processes of change in American universities as well as in the larger society of which universities are a part.

Organized protest is an eminently allowable activity, protected by the Constitution itself against interference by public agencies. Within independent universities like Columbia it is sanctioned by long practice and deep intellectual conviction of its worth. The permissible means of expressing disagreement with existing laws or policies are not, however, limitless. The limits are overstepped when protesters seize buildings or physically restrain the freedom of personal movement, in order to manifest dissatisfaction.

We do not assert that every act of "civil disobedience" is reprehensible. One way to challenge the validity of a statute is to ignore its commands, undergo arrest and prosecution, and then argue that the law is unconstitutional.

We recognize, too, that in rare instances persons whose voices might otherwise not be heard at all may engage in concerted violation of an admittedly constitutional law in order to proclaim their disapproval of it. In that situation, the violators are prepared to pay the penalty for their disobedience, hoping thus to drama-

STRIKE FOR THE EIGHT
DEMANDS STRIKE BE
CAUSE YOU HATE COPS
STRIKE BECAUSE YOUR
ROOMMATE WAS CLUBBED
STRIKE TO STOP EXPANSION
STRIKE TO SEIZE CONTROL
OF YOUR LIFE STRIKE TO
BECOME MORE HUMAN STR
IKE TO RETURN PAINE HALL
SCHOLARSHIPS STRIKE BE
CAUSE THERE'S NO POETRY
IN YOUR LECTURES
STRIKE BECAUSE CLASSES
ARE A BORE STRIKE FOR
POWER STRIKE TO SMASH THE
CORPORATION STRIKE TO MAKE
YOURSELF FREE STRIKE TO
ABOLISH ROTC STRIKE BECAUSE
THEY ARE TRYING TO SQUEEZE
THE LIFE OUT OF YOU STRIKE

Poster created and produced by striking students at Harvard's Graduate School of Design, Harvard University, April 1969.

tize opposition to the operative policies. Having in mind the difficulties sometimes experienced in drawing attention to public issues and to dissenting views, we cannot condemn this form of civil disobedience in every conceivable circumstance.

The Columbia episodes at the outset did not involve civil disobedience, but an effort to impose opinions by force. Without ascertaining whether other students shared their thoughts about academic and social issues, a relatively small group of students sought to immobilize the University until their conceptions of sound policy were adopted. Tactics like these have nothing in common with principled opposition or with democratic processes. They represented attempted intimidation.

The force of reason rather than the force of massed bodies must be the reliance of those who wish to influence a community guided by intelligence, as is Columbia. Disrupting institutional proceedings is an impermissible substitute for rational persuasion. Using muscles instead of minds to express dissent has no place in the academic setting.

We are confident that American students will themselves recognize the unwisdom of attempting to gain goals by illegal force. Violence begets violence. It beclouds rather than illumines issues. No problem that confronts Columbia or other American universities is beyond the capabilities of men who use the tools education has given them. . . .

From a resolution by the Board of Trustees, Stanford University, May 16, 1968.

Resolution on Disruption

WHEREAS Stanford University exists to increase human knowledge and to develop understanding and respect for truth, especially among its own faculty and students;

WHEREAS the pursuit of knowledge requires the free exchange of ideas, however unpopular, among all members of the academic community;

WHEREAS all recent experience shows that confrontation tactics, whether involving sit-ins or other coercive devices, invariably subvert the very nature and purpose of a university by substituting coercion by a militant minority for orderly academic procedures, by making impossible the rational evolution of the university to meet changing conditions, or by denying legitimate freedom of speech or action to those with whom that militant minority disagrees; and

WHEREAS confrontation tactics inevitably disrupt the proper activities of the university and therefore waste priceless intelligence which should be contributing to a solution of the world's problems; BE IT RESOLVED, THEREFORE, THAT:

Sit-ins and other activities by any member of the university community that disrupt or attempt to disrupt the activities of the university must no longer be tolerated at Stanford; And be it further resolved that:

This board requests that the president, faculty, and students at Stanford continue with the greatest sense of urgency their efforts to achieve means of eliminating such disruptive activities, which strike at the very existence of the university. . . .

Letter from the faculty Committee of Fifteen, Harvard University, to those disciplined, June 4, 1969.

The Necessity for Discipline

The Committee of Fifteen is fully aware of the diversity of motives that led students to participate in the forcible occupation of University Hall. Many had not approved of the decision to occupy the building or joined in any planning of the seizure. Some entered University Hall, and remained there, out of a desire to bear witness against evils or injustices which pervade our society or state policies. Some were unhappy about acts or statements of members of the University administration or governing boards, or impatient with what they regard as the slowness or bias of procedures for the redress of grievances. Some felt a deep urge to assert their solidarity with those who had taken a grave and perilous step and to establish a community in the midst of what many students deem a cold and impersonal University. Such motives were, on the whole, honorable and sometimes noble. However, the act itself—joining in the forcible occupation of University Hall—must be severely judged. Those who joined a given group because they share some of its purposes cannot absolve themselves of all responsibility for the actions and tactics of the group.

One may sympathize with the motives of many of the occupiers, or share their views about the University or about American society. But there are more constructive ways of pursuing goals. The University had responded, however imperfectly or tortuously, to student concerns and initiatives in the months that preceded these events. If many felt that the response was inadequate, there were peaceful ways of convincing others of the rightness of one's cause, or of the need to transform Harvard's relations with the world at large, or Harvard's procedures of decision. The best way is to put forth intelligent proposals, to use existing mechanisms in order to persuade others, to suggest and promote new mechanisms, to mobilize support behind such proposals—in other words, to make use of all the opportunities provided by the University without violating its basic commitment to reasoned discourse. The previous argument would not be valid had this University been a totally coercive institution. But whatever Harvard's flaws and failures, about which this committee intends to speak clearly and firmly, there were other ways of dealing with them than the forcible occupation of University Hall.

As for those whose target was society, an evil and unjustifiable war, and the University's supposed connections with social injustice, they often argue that students who feel impotent both as citizens and as a minority with limited rights and powers can make their influence felt only in the University. But the fact remains that striking at the University is likely to produce not a better society but one more repressive and not at all more enlightened. Whatever else may be said of Harvard, its intellectual life serves to generate criticisms of society and, to a considerable degree, to provide catalysts of constructive social change.

Even if one believes that the ends justified the means, those who today assert that the seizure produced worthwhile results must realize that the costs themselves were too high. These results, insofar as they are due to force, derive at least as much from the shock of the bust as from that of the seizure. In the wake of these shocks, what put the place together again and made it move forward was a generalized and passionate display of the good uses of reason: colloquia, meetings, discussions, negotiations, most of which proved constructive and orderly. Surely the price paid by the University—animosities, divisions, sanctions, fatigue, the genuine suffering inflicted by the events on so many, and the diversion of energy from the essential functions of the University—

proves that disruptive tactics cannot become a recurrent method of government or progress. Surely, the members of this community and especially the students have enough imagination to produce the benefits without the costs. Confrontation, violent action and reaction, the radicalization of some and the alienation of others are not constructive in themselves.

Finally, some of the means were bad in themselves. An academic community must be committed to the use of reason and the avoidance of violence. To be sure, there was more violence during the bust than in the seizure; this Committee has no intention of endorsing this bust and addresses itself to this matter in a separate document. But had there been no forcible seizure of the building, there would not have arisen any reason to call the police; had this seizure not been accompanied by intolerable acts of force and violence, the idea that an early call was necessary would not have arisen in the minds of some. The resort to the police, while it may have momentarily erased in the minds of many the responsibility of those who had seized the building, does not in fact excuse them.

Violence is simply not compatible with the serious and sustained intellectual work which is the essence of a University. The very intellectual processes on which study, teaching and research depend cannot proceed in the atmosphere of destructive emotions which invariably accompany violence and which are too often unleashed by it. If the University is to make any contribution toward reducing or overcoming the violence that prevails in the world it must itself remain an oasis of non-violence. This does not mean that even the subtle forms of repression and authoritarianism which any hierarchical (or for that matter "participatory") organization creates must be accepted; it means that they must be fought in ways that are not self-defeating.

Of course, many will argue that their presence in the building was entirely peaceful, and that the only violence was that which occurred at their expense at 5:00 A.M. But those who joined in what had begun as a violent take-over and who asserted through their presence their solidarity with the small group that had seized the building (a group many members of which broke that solidarity by seeing to it that they, at least, would be out before the police came in) made themselves willy-nilly the pawns of that group. The non-violent ones thus placed themselves at the mercy of the more violent ones and aligned themselves with the most intransigent. Those who came in to protest against the lack of dialogue in the University abetted those who refused any dialogue at all. Those who came in with the hope of improving the University, served those who wanted to shut it down. Those who came to protest against Vietnam, the very symbol of violence, became the hostages of those who favor violence as the method of change.

For there were at least two symbolic dimensions to the affair of University Hall. One may have been Vietnam, which is what many students saw. But another was the breakdown of the rule of non-violence, without which no University can survive. The fact that this rule was broken on both sides certainly cannot excuse those who broke it first. Many students who participated in the seizure may not have seen in it anything but a sit-in, or an act of militant non-violence or civil disobedience. But there is a difference between a sit-in—and unauthorized presence in a building—and a forcible seizure of a building accompanied by a lock-out. And there are differences between the acts of a Gandhi or a Martin Luther King and the events of April 9. The former condoned no acts of violence—indeed Gandhi interrupted many of the protests he led as soon as acts of violence had occurred. Moreover, Gandhi and Dr. King fully accepted the disciplinary implications of their acts: they acted in order to change rules they deemed unjust, but they fully expected to pay a price—because they knew that, whereas one must appeal against unjust rules, there can be *no* society without rules.

It is not the intention of this Committee to blame only one group for recent events, or to pretend that there is some group that made no mistakes. Our purpose is to reunite the University community or, as some may say, to help Harvard become a genuine community. You are a member of it. We expect you to participate actively in the colossal task of reexamination which will affect the curriculum as well as the structure of the University; but you must understand that no valid reforms can be made without adequate procedures for discussion and persuasion. We expect the role of students in the University to grow; you must understand, however, that rights must be accompanied by obligations. Only if the University can establish its own code of behavior, and apply it, will it be able to prevent others, be they the Federal government or the local police, from imposing their code on us. The disciplinary decisions of this Committee are only part of an overall effort which includes an assessment of the causes of recent events, the establishment of a code of behavior, and planning for reconstruction.

If you find our disciplinary decisions unjust, you should remember these words of Albert Camus: "If it is true that in history . . . values do not survive unless they have been fought for, the fight is not enough to justify them. The fight itself must be justified and enlightened by those values. When fighting for your truth, you must be careful not to kill it with the very weapons you are using to defend it . . . Knowing that, the intellectual has the role of distinguishing in each camp the respective limits of force and justice . . . in order to disintoxicate minds and to calm fanaticism." What Camus said of the intellectual applies to all members of this community.

By Direction of the Committee of Fifteen

Letter to the editor from Benjamin R. Barber, Assistant Professor of Political Science, the University of Pennsylvania, in The New York Times, *May 12, 1968.*

More Frightening than Militant Tactics

There are few Americans who welcome the increasing dependence of political activists on extralegal and violent methods of protest and change. Such means seem especially inconsistent with the principles of academic life.

But more frightening than the militant tactics of young radicals (whether in our colleges or our ghettos) are the duplicity and misunderstanding with which these tactics have been condemned by moderates. For although the liberal response to violence (exemplified by the editorial posture of *The New York Times*) has been couched in democratic rhetoric, it misreads the procedural requisites of democracy.

In a democracy men need not agree, but they must agree about the ways in which they will disagree; they must cooperate in seeking means to compete; ultimately, each man—each minority—must believe that his interests and views, even if they do not prevail, will have an effect on the system.

What we are witnessing today is a breakdown of this procedural consensus—a breakdown precipitated not by the unwillingness of minorities to utilize democratic methods, but by the apparent unresponsiveness of such methods (or of those who defend them) to legitimate and pressing minority needs. Indeed, the procedures of democracy have not only failed to provide for change, but have become convenient legitimizing symbols for the *status quo.*

This use of democracy as an ideology has destroyed the faith of many Americans in the ability of the system to serve even partially their needs.

Far from being naive, student activists have become hardened cynics. Like so many black Americans who refuse to cooperate with a society which systematically excludes them from its benefits, many students have grown weary of being admonished to respect democracy and academic sacrosanctity by the administrative officers of universities which are hierarchically structured, undemocratically governed and increasingly subordinate to the intellectual tyranny of government and corporate research.

They are understandably unwilling to heed the call for peaceful solutions from governmental authorities who rely on organized, "legitimate" coercion to solve problems—at home and abroad. They blink incredulously at a society which condemns the damaging of property in the ghetto or in college buildings while condoning the destruction of entire cities (Ben Tre, Hue) and the decimation of a people.

Civil disobedience and violence, then, are symptoms, not causes, of political malaise; like medical symptoms, they may even represent the system's effort to cure itself. In any case, they are effects, not causes of malignancy; inveighing against them, even treating them successfully (shooting rioters? expelling student activists?), will only mask the real disease, condemning the democratic body politic to a certain death.

Article by Jerry L. Avorn, a student at Columbia College and an editor of the Columbia Daily Specatator, *in* Look, *May 13, 1969.*

To Be a Revolutionary or Not to Be?

It's been just a year since the Spring Revolution at Columbia, and many of us who were involved—as activists, observers, and reporters—are now able to look back at the eruptions with a peacetime perspective. During those months of April and May, 1968, many people were enraged because formal educational activities of much of the university had come to a halt. But some of us learned more in those six weeks than we would have if the demonstrations had never taken place.

There was a special dimension to our education last spring. It had little to do with textbooks or traditional academic subjects; it dealt with politics, with power, with the way Real Life works. Through elementary and high school, we had grown up with the traditional fables: that major American institutions—the government, the university—are delicately balanced structures designed to provide the greatest good for the greatest number, that they contain mechanisms to correct any major flaws that might develop. For many of us, that myth had begun to crumble even before we came to Columbia; the Vietnam war, perhaps more than any other factor, had made it clear how perverted American policy could become, how the safeguards and corrective mechanisms didn't always work.

The war was not the only event that shaped our ideology of mistrust. We looked at the history of blacks in this country and saw that real change began to take place only after Martin Luther King was thrown into jail for leading "illegal" sit-ins. We looked at the way American cities had been left to rot and noticed that those in power became concerned enough to change things only after several summers of bloody rioting.

Against this historical background, spring came to Columbia last year. Earlier, students had presented President Kirk with a petition calling for the university to disaffiliate from a think tank doing weapons research for the Vietnam war. Kirk had never answered the petition. Construction continued on a gymnasium in nearby Harlem parkland, even though many people argued that Columbia had no right to gobble up the open space surrounding it without consulting the community. But these issues were only symbols of larger problems that underlay them: the university's growing bondage to Government- and military-related research, and its often heartless expansion into the surrounding black community. On a deeper level lay the broadest issues we were fighting: the Government's commitment to an evil and senseless war, and the racial prejudice that pollutes American life.

Soon after the occupation of the buildings at Columbia, I spoke to a middle-aged business executive about the revolt on campus.

"I agree with what you kids want," he assured me, "but why can't you go about getting it in a *socially acceptable* way?" Leaders of the student movement have called this objection the Liberal Hang-up. It appears again and again in the report of the Cox Commission, the blue-ribbon panel set up last spring by the faculty to investigate the causes of the Columbia demonstrations.* The reforms the students demanded were for the most part necessary and long overdue, the report conceded, and it was clear that they had little chance of accomplishing anything through ossified "legitimate channels." But, the report insisted, the students still should not have resorted to extralegal action to win their demands.

A great many young people today are infuriated by the priorities and values that govern American life. We'd like to believe that rational discourse is all that is necessary to right wrongs. But the world we see around us just doesn't bear that out. I was a big fan of the America that I found in my high school textbooks—any kid can become President, justice triumphs in the end—and I was bitterly disappointed when I saw how poorly it measured up to the truth. Something has gone wrong; one need only to walk through Harlem or read the daily casualty statistics to be aware of that. And to judge from some of the good and healthy changes that have come from the "illegitimate" protests of the early civil rights movement, the Northern ghetto riots and the Columbia demonstrations, many of us wonder whether the best way to improve things is necessarily the most respectable. The university, like the nation, seems to be like a great, complex vending machine that has become rusted with age: the only way to make it work right is to kick it hard.

Some people argue that radical tactics are evil. I, too, am bothered by the violence and abrogation of free speech that have begun to tinge the leftmost edges of the student movement. And I am worried that civil disobedience is becoming the tactic of choice on many campuses when it should be used only as a last resort. I reject the notion of some ultra-Leftist students that one goal of campus protest should be the destruction of the university. But I confess that I'm more worried about the kind of damage done to a university by trustees who involve it institutionally in war research than I am about the damage done to it by students

* For text, see pp. 386–95.

who take over its buildings for several days. So I cannot share the righteous indignation many of my elders feel about campus protest. The anti-war movement faced the same problem: Americans become more upset over burnt draft cards than over burnt babies.

It is interesting to see what has happened in the year since the Spring Revolution to the "unrealistic" demands that formed the backbone of the Columbia sit-ins. The students demanded that the university halt construction of its gym in Morningside Park. In March of 1969, Acting President Andrew Cordier and the trustees concurred that it would be inappropriate to build a gym there if the community did not want one. The radicals had argued that the disciplinary structure of the university was authoritarian and unjust. That structure has, in response, been revamped. Discipline is no longer administered unilaterally by a dean; the accused student may appeal to a tribunal of students, professors and administrators. Even the most unthinkable demand of all—amnesty—has been all but granted, with the university belatedly dropping most criminal and disciplinary punishment pending against demonstrators. There has been another direct by-product of last spring's turmoil—the creation of a university senate, dominated by faculty and students, to make university policy. I know of no one familiar with Columbia who would maintain that these reforms would now be realities if the events of last spring had not happened.

Few of us saw last spring as the staunchest SDS ideologues did —as the opening shot in a national revolution. But it did serve the quasi-revolutionary function of shaking up the status quo so thoroughly that a wave of relatively peaceful change would take place. Maybe this is the greatest contribution of the radical and black militant movements: to act as a catalyst of social change by scaring the hell out of those who are so sure that things are good enough as they are. Of course, the possibility remains that all of these "reforms" will, in the end, merely gloss over the basic problems that brought about the revolt. If "reform" turns out to be a veneer, then the future looks pretty dismal.

Those of us in my generation who are deeply committed to creative, constructive change face an existential choice between radical tactics and within-the-system reform. Some might still be willing to work through the accepted political channels—within the universities and in the world at large. But those who control that system of channels must first convince us that, if we do, genuine change is possible. Their record has not been good and shows little promise that it will change. If some of the most idealistic and capable members of my generation end up on the barricades instead of changing things from positions of legitimate power, it will be because of the Grayson Kirks of this world, not because of its Mark Rudds. Perhaps this is the real lesson of last spring at Columbia.

From a statement by the American Civil Liberties Union, April 3, 1969.

Campus Disorders

Student protests and demonstrations in high schools, colleges and universities have mounted in volume, scope and intensity. Many of them have raised issues of fundamental importance about the nature and goals of our country and its institutions.

Student demonstrations have shown deep concern about the materialism of our society and the plodding pace toward desegregation and equal rights. They have raised questions about the moral bases of the Vietnam war, the power of the military-industrial complex, and the perversion of the university's purpose to serve military ends. They have sought a participatory role for faculty and students in the running of educational institutions and the revision of curricula to increase their relevance to the problems of life in our society.

On many college and university campuses there have clearly been grave violations of principles of sound academic governance. Administrators have denied to faculty and students a significant voice in the making of policy so vitally affecting them. Administrators and faculties both have frequently proved indifferent or slow to recognize the legitimate needs and aspirations of students. And, all too often, governing authorities have failed to give rigorous priority to academic, moral and human considerations over financial and organizational ones.

In general, whatever differences of opinion exist on how best to serve the causes of peace, equality, justice and freedom, it is well to recognize, too, that the student protests have in great degree been motivated by extraordinary selflessness, idealism and altruism. Speaking of a student demonstration in support of opening up opportunities for blacks in the construction of Buffalo campus buildings, Governor Nelson D. Rockefeller on March 21, 1969, said "I think that students have assumed a share of social responsibility in the life of our community and I applaud them for it." So do we.

We are aware of the fact that student dissenters are handicapped by lack of funds and of direct access to media of mass communications as well as by stubborn and often recalcitrant resistance to desirable change. Many have used, therefore, dramatic forms of protest to call attention to their grievances.

We believe in the right and are committed to the protection of all peaceful, non-obstructive forms of protest including mass demonstrations, picketing, rallies and other dramatic forms. However, we are deeply disturbed about some methods that some student activists have used in the attempt to achieve their ends; methods which violate and subvert the basic principles of freedom of expression and academic freedom. Protest that deprives others of the opportunity to speak or be heard, or that requires physical take-over of buildings to disrupt the educational process, or the incarceration of administrators and others are anti-civil-libertarian and incompatible with the nature and high purpose of an educational institution.

In December of 1968, students at New York University's Loeb Student Center stopped an address by Nguyen Huu Chi, the South Vietnamese Permanent Observer at the UN, by draping a Nazi flag across him, hurling an egg and pouring a pitcher of water over him. They then invaded another room, seized the notes of James Reston, executive editor of *The New York Times,* and tore them to bits. He left without delivering his address.

In January 1969, at a symposium at Northwestern University on confronting change, student activists shouted down all but the most radical speakers.

In February at Harvard University students disrupted a course whose focus they resented.

In March, Professor John H. Bunzel, of San Francisco State College, whose views are unpalatable to some student activists, was drowned out in a flood of shouts and questions in his classroom.

At a conference on "World Problems and American Change" on March 22, 1969, Arthur J. Goldberg, former Supreme Court Justice and United States ambassador to the United Nations, was shouted down by about 30 youngsters who dumped the head of a pig on the speaker's table.

Fundamental to the very nature of a free society is the conviction expressed by Mr. Justice Holmes that "the best test of truth is the power of the thought to get itself accepted in the competition of the market." When men govern themselves they have a right to decide for themselves which views and proposals are sound and which unsound. This means that all points of view are entitled to be expressed and heard. This is particularly true in universities which render great services to society when they function as centers of free, uncoerced, independent and creative thought and experience. Universities have existed and can exist without bricks and mortar but they cannot function without freedom of inquiry and expression.

For these reasons, the American Civil Liberties Union has from its very inception, defended free expression for all groups and all points of view, including the most radical and the most unpopular within the society and the university. To abandon the democratic process in the interests of "good" causes is to risk the destruction of freedom not just for the present but for the future, not just for our social order but for any future social order as well. Freedom, the world has learned to its sorrow, is a fragile plant that must be protected and cultivated.

We speak out of faith in our conventional wisdom—commitment to the principles of free expression embodied in the Bill of Rights—principles which are still essential, exhilarating, dynamic and even revolutionary. Free expression, academic freedom, habeas corpus, due process of law, and other liberties painfully won after centuries of struggle are worth preserving and extending.

It is well to remember, too, that violence and the threat of violence may be used in "bad" causes as well as "good" causes. They were employed by the Nazis in Germany and by Hungarian fascists to shut down universities or oust particular faculty members or students. They were used in the attempt to block the admission of James Meredith to the University of Mississippi and to block integration widely across the South. And there are those who today would use these methods to destroy our universities, not to reform them.

There are dangers, too, that violence and the threat of violence will breed a counter-violence and backlash that will defeat or set back the very objectives student activists seek to serve and lead to repressive counter-measures. . . .

We believe that the discussions between open-minded trustees and students which brought changes at the University of Pennsylvania set an admirable example. Similarly, we commend the experimentation in shared governance at Antioch College and Richmond College of the City University of New York. In general, we are convinced that universities must draw upon the whole academic community—trustees, administrators, faculties, and students—to effect desirable changes. Where existing processes are inadequate or unrepresentative, creativity and imagination must be summoned to the task of developing new mechanisms for peaceful communication and decision-making that will prove responsive to just demands.

Let us recognize, finally, that some student activists have been moved by conscience to use extraordinary means in the belief that ordinary means have failed to build a just and equal society and secure peace. We in America have the burden of changing and adapting our social institutions and policies to demonstrate that we have the capacity and will to redress the evils of our social order.

From an article by Professor Staughton Lynd, in The Radical Teacher, *published by the New University Conference, 1969.*

Academic Freedom and the First Amendment

. . . Clearly current doctrine with respect both to academic freedom and civil liberties remains: Talk but do not act; instruct but do not obstruct; discuss but do not disrupt.

I want to challenge this doctrine. I want to challenge it in the light both of my research as a historian and of my experience as a practicing radical. I want to challenge it in its application both to the campus and to the larger society. And I want to challenge it within the framework of the rule of law and classical democratic theory.

Historically, secular free speech developed from religious free speech: for instance, from Milton's *Areopagitica.* But free speech about religion was gained only at a price. The price was that men had to agree not to translate their beliefs into action, a restraint which, viewed from a different angle, is known as "hypocrisy." Today, we rationalize the separation of speech from action on the ground that speech should not be translated into action until a majority has been won to the speaker's outlook. But this democratic rationale was not the original rationale. The original rationale was that religion and secular society were two separate and mutually-exclusive spheres. Thus in his *Letter Concerning Toleration,* Locke asserted that while liberty of conscience "is every man's natural Right," he esteemed it "above all things necessary to distinguish exactly the Business of Civil Government from that of Religion, and to settle the just Bounds that lie between the one and the other." *

Carried over into contemporary life, the distinction between thought and action prevents a man not only from being a good citizen but also from being a good academic. At least in the social sciences, action may be essential to the search for truth itself. Paul Goodman puts the case this way:

> Certainly if we consider the masters of the century prior to our generations—whether Comte, Marx, Proudhon, Durkheim, Kropotkin, Sorel, Veblen, Lenin, Freud, Dewey, etc., etc.—we are struck by their activism, their actual or projected experimentation on a civic scale. Some of these men are unthinkable as academics and some had uneasy academic lives. The present-day preoccupation with careful methodology is academically praiseworthy, but it does not lead to intensely interesting propositions. One cannot help feeling that a good part of the current concern with statistics and polling is a way of being active in the "area" without being actively engaged in the subject matter. There is a good deal of sharpening of tools but not much agriculture.†

Goodman and others add that the teacher must also be able to act, politically and socially, because "what is learned in the class-

* John Locke, *A Letter Concerning Toleration* (London, 1689), 48, p. 6.

† Paul Goodman, "The Freedom To Be Academic," in *Growing Up Absurd* (New York, 1960), p. 261.

room is *him,* the teacher," ‡ and his students look to him as a model for a whole life.

I believe that a teacher should be free to act as he wishes outside the classroom so long as he continues to perform his academic duties. I reject the distinction between thought and action which would protect the teacher so long as he talks and would fire him if he acts illegally. For one thing, what is an illegal act? My trip to Hanoi was widely described as illegal, but in the end, the courts held it protected action under the First Amendment. If a teacher is sent to jail, he will be unable to meet his classes. At that point, his academic employer might understandably conclude that the teacher's public activities temporarily interfered with the performance of his academic duties, and, if charitably inclined, give him a leave of absence. But academic employers should eschew appointing themselves judges, and convicting a man before the courts themselves have acted. Teachers, like other citizens, should be innocent until proven guilty.

How can the teacher's freedom of action be protected? Not by the AAUP [American Association of University Professors] alone. My experience leads me to believe that, at best, AAUP action may induce an administration to act differently the next time. What it rarely does is to save the job of the aggrieved individual. In my opinion, the only hope for a mistreated teacher is to think of himself as a workingman trying to organize a factory. If such a man were fired because of his radicalism, his fellow-workers would go on strike until the grievance was settled. In exactly the same way, the students at San Francisco State, whatever the incidental excesses of their action, are right in principle to try to shut down a university to save the job of a discharged teacher. To say that they may never do so is no different from a permanent injunction forbidding civil rights demonstrators to march or workingmen to strike.*

Now how can obstructive or disruptive action be reconciled with a commitment to the rule of law and democracy? If it remains nonviolent. The usefulness of nonviolent civil disobedience as an aspect of democratic process is its enabling individuals to act on their deep convictions without destroying law and order it-

‡ Leslie Fiedler, "Academic Irresponsibility," *Playboy,* December 1968, p. 275.

* See the incisive comment on injunctions by Anne Braden, "How Injunctions Crush Peaceful Protest," *The Southern Patriot.*

self. If you tell a man not to act on his beliefs until a majority agrees with him, you compel him to be a hypocrite. If you permit him to act on his beliefs by violent means, you invite anarchy. Nonviolent civil disobedience offers a third alternative. What makes it particularly congruent both to democracy and to the spirit of academic life is its satisfying the criterion of universality. I do not ask that only I be permitted to break the laws. If you feel compelled to refuse a portion of your taxes to protest the enforcement of civil rights laws, I do not find this threatening. Clearly you feel deeply, for you are risking going to jail for the sake of your beliefs. In acting, you have not physically injured any other human being. Had you merely spoken or written, I might have hastily dismissed your concerns, but the fact that you have "put your body where your mouth is" inclines me to pay a little more attention.

Admittedly, disruptive disobedience—sitting down in the middle of a street or occupying an administration building—raises an additional issue. If I refuse to be inducted, I say in effect: Have your war if you want to, but without me. However, if I stand in front of troop trains, block the doorways of induction centers, and surround the cars of campus recruiters, I say something different, namely: What you are doing is so wrong that I shall try to stop you. Both are forms of nonviolent civil disobedience. But the first is disobedience by withdrawal, the second disobedience by obstruction. The latter has been condemned not only by constituted authority but also by national AAUP. Denouncing General Hershey's advice that obstructers be drafted, the AAUP nevertheless stated that "action by individuals or groups to prevent speakers invited to the campus from speaking, to disrupt the operations of the institutions in the course of demonstrations or to obstruct and restrain other members of the academic community and campus visitors by physical force is destructive of the pursuit of learning and of a free society."

Radicals have not adequately justified disruptive civil disobedience against this argument. Their tendency has been to agree with their conservative antagonists that disruption, even if nonviolent, is essentially revolutionary in the sense that it challenges the whole structure of law and order. Disruption, in this view, presupposes a readiness for Locke's "appeal to Heaven." He who disrupts expects no protection from the law. His action is insurrectionary. He will win or die.

The outstanding recent argument along these lines is Herbert Marcuse's essay on "Repressive Tolerance." Insisting that indiscriminate tolerance bolsters the status quo, Marcuse justifies:

> withdrawal of toleration of speech and assembly from groups and movements which promote aggressive policies, armament, chauvinism, discrimination on the grounds of race and religion, or which oppose the extension of public services, social security, medical care, etc. Moreover, the restoration of freedom of thought may necessitate new and rigid restrictions on teachings and practices in the educational institutions which, by their very methods and concepts, serve to enclose the mind within the established universe of discourse and behavior . . .†

To justify such extensive repression of the speech and action of one's opponents, so that one may oneself come to power, is to invite one's opponents, who presently have the power, to use it in the same spirit. For all practical purposes, Marcuse's argument amounts to saying that whichever side is strongest, wins.

But I believe Marcuse's rationale to be unnecessarily drastic, an instance of intellectual overkill. So long as we are speaking of nonviolent disruptive disobedience rather than armed insurrection, a better defense is simply to offer the same opportunity to one's opponents. If I block your doorway one day, you may block mine the next. Seen in this light, nonviolent obstructive disobedience remains a kind of dialogue. "Speaking," to be sure, in which the interlocutors are concerned so deeply that they act out their convictions with their lives and bodies; but for all that, an exchange in which a sense of reciprocity is preserved, in which the awareness of one's opponent as a human being and of oneself as conceivably fallible is not yet abandoned. Such disobedience remains within the framework of democratic process.

If, despite all the special features of the campus community, disruptive disobedience can be justified on the campus, its rationale in the community at large is more straightforward. Classical democratic theory offers no intermediate steps between politics-as-usual and revolution. According to Locke's *Second Treatise,*

† Herbert Marcuse, "Repressive Tolerance," in *A Critique of Pure Tolerance* (Boston, 1965), pp. 100–101.

for example, one either strives for change through the existing structure or seeks to overthrow the government. But what about the case where a particular policy of the government is resented with that pitch of intensity which would ordinarily justify revolution, and yet a total overthrow is not desired? Chattel slavery was such a policy, and Thoreauvian disobedience was improvised in response. The Vietnam war is another such policy which the draft resistance movement strives to prevent.

Nonviolent obstructive disobedience explores the twilight zone between reform and revolution. Without yet seeking to overthrow the government, resisters declare their determination to overthrow a given policy or complex of institutions by refusing to obey them or to permit them to function. The resister does not rely on the electoral process or the courts to bring about the change he seeks, but he leaves open the possibility that these conventional institutions can adapt themselves to changes brought about by more direct means.

From the standpoint of society as a whole, such resistance by nonviolent obstructive disobedience might be seen as an experiment or probing operation to determine whether revolution is required. It is a means of assessing the nature and degree of social crisis which at the very least valuably supplement the electoral process. Perhaps the obstructor will receive so little popular support, or be repressed so harshly, that he will conclude that resistance from within the society is hopeless. Perhaps the obstructor and his associates will make so deep an impression—on national opinion, or on the armed men sent to suppress them, or on a significant number of potential draftees and defense workers—that they will sense the possibility of becoming a majority through conventional means more rapidly than they had previously supposed possible, and for this reason lay aside extreme tactics. Perhaps the obstructive action will lead both to harsh repression and a rallying of wide support behind the obstructors and so to deepening revolutionary crisis of the traditional variety. The essential thing to recognize is that this disobedience, far from representing an alternative to politics-as-usual, is a third course men can adopt when in frustration and despair they might otherwise turn to insurrection.

Nonviolent civil disobedience, even obstructive disobedience, seems to me then an essential corollary concept to the theory of academic freedom and civil liberty.

CHAPTER 2

The Anatomy of Confrontation Politics

Inevitably, political activity in the universities became a subject of academic analysis. One popular interpretation of student revolts, presented by Professor John Searle of Berkeley, sketched the development of upheavals. Searle saw confrontation politics as a self-contained process with its own internal dynamic. In the manner of a natural scientist describing the life cycle of a species, Searle analyzed rebellions as three-stage developments, with each stage providing radical leaders with the opportunities necessary for elevating their protest to the next highest level. Manipulation by the radical leaders was a central element in his theory.

In a critique of Searle's article, Berkeley student Jeff Lustig argued that the narrow scope of the author's model prevented him from dealing with certain crucial questions. For example, Searle stated that one of the reasons that student revolts succeed was "the pervasive distrust of authority," due to unnamed historical forces. However, as Lustig pointed out, to say that revolts against authorities succeed because authority is distrusted does not add to our understanding. The important question to ask is *why* authority is distrusted. But since Searle did not place campus revolts in any historical or social context, Lustig said, he could not deal with this problem. Lustig's commentary on Searle's approach becomes a critique of the orientation of much contemporary social science, recalling the ideas broached by Richard Lichtman in his essay, "University: mask for privilege?" (See Volume I, Chapter 2).

Article by Professor John R. Searle, Department of Philosophy, the University of California, Berkeley, in The New York Times Magazine, *December 29, 1968.*

A Foolproof Scenario for Student Revolts

In several years of fighting for, fighting against, and simply observing student revolts in the U.S. and Europe I have been struck by certain recurring patterns of action and internationally common styles in the rhetoric of confrontation. Leaving out student revolts in Turkey, Czechoslovakia, and Spain—all of which have rather special features—and confining ourselves to the U.S. and the advanced industrial democracies of Western Europe, it seems to me to be possible to discern certain family resemblances in the successful campus rebellions. In general, successful student revolts in these countries tend to occur in three separately identifiable phases or stages.

Stage One: The Creation of the Issue

In the beginning, the campus always has—at least in the mythology of local administrations—the same two features: there is only "a very small minority" of troublemakers, and "they have no legitimate grievances." These conditions, I have found in visits to campuses all over the U.S. and Western Europe, are, by common administrative consent, universal. They are so universal that they are also the reasons why, "it won't happen here"; that is, they are always the reasons why "this campus won't become another Berkeley," or lately, "another Columbia." I have discovered, incidentally, that a legitimate grievance is defined by the general public as one on which the students win. If you win, it turns out that your grievance was legitimate all along; if you lose, then alas for you, you had no legitimate grievance.

The small-minority-with-no-legitimate grievance starts out by selecting an issue. Now, curiously, almost any old issue will do. In Berkeley it concerned the campus rules on political activity, in Columbia it was the location of a gym, at Nanterre, a protest against TWA and the Chase Manhattan Bank, in Essex, it was a visit by a representative of the Ministry of Defense, and many places have used recruiters from the Dow Chemical Company and other variations on the theme of the war in Vietnam. Almost any issue will do provided it has two crucial features: (1) It must be an issue that can be somehow related to a Sacred Topic. In the U.S. the Sacred Topics are the First Amendment, race, and the war in Vietnam in that order, though I believe that in the past year race has pulled ahead of the First Amendment into first place. (In France "La révolution" is itself a Sacred Topic.) If the issue can be related to a Sacred Topic then the majority of students even though they would not do anything about it themselves, will at least be sympathetic to the demonstrators' position in the early stages. (2) It has to be an issue on which the university authorities cannot give in. The authorities must initially refuse your demands. If you win, you have lost. If the authorities give in to your demands there is nothing for it but to pick another issue and start all over.

The demand, therefore, has to be presented in the maximally confrontationalist style. This usually requires a demonstration of some sort, and sit-ins are not uncommon at this stage, but a "mass meeting" or march for the purpose of presenting your demands will often do as well. The numbers in stage one are usually small but they serve to "educate" the campus, to "dramatize" the issue. It is a good idea, though not always necessary in stage one, that in the course of the initial presentation of your demands, in your first demonstration—you violate as many campus rules or civil laws as you possibly can, in as visible a manner as you possibly can. In other words, you should challenge the authorities to take disciplinary action against you, and generally they will oblige by suspending a few of your leaders.

Stage one closes when the administration rejects your demands, admonishes you to better behavior in the future, and if possible brings some of your leaders to university discipline for rule violations in the first demonstrations. Berkeley 1964, and Paris 1968, are the models of a well-managed stage one.

Stage Two: The Creation of a Rhetorical Climate

In stage two the original issue is transformed so that the structure of authority in the university itself is the target. This is achieved by the following method. The fact that the university rejected the original demands, and even more the fact that the university disciplined people for rule violations in making those demands are offered as conclusive proof that the university is the real enemy of the forces of truth and justice on the Sacred Topic. Thus, if the original demand was related to the war in Vietnam the fact that the university disciplines a student for rule violation in making the demand is proof that the university is really working for the war and that it is out to "crush dissent." If, for example, the demonstrations were against the Dow Chemical Company recruiters on campus, the fact of university discipline proves that the university is really the handmaiden (or whore) of the military industrial complex. And the fact that the university refuses to cancel plans for the gym (Columbia) or does cancel plans for the Cleaver course (Berkeley) demonstrates that the university is really a racist institution. Why else would anybody try to discipline our fellow students and refuse our just demands if they weren't racists, warmongers, or dissent-crushers, as the case might be? And indeed can't we now see that the university is really just a part of much larger forces of oppression (imperialism, racism) in Murkensociety? In the face of such proof only the most callous or evil would fail to join us in our struggle to make this a livable university, a place where we can be truly free.

Depending on the success of this shift in the issue to make the university the primary target, the numbers of people involved in stage two will increase enormously. Large numbers of students who will not demonstrate illegally against the war in Vietnam or for free speech will demonstrate illegally if they can demonstrate against someone's being disciplined for illegally demonstrating against the war in Vietnam or for free speech. The original issue is made much more personal, local, and "relevant" to their life as students by being redefined with the university authorities as the main enemy. The war in Vietnam is a long way away, but Grayson Kirk's office is just across the campus. This redefinition of the issue so that the university authorities become the main target is crucial to the success of the entire operation, and is the essential characteristic of a successful stage two.

Speeches, leaflets, meetings, articles in the student papers all serve to create a certain rhetorical climate where charges that would normally be thought to verge on the preposterous can gain currency and acceptability. Thus, the president of the university is a racist, the board of regents is trying to run the university for its own personal profit, the university is fundamentally an agent of the Pentagon, and so on. Anyone who remembers the witch hunts of the 1950's will recognize the distinctive features of this rhetorical atmosphere: the passionate conviction that our side is right and the other side not only wrong but evil, the urgency of the issue, the need of all of us to stand united against the threat (of Communism, or the military industrial complex, depending on your choice of era) and most important, the burning sincerity of all but the most intelligent. To accuse a professor of doing secret war research for the Defense Department nowadays has the same delicious impact that accusations of secret Communist party membership did a decade ago. And one even reads the same sort of nervous apologetic prose on the part of the accused: "I was consultant (to the Institute of Defense Analysis) from 1964–1967 when I went to meetings and listened and offered comments; however, you will not find my name on the reports," he said (*The Daily Californian,* Tuesday, November 5, 1968, p. 1). The ultimate in such accusations—leaving out such horrendous charges as "He worked for the CIA"—are "He's a racist," and "He is in favor of the war." We are incidentally going to see a great deal more of this left McCarthyism in the next few years on college campuses, especially in the United States.

In stage two certain new and crucial elements enter the fray—television and the faculty. It sounds odd to describe the jobs television does, but here they are: it helps to provide a leader, and it dignifies the proceedings. The mechanisms by which television helps the movement pick a leader are not generally well understood. It looks like the movement chooses a leader and he then addresses the TV cameras on its behalf. But that is rarely what happens; in fact that almost never happens. What happens is that among the many speakers who speak at rallies and such, some are more telegenic than others; and the TV reporters and cameramen, who can use only a small amount of footage anyway, are professional experts at picking the one who will make the most interesting news shots. The man they pick then becomes the leader or spokesman or symbol of the movement. Of course, his selection has to be approved by the movement, so any TV selection is subject to ratification by the crowd. If they don't like him, the TV people have to find somebody else, but among the many leaders who are acceptable to the demonstrators, television plays an important role in the eventual success of one or another. Thus Savio in Berkeley, Cohn-Bendit in Paris, and Rudd at Columbia—all were people with relatively little leadership position prior to stage one, but who, as a result of their own qualities and the fact that the television people chose them to present to the world as leaders, were elevated to the status of, at least symbolic, leaders of the movement. Both Savio and Rudd have complained of this television exaggeration. Actually, Cohn-Bendit is the purest case of mass publicity as a factor in selecting a leader, for Sauvageot and Geismar were both authentic campus leaders and organizers well before stage one ever got going, but neither is much good on TV so never attained Cohn-Bendit's symbolic stature. In a way, the fact that television plays such an important role in the selection of the leader doesn't much matter, because it is a feature of this type of political movement that leaders don't lead (they may manipulate, but lots of people who are not "leaders" do that as well). This type of political movement rejects hierarchical forms of organization in general and direction from above in particular.

Also, television, in a crazy kind of way, dignifies the proceedings. If you are at a demonstration at noon and you can go home and watch yourself on the six o'clock news, it suddenly means that the noon behavior is lifted out of the realm of juvenile shenanigans and becomes genuinely historical stuff. If you are there on the box, it must be pretty serious, an authentic revolutionary event. This is a McLuhanite generation, raised and bred with a feel for publicity in general and TV in particular. When I was an undergraduate if you got kicked out of school you went somewhere else and tried to forget about it; nowadays you would immediately call a TV news conference and charge that you did not get due process. As a news medium, television requires the visually exciting, and campus demonstrations are ideal telegenic events; they are dramatic, colorful, often violent, and even in slack moments the cameras can rest on the bearded, barefoot hippies or the good-looking, long-haired girls. In return for the useful footage the media men provide the dignity and self-respect that ordinary people derive from mass publicity.

It is very important in stage two that a few faculty members should side with the demonstrators "on the issues." In general, they will not directly condone rule violations, but by supporting the issues of stage one they add a stamp of approval to the whole enterprise and thus have the effect of indirectly excusing the rule violations. "It is unfortunate that there should be any disruption of the university, but it really is awful that the administration should kick poor Smith out just for sitting peacefully and nonviolently on the dean's desk for a few hours, especially when Smith was only trying to end racism and the war in Vietnam."

More important, the approval of faculty members provides a source of security and reinforcement of convictions. An undergraduate engaging in a disruption of university operations is not (anyhow not yet) engaging in a conventional and established form of political behavior. He feels deeply insecure, and the stridency of his rhetoric should not conceal the depth of his insecurity from us. The apparently passionate convictions of many university demonstrators are in fact terribly fragile, and when away from the crowd they are fairly easily talked out of their wildest fantasies. A few faculty members can provide security and reinforcement, and are therefore also a great aid in recruiting more student support. Old-fashioned people, Freudians and such, would say that the student needs the faculty member to play the role of an older sibling in his revolt against the administration-parent.

At the end of stage two there is a large scale demonstration against the university on the issue of stage one as transformed by the rhetorical impact of stage two. In the U.S. it takes the form of a large sit-in, though this has recently been developing into the seizure ("liberation") of a building, complete with barricaded doors and windows. In Paris it was also a matter of building street-barricaded doors and windows. (In Paris it is French tradition, not easily exportable, that somehow manages to survive, in spite of Haussmann, even in wide streets like the Rue Gay-Lussac. The survival of the tradition is aided by the presence of small cars to be used as barricade building material.) When the sit-in or seizure occurs the university authorities are strongly inclined to, and usually do, call out the police to arrest the people who are sitting in the building and move them out physically. When that happens, if all has gone according to the scenario, we enter stage three, and we enter it with a vengeance.

Stage Three: The Collapse of Authority

The first thing that happens in stage three is an enormous and exhilarating feeling of revulsion against the calling of the police. The introduction of hundreds of police on campus is regarded as the ultimate crime that any university administration can commit, and a properly led and well organized student movement will therefore direct all of its efforts in stages one and two to introducing a situation where the authorities feel rightly or wrongly that they have no choice but to call the police. Large numbers of faculty members who have so far watched nervously from the side lines, vaguely sympathetic with the students' rhetoric, but unwilling to condone the rule violations are suddenly liberated. Suddenly, they are rejuvenated by being able to side with the forces of progress against the forces of authority; and the anxieties of stages one and two are released in a wonderful surge of exhilaration that we can hate the administration for calling the cops instead of having to tut tut at the students for their bad behavior. On the students' side there is a similar euphoria, and in Berkeley at least the student health service reported a sharp decline in the number of students seeking psychological and psychiatric help in stage three in 1964. For excitement, meaningful participation, intensity of noble feeling and simple all around fun the modern university offers nothing that can compete with stage three.

In the transition to stage three the more police brutality you can elicit by baiting and taunting the police or the police are able to provide by themselves in the absence of any such incitement, the better; but, as any competent leader knows, police brutality is not strictly speaking necessary because any large-scale mass arrest will produce accusations of police brutality no matter what happens.

In the face of the sheer horror of the police on campus the opposition to the movement, especially the opposition among the liberal and moderate students, becomes enfeebled and usually collapses altogether. At this point, there is a general student strike, with fairly strong faculty support, and quite often the campus will be completely shut down.

Furthermore, the original demands of stage one are now only a small part of a marvelously escalated series of demands. Sometimes, as in Paris, the stage one demands may be pretty much forgotten. Who, for example, could remember on the barricades what Cohn-Bendit was agitating for back in stage one? A typical list of stage three demands would comprise:

- The president must be fired (he usually is, in fact);
- There must be amnesty for all;
- The university must be restructured so as to give the students a major share in all decision making;
- The administration has to be abolished, or at any rate confined to sweeping sidewalks and the like;
- The university must cease all cooperation with the Defense Department and other official agencies in the outside community;
- Capitalism must end—now;
- Society must be reorganized.

Meanwhile, interesting things are happening in the faculty: committees are meeting and drafting resolutions, alliances are being formed and petitions circulated. The faculty government, by tradition a sleepy and ill-attended body that gently hassles about parking and bylaws, is suddenly packed with record numbers of passionate and eloquent debaters. There are endless amendments and fights over the symbolism of a *"whereas"* clause. Great victories are won and symbolic defeats sustained. Also, in the general unhinging of stage three many faculty members discover all sorts of long forgotten grievances they have against the administration. There is simply no end of good grievances; and indeed in our best universities I believe this could be one of the conditions of continued employment: if you can't think up half a dozen really good grievances against the place you are probably not intelligent enough for continued employment in a university of top caliber. More important, deep and abiding hostilities and hatreds grow up among various factions in the faculty. Those who are active find that their political role is more important to their standing in the community than their scholarly achievement. No matter what the issues, more faculty energy is expended on hostilities within the faculty than at any nonfaculty targets, and the passionate feelings and hostilities usually go far beyond what is found in democratic politics of the real world. Like nuns struggling for power in a convent, many professors seem to lack the distance and detachment to see stage three university politics for the engagingly preposterous affair it usually is.

So now we have come from the halcyon days of stage one where there was only-a-small-minority-with-no-legitimate-grievances to the full-blown revolutionary ecstasy of stage three where the place is shut down, the president is looking for a new job, and the *effective* authorities are a handful of fairly scruffy-looking and unplausible sounding student leaders. How does it work? What is the fuel on which the mechanism functions?

Before I answer that, I need to make the usual academic qualifications to the model: it is intended only as an analytical framework and not a complete empirical generalization. Certainly, not all successful student revolts go through these three stages, and I can think of many counterexamples, and so on. Furthermore, I do not mean to imply that anybody on either side actually plans his behavior with these three stages in mind; I am not suggesting that student leaders sit in cellars asking themselves, "Are we in stage two yet?" Furthermore, I am not saying that the demonstrators are either in the right or in the wrong on the demands they make. Student demonstrators, like university administrators, are sometimes right, sometimes wrong; on some occasions such as the FSM in Berkeley the demonstrators have in my view been overwhelmingly in the right. I am just trying to describe a common pattern of events that has recurred in many places and over quite different issues, but it will be obvious from what I have said that I find it at least an *inefficient* method of resolving disputes on college campuses.

Getting back to the question, what makes it work? The unique feature of the present situation in universities is the pervasive dislike of and distrust of authority. Far more students in the Western democracies today, than say ten years ago, hate their governments, police forces, and university administrations (there are complex historical reasons for this, most of which have nothing to do with universities). I can, for example, remember when it was quite common for university presidents to be respected and admired even on their own campuses. Now it is almost unheard of (except after they have been fired). The strategy of a successful student movement is to unite this existing mistrust of authority with genuinely idealistic impulses on one of the Sacred Topics in such a way that assaults on university authority become a form of expressing that idealism. Each new exercise of authority then becomes further proof that the authorities are enemies of the idealism, and this serves to further undermine authority. The transition from each stage to the next, remember, is produced by the exercise of authority; and eventually with the use of mass police, if all has gone according to plan, campus authority collapses altogether. The strategy in short is to pit "the students" (the semantics, incidentally, are of some importance; it has to be "the students" and not "the radicals" or "the small minority") against "the administration" on an issue where it can appear, correctly or incorrectly, that the fight is about a Sacred Topic, and then to undermine the administration by provoking exercises of authority of a sort that serve to discredit it. The three stages then should be seen as a continuous progression beginning with the creation of an issue (or issues), and ending with the collapse of authority.

The demonstrators are always puzzled by the hostility they arouse among the liberal intelligentsia outside the university. But what the demonstrators perceive as the highest idealism often looks from the outside like a mixture of vandalism and imbecilic dogmatism. And though they can convince *themselves* that, say, Columbia, Stanford and Berkeley are racist institutions, few on the outside ever accept this view.

When administrations are defeated, they almost invariably go down as a result of technical mistakes, failure to grasp the nature of the struggle they are engaged in, and, most important, their own demoralization. A confident administration bent on defending intellectual values and consequently determined to destroy the power of its essentially anti-intellectual adversary, can generally win. Victory for the administration requires a readiness to deal with each of the three stages on its own terms and certain overall strategies involving internal university reforms and the intelligent use of discipline (even including the police when it comes to the crunch). Curiously, many college administrations in America don't yet seem to perceive that they are all in this together. Like buffaloes being shot, they look on with interest when another of their number goes down, without seriously thinking that they may be next.

Response by Jeff Lustig, graduate student, University of California, Berkeley, in The Daily Californian, *January 20, 1969.*

Not Foolproof, but Foolish

There are schools of political criticism, as there are of literary criticism, which by their very nature reveal more about the mind of the critic than about the qualities of the subject at hand. This is especially true of that type of criticism known as "debunking"—the attempt to deal with large events by hacking them down to some sort of manageable but crippled size. I am reminded of Savio's rejoinder to Lewis Feuer's classic "critique" of the FSM [Free Speech Movement]. As a basis for his explanation of the FSM, Professor of Philosophy Feuer had used a sexual interpretation of Savio's discussion of "mounting" public action. Savio asked, in response, whether the important questions revolved less about his use of the phrase than about the sort of mind which heard only this word and nothing else that was said.

John Searle's article reminded me of this exchange. For despite his original opposition to Feuer's position, Searle's current article shares many qualities of Feuer's approach. It's not that the article is without *some* resemblance to reality. But we are forced to think about the world-view which looks into the complexity of campus demonstrations, and finds only the events of this scenario to talk about.

Searle's discussion is not distinguished by any account of the issues, nor any hint of the real conflicts of value, no recognition of the historical context or political alternatives within the university, and hence, no explanation of the structures and uses of power. The scenario achieves its effect (which is a discrediting effect) *not* through explicit argument leading to a conclusion, but rather indirectly and by implication. The assertion that student revolts are only of passing interest, that they are illustrative only of the state of mind of a few students; this assertion is never stated clearly and weighed against other explanations. Searle *assumes* its validity as a premise of argument.

One way of understanding a demonstration, Searle tells us, is to see it as a three-act play. In this drama, the initial actors, who constitute a minority of students on the campus, attempt—by demanding the unobtainable and by provoking the administration to violence—to engage the larger student body, the faculty, and the press in a grand, exhilarating, free-for-all. What are the objects of this exercise? Searle discerns two: the desire to close the university and to have the head of the ritual scapegoat, the President.

The small band of (inside) agitators accomplishes its aims by hitching their wagon to what Searle refers to as a "Sacred Topic"; he adds that "almost any old issue will do." His examples of "any old issue" are "the First Amendment, race, and the war in Vietnam." Because demands relating to these issues are demands on which the university "cannot give in," the administration has no alternative but to call the cops and thereby "discredit" itself.

Searle's model is clean and economical. There are no contingencies, no serious arguments amongst the students, none of the tortured and messy dilemmas of commitment in which students wrench their lives into new directions. One can only wish that it were easy to consolidate power and to discredit the authorities, and also that mere discrediting were all that was required.

Even within its own terms Searle's model is far from satisying. Too many crucial questions go unanswered. Why don't the authorities, for example, merely refuse to call the cops? Why don't they refuse to be provoked, break out of the chain-link of stimulus-response logic, and cleverly confound the radicals? Better, why don't they invite the students to air their grievances, and grant them power to attempt solutions? What better device for isolating the trouble-makers! And, secondly, what gives these trouble-makers their particular powers of seduction? The dupes are, after all, products of the educational system of which Searle is so proud. And why do the activists live in a student body which feels so little loyalty to its institutions, which in fact share a "pervasive dislike and distrust of authority?" The answer lies outside Searle's frame of reference. Students dislike and distrust authorities because universities—far from being intellectual havens—are reflective of the society in which they live: reflective of its racism, its manipulation, and its current ties with the War in Vietnam; the institutions are felt, in short, to be structures of humiliation.

The foolproof scenario helps us to understand campus revolts about as much as an explanation of an industrial strike would if it told us that the workers were striking *in order* to close the plant, and to stop production. The account would be "true" by positivist standards; but it would nevertheless leave us ignorant of the reason the workers had risked their jobs; and it would leave us unprepared for future outbreaks of discontent.

In order to understand what really moves the students to revolt and what *will continue* to move them in new expressions of discontent, it would be necessary to deal with what the university *is,* what it should be, and where it is going. One would have to deal with questions of history, of educational theory, and of students' expectations. Of course it's possible to avoid these tasks; one merely narrows his perspectives. This is what Searle does—and what most social scientists do in similar situations. We are told that the model really was not meant to "explain" or to deal with these broader questions. "It is intended only as an analytical framework"—offered merely as an attempt to describe a common pattern of events . . .

This is a familiar sort of statement—especially to those in the social sciences. But it does not really dispose of objections. In the first place, the reader wonders why some patterns have been chosen rather than others; he wonders which values have been introduced *into* the analysis. In the second place, the reader is never sure about the significance of patterns which have been abstracted from historical and institutional milieus.

It would be entirely possible, to use the old example, for a man who had observed a concert to "explain" it in terms of common patterns which were absolutely meaningless; the concert consisted of the actions of one guy who waved a reed at others who scraped sticks on cat entrails and blew tin horns in response. What this "model" would leave out would be the most important aspects of the event—precisely what was necessary to understand it. The model would leave out the historical traditions and cultural context in which the concert was meaningful. It would ignore the intentions, the standards and the sensibilities of the people involved.

The function of this method, as often practiced by social scientists, is to smuggle an administrative ideology into research under the guise of a "value-free analytic framework." This seems also to be the function it fulfills for Searle.

The premise of the scenario is that nothing is really wrong with the University. There are no internal tensions, no actions which create hostility; there are no traces of the maladies which have been chronicled by every commission since the FSM: maladies pertaining to size and impersonality, to centralization, to the structure of governance.

This bias in approach would thus identify the political purposes behind this model, even if Searle did not himself admit them in his closing paragraphs. Searle's goal is, simply, to rally University authorities to destroy their "anti-intellectual adversaries."

For members of the Berkeley community, the fact that these purposes precede and direct the analysis comes as no great surprise. What is more intriguing is the ways that Professor Searle's purposes are entwined with the *manner* in which he pursues them. His devices are those we have come to identify with the administrative frame of reference. These are the devices, the modes of thought which—despite individual claims of neutrality or liberal values—invariably place administrators and their spokesmen squarely in the camps of reactionaries. This manner of thinking constitutes a new vocabulary of Reaction: one appropriate to the epoch of corporate, administered capitalism. Professor Searle's scenario is part of a new literary and political genre which has arisen in response to the new stage of student activism.

A glance at Searle's techniques of argument can therefore tell us of something not only about modern logicians and administrators, but also about the modern logic of administration.

The main thing to understand is that this logic attempts to render the whole world in its own image. As greater areas of the society become corporatized, the logic of administration encroaches on other logics, cultures, and points of view. Its "order" becomes the only possible order: its rationality is presented as the only legitimate rationality. The techniques it uses to deny the validity of others' interests included the refusal to listen to their expressions of discontent, the glossing over of inadequacies or mistakes within the administrative order, and the outright perversion of common sense concepts so as to deny them the ability to criticize administered reality.

The use of these devices is not restricted to university administrators. The problems of Blacks and workers have traditionally been explained away by their antagonists with just these methods. The strikes of the Thirties were originally attributed to a few foreign subversives; this was easier than analyzing the priorities and contradictions of industrial organization. Black attitudes are frequently explained in terms of a "lack of motivation" or a "culture of poverty," rather then as the results of actual institutions of racism and oppression.

These habits of analysis have been adopted by modern movement watchers. Armed with the tools of vulgar psychology, sociology, or political paranoia, many observers come to conclude that the rebels are never doing what they say they are doing. Instead, they are "really" acting out some unsuspected father rebellion, sexual liberation or totalitarian nihilism. Though Searle does not go this far, his scenario *is* premised on the assumption that the terms in which demonstrators explain their actions are irrelevant for an understanding of those actions. But public issues are never explained with this approach. They are explained away as some sort of private deviance.

A corollary aspect of this approach (also mentioned above) is its congenital blindness to the policies and politics of the institution. Initiative and responsibility seem to lie solely with the students. For example, Professor Searle suggests that it is the *students* who present (the demands) in the "maximally confrontationist style." By narrowing his focus to the empirically obvious sit-ins and marches, he removes attention from the less visible, but systematically confrontationist policies of the administration. But Berkeley students do not have to rack their brains for ready examples of administration-inspired confrontation. In October, 1964, University authorities confronted students by trying to censor the content of speech, under the guise of providing for access to campus grounds; in 1966 it did the same thing by attempting to close Sproul Steps to noon rallies. The history of the last few years may in fact be seen as one long confrontation between the students' needs and the imperatives of industrialization (e.g., by the speed-up of the Quarter System, the emphasis on technical at the cost of creative and critical studies, and the centralization of authority).

The effects of this jaundiced approach are also apparent in Searle's whimsical account of the selection of Sacred Topics. Granting that he meant to be humorous and not to imply that free speech or racism were equivalent to "any old issue," nevertheless his scenario obscures the primary role the administration plays in the selection of these issues. It has played this role at times by moving directly against student politics (as in FSM, Black Power Day, and Stop the Draft Week), and at other times by hypocritically taking away with the left hand what it protects with the right. (For instance, in October, 1966, Black Power advocates had to fight to hold a program on campus, while Marine Power recruiters were invited to the Plaza.)

That these forceful actions were "provoked" is no doubt true. That they were provoked by *students* is a patent falsehood. Rather, as with 139X * (and the FSM), the provocations came from *off* the campus. (And far from being resisted, they were usually invited by the administration.)

To overlook this—as well as the fact that administrators *chose* to call police on campus at two year intervals—is to deny that administrators are responsible for their actions. This imputation of inevitability, this masking of human agency, is the third of Searle's analytic devices. He implies that administrators had no alternative, exercised no choice, and acted automatically in the calling of the police. Instead of recognizing their real roles and responsibilities, Searle prefers—in writing his scenario—to ignore this entire body of protagonists. Their roles are accordingly either miscast, denied (through the fiction of the automatic response), or assigned to the limbo of the passive voice. In Searle's "Stage Two," for example, "The original issue is transformed so that the structure of authority in the University is itself the target." "Is transformed" by *whom?* By a small number of extremists? Or transformed by the actions of the authorities themselves, and their *decision* not to "give in"?

Belief in the pristine innocence of the Insitution is maintained, finally, by a fourth technique. This is the ultilization of concepts which appear to be neutral, but which in fact have been distorted in such a way as to lose the context we assign them in ordinary speech; the utilization of mental tools whose cutting edge has blunted. For example, whatever present situation exists on campus is called "order"; whatever opposition occurs is "disruption." There is no clarification of these criteria which distinguish an educational order from any other kind of order (for instance, the order of a well-run machine, or of a city under martial law). This refusal to make qualitative, substantive distinctions is a main characteristic of administrative logic. It also marks the paralysis of critical thought.

The most familiar use of this technique is the current statesman's or police chief's invocation of a Hobbesian "law and order."

* The course Eldridge Cleaver was invited to teach.

The corollary in Searle's article is his disposal of the complex, ancient problem of political legitimacy. "If you win, it turns out that your grievance was legitimate all along. If you lose, then, alas . . . you had no legitimate grievance." There are no standards aside from those of power. The ramification of thus "establishing right from fact" were pointed out by Rousseau's remark: "One might employ a more logical method, but not one more favorable to tyrants."

Of course University administrators never think of themselves as tyrants. They prefer to apply the label to students. The spectre of "left-McCarthyism" has thus become a familiar one. It was first raised by Mr. Feuer before being taken up by Professor Searle and former Special Assistant to the Chancellor Robert Cole, and before finally being baptized in fire by the honorable Mayor Alioto. The use of this ploy requires merely the indication of superficial similarities between Joe McCarthy and a modern student rebel (e.g., "passion"), and the neglect of substantive differences. The effect of this exercise is to redefine fascism; those who oppose the corporatization of life and the influence of secret agencies, become—by virtue of their passionate commitment—"left-McCarthyists." But just because the students oppose the Central "Intelligence" Agency doesn't mean they are anti-intellectual; only that they are against the secret, irresponsible sort of "intelligence" that has always been the adjunct of repression.

Because Searle's scenario obscures an understanding of the real problems of the University, and because it ignores the context and responsibilities of the participants, it turns out to be a foolish, rather than a foolproof scenario of student revolts.

It is far inferior in explanatory power to the model the students carry around in their heads. This model conceives of the University as reflecting the structures of power and the conflicts of interest within the larger society. It sees the same two options open to university authorities as are available to any other authorities now that the contradictions of liberalism are coming to the surface: either loyalty to formal principles of democracy and "experimental reform," or loyalty to the structures of privilege which have always been masked by liberal rhetoric. In the first case, a willingness to make fundamental changes; in the second, repression. . . .

For all its roughness, this analytic framework accounts for phenomena which remain anomalous for Searle. It explains the authorities' preference for the apparatus of coercion rather than for the mechanics of reform; it explains the increasing rigidity of University rules. It also accounts for the defection of the youth. The reason "it is no longer common for university presidents to be respected and admired even on their own campuses" is that the campuses have become "plants" instead of communities. Presidents act as administrative agents of a repressive and militaristic technology, rather than as educators. Why should Hitch be admired as an educator? His background qualifies him only to do some sort of cost-analysis of bombing for the Rand Corporation and the Department of Defense. Why should Heyns be respected? His professional training was in the particularly manipulative Human Relations school of social psychology. The reason these men lack respect, in addition, is because students are no longer content to become functionaries of the given order. They are demanding an education which really informs them of the world's ills, and an education that prepares them to participate in the cure of those ills.

Searle's foolproof scenario does not help us to understand student revolts. But it is not for that matter worthless. It does tell us something about the administrative reaction to those revolts.

Managers and administrators are basically expeditors. Their social function is to make sure that machines run smoothly. Politically, therefore, an administration is rigid. Its vocabulary does not permit political discussion. Its mechanisms provide no way for dealing with fundamental disagreements. Such disagreements interfere with its efficiency. Hence, a world-view or set of needs that cannot be codified and catalogued in its terms is dangerous—not only to the administration, but to the administrators, whose "normal functioning" is at stake. The dissenter stands as a disturbing reminder that the world may not fit into the filing cabinet. His rationality exists as an alternative to the manager's; his problems cannot be solved, and for that reason cannot be acknowledged, in the manager's terms. His very existence is a stubborn reminder that the administrative order may distort rather than represent the needs of its constituents. For these reasons, there is a basic tendency to crush dissent—not in the sense that Joe McCarthy crushed the Left, but in the more vicious sense that the agency of Minitrue rewrote history in *1984.* The recalcitrant parts of reality must be wiped away—as a *precondition* for the continued operation of the institution.

When social crises arise, as at the present, this logic becomes emphatic. The liberal theories of education and formal democracy have always served to mask rather than to deal with the realities of capitalist society. As that society encounters opposition, the formal trappings of "liberal education" and "free speech" are sloughed off. The administrators, especially in a college which constitutes a main forum of opposition, become the *de facto* overseers of social transformation. And in this process, the administrative order adds its imperatives to the logic of class repression. This, to me, is the larger meaning both of Chancellor Heyns' new attitudes towards political conflict, and of John Searle's scenario.

For a faculty member or university administrator to avoid this logic and these tendencies, he would have to recognize the reality of dissent and of the issues which gave rise to dissent. Short of this, he will find himself participating in those Orwellean inversions which seem to mark this stage of our history. (Remember that Hitch was working in the Department of "Defense".) We are living in a period when "education" is coming to mean "that which takes place in a vocational institute." Where traditional educational theory sought men who could criticize, this seeks men who will obey; where it wished to create men who could shape their society, this wants men who will agree to be shaped by others.

It is only by seeking Searle's article as a part of this War is Peace campaign that we can understand how he announces in the same paragraph that the University can defend "intellectual values" by instituting internal reforms (the need for which he has not admitted), *and* by "the intelligent use of discipline—even including the police when it comes to the crunch."

A model is usually evaluated according to how well it helps to "explain, predict, and control" the phenomena with which it deals. Because this scenario fails to explain student revolts, it also fails to predict future expressions of student dissent. Purely on the basis of this scenario, for instance, readers would have been unable to foresee either the advent of a new stage of student rebellions in the nation, or the creation of new forms of protest in the Bay Area. (I refer to the militant strike at State, and the promising Radical Student Union at Cal.) Because the model failed to explain, or predict, it must also fail to achieve its major goal—the facilitation of administrative *control* over student revolts. To the extent Searle and his colleagues continue to regard university problems in the same ways, they will necessarily "fail to grasp the nature of the struggle they are engaged in." This, along with "demoralization" (which has usually accounted for the failure in understanding) are cited by Searle as two of the main causes of administration defeats.

As indications of this demoralization rather than as aids to understanding, we therefore welcome such administrative scenarios. And we hope that those of the future may be distinguished by the same cleverness and vacuity.

CHAPTER 3

Disruption as a Tactic

Although mass confrontations have drawn the greatest attention from the national press, disruptions of social affairs and individual classrooms by small numbers of students have been equally important. The arguments for and against these smaller disruptions are different from the ones over mass obstruction.

The rationale for disruptive action is set forth by ten SDS members in their description of a banquet held in 1968 by the trustees of the University of Chicago in honor of the incoming president, Edward Levi. "We did not regard the Hilton dinner as a harmless social event," the SDS members wrote, "but rather as a meeting of our enemies and the enemies of dominated peoples throughout the world. These men threaten us. We could not let their threat go unchallenged." The SDS members decided they would strip the guests of "their cultural pretenses" and lay bare the vulgarity of the dinner beneath its "veneer of civility."

Classroom disruption has been a particularly sensitive issue linked to questions of academic freedom and professorial authority. At Columbia in the fall of 1968 a group of cultural revolutionaries called the Radical Action Cooperative disrupted the class of one of the university's most popular and liberal teachers,

Professor James Shenton. In an interview with reporters from the campus radio station WKCR, the disrupters responded to objections raised by students in the course. They explained that they chose Shenton as a target precisely because he was liberal and popular, arguing that it is men like him who have made an evil system tolerable. (Five students in RAC were subsequently arrested at Harvard for disrupting a course there and received heavy jail sentences.)

Although the disruption of Shenton's lecture at Columbia was disavowed by SDS members in the course, the following spring SDS disrupted a series of classes one morning to publicize a demonstration scheduled for the next day. In response, one hundred senior professors at Columbia issued a statement denouncing classroom disruptions as a threat to academic freedom. The faculty members called disruptive tactics "fundamentally inimical" to university life and insisted that education could not take place "if teachers and students are cast in an adversary role."

In answer to similar arguments at Cornell, radical economist Douglas Dowd suggested that disruptive actions were only now being construed as threats to academic freedom because they were challenges to people in the center and on the right. Dowd told a Cornell faculty committee investigating the effects of the 1969 spring crisis that harassment has for years been a normal matter for him and that he has never considered his academic freedom threatened.

Article by ten members of the University of Chicago SDS reprinted in The Hard Core, IV (*Columbia SDS*), *December 20, 1968.*

Work! Study! Get Ahead! Kill!

THE STORY OF THE INDELICATE DINNER

CHICAGO—The banquet hall filled with rich people in fine clothing grew silent as the dishes were cleared and speeches began. Suddenly a student seated at one of the tables got to his feet and cried out:

"McGeorge Bundy, you are responsible for the genocide in Vietnam. You're soaked in blood and your stench of death fills the room. I'm going to join my brothers in the street where the air is cleaner."

And, five minutes later, "University money in Trustee David Kennedy's bank supports racism in South Africa. That's liberal. Trustee David Kennedy is on the Non-Partisan Committee to Re-Elect Mayor Daley. That's liberal. This is business as usual for this liberal university and that's what we don't want any part of."

The setting was the Conrad Hilton Hotel, Nov. 13, as the ruling elite of the University of Chicago and its wealthy, politically-important friends dined together in honor of incoming university president Edward Levi.

The guests, expecting a gala social affair, were soon put totally up-tight by continuous student disruption. The diners' veneer of civility dissolved, baring an ugly vulgar reality.

It all started late in September, when SDS learned that the university was planning a huge, inaugural dinner for the new president to which were invited 2,000 of the country's top business and political leaders—and a handful of students.

Among those invited were Mayor Richard J. Daley, of Pig City, a man noted for his actions during a certain recent convention; Avery Brundage, internationally known racist sportsman, a close friend of A. Hitler; Robert McNamara, Edward Kennedy, Arthur Goldberg, Abe Fortas, Otto Kerner, Everett Dirksen, seven (count 'em, seven) members of the Rockefeller dynasty, plus the trustees, administration and selected faculty. Billed as main speaker was McGeorge Bundy, a key figure in engineering U.S. imperialism in Vietnam and now President of the Ford Foundation.

The dinner made it obvious that to whatever extent a power elite exists in this country, the university carefully cultivates relations with it. These are the men on whom the university depends for financing. That the relationship involves obligations in return is evident from the membership of the Board of Trustees, filled as it is with corporate leaders. Although they may leave the University alone in its day-to-day operations, they have final authority in all decisions concerning the direction and policy of the University. Such decisions include those on university expansion resulting in the destruction of housing in the South Campus area and the expulsion of 10,000 lower-class blacks from the University neighborhood; the choice of a new president; what new academic and research facilities are built; co-operation with Federal aid programs, and with the controls they impose; and even student housing—trustees, for example, rejected a plan for low-cost student housing in the neighborhood because this would lower property values.

These decisions are NOT socially or politically neutral, and the University knows it. "Within the framework of the law," reported a faculty committee appointed in 1967 to report on the disclosure of a case of political bias in admissions policy, "and in cognizance of the general value consensus prevailing in our society, it is the right of the University faculty and administrative officers to determine what shall be the culture, curriculum, and education goals of the University." This was to be done in part "through the choice of the succeeding generations of scholars."

It operates not only through specific decisions, but through fostering a general atmosphere in the University—an atmosphere friendly to sociology professor Morris Janowitz's "Social Control of Escalated Riots" and hostile to radical ex-UC professor Jesse Lemisch's "Merchant Seamen in the Politics of Revolutionary America."

This atmosphere shapes us as students and guides us toward roles we are intended to assume in later life—roles friendly to the ultimate purposes of McGeorge Bundy, Richard Daley, and seven members of the Rockefeller family.

We don't think that the University of Chicago serves purposes different from those of other American universities, or that these purposes make it in any way more sacred than any major American corporation. Like any institution in our society, this one can be defended only to the extent that it helps restructure our society to satisfy the aspirations of those at its bottom and those in other countries whom it milks for its prosperity. To the extent that it does not do this—indeed, serves purposes directly opposed to these—it is subject to criticism, and to attack.

It does not do so now. We did not regard the Hilton dinner as a harmless social event, but rather as a meeting of our enemies and the enemies of dominated peoples throughout the world. These men threaten us. We could not let their threat go unchallenged.

Administration and faculty response to a radical faculty member's endorsement of the dinner protest exposed even more clearly the fraudulent nature of the claim of University neutrality.

There were primarily two types of responses. First, those which justified the dinner as "University tradition" and "an appropriate means of reaffirming relationships with the community." These faculty described Bundy simply as "a former government official," totally ignoring his role in fashioning the war in Vietnam.

The second group consisted of liberal faculty who tried to make excuses for the dinner. Mayor Daley was invited in April, they argued, and one certainly couldn't expect those who made the guest list to be prophets of what they themselves described as "one of the worst political crimes of the decade." What they don't recognize is that when you sleep with dogs, you get fleas.

SDS called for a massive student protest outside the Hilton. We wanted to say that the time has passed when 2000 fat-cats can get together for a pleasant evening of wining and dining and expect it to go smoothly. We set up our picket line in front of the Hilton's main entrance, with over 150 students, carrying signs like "Welcome to Pig City," "Is it Plato that U of C Really loves?" and "Free Speech for Capitalists and Imperalists." Chanting "Work, Study, Get Ahead—Kill!" the pickets, who were not invited to the President's banquet, held their own festivities in the streets for four-and-a-half hours.

Early in the evening the cops tried to get the picket line away from the entrance of the hotel. Threatening arrest in their attempt to disperse the demonstrators, they were answered by a unanimous vote to continue the picket. The university, again proving its lack of political power, sent an official down to ask the cops not to arrest anyone. And no one was arrested.

Meanwhile, several radicals had managed to receive invitations to the dinner being held inside. Determined that the ruling elite no longer have care-free get-togethers, the invited SDSers planned a continued disruption of the speeches which came after dinner. Typical dinner conversations between radical students and the administrators invariably seated next to them were as follows:

Adm: (Pleasantly and with total condescension) Are you a student in the college?
SDS: (Smiling) Yes I am.
Adm: (Same as above, shaking head affirmatively) Do you like the University?
SDS: (Smiling broadly) No, I think it eats shit.

Dishes were cleared and the speeches began. The disruption was planned so that every five minutes, students dispersed throughout the enormous room would stand up and scream a political rap to the audience.

One student shouted, "McGeorge Bundy, you developed that atrocity that is our policy in Vietnam; now I've been called to fight in that atrocity. Here is my draft card and here is my answer to that call!" and ripped up his draft card. One girl yelled, "You spend $150,000 here tonight that could be used to establish a child day-care center for the university community." After each student gave his rap, he stomped out of the room, shouting, "Work, study, get ahead—Kill!" and joined the picket line outside. Disruption lasted until the end of the dinner.

The audience responded at first by screaming, "Get out of here," "Sit down!" and "Shut up!" Comments to one another were, "This university is too free, get those communists out of here!" As the audience realized it was in for a full night, they became increasingly venomous and vulgar. Guests began to hit and kick the students as they left the hall. They jumped out of their seats to grab demonstrators before they could speak, and cursed, and shrieked, and waved their fists at us.

One girl had water thrown at her while shouting to the audience. By the end of the evening, those who financially support our "Great University" had been shorn of all their cultured pretenses. When confronted with student opinion, all McGeorge Bundy could do, interrupting himself, was shout, "You're . . . you're . . . SILLY!" And Julian Levi, brother of the new President and a power by his own right, spat in a student's face.

During the dinner, the hotel's kitchen staff, who were digging the disruption a lot, helped uninvited students to infiltrate the ballroom through the kitchen entrance. The evening ended with a sense of victory and success for the students, both inside and out. The demonstrators retired after four hours of picketing but confronted the departing guests with the spirited chant of "Work, study, get ahead—Kill!"

The faces of the ruling elite were so drawn and expressionless that they looked like powdered pulp.

Transcript of a dialogue from WKCR tapes, Columbia University, fall 1969. The comments in quotes were made by students in a course taught by Professor James Shenton after it was disrupted by the Radical Action Cooperative. A, B and C were members of RAC who took part in the distruption.

A Dialogue on Classroom Disruption

1. "Why did you pick on Shenton? After all, he's doing the best he can in the situation."

"It's an insult to his radicalism."

"He's a good professor. I like his lectures."

"I was interested in what he had to say about the War of 1812."

"There's lots of room for creativity in his class. He doesn't give silly exams. In fact, you can write a paper instead."

A. We do not aim to criticize James P. Shenton as an individual; rather, we aim to criticize our insane, repressive, and inhumane society. Within our society, the University serves as an "Officers' Candidate School," socializing tomorrow's leaders. Shenton is one of the more appealing functionaries in this school. Like the smiling recruiting officer, he is doing his socially-prescribed job in the best way he knows how. It is precisely because he is a "good teacher" and a "nice" fellow that he is dangerous. The point is that gentle Jim Shenton is doing violence to you, and to himself, by creating a false consciousness of security within the University.

> Exploitation must not be seen as such. It must be seen as benevolence. Persecution preferably should not need to be invalidated as the figment of a paranoid imagination, it should be experienced as kindness. Marx described mystification and showed its function in his day. Orwell's time is already with us . . .
>
> In order to rationalize our industrial-military complex, we have to destroy our capacity to see clearly any more what is in front of and to imagine what is beyond, our noses. Long before a thermonuclear war can come about, we have had to lay waste our own sanity.

Shenton, of course, appears late in this process of organized mystification that started with kindergarten.

> We begin with the children. It is imperative to catch them in time. Without the most thorough and rapid brainwashing their dirty minds would see through our dirty tricks. Children are not yet fools, but we shall turn them into imbeciles like ourselves, with high I.Q.'s if possible.
> (R. D. Laing, *Politics of Experience,* pp. 57–58)

B. Some have called Shenton a "radical." His "radicalism" conceals the reality of his role. He accepts a position within the existing hierarchy. He lives the status of "professor" and thereby perpetuates the inferior status of the student and the custodian (who may have five kids but only one tenth of a professor's salary). We seek a classless society in which all men will have control over their own lives and not be competing for wealth, prestige and power over others.

2. [Comments not transcribed.]

A. Maybe it's not so ineffective. About half the class stayed, and only a few were overtly hostile. Of the students who left, we interviewed about a dozen later and none felt the intervention illegitimate. How many do you suppose read the handout? Isn't that a hell of a lot higher percentage than the usual leafleting on campus walk? But suppose not a single leaflet was read. The sacrosanct image of the classroom has been cracked. People have expressed real emotion (even if hostility toward the interventionists). People talk, ask questions. Something is happening.

B. If it's not so effective, can you suggest a more effective tactic? What have *you* been *doing* to transform American society? If you're a cynic, we have nothing more to say to you, since you have accepted your own impotence. We've been experimenting with a variety of intervention styles, of which the imposing style of our Academic Game skit is only one. Maybe other styles will prove more effective, but we'll only find out by trying. Maybe different styles are more effective for different situations (e.g., physical science vs. social science lectures, domineering vs. "nice guy" profs, conservative schools vs. liberal schools, high school vs. college).

3. "You're violating the rights of the other students." "You're

violating academic freedom." "We wanted to hear Shenton, and you wouldn't let us."

A. Of course, you have the right to do what you want, but you also have the responsibility to ask yourself whether you *really* want what you think you want. If market research can create artificial needs (alienated desires) such as fatless fat and sugarless sugar, isn't it also likely that a similar technique has created an artificial need for a university education? Why would you want to sit in on a lecture (which could just as well be tape-recorded) if there was anything better to do. Of course, the answer may be that you have nothing better to do. If so, it goes to show just how far our "advanced" society has succeeded in raising the Level of Boredom. For most of us, a university education is a lesser evil. For a young man, the alternatives are Army, Navy, Air Force or Marines, loss of job opportunity, loss of prestige, loss of self-esteem ("You're a chickenshit and couldn't make the grade") etc. For women the alternatives are boring work or housewifery. True we imposed on you. Our purpose in doing so was to point out how "legitimate authority" imposes on you every day in a thousand ways; so much so that their impositions are accepted as "natural," while ours was disturbing because unusual.

B. Your right to do what you please is always qualified by your responsibility not to violate the same right of others (to life and sanity, for example) both in this country and abroad. Your passivity in accepting this part of the system is a political act for which you are responsible. We challenge your action.

4. "Your actions violated the norms of etiquette and politeness." "You demonstrated disrespect for both the prof and your fellow students." "You were rude and discourteous."

A. As we said above (1) we do not aim to criticize either the prof or the students as individuals, but rather we criticize the roles they play in the larger system. The difficulty is raised by the fact that so many people have defined themselves in terms of their societal roles rather than as human individuals. If you can help us design tactics which avoid the confusion of these two criticisms without compromising the effectiveness of the social criticism, please let us know.

B. Such norms (as falling silent when the professor speaks, accepting his control of discussion, refraining from writing on the blackboard, not entering or leaving the classroom except at prescribed times, not discussing "personal" matters, etc.) serve to perpetuate the existing system and its inhumanity and injustices. All norms are inherently restrictive and must be subordinate to the freedoms they supposedly protect. Your cry is like that for "Law and Order" without mentioning the injustices which our legal system perpetuates. In transforming the existing system it will be necessary for people to free themselves from such norms of etiquette. Free men will not respect norms and laws which violate freedom in her own name.

C. You say "It's rude" to interrupt your class for ten minutes, but you probably don't bat an eye to hear that 2000 Vietnamese have been killed and 5000 Biafrans have starved this week. How are you protesting these "insults" to humanity?

5. "If you critics of the existing system could come up with a better alternative I'd listen to you. But as long as you criticize without being creative, don't bother me."

A. It's not necessarily the responsibility of the critic to produce a solution to the problem he sees. We feel that the existing society is repressive (tolerant though this repression may seem). We seek to end this repression. This is ample work for the present. Would you ask the prisoner escaping from a concentration camp to produce a "better alternative"? (Better what? A better concentration camp?)

B. It would be premature and unrealistic for us to suggest an alternative to the present structure. We (the critics) are not entirely free from the debilitating effects of our socialization. Furthermore, the acceleration of our "civilization" (such as it is) makes any static solution obsolete the moment it is devised.

C. But most fundamentally, it would be paternalistic for us to give a solution which we expected others to follow. When men and women are free, they will decide their own fate, will create their own structures appropriate to their own *unalienated* desires. In the meantime, we will do what we feel we must to achieve our own freedom and to unmask the present repressive society.

6. "Your skit was humorous, and I've heard those old jokes before (like about academic castration)."

A. If you think our humor indicates a lack of seriousness, you are mistaken. If you place yourself in the role of drama critic, you are merely expressing your own alienation. We do not set ourselves up as a spectacle for your amusement; rather we mimic the spectacle that you "buy" daily, the spectacle of the American commodity system which makes a wasteland of your life. The joke is on you!

For them that obey authority
that they do not respect in any degree,
who despise their jobs, their destiny,
speak jealously of them that are free,
do what they do to be
nothing more than something they invest in.

—Dylan

Classrooms confine students.
They can't hold a free man.

Statement by over 800 faculty members of Columbia University, April 21, 1969.

The University as a Sanctuary of Academic Freedom

The tradition of the university as a sanctuary of academic freedom and center of informed discussion is an honored one, to be guarded vigilantly. The basic significance of that sanctuary lies in the protection of intellectual freedoms: the rights of professors to teach, of scholars to engage in the advancement of knowledge, of students to learn and to express their views, free from external pressures or interference. These freedoms can flourish only in an atmosphere of mutual respect, civility and trust among teachers and students, only when members of the university community are willing to accept self-restraint and reciprocity as the condition upon which they share in its intellectual autonomy.

Academic freedom and the sanctuary of the university campus extend to all who share these aims and responsibilities. They cannot be invoked by those who would subordinate intellectual freedom to political ends, or who violate the norms of conduct established to protect that freedom. Against such offenders the university has the right, and indeed the obligation, to defend itself. Nor does the sanctuary of the university protect acts violating civil or criminal law, which are illegal whether committed on or off the campus.

Current attempts to disrupt or prevent the holding of classes are a matter of urgent concern to us. These tactics are fundamentally inimical to university life. No genuine education can take place if teachers and students are cast in an adversary role. Disruptions deny students their right to an education and scholars their right to be heard.

The claim is false that only by disruptive tactics can criticism be made effective and university policies changed. In the past important policy and curriculum changes have been made through faculty and student action, in which rational discussion has been used to find constructive solutions to our problems. We recognize the need for further reforms and hope that all members of the university community will join in the process of orderly discussion leading to such changes, but we cannot accept force as a substitute for reasoned argument in deciding matters affecting the curriculum, instruction, and administration of the university.

In September of 1968 the faculty of this University adopted interim rules in order to insure the right to demonstrate peaceably and at the same time guarantee that the normal functioning of the university would not be impeded. It is desirable that university discipline be administered through bodies representative of the academic community, but this can be effective only if their members accept their responsibility to protect each other's rights and demonstrate the will to act. The argument that "justice delayed is justice denied" applies to the university community as well as to persons charged with violations of campus rules. Justice is denied the community if disciplinary cases go unresolved and all proceedings are subsequently abandoned.

We hope that present judicial bodies and any university-wide senate to be established will not shirk their responsibility in these matters. Teachers and students are entitled to meet their classes without interference, and the university is obliged to secure that freedom. We call upon all members of this and other universities to defend by example and by action the fundamental principles of a free university. It is our intention not to surrender the safeguards of freedom that men have erected at great sacrifice over several centuries.

Statement made to the Committee on Academic Freedom and Tenure of the Cornell Constituent Assembly by Professor Douglas F. Dowd, Department of Economics, Cornell University, May 1969. Professor Dowd was at the time co-chairman of the National Mobilization Committee to End the War in Vietnam.

Whose Academic Freedom?

This is a response to the memo of May 5 from the Committee on Academic Freedom and Tenure. I should like to provide your Committee with some excerpts from my own history at Cornell, along with some interpretative comments on that history and on the present situation, as regards the question of academic freedom. . . .

I probably do not have to tell you that my viewpoint and my activities both in and outside the classroom have been controversial. As an economist, I am a radical (or seen as such), and my "extra-curricular" activities have been in accord with that professional stance, making me something of an activist—as regards matters of war and peace, arms, race questions and the like. The diverse attacks on me have come from people to the "right" (an imprecise term, of course) of me, people who have been encouraged to be vocal and even abusive over the past twenty years or so by an environment that seemed to make of people on the "left" something beyond the pale. More recently, harassers have apparently been stimulated by a sense of contest and conflict, there now being something increasingly substantial in the way of movement coming from what were earlier silent quarters. But now, of course, people in the center and on the right are finding their views contested. In my view, they see this contest as a threat to their freedom. In fact, I believe that they are simply unused to serious challenges. The latter, as you will see, have been a normal matter for me. . . .

In the past ten years or so at Cornell, a period during which the almost total political apathy of the 1950s has been increasingly replaced by political involvement—beginning with arms control and disarmament, and moving into civil rights, the Vietnam War, and now the whole range of issues raised by black and white students concerning the university itself—the following kinds of incidents have been a continual part of my life here:

—Several times during the Malott period, I was called into the President's office and asked, in effect, "Did you really say these things?" The "things" I was asked about had to do with public talks on Cuba, on the American economy, on the American educational system, and so on. Had I chosen to do so, I could have construed those requests as intimidation.

—More than once, in the early 1960's, I was pelted with eggs, tomatoes, and on one occasion stones, while giving public talks on the campus and off the campus in Ithaca.

—In the years 1963–1965, while active in a civil rights project organized by Cornellians (for work in the South), I was frequently harassed in and out of the classroom, received threatening letters, had my office broken into, and had my car damaged—*inter alia.*

—I receive at least one letter a week, on the average (and have, for years), from students, parents, unidentifiable persons, telling me of their desires to have me removed from the campus, of removing their children from the campus, of having me chained to a tree and burned alive, etc.

—In the past six months, on the average of once a week, a young white man comes to my office, stands in the door, and says "pig!" I am able to identify him by name, if that is not believed.

—Middle of the night and early morning calls have been intermittent over the years; in the past few weeks they have taken place hourly every night. The telephone company is now investigating this case successfully, by virtue of its regularity and predictability.

. . . I do not consider these events, or others unmentioned like them, to be threats to my academic freedom. Perhaps I should; but that I have continued to teach, research, write and speak as I choose would seem to indicate that in fact the existence of such actions does not by itself weaken academic freedom for those harassed.

Finally, and as I suggested earlier, I believe that much of what many faculty members consider to be threats to their academic freedom is rather their difficulty in coping with what is for them a new situation; namely, a situation in which moderate people are finding their ideas challenged, and in which moderate people find themselves occasionally receiving threats. Those who threaten, like the bomb that one hears explode, seldom do damage of any serious variety. In the classroom, ideas should not be put forth that are indefensible. If they are defensible, the class is improved by the discussion. . . .

CHAPTER 4

Politicizing the Universities

The debate on legitimate procedures for change has not been exclusively concerned with forms of protest. Beyond the question of whether or not obstructive tactics are justified is another issue: Is the campus the right place to organize a social movement? Is it right to "politicize" the universities?

For liberals, like John Bunzel, politicization means the "intrusion of politics onto the campus." For others, like Leo Litwak, politicization means an awakening to politics. The accounts by these two professors at San Francisco State of the events at their college in 1969 illustrate the differences between their positions. Bunzel stresses the cost of politicization in terms of lost academic freedom, while Litwak emphasizes the possibilities for change through increased political awareness. What Bunzel sees as a tragedy for the university, Litwak sees as a liberating experience.

In "The university politicized," the editors of Columbia's student paper argue that although the university is worth preserving, its politics must be changed "by whatever means necessary" so that it plays a part in radically transforming American society. Replying to the editorial and to the "The university as a sanctuary of academic freedom" (see pages 61–62), Professor Allan Silver objects to both the students' desire to politicize the university "by whatever means necessary," and the "defensive pieties" of the faculty declaration.

San Francisco State

Statement by Professor John H. Bunzel, Department of Political Science, San Francisco State College, to Special Subcommittee on Education of the House Committee on Education and Labor, March 25, 1969.

Costs of the Politicized College

I would like to address myself to some of the problems that have emerged on our campus (but not ours alone) as a consequence of certain developments which, in my judgment, need serious attention. Put briefly, I am deeply concerned about the intrusion of politics onto the campus and the enormous strains and tensions which an increasingly wide range of political activities are creating for our academic communities. This issue, it need hardly be said, transcends one's political allegiances and party loyalties. Nor is this a liberal issue or conservative problem. I have in mind, rather, the delicate and complex idea of academic freedom in the most profound sense of that term and, more specifically, the political pressures and passions which are now being generated at such a fever pitch on our campuses that the climate conducive to orderly procedures and rational inquiry is now in jeopardy.

The situation at San Francisco State, if one can step back from the immediacy of day-to-day events and their attendant difficulties, is a clear case in point. We have had to pay a terrible price for the mindlessness that has run rampant on our campus, to the point where threats, intimidation, and violent behavior have become part of our ways of life. The consequences of disruptive demonstrations, bomb scares (as well as real bombs), arson, roving bands of vandals, breaking into classes that are in progress—these are only the most dramatic, but nonetheless real, occurrences which have worked to politicize our campus, to polarize the faculty, and to charge the atmosphere with passion, bitterness, and enmity. The tragic irony, of course, is that San Francisco State, once so open and free to everyone, is now exposed like a raw nerve—exposed to anyone who wants to tear it apart. What must be understood is that the academic community rests and depends on very fragile understandings. It has no elaborate mechanisms of self-protection, which is simply to say it is all too vulnerable to those who would use power, pressure, and muscle.

Let me turn now to certain dimensions of our general malaise and try, at the risk of great oversimplification, to illuminate what, to me at least, are some of their major implications for both the short and the long run. If nothing else emerges, I hope it will become clear that I have a tender regard for what a university community is and for the special values it represents. At the very least my idea of an academic community is very different from that of those who want to turn it into a political staging area, or who insist that it become exclusively an instrument of social reconstruction.

Consider the recent teachers' strike at San Francisco State. I opposed the strike, although I have been a strong trade union supporter most of my life. For one thing, I have always felt that a strike, if it is to be effective, should have solid backing, and that is precisely what the striking teachers did not have and have never had. A year or so ago the American Federation of Teachers union was specifically rejected, in a democratic written secret ballot, as the faculty's bargaining agent, and during the strike about two-thirds of the faculty voted against it. Besides, I have some reservations about a teachers' union treating a college in the same way an industrial trade union might treat a reactionary employer. The use of confrontation, the weapon of the strike by a minority against the majority of its faculty colleagues, the withholding of students' grades at the end of the semester as if students were an economic commodity—these tactics could do serious damage to an academic community if they became a permanent way of life.

But there were even more serious reasons why I felt this was the wrong strike at the wrong time—and led by the wrong people. A single incident will serve to make the point, especially since it outraged the great majority of the faculty and also resulted in many resignations from the union. The president of the teachers' union, in a letter to all members of the faculty, arbitrarily divided them into (his words) "friend versus enemy." Arrogantly and belligerently he pronounced the union's attitude: "You will not have the luxury of nice distinctions or Byzantine excuses," he told us, overlooking the fact that a community of scholars has a specific responsibility to make distinctions—nice, Byzantine, or otherwise. "He who observes our picket line is a friend anyone who plans to cross will be subject to moral force." I for one was subject to more than moral force, unknown in origin but revealing the conditions which, unhappily, have become all too familiar. One night after my wife and I had gone to bed someone slashed the tires of both cars and painted all over them "fascist scab."

My argument should not be misunderstood. Some of the demands of the union were and are shared by many members of the faculty, but that is not the point. As one of the oldest members of the union put it himself, "I think it is not intellectually honest for us to argue that the trustees should negotiate with us. How righteously would we scream if the trustees sat down and negotiated with AAUP, for example? Our right to negotiate for the faculty is no better founded than theirs. I am sorry that this is true. But it is true. And, as long as it is true, I cannot honestly argue that we have a right to expect the trustees to bargain with us. . . ." For me and most of the faculty a significant and overriding question has been clear from the beginning of the strike: by what right did a small minority feel it could try to impose its ideology on the rest of us? These were the political moralists who, with little support from their colleagues, regarded every rejection of their demands as further confirmation of their right to call a halt to all teaching and to suspend the academic program. The real danger lay in their wish and determination to politicize the college or, failing that, to shut it down.

Or take the student strike that began last November when the Black Students Union and the Third World Liberation Front presented 15 "non-negotiable" demands. Apart from the demands themselves, some of which are reasonable and others of which are not, the key term is "non-negotiable." No one on this committee needs to be told that there is no such thing as a non-negotiable demand if one is seriously interested in realistic, achievable goals. Reasonable men who have differences and disagreements have a better chance of accommodating each other if they can discuss concrete issues that can lead to concrete results.

I think it has to be made clear that San Francisco State has been a victim of exploitation by intransigent radicals. When I say this I have some specific thoughts in mind about the tactics that have been used on our campus. Many student groups on other campuses around the country have used a variety of tactics designed to bring about reforms in the educational system at their college. They wanted to make changes, and they wanted to be a part of those changes. But on our campus the militant student leaders from the beginning have used tactics that were intended not to bring about changes but to shut the place down. The distinction is important, and it has to be understood if one wants to understand what has taken place here.

Whatever the faults of our college—and we have plenty of them, from the typical administrative lethargy that is slow to change, to a lack of urgent attention to many legitimate student grievances about the curriculum—we are not a reactionary place. We are, on the contrary, very liberal. The faculty is liberal, the student body is liberal; in fact, I have never seen a place with so much permissiveness and so few rules. But for the hard core revolutionaries on this campus that is not enough. To put it simply, they have to use confrontation tactics on the college so that they can confront its power. More than that, they must force the power of the college to show its ugly face. They know, of course, that the college, because it is liberal, wants to show a friendly and moderate face; it wants to discuss, to hold meetings, and to have forums and convocations. But the radicals also know that this whole method of convocations and discussions will help maintain the evil system. Thus, what they have to do is make the college show that it is an ugly fascist beast. How do they do this? By forcing the college to call the police, and then by forcing the police to use clubs and violence. Stokely Carmichael once said that any demonstration in which police are not involved is a failure for demonstrators.

One expects this kind of exploitation and tactics from such groups as the Students for a Democratic Society. What has been more perplexing is the militant black leadership on our campus: it does not precisely fit the pattern of behavior of black militants on every other campus around the country. What has been missing among the hard core black leadership here is an operating principle of reality—a clear, realistic sense of what is possible and achievable. This is what I mean when I say that no one with any real political sense would insist that their demands were non-negotiable. As a matter of fact, there are already some signs that, finally, the militant student leaders have discovered that their non-negotiable demands are, in fact, quite negotiable. If and when this happens, it would be a big step forward from the tiresome intransigence of "Either we get all our non-negotiable demands met or we will shut you down."

In a small way my own case may be illustrative here. For many years I have been committed to the development of a sound program of ethnic studies at San Francisco State. However, the problem this year has been that my concern for some measure of academic substance and integrity in the program of Black Studies has gotten lost in the fierce level of rhetoric in which the bullhorn replaced conversation and listening gave way to diatribe. At the beginning of the fall semester I was informed by the vice president for academic affairs that I might become a "target" in the months to come. As it turned out, he was right. My troubles started with an article I had written on Black Studies at San Francisco in which I was critical not of the idea of Black Studies but of the *particular* perspective of Nathan Hare, who put together the proposal for Black Studies. Mr. Hare has been very clear about the kind of program he wants—this was long before he was suspended for jumping up on the stage and interrupting President Hayakawa's address to the faculty. He has said he wants teachers in his model of a Black Studies Department who will work solely within a "black revolutionary nationalist framework. I don't want any assimilationists," he says, by which he means Negroes. My article simply raised questions about his approach, because I do not agree with it. In a public speech a few months ago Mr. Hare said, "I think this is a time for hate." I do not agree with that, and I am not persuaded that that sentiment has any place in a college program. But in the kind of polarized, combustible environment we have had on the campus, one either supported Mr. Hare's program entirely, or he was tagged an enemy.

One morning in October around 8:30 a bomb was found leaning against my office door by one of my colleagues who happened to pass and heard it ticking. The building was immediately evacuated, and the demolition crew from the nearby Army post was called. Fortunately, no one was hurt. I have no idea who put the bomb there, nor have the police ever found out. But the important point is this: In an academic community it is ideas that should triumph, not power, or some group's interests or demands, or the tactic of physical pressure or emotional duress.

My most recent experience demonstrates, I think, the extent to which this delicate and complex notion of academic freedom can be endangered in the classroom itself by those who have no understanding of or commitment to the right to free intellectual inquiry in the pursuit of knowledge. During the preregistration period at the opening of this semester about 50 students, including many of the leaders of the Black Students Union, the Third World Liberation Front, and other student radicals and known supporters of the four-month-old strike, enrolled in my upper division course on Community Power and the Politics of Leadership. The next day majors in political science and others who wished to take the course were admitted to the class, bringing the final enrollment to one hundred.

At the first meeting it immediately became obvious that about half of those present had no legitimate interest in the course and were there for other reasons. I attempted to begin the course and explain what it would be about, but never got beyond the first sentence when the room erupted into shouts and other forms of verbal abuse from 25 or so militant students. One student jumped to his feet time after time and shouted quotations from Chairman Mao. Others were more shrill and personal in their denunciations. For some 20 minutes I tried to make myself heard over their torrent of invective. Unsuccessful, I finally had to dismiss the class.

On Wednesday I tried again, this time to begin the first lecture. I indicated that I would remain at the end of the hour to answer any and all questions. But the barrage of invective commenced once more, and after a half hour of asking the disrupters to permit me to speak, I had to dismiss the class for the second time. On Friday the disruptive tactics started again. The students this time were warned that, if they did not stop their continuous and purposive interruptions, disciplinary action would be taken. They did not, at which point two students were suspended. Another was suspended in my class the next day for similar behavior.

Ernest Besig, executive director of the American Civil Liberties Union of Northern California, was an invited guest in the class on Friday, February 21, and observed what took place. He was a witness to the disturbances in the classroom and has told me he was amazed that only two students were suspended. It is his belief that eight or ten others could have been suspended for disrupting the class and for interfering with the academic freedom of the professor and the other students. He has informed me that the ACLU will not intervene in behalf of those who have been charged with disruptive behavior in my class.

The paramount issue is unequivocally clear and of fundamental importance to the academic community, which includes faculty and students alike. The inviolability of the classroom is a principle that cannot be compromised. It involves nothing less than the integrity of the academic process and, in the most profound sense, is at the heart of academic freedom.

What is particularly distressing to me and, I am sure, the great majority of the faculty, is that this view and commitment is not unanimously shared by our colleagues. I find this personally very disturbing. During the week of my difficulties a resolution was introduced in the Academic Senate reaffirming the right of the student to learn and the teacher to teach in the classroom. It further asserted that any denial of such rights is not acceptable to the college community and that the senate will support the obligation of the college administration to protect these rights. Nineteen members of the senate voted to support the resolution; four voted against; eight abstained. No phraseology of a resolution is ever completely satisfactory. But surely the principle at issue here far transcends in importance any other divisions among us and is an irreducible minimum deserving support of every faculty member. I find it hard to believe, but, regretfully, not surprising, that 12 members of the Academic Senate could not support the resolution. If the faculty cannot agree that the classroom is inviolate, then I think we have moved a step closer to turning the academic community into a cockpit of ideologues.

I come, then, at this precise juncture, to the nub of the issue of academic freedom. When freedom to teach and freedom to learn are imperiled, when libraries are ransacked, when professors are harassed by anonymous phone calls, when ungovernable passions are deliberately inflamed, it is not for us, in the words of my colleague, Professor Philip Siegelman, "to inquire too much whether such extraordinary attacks come from the far left or the far right. They become facts of our existence, and we would be criminally negligent to condone or approve them because of their particular source." On this particular point it should be noted that while the militants of the left have always jealously guarded against any incursions from the far right, they have not shown an equal determination or readiness to react to the more novel threats in this area coming from within their own ranks. This moral duplicity and double standard has the suggestion of fanaticism at its worst.

I take it as an article of faith that has its roots in the long history of the liberal tradition that when freedom is attacked or suppressed, liberals must take their stand in opposition. It used to be that the severest threats to academic freedom came from above and outside—in a word, from the avenging furies of the far right—with the result that the faculty was almost instantly united. But now, when the assaults come from the inside and from the new brand of left-wing political moralists, the faculty is just as instantly divided. In the blunt words of a perceptive associate, if the threat were white and right instead of black and left, we on the faculty would always be close to unanimous. The attack on academic freedom from the left, of course, is by no means always tied to black militancy and extremism. But the basic question remains: when principles that are fundamental to the academic community are cynically exploited by the extremists of the left, why do the liberal and moderate members of the faculty not stand firm in their opposition to those who would impose their will by threats or coercion? It is a phenomenon which deserves more than passing notice.

For one thing, there is a failure of nerve, a lack of moral courage, on the part of many faculty members who become, consciously or unconsciously, victims of a form of psychological and moral intimidation exercised by the left-wing radicals. It has the immediate and practical result of silencing the middle, or, to put it another way, of engendering the feeling on the part of a great number of the faculty that there is something shameful about speaking out or being in opposition. This has nothing to do with physical coercion. It is a subtle but powerful control over people who might normally speak out but who, in an increasingly politicized and polarized arena, impose their own self-restraints and remain silent or otherwise preoccupied. Some resolve whatever personal dilemma they may feel by simply withdrawing altogether—"the problems are too massive."

There is, however, another consideration that also must be noted. Traditionally, college faculties have never been organized for internal self-defense. Thus, when an academic community is faced with student demands that are accompanied by the "body-on-the-line" tactic, it responds, not surprisingly, in the only way it knows how: by concessions, by pleading for time, by setting up committees, by trying to persuade the radicals of its good faith and intentions. But what we have all discovered is that the university is simply not equipped to deal with the well-organized groups of political students, encouraged by their faculty supporters, who know that the vacillating and clumsy responses of the administration are no match for their policies of confrontation.

Let me return to the minority of striking professors at San Francisco State to make a point. Those faculty members who went out on strike will now carry on their union activities *inside* the campus, welded together, as it were, by the high-intensity heat of the strike. The tactic will be to operate as an organized political party—to run committees, to organize politically within departments, to try to take over the Academic Senate, to call faculty meetings where they will turn out their troops and try to make college-wide policy decisions; in short, to bend the college to their own political purposes.

The cost to the college community will be heavy, essentially because such concerted tactical behavior can only increase the politicization and polarization of the campus. Instead of being concerned with educational programs and problems, we will constantly be involved in political activities that will divide the faculty into ideological groups which, in turn, will deepen the hostilities and divisions. To oppose the faculty minority on even remotely equal terms, the rest of the faculty will have to organize, in effect, a political party of its own, something most faculty members are reluctant to consider, because they feel strongly that the amount of time, energy, and commitment it would take to organize politically runs counter to the very reasons they are there, on the faculty. That is not why they went into teaching, which is to say, they regard political activism and ideological factions as contrary to the purposes of a university.

One additional observation should be made, particularly in relation to the feeling and predispositions of those on the faculty who are committed to the liberal persuasion and outlook. There is today a complicating matter that most faculty members simply would prefer not to have to deal with and over which they certainly do not want to feel in any way compromised; namely, any organized opposition might immediately be manipulated in such a way that it would be tagged as racist and regarded as further evidence of the Establishment's antagonism to the needs and aspirations of black students.

It cannot be emphasized too much—and this goes to the heart of my principal concern—that faculties around the country are for the most part liberal in their basic orientation. With this in mind, the point I am trying to make is that the assaults on academic freedom today are likely to come not only from within the academy but, more important, from individuals and groups with which most members of the faculty have some overlapping sympathies. To use a term that has some currency among social scientists, faculty members with liberal values become extremely cross-pressured. There are other values with which they are in general sympathy, e.g., an academically defensible program of ethnic studies, the equalitarian ethic, social justice, and so on. In other words, they share these same values with many of their colleagues on the faculty who, however, at this point in time, make up a well-organized political minority that insists on the moral superiority of its goals and seems bent on the total politicization of the university. It is the kind of cross-pressure that elicits in many faculty members the desire to remain "uninvolved."

I have been talking of the consequences that accrue to an academic community when its members are increasingly forced to make decisions and choices in the heightened political atmosphere that characterizes my own campus today. The fundamental proposition I have been advancing is that academic freedom is seriously and directly threatened in a highly politicized environment. Reasoned inquiry gives way to passion and partisanship, and the end result is polarization and confrontation. The signs are everywhere. At San Francisco State the college community is being torn apart from the inside by the militants of the left, while off campus, watching and waiting, are the forces of the right. The striking teachers and student radicals keep saying that what they have been doing all year is "saving" higher education in California. The political truth of the matter is that they have helped galvanize all of the conservative and reactionary forces in the state into a kind of mass public that is motivated to act not with interest, patience, and constructive concern, but out of fear, anxiety, and anger. When the student militants on campus keep shouting, "Power to the people!" I get depressed when I think of the people who really have the power.

A different view of the events at San Francisco State College, by Leo Litwak, novelist and Associate Professor of English, in Look, *May 27, 1969.*

We Needed a Revolution

Returning from Europe after World War II, I joined the swarm of GI's seeking academic careers. The college campus seemed a likely place to find peace and security. But it was every man for himself. We pursued our degrees in competition with others: our grades against theirs, our ability to charm professors against theirs. The curriculum was designed mainly to weed out the less worthy, and our intellectual life existed mostly beyond the academic walls.

After 18 years, I was secure. I did my job. I had tenure, an adequate salary. I worked hard. Others made academic policy, but I didn't care. I was reconciled to the fact that my significant life was off-campus. I had no strong sentiments for my institution.

Then, last November, all this changed. The Black Students Union began a strike at San Francisco State College that ended my detachment and imperiled my security. The BSU came at us with nonnegotiable demands. It indicted the college as a racist institution, abused state and local officials as "racist pigs" and "slavemasters." Groups of militant blacks entered classrooms shouting, "On strike! Shut it down!" They jostled professors, shoved students, ordered classes dismissed. Some smashed windows, broke lab equipment and set off fire alarms.

The objective of the strike was to close the college until the BSU demands were met. A coalition of other minority groups, called the Third World Liberation Front, joined the revolt and tacked on more demands.

I felt that the intrusion of the blacks into the classrooms was outrageous, that their bellicose demands were irrational and therefore frightening. They wanted an autonomous Black Studies Department and an Ethnic Studies School, with minority-group faculty and students having sole authority to hire, fire and determine policy. I listened to the BSU strike leaders and was repelled by their rhetoric. "Power to the people!" Wasn't that a Maoist line? "Racist pigs!" Did they mean our innocuous deans and administrators? The crowd chanted simple slogans that turned me off. "Shove the puppets against the wall!" If they reduced men to puppets, they might indeed be able to shove them against the walls. I decided to stay clear of the mess. While I resented the strikers, I shared some of their grievances. I might become involved and imperil my cozy academic status.

Plainclothesmen were guarding campus buildings. Blacks held class everywhere. A black youth with a West Indian accent warned, "Don't think about returning this campus to normal. Your education is going on right now. We black students are your teachers." The subject they taught was Power. "For too long we've politely requested what should always have been ours. No one has the power to *give* us freedom. And we don't *request* you people for our rights. We *demand* them." The students considered talks with the local administration useless. "You people have no power to give us what we demand. We been talking to you for two years, and we got nothing. We just get tricked. Now we will only talk to educate you, but our demands are nonnegotiable. This strike will be over when our demands are met."

The faculty was powerless. The Governor and state legislature gave power to the Board of Trustees and the Chancellor's office. Little reached the college president and less went to the council of deans and department chairmen. There was nothing left for the faculty and students. In our time of crisis, we discovered that the system allowed us no solutions.

A general faculty meeting remained in session for several weeks and passed 70 resolutions with no visible influence on the strike. Instead, we were accused of being soft on student radicals. Superintendent of Public Instruction Max Rafferty and Gov. Ronald Reagan wanted these dissidents handled like a bunch of rowdies in an Old West saloon. Enough resolutions; enough talk; throw the bums out.

A small band of faculty militants called a short-lived strike against state interference, but a far larger group, while not joining that strike, had soured on the administration's unimaginative doctrine of "classes as usual." They wanted to suspend regular instruction, move out of the classrooms and onto the campus. I began to wonder why we couldn't use this scary energy for some new kind of education, rather than clamp a lid on it.

The majority of my colleagues, however, didn't want to surrender formal instruction. They asked, what about grades? What about teaching credentials? What about jobs that require a degree? Wasn't that what education was *really* about?

I decided, no. Not really. I questioned whether the contradiction between campus experience and community experience was any longer tolerable. I'd once welcomed the benign order of campus life. But did I want to continue paying the price for that security? I was subjected to educational policies that made no sense to me. I didn't feel there was anything sacred about our curriculum. On the contrary, it was my impression that most programs have no inherent justification but simply reflect campus politics. I agreed with those who wanted regular instruction suspended in favor of a different mode of encounter.

Only a minority of the faculty shared my view. There was considerable support for Prof. S. I. Hayakawa, who announced that no student would interfere with the conduct of his classes. He urged strong police measures, and strong police measures were what we got.

Leaving a faculty meeting about that time, I heard screams. Two officers from the Tactical Squad hauled a BSU leader across the campus through hundreds of milling students. Both cops had revolvers out. One wheeled around to cover everyone, including me. Dozens of reporters and television crews were watching. A half-dozen police found themselves in a tight spot. Suddenly, they lashed out. They beat a frail, bespectacled BSU leader to the ground. They swung their batons like baseball bats. They clobbered everyone in their way, including innocents. Soon I found myself aligned with colleagues trying to separate students and police. The Tac Squad photographer snapped my picture. Like it or not, I was involved.

The campus mayhem finally forced the faculty to suspend formal instruction, and the entire college was convoked to discuss the strike issues. Strike leaders confronted college faculty and administration on the stage of the main auditorium. All together—students and faculty—we faced the vital issues of our college.

The minority students presented a strong case in strong language. Could we be made to understand, they wondered, why they would never allow themselves to be absorbed into the traditional campus life while their people continued to suffer in the ghetto? They demanded an education that would enable them to serve their community. The existing curriculum was irrelevant to their purposes. They didn't balk at obscenity. They insulted their opposition and made open bids for audience sympathy. Our administrators responded to this passion with the tedious precision of accountants, citing the limitations of state codes, budgetary policy and a fiscal crisis.

The students, accusing the college administration of bad faith, brought the convocation to a premature end. Next, the trustees forced President Smith to resign and replaced him with Dr. Hayakawa, of the colorful tam-o'-shanter and hard line. Official California had chosen to ignore the basic dissatisfactions and possibilities for reform that lay beneath the rebels' furious rhetoric.

The Governor—with popular support, it's true—wanted to restore the college of his Hollywood fantasies, a benign place for cheerleaders and absentminded professors.

Acting President Hayakawa declared all assemblies illegal unless authorized by him. Professors who did not hold classes as scheduled risked being fired. He announced that all necessary force would be employed to keep the campus open. He refused to negotiate with those he regarded as hooligans. Both sides chose *High Noon* as the kind of confrontation they preferred.

Six hundred cops assembled near the campus. Three thousand students gathered on the commons. Dr. Hayakawa piped from loudspeakers to everyone, "This is a warning. All innocent bystanders leave this vicinity. Go to your classes. Go to the library. Leave the troublemakers to the police. Those of you who want trouble, stay there; the police will see that you get it." For two weeks, there were daily confrontations. The script never changed. The cops approach; students taunt them; clods of turf and pinecones are flung. Suddenly, a cop lets go and flails away, and the movement spreads down the line. When they swing, they put their weight behind the sticks. I see them still flailing away after the kid is downed.

One of my colleagues, protesting a brutal arrest, was thrown down, handcuffed, led away with a riot stick pressed to his throat. An officer squirted Mace in his eyes. Another came from behind —"How do you like this, you fancy-pants professor?"—and cut his head open with a blow from a riot stick that knocked him cold. The professor was charged with resisting and interfering with an arrest.

One of my students told me she was striking "because of the PIGS!" Her boyfriend had been photographing arrests behind the gym. A cop seized his camera and stripped the film. Another said, "No one's looking." They fractured his ribs, damaged a lung, thrust a riot stick under his genitals and hoisted up and down. They charged the boy with attempted murder. PIGS!

Hayakawa announced after a particularly bloody day: "This has been the most exciting day since my tenth birthday, when I rode a roller coaster for the first time." It was a callous statement. Yet it reflected what everyone experienced, a new energy that changed our connections to each other and to our institution. What a loss if we simply resumed teaching as before and didn't profit from these new connections. Should we simply repair broken windows, wash away strike slogans from building façades and plant flowers? Should we get back to Keats and California state history, and drama classes, and allow the performance of *Little Me* that had been interrupted by strike action? If students wished to participate in the fundamental design of my courses, why not? If my work could become relevant to my experience and theirs, perhaps teaching and learning could become more joyful.

Those of us who wanted to profit from the new energies on campus had no alternative but to join the American Federation of Teachers strike. We had no illusions that we could defeat the overwhelming power the state would muster against us. We were a minority of the faculty. Public sentiment strongly favored repressive measures. We were the villains; Hayakawa was the hero. But we felt that submitting to the old routines without any resistance would be degrading. We had everything to lose—rank, tenure, jobs, homes—yet we struck. We established a picket line around campus and marched through one of the wettest winters in San Francisco history. At times, we were frightened; often, we were exhilarated. Yet we became united, with a new commitment to our work and to our institution.

The strike finally ended, but a volatile situation remains. The administration is still intransigent. But we are changing things in our classrooms. Students are collaborating in the design of courses. In some departments, we are moving away from the old hierarchical structure toward more democratic participation. Perhaps, through our strikes, we faculty and students have chosen a new and hopeful direction for higher education in America.

Columbia

Editorial in The Columbia Spectator, *student newspaper, Columbia University, March 14, 1969, while under the editorship of Robert Friedman.*

The University Politicized

I

In the middle of the occupation last spring, Professor of Sociology Allan Silver posed a sphinx-like question to several SDS members who were addressing the Ad Hoc Faculty Group. Attempting to force them to define their priorities, he asked whether there was anything worth preserving in the University. The SDS members, sensing the delicateness of the question, declined to answer. Now, nearly one year later, with the possibility of another spring of confrontation upon us, little has changed at Columbia and Professor Silver's question remains unanswered.

As we relinquish editorial control of this newspaper today, we sense around us a grave lack of consciousness about the direction this University is taking, and an inability to focus on the critical questions of just what the function and role of the University ought to be. Last year at this time we expressed guarded optimism about the future of Columbia; today we feel pessimistic. What, more than anything else, has led to this change in attitude is that despite the opportunities for rediscovery that were abundant last spring, the administration, faculty, and even the students have continued to look at Columbia with their old, myopic eyes and have avoided confronting the new political character of their University.

II

Columbia is a liberal institution. It espouses the liberal values of academic freedom—freedom of inquiry and exchange of ideas; it follows the dictates of liberal politics—offering the services of civilian intellectuals to the military establishment and offering to build community gymnasium facilities in a public park. That is to say, Columbia is neither value-free nor apolitical. Everything it does, supports, or allows as an institution, is a product of the University's liberal ethos.

Liberalism, which once appeared to satisfy this nation's needs and desires, is now bankrupt; liberalism, which once appeared to satisfy this University's needs and desires, is now leading it to chaos. The liberal can accept turmoil and conflict only in the realm of ideas; he shields himself with a veneer of passivity from the crimes of a war in Vietnam and from the racism eroding our society. The liberal must bear the blame for having sat back behind the guise of academic freedom while Columbia University became increasingly implicated in the nation's military ventures and became a spectator to the nation's urban and racial decay.

In the past year we have seen the gradual demise of the University as a liberal institution. It cannot follow its present course much longer for the liberal institution can only survive and thrive when insulated from the pressures of the federal government, the local community, and political action. Columbia is not resilient enough, either financially or spiritually, to keep bouncing back after repeated and prolonged political upheaval.

III

Within the past year, two responses to this new, critical situation in which the University finds itself have begun to take shape. The first of these crystallized Monday when one hundred senior faculty members held a press conference to affirm the values of academic freedom and to denounce disruptive tactics. Using as their motto the Cox Commission's assertion that the fate of Columbia lies in the hands of liberals, the one hundred professors called for a concerted effort to return to the concept of a University sheltered from politics. Their stern approach would necessitate cracking down on all disruptive elements by swift, firm discipline, suspensions and expulsions.

This hard-line response is understandably attractive to a large segment of the liberal Columbia community, but is one which we cannot accept. In terms of the literal survival of the University, it is perhaps the most practicable. Yet, it would involve the repression of large numbers of our generation—an action which we find reprehensible and criminal. Furthermore, the history of the past few years shows rather clearly that such repressive action in defense of academic freedom only generates further unrest and resistance. Finally, the type of University that would emerge after clipping off its left wing would not be worth preserving. It is impossible to deny the political nature of the University—in terms of institutional actions and personal commitments—as our senior faculty members would have us do. Their answer to Professor Silver's telling question is far too easy: that there is nothing of the recent political transformation of the University worth preserving.

The second response, which remained beneath the surface throughout most of last spring, is that put forward by a number of self-styled revolutionary students. It is predicated on the belief that Columbia is so intimately bound up with a corrupt and repressive society that the only legitimate action that can be taken is to shut down and destroy the University as the first step toward revolution.

There is no doubt in our minds that much of the analysis and the ideals on which this response is founded are correct. Yet to believe that this society is on the verge of revolution is to be deluded, and to answer Professor Silver's question by saying that there is absolutely nothing worth preserving in the University is also too easy.

IV

There is a third response to the changing University, one which is still nascent and not yet clearly defined. It is not a middle road and it does not offer sure salvation. Yet, while we are pessimistic about the success of this approach, we believe it well worth considering.

Given the fact that the University is and will continue to be a political institution which plays an important role in society, and given the fact that the liberal politics of the University have cast it in the role of supporting a sick society, we must commit ourselves to transforming the politics of the University by resorting to whatever means prove necessary. This response not only recognizes and adapts itself to the political nature of the University, but it presumes that there is some value in the existence of the University. Specifically, we believe that in addition to certain academic values which should be preserved, the University must undertake a transformative role in society. To accomplish this, its politics must be changed.

Since it is clear that the Trustees and administrators who currently shape University policy are so entrenched in their liberal and outmoded ways of looking at the world and are not likely to change their beliefs on their own accord, those who disagree with their politics will have to engage themselves in a long and perhaps unsuccessful struggle. The problem is no longer one of faulty communication, but one of different viewpoints; the struggle must necessarily be a political one waged on many fronts.

First of all, if democratic decision-making procedures at Columbia are instituted, the Left may be able to exert considerable pressure, through "legitimate" channels, on the nature of decisions made. It is uncertain however, whether this would be sufficient or even effective, since "student power" is, in most cases, as bad as administrative or faculty power. Thus, it may also prove necessary to exert pressure through the threat or reality of political action, demonstrations, strikes, and so on. There are dangers in this as well, particularly in the possibility of a strong reaction, but these risks must be taken if there is to be any change or any victory.

V

We are now on the verge of another spring. Spring at Columbia means renewed political activity, and the prospects for calm this spring are not promising. Yet whatever happens in the next few months—whether it be quiet or violence—members of the University community will have to address themselves to the directions Columbia should take, and particularly to how they should respond to the political nature of the institution. This has not been done. We are skeptical that new and valuable directions will emerge, but the existence and success of this University depend upon it.

A reply to the Spectator *editorial by Allan Silver, Associate Professor of Sociology, Columbia University, published in* Spectator, *March 17, 1969.*

Orwell, Thou Should'st Be Living at This Hour!

I was struck by *Spectator*'s editorial of March 14—the last, major statement of the departing editors—because of its significance and importance; and also I admit, because its discussion of the University's situation and future was largely organized around an incident last spring in which I was involved. In the editorial's words, "In the midst of the occupation last spring Professor of Sociology Allan Silver posed a sphinx-like question to several SDS members who were addressing the Ad Hoc Faculty Group. Attempting to force them to define their priorities, he asked whether there was anything worth preserving in the University. The SDS members, sensing the delicateness of the question, declined to answer. Now, nearly one year later, with the possibility of another spring of confrontation upon us, little has changed at Columbia, and Professor Silver's question remains unanswered."

Actually, neither the editorial nor *Up Against the Ivy Wall* gets the incident quite right. Essentially, my question fell into two parts; minus rhetorical elaboration, I recall it as follows: Is there anything about Columbia University—even in its current, unreformed state, with all its imperfections on its head—which you find precious, and even indispensable? If yes, does that answer place any restraints whatever on the tactics you are prepared to use, or the lengths to which you are prepared to go? I do not recall that the student leaders of whom it was asked "declined to answer." I recall that one of them tried, invoking a political justification of the uprising, but he ceased when his audience told him he was being irrelevant. Further, that as a group the students then tried, huddling among themselves, to formulate an answer. Some time passed, after which I said that the question was difficult and that I was prepared to wait for an answer; but that I hoped the students would think about it, and that an answer would come. In *Up Against the Ivy Wall,* Mark Rudd is quoted as saying that "We had no answer to this huge question . . . We had to go and formulate a policy on the University." Apparently, the leaders of that massive convulsion had not considered the need for such a policy. Later, during the first mediation session, Mr. Rudd was to indicate that he was angry and "humiliated" because the question had been put to him—a question which, in his own words at the time, "we couldn't answer."

The question was not intended to be "sphinx-like," if by that is meant that it is humanly impossible to answer, and that the penalty for failing to answer is very severe. It was intended to "confront" the student leaders with a dilemma—or, rather to ask if they were capable of experiencing dilemmas in any terms other than merely tactical. A dilemma, especially a moral one, consists in recognizing that one cannot optimize all values; that action for the good involves the risk of very painful costs; and that, in this instance at least, one always had to be mindful of the predictable consequences of one's acts, even if those were undesired—and take some measure of responsibility for them. My question was only the vehicle for raising this issue. Let us now consider it further.

Much has been hard to take at Columbia. The old indifference and fragmentation of colleagueship among many faculty; the obtuseness of trustees; the piety of uncritical liberalism; the aloof insensitivity of administrators, some of whom apparently thought of their silence in the face of critical issues as a form of dignified virtue. The moral arrogance of many radical student leaders has been among these afflictions. It is possible to talk to some purposes—including those of enlightenment and politics—with people with whom one strongly disagrees; it is impossible, literally impossible, to do so when they declare that they are not in the same moral universe as you, that they do not share some of the basic dilemmas that human flesh is heir to.

Many radical students seem to cling to the university. Here there is an arena of significant, though far from total, "apartness" from the pressures of employment, family, class and even those of the dropout cultures; there are books, a concentration of intelligent people interested in ideas, and a level of tolerance—"repressive tolerance," to be sure—unlikely to be encountered elsewhere in America. There are teachers—some of them genuinely learned, serious and dedicated, and dependent on the university to do research. Remaining at the university, despite all, one has not irreversibly cut oneself off from America: degrees and certifications are still to be had. Meanwhile, there is the prospect of politically mobilizing the institution.

Very well. I have asked whether some of these goals do not place certain restraints upon the pursuit of others. Not only whether politicization places restraints upon the traditional obligations of studenthood, but also whether taking advantage of some of what a university offers—for example, the prospect of learning something about disciplined inquiry—places some restraints upon political tactics. I think it does, and must. That man is a child (whatever his age) who thinks that he can, should or must get something—anything—for nothing.

Radical students—and this is hardly a homogeneous category—have not returned a collective response to these questions. But Spectator's editorial of March 14 did, albeit in "nascent" form: "Given the fact that the University is and will continue to be a political institution which plays an important role in society, and given the fact that the liberal politics of the University have cast it in the role of supporting a sick society, we must commit ourselves to transforming the politics of the University by resorting to whatever means prove necessary."

I pass over the intellectual and moral coarsening that comes from depicting vital and complex matters of judgment and value as "fact," and concentrate on the words "whatever means prove necessary." Are these words meant seriously? I don't know, for I find shortly after them other words: ". . . in addition to certain academic values which should be preserved, the University must undertake a transformative role in society." (I pass over the stylistic and intellectual vulgarity of "transformative.") I suppose that among these "academic values" are science, reason, disciplined inquiry, and the working relations of academic men, whether students or teachers. Is it that they should be "preserved" or that they must not die? What if some means that "prove necessary" involve attacking them, or the risk of seriously damaging them? How reckon these costs, how cast these moral accounts?

Further: the language of "preservation" is not only curious but misplaced. I thought it was "liberals" who were always talking about "preserving" things like the Bill of Rights and Academic Freedom, as though they were especially precious pickles. (I suppose the image's origins lie in the Constitutionally specified presidential oath—to "preserve, protect and defend".) Has it occurred to the editorial's writers that matters like science, reason, and disciplined inquiry are not so much preserved as constantly re-created? That the means to re-create them—and, more important still, extend them in areas where they are weakly developed, many of which are of special interest to ideologically concerned students—that these means consist above all of understandings among men about the behaviour indispensable if a university is to live?

In this light, no one who claims to belong in some way to the university—and I mean no one at all, whether trustee, administrator, faculty or student—can easefully speak of using "whatever means prove necessary," whether those means involve discipline or disruption. For some means may violate or threaten the set of understandings—for example, that there is something special that invests the assembly of those who come together to learn—without which a university cannot live as an institution marked by some purposes and means distinguishing it from others in society. One cannot expect to violate those understandings without opening himself to judgment.

Let us now consider judgment and the prospects thereof. In an editorial on March 12, Spectator attacked the hundred faculty, almost entirely senior, who have announced their opposition to the interruption or disruption of classes. Some of this attack has force. Elaborate and stately concern with this matter does indeed contrast badly with the faculty's slowness to seize "the initiative and improve rather than just preserve." (Hear, hear!) Moreover, the statement of the hundred is full of the reified abstractions that make possible such metaphors as "preservation." It refers to the University as a "sanctuary of academic freedom," a phrase that serves as its title.

If these references were to an aspiration as yet unrealized, I might accept them, though with many rhetorical reservations. But they appear to refer to some historical and contemporary realities. Was Columbia a "sanctuary" some decades ago, when President Butler formally suspended academic freedom for the duration of World War I? I do read in the statement that the safeguards of freedom have been "erected at great sacrifice over several centuries." True enough. But the statement reads—if only by omission and style—as though "freedom" now exists in a sufficiently satisfactory state. Further, that its character is rendered by such quiescent images as "sanctuary." But "sanctuary" seriously underplays the constant tension and delicate interplay between the institutionalization of disciplined learning in the universities and the state of affairs, contentious and otherwise, in the societies that sponsor them.

These inadequacies are not compensated for by an unelaborated, passing reference to "the need for further reforms." An adequate response to the political disruption of classes must refer to the novel problems that face the university today. Have struggles for intellectual freedom ended, and is their only concern the behavior of disruptive students? Does not the rather new structure of universities' relations with government also cause concern—less inflamed, less acute, but all the more pervasive and troublesome? Are the canons of scholarship in all fields sufficiently clear to minimize the prospect of excluding new knowledge, whatever its ideological clothes or substance? How many students have satisfactory intellectual relationships with their teachers at Columbia? Thus, despite my great agreement with central parts of the statement of the hundred, I cannot sign it because of its essentially complacent tone, which omits sustained reference to such matters.

But back to Spectator, which on March 12 was editorially critical of the hundred because they were excited about "an infringement on a few minutes of their precious class time . . . Too many professors are so possessive with their fifty minutes of class time that they are unable (sic) to recognize or accommodate themselves to the fact that in the past year Columbia has become a highly politicized institution." How utterly inadequate! Must all facts be accommodated to? Did the hundred professors claim that those fifty minutes were their sole possession? Are they not a space of time in which professors and students are—or are supposed to be—linked by the concerns of science, reason, disciplined inquiry, learning, including—where "relevant"—the concerns of moral passion and political ideology? Are they not the resource of all in the classroom?

Further, are they any fifty minutes? Are they not a space of time that expresses the idea of what a university is in the very bones of its spirit, if it is to exist at all, whether in this society or in a better one to come? They are not alone in this: libraries, offices, laboratories also express it. That classes are sometimes boring, or worse, is sad—and worse than sad. I have given lectures, even courses, that make me blush to scan the names carved around Butler Library. That is not—for the moment—my point. I ask, rather, whether professors are not at least as free as radical students to define reality in terms of symbols.

For was not IDA a symbol of the "garrison state," and the gym of "racism"? May I not—together with my colleagues, emphatically including the hundred—see a symbol in the political interruption or disruption of the classroom? Unlike the editorial of March 12, I do not see in these acts only "a counter-productive tactic, alienating large numbers of faculty members and students." Nor do I think it especially forceful to observe that "only" 25 out of 110,000 classes have been disrupted or interrupted. Symbols are sometimes small things, though large portents.

In the days when the Peace Corps was widely considered a good thing on campuses, I never permitted their unfailingly polite representatives to take five minutes to address my students. Not because those five minutes were "mine," but because when people in a university assemble for the purposes of learning, they should not be used as a captive audience for another purpose. Nor may they be imposed on disruptively for another purpose, because doing that is an attack on the prospects of disciplined inquiry itself. I do not speak of all purposes in society nor all thinkable ones. I too have a point where I must stand and say I can do no other. But those in a university, who claim—if only by their continued presence—to be a part of some, at least, of its purposes—

cannot impose their own purposes on classrooms without exposing themselves to judgment.

Those who interrupt or disrupt the attempts of teachers and students at sustained learning must answer to the University for their acts. Judgment arrived at through legitimate procedures is a way—indispensable, but not the only way—of instituting moral accountability. The statement of the hundred is deficient in not seeing that the "justice delayed" of recent months represents not only an unwillingness to act in defense of the university, but also expresses the breakdown of moral consensus last spring that in itself renders the imagery of the "sanctuary" misleading. Yet those who interrupt or disrupt classes—or perform equivalent acts—are not the sole judges of legitimacy; nor can they claim the dignity of a moral imperative for what is usually a tactical experiment. The re-creation of a moral consensus must not be equated with new and effective forms of justice and judgment, but these are indispensable to it. . . .

So we stumble into the spring, the season of indignation and memory. Classes are interrupted, evoking pieties, evaluations of tactical efficacy and statements about discipline . . . Language coarsens—sanctuary, law and order, spring offensive, class and racist nature of the university. Once again, the university sees itself—radicals and "power holders" alike—as the critical political arena. Stakes rise, prophecies are pronounced.

Those who wish little or nothing to change in America should rejoice at this new form of political containment. Let the battles rage within the universities! So what if a few universities die, now and then? Men of property and power have only rarely valued learning, and certainly few of them in America do. Let the forces of change hurl themselves against academics, administrators and trustees, seeking symbolic victories and a "revolutionary base" subsidized by society itself! Deprived of any constituency, except that of fellow-students—or unwilling to take on the burdens and realities of relating to a real constituency—radicals often convert the university into the central arena of our time, while refusing to acknowledge that the institution has any claims upon them until it meets their moral requirements. Cut off by location, age and status from other arenas—the political parties, the unions, the ghettos and areas of rural poverty, the organization of work and community—they often seek to attack the larger problems in microcosm, and at a "strategic" point—the universities.

Those larger problems are reflected plentifully in the universities, of course, but universities are also special sorts of institutions with special claims upon their members. I beseech students to think that just as no one can escape the moral web that encompasses all Americans, so they cannot escape those dilemmas that are imposed on all in the university. And I implore my colleagues to think less exclusively in terms of a received wisdom that too easily becomes, under pressure, a set of defensive pieties; and to be more concerned to show how reasonable and educated men, differing widely, may unite to regenerate new kinds of intellectual freedom and substance for students and teachers alike, in a time when the wisdom and rhetoric of the past are both indispensable and insufficient.

PART II

SDS AND THE LEFT: HOW TO BUILD A MOVEMENT

In the period between 1966 and 1970, the major tactical debates on the student left occurred within its most important organization, Students for a Democratic Society. SDS began as the student branch of the League for Industrial Democracy, a democratic socialist group, and barely limped through the fifties. In 1962, under the leadership of Tom Hayden and Al Haber, SDS made itself independent of its parent organization. Its initial activities were focused on the civil rights movement and community organizing. Not until 1965, however, when SDS organized the first march on Washington protesting the Vietnam War, did the group gain much attention.*

At this point in its history SDS had several alternatives. It could have devoted its efforts to building a national anti-war campaign, continued its involvement in the Black struggle, or turned to radical electoral politics. Various left-wing groups did pursue these activities, but SDS chose to move in a different direction. A belief in "grass-roots" organizing and participatory democracy discouraged SDS from abandoning local problems and committing itself to a succession of large-scale national protests like the 1965 Washington march. On the other hand, the rise of "Black power" and the decline of SDS's own community action projects militated against working in the urban ghettos. The experience of the 1964 election, when SDS had gone "part of the way with LBJ," suggested that alliances with the Democratic Party would be fruitless. And since SDS did not see much hope at that time for a new radical party, it spurned independent electoral politics.

So instead of adopting one of these strategies, SDS decided to turn its full attention to university issues and concentrate on building a campus-based *student* movement. The war in Vietnam would be linked with various aspects of the university, including cooperation with the Selective Service and even paternalistic dor-

* For a detailed history of SDS, see James O'Brien, *A History of the New Left, 1960–1968* (Boston: New England Free Press, 1969).

mitory rules. In other words, SDS sought a synthesis between radical issues and student grievances in the hope that students fighting for their own interests would become radicals. The belief that this strategy would work lasted roughly until the spring of 1968.

Prior to the breakdown of this strategy, SDS went through two phases. In the first phase, in late 1965 and 1966, the group emphasized local campus problems and called for more "student power" in the university. Although a few successful campaigns were launched, the program was not very successful. In the second phase, from 1967 through mid-1968, SDS tied its protests much more closely to the war in Vietnam through a campaign to "expel the military from the campus" that united anti-war sentiment with the drive to reform the university. From "student syndicalism," SDS moved to "institutional resistance."

The resistance strategy, though it was more militant than student power, did not represent a complete break with liberals on the campus. SDS had begun to develop a radical analysis of American society that liberals did not share, but the group was still able to unite with left liberals on specific questions such as the Vietnam War and racial injustice. Consequently radicals, anti-war liberals, and Blacks were able to join in a loose coalition for a series of large, dramatic student protests in 1967 and 1968.

But the spring of 1968, which saw both the uprising at Columbia and a near-revolutionary upheaval in France, signaled an important turning point. At Columbia, SDS leaders concluded from the '68 experience that they could carry off a major revolt without accommodating liberals. Moreover, SDS now regarded university reform not as a useful issue that could win students to the radical movement, but instead as a subtle threat that might divert students away from it ("co-optation"). Columbia SDS, therefore, decided to reject "mass politics," that is, the belief in organizing a mass student movement by drawing in non-radical groups. At the same time that SDS rejected mass student organizing, the French uprising stimulated hopes that the working classes in industrial countries could still be mobilized into a revolutionary force. The closest approximation to revolutionary activity in the United States was the Black movement, and in the months after spring 1968, racism became the preeminent issue for the left. SDS began to look beyond the universities; it no longer defined its task as the creation of a student movement.

As SDS drifted away from the campus, it sought to relate student protest to social revolution through a theory of "exemplary action." According to this theory, which had been encouraged by the French experience, students could "set in motion" other groups in the society by taking action around their own interests. But within a few months, the same SDS leaders who had been advancing this theory decided that such an indirect approach to revolution was inadequate.

Through 1968 and 1969, SDS began to talk explicitly about "shutting down the universities"—not to win reforms, in which it no longer saw any value, but to stop the universities from carrying out their functions.

By this time, SDS no longer had any interest in winning support from liberal students; its objectives were to gain support among the Blacks and the white working class. Disagreements among SDS members over how to relate to these groups led to intense divisions in the organization, and finally an open split in the summer of 1969. By this time SDS members in the two major factions had adopted an explicitly Marxist framework, though many of their ideas were far from orthodox. By the close of the decade, SDS had splintered into several factions, each calling the others reactionary, and none of them any longer seeing the universities as their chief concern.

CHAPTER 5

Organizing Students on Campus

SDS's decision to return to the campus in 1966 and abandon its program of community organizing was made at a national convention in August at Clear Lake, Iowa. Carl Davidson, then working for SDS in the Great Plains region, presented the key paper at the conference: "Toward student syndicalism, or university reform revisited." Davidson urged that SDS mount campaigns for student power on the thesis that by opposing university regulation of students' lives, they would strike at one of the mechanisms that turn students into uncritical components of the society.

Through the next year, 1966–67, Davidson and others in SDS developed a more comprehensive analysis which viewed students as trainees for a "new working class" of technicians and bureaucrats. In "The multiversity: crucible of the new working class," Davidson clearly stated what SDS then believed was the point of student protest: "If there is a single over-all purpose for the student power movement, it would be the development of a radical political consciousness among those students who will later hold jobs in the strategic sectors of the political economy."

Neither student syndicalism nor the new-working-class program ever succeeded in its stated aims, and they were both subsequently repudiated by SDS. Nevertheless, they left a deep impression on radical thought and many elements of the theories remained after the frameworks had been abandoned.*

Position paper by Carl Davidson, SDS leader, delivered at the SDS National Convention, August 1966.

Toward a Student Syndicalist Movement, or University Reform Revisited

In the past few years, we have seen a variety of campus movements developing around the issue of "university reform." A few of these movements sustained a mass base for brief periods. Some brought about minor changes in campus rules and regulations. But almost all have failed to alter the university community radically or even to maintain their own existence. What is the meaning of this phenomenon? How can we avoid it in the future? Why bother with university reform at all?

It is a belief among members of Students for a Democratic Society that all the issues are interrelated. However, we often fail to relate them in any systematic way. What, in fact, is the connection between dorm hours and the war in Vietnam? Is there one system responsible for both? If so, what is the nature of that system? And, finally, how should we respond? These are the questions I will try to answer in the following anaysis.

Why university reform?

SDS has named the existing system in this country "corporate liberalism." And, if we bother to look, its penetration into the campus community is awesome. Its elite are trained in our col-

* For more on the "new working class" debate, see below Greg Calvert, pp. 247–56, Staughton Lynd, p. 229, and Carl Oglesby, pp. 303–07. In a 1967 supplement to *New Left Notes* called "Praxis," Bob Gottlieb, Gerry Tenney, and Dave Gilbert, who first expounded the "new working class" theory in SDS, stated that it had its origins in the works of Antonio Gramsci, Serge Mallet, and André Gorz. The theory was popularized most by Calvert, through a speech entitled "In White America: Radical Consciousness and Social Change," originally given at Princeton in February 1967, and reprinted in the *Guardian*, March 27, 1967.

leges of business administration. Its defenders are trained in our law schools. Its apologists can be found in the political science departments. The colleges of social sciences produce its manipulators. For propagandists, it relies on the schools of journalism. It insures its own future growth in the colleges of education. If some of us don't quite fit in, we are brainwashed in the divisions of counseling. And we all know only too well what goes on in the classrooms of the military science buildings.

This situation takes on more sinister ramifications when we realize that all these functionaries of "private enterprise" are being trained at the people's expense. American corporations have little trouble increasing the worker's wage, especially when they can take it back in the form of school taxes and tuition to train their future workers. To be sure, many corporations give the universities scholarships and grants. But this is almost always for some purpose of their own, if only for a tax dodge.

Furthermore, the corporate presence on campus grotesquely transforms the nature of the university community. The most overt example is the grade system. Most professors would agree that grades are meaningless, if not positively harmful, to the learning process. But the entire manipulated community replies in unison: "But how else would companies know whom to hire (or the Selective Service whom to draft)?" And we merrily continue to spend public money subsidizing testing services for private enterprise.

What we must see clearly is the relation between the university and corporate liberal society at large. Most of us are outraged when our university administrators or their student government lackeys liken our universities and colleges to corporations. We bitterly respond with talk about a "community of scholars." However, the fact of the matter is that they are correct. Our educational institutions *are* corporations and knowledge factories. What we have failed to see in the past is how absolutely vital these factories are to the corporate liberal state.

What do these factories produce? What are their commodities? The most obvious answer is "knowledge." Our factories produce the know-how that enables the corporate state to expand, to grow, and to exploit people more efficiently and extensively both in our own country and in the third world. But knowledge is perhaps too abstract to be viewed as a commodity. Concretely, the commodities of our factories are the *knowledgeable.* AID officials, Peace

Corpsmen, military officers, CIA officials, segregationist judges, corporation lawyers, politicians of all sorts, welfare workers, managers of industry, labor bureaucrats (I could go on and on): Where do they come from? They are products of the factories we live and work in.

It is on our assembly lines in the universities that they are molded into what they are. As integral parts of the knowledge factory system, we are both the exploiters and the exploited. As both the managers and the managed, we produce and become the most vital product of corporate liberalism: bureaucratic man. In short, we are a new kind of scab.

But let us return to our original question. What is the connection between dorm rules and the war in Vietnam? Superficially, both are aspects of corporate liberalism, a dehumanized and oppressive system. But let us be more specific. Who are the dehumanizers and oppressors? In a word, our past, present, and future alumni: the finished product of our knowledge factories.

How did they become what they are? They were shaped on an assembly line that starts with children entering junior high school and ends with junior bureaucrats in commencement robes. And the rules and regulations of *in loco parentis* are essential tools along that entire assembly line. Without them, it would be difficult to produce the kind of men that can create, sustain, tolerate, or ignore situations like Watts, Mississippi, and Vietnam.

Finally, perhaps we can see the vital connections that our factories have with the present conditions of corporate liberalism when we ask ourselves what would happen if the military found itself without ROTC students, the CIA found itself without recruits, paternalistic welfare departments found themselves without social workers, or the Democratic Party found itself without young liberal apologists and campaign workers? In short, what would happen to a manipulative society if its means of creating *manipulable* people were done away with?

The answer is that we might then have a fighting chance to change that system. Most of us have been involved in university reform movements of one sort or another. For the most part, our efforts have produced very little. The Free Speech Movement flared briefly, then died out. There have been a few dozen *ad hoc* committees for the abolition of this or that rule. Some of these succeed, then fall apart. Some never get off the ground.

However, we have had some effect. The discontent is there. Although the apathy is extensive and deep-rooted, even the apathetic gripe at times. Our administrators are worried. They watch us carefully, have staff seminars on Paul Goodman, and study our own literature more carefully than we do. They handle our outbursts with kid gloves, trying their best not to give us an issue.

We have one more factor in our favor: We have made many mistakes that we can learn from. I will try to enumerate and analyze a few of them.

1. *Forming single-issue groups.* A prime example here is organizing a committee to abolish dorm hours for women students over 21. This tactic has two faults. First, insofar as relevance is concerned, this is a *felt issue* for less than 10 percent of the average campus. Hence, it is almost impossible to mobilize large numbers of students around the issue for any length of time. The same criticism applies to student labor unions (only a few hundred students work for the university), dress regulations (only the hippies are bothered), or discrimination in off-campus housing (most black college students are too bourgeois to care). The second fault is that most of these issues can be accommodated by the administration: After months of meetings, speeches, and agitation, the dean of women changes the rules so that a woman over 21, with parental permission and a high enough grade average, can apply, if she wants, for a key to the dorm. Big deal. At this stage, the tiny organization that worked for this issue usually folds up.

2. *Organizing around empty issues.* Students often try to abolish rules that aren't enforced anyway. Almost every school has a rule forbidding women to visit men's apartments. But it is rarely enforced, even if openly violated. Since most students are not restricted by the rule, they usually won't fight to change it. Often, they will react negatively, feeling that if the issue is brought up, the administration will have to enforce it.

3. *Fear of being radical.* Time and time again, we water down our demands and compromise ourselves *before we even begin.* In our meetings we argue the administration's position against us before they do and better than they will. We allow ourselves to be intimidated by the word "responsible." (How many times have we changed a "Student Bill of Rights" to a watered-down "Resolution on Student Rights and Responsibilities"?) We spend more energy assuring our deans that we "don't want another Berkeley" than we do talking with students about the real issues.

4. *Working through existing channels.* This phrase really means,

"Let us stall you off until the end of the year." If we listen to it at all, we ought to do so just once and in such a way as to show everyone that it's a waste of time.

5. *Waiting for faculty support.* This is like asking Southern Negroes to wait for white moderates. We often failed to realize that the faculty are more powerless than we: They have the welfare of their families to consider.

6. *Legal questions.* We spend hours debating among ourselves whether the university can legally abolish *in loco parentis.* They can if they want to, or if they have to. Besides, suppose it isn't legal. Should we then stop, pick up our marbles, and go home?

7. *Isolating ourselves.* Time and time again we fall into the trap of trying to organize independents over the "Greek-Independent split." This should be viewed as an administration plot to divide and rule. On the other hand, we shouldn't waste time trying to court the Greeks or "campus leaders." They haven't any more real power than anyone else. Also, SDS people often view themselves as intellectual enclaves on campus when they should see themselves as organizing committees for the entire campus. We retreat to our own "hippy hangouts" rather than spending time in the student union building talking with others.

8. *Forming Free Universities.* This action can be a good thing, depending on how it is organized. But we run the risk of the utopian socialists who withdrew from the early labor struggles. We may feel liberated in our Free Universities; but, in the meantime, the "unfree" university we left goes on cranking out corporate liberals. In fact, they have it easier since we aren't around making trouble.

9. *Working within student government.* We should do this for one and only one reason: to abolish the student government. We should have learned by now that student governments have no power and, in many cases, the administration has organized them in such a way that it is impossible to use them to get power. (In a few cases, it might be possible to take over a student government and threaten to abolish it if power isn't granted.)

From these criticisms of our mistakes over the past few years, I think the direction we should move in becomes more clear. Also, when we consider the fact that *our universities are already chief agents for social change in the direction of 1984,* I think we can see why it is imperative that we organize the campuses. (I do not mean to imply that we ought to ignore organizing elsewhere.)

Toward student syndicalism

In the preceding analysis of the university (by no means original with me), we can find an implicit antagonism, or, if you will, a fundamental contradiction. Namely, our administrators ask of us that we both participate and not participate in our educational system. We are told we must learn to make responsible decisions, yet we are not allowed to make actual decisions. We are told that education is an active process, yet we are passively trained. We are criticized for our apathy and for our activism. In the name of freedom, we are trained to obey.

The system requires that we passively agree to be manipulated. But our vision is one of active participation. And this is a demand that our administrators cannot meet without putting themselves out of a job. That is exactly why we should be making the demand.

What is to be done?

Obviously, we need to organize, to build on the campuses a movement that has the primary purpose of radically transforming the university community. Too often we lose sight of this goal. To every program, every action, every position, and every demand, we must raise the question: How will this radically alter the lives of every student on this campus? With this in mind, I offer the following proposals for action.

1. That every SDS chapter organize a student syndicalist movement on its campus. I use the term "syndicalist" for a crucial reason. In the labor struggle, the syndicalist unions worked for industrial democracy and worker's control, rather than for better wages and working conditions. Similarly, and I cannot repeat this often enough, the issue for us is student control (along with a yet-to-be liberated faculty in some areas). What we do not want is a company union type of student movement that sees itself as a body that, under the rubric of "liberalization," helps a paternal administration make better rules for us. What we do want is a union of students in which the students themselves decide what kind of rules they want or don't want. Or whether they need rules at all. Only this sort of student organization allows for decentralization and the direct participation of students in all those decisions daily affecting their lives.

2. That the student syndicalist movement take on one of two possible structures: a Campus Freedom Democratic Party (CFDP) or a Free Student Union (FSU).

a) *Campus Freedom Democratic Party.* This is possible on those campuses where the existing student government is at least formally democratic (that is, one student—one vote). The idea is to organize a year-round electoral campaign for the purposes of educating students about their system; building mass memberships in dormitory and living area "precincts"; constantly harassing and disrupting the meetings of the existing student government (for instance, showing up *en masse* at a meeting and singing the jingle of the now-defunct "Mickey Mouse Club"); and, finally, winning a majority of seats in student government elections. As long as the CFDP has a minority of the seats, those seats should be used as soapboxes to expose the existing body as a parody of the idea of government. It should be kept in mind that the main purpose of these activities is to develop a radical consciousness among *all* the students in the struggle yet to come against the administration.

What happens if a CFDP wins a majority of the seats? It should immediately push through a list of demands (the nature of which I will deal with later) in the form of a Bill of Rights or a Declaration of Independence or both. The resolution should indicate a time-limit for the administration (or regents or whatever) to reply. If the demands are met, the students should promptly celebrate the victory of the revolution. If not, the CFDP should promptly abolish student government or set up a student-government-in-exile. Second, the CFDP should immediately begin mass demonstrations: sit-ins in the administration buildings, in faculty parking lots, in maintenance departments, and so forth; boycotts of all classes; and strikes of teaching assistants. In short, the success of these actions (especially when the cops come) will be the test of how well the CFDP has been radicalizing its constituency during the previous two or three years.

b) *Free Student Unions.* The difference between an FSU and a CFDP is mainly tactical. On many campuses, existing student governments are not even formally democratic; rather, they are set up with the school newspaper having one vote, the interfraternity council having one vote, and so on. In a situation like this, we ought to ignore or denounce campus electoral politics from the word go, and, following the plan of the Wobblies, organize one big union of all students. The first goal of the FSU would be to develop a counter-institution to the existing student government that would eventually embrace a healthy majority of the student body. It would have to encourage nonparticipation in student government and to engage in active, nonelectoral, "on-the-job" agitation. This would take the form of organizing and sponsoring the violation of existing rules. Such violations might include staging dormitory sleep-outs and "freedom" parties in restricted apartments, nonviolently seizing the building that houses IBM machines used to grade tests, campaigning to mutilate IBM cards, disrupting oversized classes, and nonviolently attempting to occupy and liberate the student newspaper and radio station. All this should be done in such a manner as to recruit more and more support. Once the FSU has more support than the student government has, it should declare the student government defunct, make its demands of the administration, and, if refused, declare the general strike.

Obviously, the success of either a CFDP or an FSU depends upon our ability to organize a mass radical base with a capacity for prolonged resistance, dedication, and endurance. Bearing these needs in mind, one can easily see why such a student syndicalist movement must be national (or even international) in its scope. There will be a need for highly mobile regional and national full-time organizers to travel from campus to campus. When critical confrontations break out, there will be a need for sympathy demonstrations and strikes on other campuses. There may even be a need to send busloads of students to a campus where, because of mass arrests, replacements are required. Again, we can learn much from the organizing tactics of the Wobblies and the CIO.

3. That the student syndicalist movement adopt as its primary and central issue *the abolition of the grade system.* This is not to say that other issues, such as decision-making power for student governing bodies, are unimportant. They are not; and, in certain situations, they can be critical. But to my mind, the abolition of grades is the most significant over-all issue for building a radical movement on campus. There are three reasons why I think this is so.

a) Grading is a *common condition* of the total student and faculty community. It is the direct cause of most student anxieties and frustrations. Also, it is the cause of the alienation of most faculty members from their work. Among our better educators and almost all faculty, there is a consensus that grades are, at best, meaningless, and more likely, harmful to real education.

b) As an issue to organize around, the presence of the grade system is *constantly felt.* Hour exams, midterms, and finals are always cropping up (whereas student government elections occur only once a year). Every time we see our fellow students cramming for exams (actually, for grades), we can point out to them that they are being exploited and try to organize them. In every class we take, throughout the school year, every time our professors grade our papers and tests, we can agitate in our classrooms, exposing the system and encouraging both our classmates and our instructors to join with us to abolish that system.

c) The abolition of the grade system is a demand that cannot be met by the administration without radically altering the shape and purpose of our educational system. First of all, if there were no grades, a significant part of our administrators would be without jobs, for they would have nothing to do. Also, large mass-production TV classes and the like would have to be done away with. Since education would have to take place through personal contact between the student and his professor, classes would necessarily be limited in size. Since the evaluation of a student's work would not have to be temporally regulated and standardized, independent scholarship would be encouraged, if not necessitated. As a result, the corporate system might have some difficulty in finding manipulable junior bureaucrats. Finally, the Selective Service would have a hell of a time ranking us.

For these reasons, it is my feeling that the abolition of the grade system should serve as the "umbrella" issue for a student syndicalist movement, much in the same manner as the abolition of the wage system served the syndicalist trade union movement. Under this umbrella, many other issues can be raised, depending upon which segment of the student community we were appealing to and upon what degree of strength we might have at any one time.

4. That the student syndicalist movement incorporate in secondary issues the ideology of participatory democracy. This can be viewed as an attempt on our part to sabotage the knowledge factory machinery that produces the managers and the managed of 1984. There are numerous ways to go about this. I will list a few:

a) Approach students in teachers colleges with a counter-curriculum that is based on the ideas of Paul Goodman and A. S. Neil for the radical education of children.

b) At the beginning of each semester, request (or demand) of the professors that you and your fellow classmates participate in shaping the structure, format, and content of that particular course.

c) Sign up for, attend, denounce, and then walk out of and picket excessively large classes.

d) Organize students and liberated faculty members in certain departments to work out a model counter-curriculum and agitate for its adoption, *mainly because students participated in shaping it* rather than because of its merits.

e) Hold mock trials for the dean of men and dean of women for their "crimes against humanity."

f) In the case of women students, organize a decentralized federation of dormitory councils (soviets?) where each living unit would formulate a counter-set of rules and regulations; and then use them to replace existing rules *on the grounds that the women themselves made the rules.*

I am sure that if we use our imaginations, we can extend this list indefinitely. And because they embody the philosophy of participatory democracy, these suggestions, to my mind, are of intrinsic worth. And I also believe that they might have far-reaching effects. For participatory democracy is often like a chronic and contagious disease. Once caught, it permeates one's whole life and the lives of those around. Its effect is disruptive in a total sense. And within a manipulative, bureaucratic system, its articulation and expression amounts to sabotage. It is my hope that those exposed to it during the time they are building a movement for student syndicalism will never quite be the same, especially after they leave the university community.

From the SDS pamphlet, "The Multiversity: Crucible of the New Working Class," by Carl Davidson, early 1967.

The Praxis of Student Power: Strategy and Tactics

Socialism on one campus—an infantile disorder

Perhaps the single most important factor for the student power movement to keep in mind is the fact that the university is intimately bound up with the society in general. Because of this, we should always remember that we cannot liberate the university without radically changing the rest of society. The lesson to be drawn is that any attempt to build a student movement based on "on-campus" issues only is inherently conservative and ultimately reactionary. Every attempt should be made to connect campus issues with off-campus questions. For example, the question of ranking and university complicity with the Selective Service System needs to be tied to a general anti-draft and "No Draft for Vietnam" movement. The question of the presence of the military on the campus in all its forms needs to be tied to the question of what that military is used for—fighting aggressive wars of oppression abroad—and not just to the question of secret research being poor academic policy. Furthermore, the student movement must actively seek to join off-campus struggles in the surrounding community. For example, strikes by local unions should be supported if possible. This kind of communication and understanding with the local working class is essential if we are ever going to have community support for student strikes.

Radicalizing the new working class

If there is a single over-all purpose for the student power movement, it would be the development of a radical political consciousness among those students who will later hold jobs in strategic sectors of the political economy. This means that we should reach out to engineers and technical students rather than to business administration majors, education majors rather than to art students. From a national perspective, this strategy would also suggest that we should place priorities on organizing in certain kinds of universities—the community colleges, junior colleges, state universities and technical schools, rather than religious colleges or the Ivy League.

One way to mount political action around this notion is to focus on the placement offices—the nexus between the university and industry. For example, when Dow Chemical comes to recruit, our main approach to junior and senior chemical engineering students who are being interviewed should not only be around the issue of the immorality of napalm. Rather, our leaflets should say that one of the main faults of Dow and all other industries as well is that their workers *have no control* over the content or purposes of their work. In other words, Dow Chemical is bad, not only because of napalm, but mainly because it renders its workers *powerless,* makes them *unfree.* In short, Dow and all American industry *oppresses its own workers* as well as the people of the Third World. Dow in particular should be run off the campus and students urged not to work for them because of their complicity in war crimes. But when other industries are recruiting, our leaflets should address themselves to the interviewee's instincts of workmanship, his desires to be free and creative, to do humane work, rather than work for profit. We should encourage him, if he takes the job, to see himself in this light—as a skilled worker—and arouse his interest of organizing in his future job with his fellow workers, skilled and unskilled, for control of production and the end to which his work is directed. The need for control, for the power, on and off the job, to affect the decisions shaping one's life in all arenas; developing this kind of consciousness, on and off the campus, is what we should be fundamentally all about.

Practical, critical activity: notes on organizing

There are three virtues necessary for successful radical organizing: honesty, patience, and a sense of humor. First of all, if the students we are trying to reach can't trust us, who can they trust? Secondly, it takes time to build a movement. Sometimes several years of groundwork must be laid before a student power movement has a constituency. It took most of us several years before we had developed a radical perspective. Why should it be any different for the people we are trying to reach? This is not to say that everyone must repeat all the mistakes we have gone through, but there are certain forms of involvement and action that many students will have to repeat. Finally, by a sense of humor, I mean we must be life-affirming; lusty, passionate people are the only kind of men who have the enduring strength to motivate enough people to radically transform a life-negating system.

Che Guevara remarked in *Guerrilla Warfare* that as long as people had faith in certain institutions and forms of political activity, then the organizer must work with the people through those institutions, even though we might think those forms of action are dead ends. The point of Che's remark is that people must learn that those forms are stacked against them through their *own experience* in attempting change. The role of the organizer at this point is crucial. He or she should neither passively go along with the student government "reformer" types nor stand apart from the action denouncing it as a "sell-out." Rather, his task is that of *constant criticism* from within the action. When the reformers fail, become bogged down, or are banging their heads against the wall, the organizer should be there as *one who has been with them throughout their struggle* to offer the relevant analysis of *why* their approach has failed and to indicate future strategies and tactics.

However, we also need to be discriminating. There are certain forms of political action, like working within the Democratic Party, that are so obviously bankrupt, that we need not waste our time. In order to discern these limits, an organizer has to develop a sensitivity to understand where people are. Many radical actions have failed on campuses because the activists have failed in laying a base for a particular action. It does no good to sit in against the CIA if a broad educational campaign, petitions, and rallies on the nature of the CIA have not been done for several days before the sit-in. It is not enough that we have a clear understanding of the oppressiveness of institutions like the CIA and HUAC before we act in a radical fashion. We must make our position clear to the students, faculty, and the surrounding community.

The cultural apparatus and the problem of false consciousness

In addition to its role in the political economy, it is important to deal with the university as the backbone of what Mills called "the cultural apparatus." * He defined this as all those organizations and milieux in which artistic, scientific, and intellectual work goes on, as well as the means by which that work is made

* C. Wright Mills, *Power, Politics and People,* p. 368.

available to others. Within this apparatus, the various vehicles of communication—language, the mass arts, public arts, and design arts—stand between a man's consciousness and his material existence. At present, the bulk of the apparatus is centralized and controlled by the corporate rulers of America. As a result, their use of the official communications has the effect of limiting our experience and, furthermore, expropriates much of that potential experience that we might have called our own. What we need to understand is that the cultural apparatus, properly used, has the ability both to transform power into authority and transform authority into mere overt coercion.

At present, the university's role in acculturation and socialization is the promulgation of the utter mystification of "corporate consciousness." Society is presented to us as a kind of caste system in which we are to see ourselves as a "privileged elite"—a bureaucratic man channeled into the proper bureaucratic niche. In addition to strengthening the forms of social control off the campus, the administration uses the apparatus on campus to legitimize its own power over us.

On the campus, the student press, underground newspapers, campus radio and television, literature tables, posters and leaflets, artist and lecture series, theatres, films, and the local press make up a good part of the non-academic cultural media. Most of it is both actively and passively being used against us. Any student power movement should (1) try to gain control of as much of the established campus cultural apparatus as possible, (2) if control is not possible, we should try to influence and/or resist it when necessary and (3) organize and develop a new counter-apparatus of our own. In short, we need our people on the staff of the school newspapers and radio stations. We need our own local magazines. We need sympathetic contacts on local off-campus news media. Finally, we all could use some training in graphic and communicative arts.

What this all adds up to is strengthening our ability to wage an effective "de-sanctification" program against the authoritarian institutions controlling us. The purpose of desanctification is to strip institutions of their legitimizing authority, to have them reveal themselves to the people under them for what they are—raw coercive power. This is the purpose of singing the Mickey Mouse Club jingle at student government meetings, of ridiculing and harassing student disciplinary hearings and tribunals, of burning the Dean of Men and/or Women in effigy. People will not move *against* institutions of power until the legitimizing authority has been stripped away. On many campuses this has already happened; but for those remaining, the task remains. And we should be forewarned: it is a tricky job and often can backfire, de-legitimizing us.

The correct handling of student governments

While student governments vary in form in the United States, the objective reasons for their existence are the containment, or pacification and manipulation of the student body. Very few of our student governments are autonomously incorporated or have any powers or rights apart from those sanctioned by the regents or trustees of the university. Furthermore, most administrations hold a veto power over anything done by the student governments. Perhaps the worst aspect of this kind of manipulation and repression is that the administration uses students to control other students. Most student government politicos are lackeys of the worst sort. That is, they have internalized and embraced all the repressive mechanisms the administration has designed for use *against* them and their fellow students.

With this in mind, it would seem that we should ignore student governments and/or abolish them. While this is certainly true in the final analysis, it is important to relate to student governments differently during the earlier stages of on-campus political struggles. The question we are left with is how do we render student governments ineffective in terms of what they are designed to do, while at the same time using them effectively in building the movement?

Do we work inside the system? Of course we do. The question is not one of working "inside" or "outside" the system. Rather, the question is do we play by the established rules? Here, the answer is an emphatic no. The established habits of student politics—popularity contest elections, disguising oneself as a moderate, working for "better communications and dialogue" with administrators, watering down demands before they are made, going through channels—all of these gambits are stacked against us. If liberal and moderate student politicians really believe in them, then we should tell *them* to try it with all they have. But if they continue to make this ploy after they have learned from their own experience that these methods are dead-ends, then they should be soundly denounced as opportunists or gutless administration puppets.

We should face the fact that student governments are *powerless* and designed to stay that way. From this perspective, all talk about "getting into power" is so much nonsense. The only thing that student governments are useful for is their ability to be a *temporary vehicle* in building a grass-roots student power movement. This means that student elections are useful as an arena for raising real issues, combating and exposing administration apologists, and involving new people, rather than getting elected. If our people do happen to get elected as *radicals* (this is becoming increasingly possible) then the seats won should be used as a focal point and sounding board for demonstrating the impotence of student government *from within.* A seat should be seen as a soap-box, where our representative can stand, gaining a kind of visibility and speaking to the student body as a whole, over the heads of the other student politicians. . . .

Reform or revolution: what kinds of demands?

Fighting for reforms and making a revolution should not be seen as mutually exclusive positions. The question should be: what kind of reforms move us toward a radical transformation of both the university and the society in general? First of all, we should avoid the kinds of reforms which leave the basic rationale of the system unchallenged. For instance, a bad reform to work for would be getting a better grading system, because the underlying rationale—the need for grades at all—remains unchallenged.

Secondly, we should avoid certain kinds of reform that divide students from each other. For instance, trying to win certain privileges for upper classmen but not for freshmen or sophomores. Or trying to establish non-graded courses for students above a certain grade-point average. In the course of campus political activity, the administration will try a whole range of "divide and rule" tactics such as fostering the "Greek-Independent Split," sexual double standards, intellectuals *vs* "jocks," responsible *vs* irresponsible leaders, red-baiting, and "non-student" *vs* students. We need to avoid falling into these traps ahead of time, as well as fighting them when used against us.

Finally, we should avoid all of the "co-management" kinds of reforms. These usually come in the form of giving certain "responsible" student leaders a voice or influence in certain decision-making processes, rather than abolishing or winning effective control over those parts of the governing apparatus. One way to counter administration suggestions for setting up "tripartite" committees (one-third student, one-third faculty, one-third administration, each with an equal number of votes) is to say, "OK, but once a month the committee must hold an all-university plenary session—one man, one vote." The thought of being outvoted 1,000–1 will cause administrators to scrap that cooptive measure in a hurry.

We have learned the hard way that the reformist path is full of pitfalls. What, then, are the kinds of reformist measures that do make sense? First of all, there are the civil libertarian issues. We must always fight, dramatically and quickly, for free speech and the right to organize, advocate, and mount political action—of all sorts. However, even here, we should avoid getting bogged down in "legalitarianism." We cannot count on this society's legal apparatus to guarantee our civil liberties: and, we should not organize around civil libertarian issues *as if it could.* Rather, when our legal rights are violated, we should move as quickly as possible, without losing our base, to expand the campus libertarian moral indignation into a multi-issue *political* insurgency, exposing the repressive character of the administration and the corporate state in general.

The second kind of partial reform worth fighting for and possibly winning is the abolition of on-campus repressive mechanisms, i.e., student courts, disciplinary tribunals, deans of men and women, campus police, and the use of civil police on campus. While it is true that "abolition" is a negative reform, and while we will be criticized for not offering "constructive" criticisms, we should reply that the only constructive way to deal with an inherently destructive apparatus is to destroy it. We must curtail the ability of administrators to repress our *need to refuse* their way of life—the regimentation and bureaucratization of existence.

When our universities are already major agencies for social change in the direction of 1984, our initial demands must, almost of necessity, be negative demands. In this sense, the first task of a student power movement will be the organization of a holding action—a resistance. Along these lines, one potentially effective tactic for resisting the university's disciplinary apparatus would be the forming of a Student Defense League. The purpose of the group would be to make its services available to any student who must appear before campus authorities for infractions of repressive (or just plain stupid) rules and regulations. The defense group would then attend the student's hearings *en masse.* However, for some cases, it might be wise to include law students or local radical lawyers in the group for the purpose of making legal counterattacks. A student defense group would have three major goals: (1) saving as many students as possible from punishment, (2) desanctifying and rendering dysfunctional the administration's repressive apparatus, and (3) using (1) and (2) as tactics in reaching other students for building a movement to abolish the apparatus as a whole.

When engaging in this kind of activity, it is important to be clear in our rhetoric as to what we are about. We are not trying to *liberalize* the existing order, but trying to win our *liberation* from it. We must refuse the administration's rhetoric of "responsibility." To their one-dimensional way of thinking, the concept of responsibility has been reduced to its opposite, namely, be nice, don't rock the boat, do things according to our criteria of what is permissible. In actuality their whole system is geared towards the inculcation of the values of a planned irresponsibility. We should refuse *their* definitions, *their* terms, and even refuse to engage in *their* semantic hassles. We only need to define—*for ourselves and other students*—our notions of what it means to be free, constructive and responsible. Too many campus movements have been coopted for weeks or even permanently by falling into the administration's rhetorical bags.

Besides the abolition of repressive disciplinary mechanisms within the university, there are other negative forms that radicals should work for. Getting the military off the campus, abolishing the grade system, and abolishing universal compulsory courses (i.e., physical education) would fit into this category. However, an important question for the student movement is whether or not positive radical reforms can be won within the university short of making a revolution in the society as a whole. Furthermore, would the achievement of these kinds of partial reforms have the cumulative effect of weakening certain aspects of corporate capitalism, and, in their small way, make that broader revolution more likely?

At present, my feeling is that these kinds of anti-capitalist positive reforms are almost as hard to conceive of intellectually as they are to win. To be sure, there has been a wealth of positive educational reforms suggested by people like Paul Goodman. But are they anti-capitalist as well? For example, we have been able to organize several good Free Universities. Many of the brightest and most sensitive students on American campuses, disgusted with the present state of education, left the campus and organized these counter-institutions. Some of their experiments were successful in an immediate internal sense. A few of these organizers were initially convinced that the sheer moral force of their work in these free institutions would cause the existing educational structure to tremble and finally collapse like a house of IBM cards. But what happened? What effect did the Free Universities have on the established educational order? At best, they had no effect. But it is more likely that they had the effect of strengthening the existing system. How? First of all, the best of our people left the campus, enabling the existing university to function more smoothly, since the "troublemakers" were gone. Secondly, they gave liberal administrators the rhetoric, the analysis, and sometimes the manpower to coopt their programs and establish elitist forms of "experimental" colleges inside of, although quarantined from, the existing educational system. This is not to say that Free Universities should not be organized, both on and off the campus. They can be valuable and useful. But they should not be seen as a primary aspect of a strategy for change.

What then is open to us in the area of positive anti-capitalist reforms? For the most part, it will be difficult to determine whether or not a reform has the effect of being anti-capitalist until it has been achieved. Since it is both difficult and undesirable to attempt to predict the future, questions of this sort are often best answered in practice. Nevertheless, it would seem that the kinds of reforms we are looking for are most likely to be found within a strategy of what I would call "encroaching control." There are aspects of the university's administrative, academic, financial, physical, and social apparatus that are potentially, if not actually, useful and productive. While we should try to abolish the repressive mechanisms of the university, our strategy should be to gain control, piece by piece, of its positive aspects.

What would that control look like? To begin with, all aspects of the non-academic life of the campus should either be completely under the control of the students as individuals or embodied in the institutional forms they establish for their collective government. For example, an independent Union of Students should have the final say on the form and content of all university political, social and cultural events. Naturally, individual students and student organizations would be completely free in organizing events of their own.

Second, only the students and the teaching faculty, individually and through their organizations, should control the academic affairs of the university. One example of a worth-while reform in this area would be enabling all history majors and history professors to meet jointly at the beginning of each semester and shape the form, content, and direction of their departmental curriculum. Another partial reform in this area would be enabling an independent Union of Students to hire additional professors of their choice and establish additional accredited courses of their choice independently of the faculty or administration.

Finally, we should remember that control should be sought for some specific purpose. One reason we want this kind of power is to enable us to meet the self-determined needs of students and teachers. But another objective that we should see as radicals is to put as much of the university's resources as possible into the hands of the under-class and the working class. We should use campus facilities for meeting the educational needs of insurgent organizations of the poor, and of rank and file workers. Or we could mobilize the universities' research facilities for serving projects established and controlled by the poor and workers, rather than projects established and controlled by the government, management, and labor bureaucrats. The conservative nature of American trade unions makes activity of this sort very difficult, although not impossible. But we should always be careful to make a distinction between the American working class itself and the labor bureaucrats.

The faculty question: allies or finks?

One question almost always confronts the student movement on the campus. Do we try to win the support of the teaching faculty before we go into action? Or do we lump them together with the administration? What we have learned in the past seems to indicate that both of these responses are wrong. Earlier in this paper, I remarked on the kinds of divisions that exist among the faculty. What is important to see is that this division is not just between good and bad guys. Rather, the faculty is becoming more and more divided in terms of the objective functions of their jobs. To make the hard case on one hand, the function of the lower level of the faculty is to teach—a potentially creative and useful activity; on the other hand, the function of most administrative and research faculty is manipulation, repression, and—for the defense department hirelings—destruction. In general, we should develop our strategies so that our lot falls with the teaching faculty and theirs with ours. As for the research and administrative faculty, we should set both ourselves and the teaching faculty against them. Also, during any student confrontation with the administration, the faculty can do one of four things as a group. They can (1) support the administration, (2) remain neutral, (3) split among themselves, and (4) support us. In any situation, we should favor the development of one of the last three choices rather than the first. Furthermore, if it seems likely that the faculty will split on an issue, we should try to encourage the division indicated above. While it is important to remain open to the faculty, we should not let their support or non-support become an issue in determining whether or not we begin to mount political action. Finally, we should encourage the potentially radical sectors of the faculty to organize among themselves around their own grievances, hoping that they will eventually be able to form a radical alliance with us.

The vital issue of teaching assistants' unions

Probably the most exploited and alienated group of people on any campus are the graduate student teaching assistants. The forces of the multiversity hit them from two directions—both as students and as teachers. As students, they have been around long enough to have lost their awe of academia. As faculty, they are given the worst jobs for the lowest pay. For the most part, they have no illusions about their work. Their working conditions, low pay, and the fact that their futures are subject to the whimsical machinations of their department chairmen, make them a group ripe for radical organization. Furthermore, their strategic position within the university structure makes them potentially powerful as a group, if they should decide to organize and strike. If they go out, a large part of the Multiversity comes grinding to a halt. The kinds of demands they are most likely to be organized around naturally connect them with a radical student power movement and with the potentially radical sector of the faculty. Moreover, these considerations make the organization of a radical trade union of TAs a crucial part of any strategy for change. We should see this kind of labor organizing as one of our first priorities in building the campus movement.

Non-academic employees: on-campus labor organizing

Almost all colleges and especially the multiversities have a large number of blue-collar maintenance workers on campus. Within the state-supported institutions in particular, these people are often forbidden to organize unions, have terrible working conditions, and are paid very low wages. Their presence on the campus offers a unique opportunity for many students to become involved in blue-collar labor organizing at the same time that they are in school. Secondly, since these workers usually live in the surrounding community, their friends and relatives will come from other sectors of the local working class. Quite naturally, they will carry their ideas, opinions, and feelings toward the radical student movement home with them. In this sense, they can be an important link connecting us with other workers, and our help in enabling them to organize a local independent and radical trade union would help tremendously. Finally, if we should ever strike as students, they could be an important ally. For instance, after SDS at the University of Missouri played a major role in organizing a militant group of non-academic employees, they learned that, were the Union to strike for its own demands in sympathy with student demands, the university as a physical plant would cease to function after four days. It is obviously important to have that kind of power.

The knowledge machinery and sabotage: striking on the job

One mistake radical students have been making in relating to the worst aspects of the multiversity's academic apparatus has been their avoidance of it. We tend to avoid large classes, lousy courses, and reactionary professors like the plague. At best, we have organized counter-courses outside the classroom and off the campus. My suggestion is that we should do the opposite. Our brightest people should sign up for the large freshman and sophomore sections with the worst professors in strategic courses in history, political science, education, and even the Reserve Officers' Training Corps counter-insurgency lectures. From this position they should then begin to take out their frustrations with the work of the course while they are on the job—i.e., inside the classroom. Specifically, they should constantly voice criticism of the form and content of the course, the size of classes, the educational system, and corporate capitalism in general. Their primary strategy, rather than winning debating points against the professor, should be to reach other students in the class. Hopefully, our on-the-job organizer will begin to develop a radical caucus in the clash. This group could then meet outside the class, continue to collectively develop a further radical critique of the future class-work, to be presented at the succeeding sessions. If all goes well with the professor, and perhaps his department as well, they will have a full-scale academic revolt on their hands by the end of the semester. Finally, if this sort of work were being done in a variety of courses at once, the local radical student movement would have the makings of an underground educational movement that was actively engaged in mounting an effective resistance to the educational *status quo.*

Provo tactics: radicalization or sublimation?

There is little doubt that the hippy movement has made its impact on most American campuses. It is also becoming more clear that the culture of advanced capitalist society is becoming more sterile, dehumanized, and one-dimensional. It is directed toward a passive mass, rather than an active public. Its root value is consumption. We obviously need a cultural revolution, along with a revolution in the political economy. But the question remains: where do the hippies fit in? At the moment their role seems ambivalent.

On the one hand, they thoroughly reject the dominant culture and seem to be life-affirming. On the other hand, they seem to be for the most part, passive consumers of culture, rather than active creators of culture. For all their talk of community, the nexus of their relations with each other seems to consist only of drugs and a common jargon. With all their talk of love, one finds little deep-rooted passion. Yet, they are there: and they are a major phenomenon. Their relevance to the campus scene is evidenced by the success of the wave of "Gentle Thursdays" that swept the country. Through this approach, we have been able to reach and break loose a good number of people. Often, during the frivolity of Gentle Thursday, the life-denying aspects of corporate capitalism are brought home to many people with an impact that could never be obtained by the best of all of our anti-war demonstrations.

However, the hippy movement has served to make many of our people withdraw into a personalistic, passive cult of consumption. These aspects need to be criticized and curtailed. We should be clear about one thing: the individual liberation of man, the most social of animals, is a dead-end—an impossibility. And even if individual liberation were possible, would it be desirable? The sublimation of reality within the individual consciousness neither destroys nor transforms the objective reality of other men.

Nevertheless, the excitement and the imagination of some aspects of hippydom can be useful in building critiques of the existing culture. Here, I am referring to the provos and the diggers. Gentle Thursday, when used as a provo (provocative) tactic on campus, can cause the administration to display some of its most repressive characteristics. Even something as blunt as burning a television set in the middle of campus can make a profound statement about the life-styles of many people. However, people engaging in this kind of tactics should (1) not see the action as a substitute for serious revolutionary activity and (2) read up on the Provos and Situationists rather than the Haight-Ashbury scene.

From soap-box to student strikes: the forms of protest

During the development of radical politics on the campus, the student movement will pass through a multitude of organizational forms. I have already mentioned several: Student Defense League, Teaching Assistants' Unions, Non-Academic Employees' Unions, and of course, SDS chapters. Another important development on many campuses has been the formation of Black Student Unions, or Afro-American cultural groups. All of these groups are vital, although some are more important than others at different stages of the struggle. However, for the purpose of keeping a radical and multi-issue focus throughout the growth of the movement, it is important to begin work on a campus by organizing an SDS chapter.

From this starting point, how does SDS see its relation to the rest of the campus? I think we have learned that we should not look upon ourselves as an intellectual and political oasis, hugging each other in a waste land. Rather, our chapters should see themselves as organizing committees for reaching out to the majority of the student population. Furthermore, we are organizing for something—the power to effect change. With this in mind, we should be well aware of the fact that the kind of power and changes we would like to have and achieve are not going to be given to us gracefully. Ultimately, we have access to only one source of power within the knowledge factory. And that power lies in our potential ability to stop the university from functioning, to render the system dysfunctional for limited periods of time. Throughout all our on-campus organizing efforts we should keep this one point in mind: that sooner or later we are going to have to strike—or at least successfully threaten to strike. Because of this, our constant strategy should be the preparation of a mass base for supporting and participating in this kind of action.

What are the organizational forms, other than those mentioned above, that are necessary for the development of this kind of radical constituency? The first kind of extra-SDS organization needed is a Hyde Park or Free Speech Forum. An area of the campus, centrally located and heavily traveled, should be selected and equipped with a public address system. Then, on a certain afternoon one day a week, the platform would be open to anyone to give speeches on anything they choose. SDS people should attend regularly and speak regularly, although they should encourage variety and debate, and not monopolize the platform. To begin, the forum should be weekly, so that students don't become bored with it. Rather, we should try to give it the aura of a special event. Later on, when political activity intensifies, the forum could be held every day. In the early stages, publicity, the establishment of a mood and climate for radical politics is of utmost importance. We should make our presence felt everywhere—in the campus news media, leafleting and poster displays, and regular attendance at the meetings of all student political, social and religious organizations. We should make all aspects of our politics as visible and open as possible.

Once our presence has become known, we can begin to organize on a variety of issues. One arena that it will be important to relate to at this stage will be student government elections. The best organizational form for this activity would be the formation of a Campus Freedom Party for running radical candidates. It is important that the party be clear and open as to its radical consciousness, keeping in mind that our first task is that of building radical consciousness, rather than winning seats. It is also important that the party take positions on off-campus questions as well, such as the war in Vietnam. Otherwise, if we only relate to on-campus issues, we run the risk of laying the counter-revolutionary groundwork for an elitist, conservative and corporatist student movement. As many people as possible should be involved in the work of the party, with SDS people having the function of keeping it militant and radical in a non-manipulative and honest fashion. The party should permeate the campus with speeches, films, and leaflets, as well as a series of solidly intellectual and radical position papers on a variety of issues. Furthermore, we should remember that an election campaign should be fun. Campus Freedom Parties should organize Gentle Thursdays, jug bands, rock groups, theatre groups for political skits, and homemade 8mm. campaign films. Finally, during non-election periods, the Campus Freedom Party should form a variety of CFP *ad hoc* committees for relating to student government on various issues throughout the year.

The next stage of the movement is the most crucial and delicate: the formation of a Student Strike Coordinating Committee. There are two preconditions necessary for its existence. First, there must be a quasi-radical base of some size that has been developed from past activity. Secondly, either a crisis situation provoked by the administration or a climate of active frustration with the administration and/or the ruling class it represents must exist. The frustration should be centered around a set of specific demands that have been unresolved through the established channels of liberal action. If this kind of situation exists, then a strike is both possible and desirable. A temporary steering committee should be set up, consisting of representatives of radical groups (SDS, Black Student Union, TA's Union). This group would set the initial demands, and put out the call for a strike in a few weeks' time. Within that time, they would try to bring in as many other groups and individuals as possible without seriously watering down the demands. This new coalition would then constitute itself as the Student Strike Coordinating Committee, with the new groups adding members to the original temporary steering committee. Also, a series of working committees and a negotiating committee should be established. Finally, the strike committee should attempt to have as many open mass plenary sessions as possible.

What should come out of a student strike? First, the development of a radical consciousness among large numbers of students. Secondly, we should try to include within our demands some issues on which we can win partial victories. Finally, the organizational form that should grow out of a strike or series of strikes is an independent, radical, and political Free Student Union that would replace the existing student government. I have already dealt with the general political life of radical movements. But some points need to be repeated. First of all, a radical student union must be in alliance with the radical sectors of the underclass and working class. Secondly, the student movement has the additional task of radicalizing the subsector of the labor force that some of us in SDS have come to call the new working class. Thirdly, a radical union of students should have an anti-imperialist critique of US foreign policy. Finally, local student unions, if they are to grow and thrive, must become federated on regional, national, and international levels. However, we should be careful not to form a national union of students lacking in a grass-roots constituency that actively and democratically participates in all aspects of the organization's life. One NSA is enough. On the international level, we should avoid both the CIA and Soviet Union sponsored International Unions. We would be better off to establish informal relations with groups like the Zengakuren in Japan, the German SDS, the French Situationists, the Spanish Democratic Student Syndicate, and the Third World revolutionary student organizations. Hopefully, in the not too distant future, we may be instrumental in forming a new International Union of Revolutionary Youth. And even greater tasks remain to be done before we can begin to build the conditions for human liberation.

CHAPTER 6

"From Protest to Resistance"

As opposition to the Vietnam War intensified during 1967, SDS laid greater emphasis on the role of the military in the university. Radicals moved from protest marches, which merely attracted publicity, toward attempts at denying the government the resources and cooperation of key institutions in the society. This shift in strategy was called: "From protest to resistance."

But the change was not only in strategy. Most SDS members now clearly differentiated themselves from liberal critics of the war by adopting an anti-imperialist position and by explicitly defining themselves as revolutionaries. Relations with liberal students, however, became a major internal dilemma for the organization. SDS debated whether it made more sense to ally with liberals and risk loss of political clarity or to insist on ideological agreement and risk isolation from broad support.

All but one of the readings that follow come from the period between November 1967 and March 1968—a period framed in radical history by the March on the Pentagon of October 21, 1967, and the Columbia revolt of April 1968. All the pieces originally appeared in *New Left Notes,* SDS's weekly organizational paper.

The selections begin with an excerpt from a short but influential article by Todd Gitlin, a founder of SDS, suggesting that SDS unite its campaign for university reform with its anti-war activities in a national effort to expel the military from the campus. An article by Carl Davidson discusses the history of anti-war protest and the full array of tactics for action against military research and recruiting. In the course of his argument, Davidson denies legitimacy to any aspect of the social order, including civil liberties. "To respect and operate within the realm of bourgeois civil liberties," Davidson states, "is to remain enslaved." The SDS leader also indicates that institutional resistance should not be considered a final strategy, but only a transitional approach. (Elsewhere he explained that radicals should aim at organizing a working class movement, but that it was premature to make the attempt.)

Following Davidson's article is the program for a spring offensive that was approved by an SDS national convention in December of 1967. The program, which embodied the resistance strategy, was passed as a compromise between different factions within the organization after a plan put forth by Davidson and Greg Calvert, SDS national secretary, had been narrowly defeated. The opposition to the resistance strategy came primarily from members of the Progressive Labor Party, who rejected the notion that organizing the working class was premature. Nevertheless, they accepted the resistance position that the immediate focus of SDS activities should be "the open use of the university for the war" (i.e., military recruiting, war research, etc.). With this area of agreement, the two factions were able to work together in the coming months.

Following the excerpts from the proposal introduced at the December convention by members of Progressive Labor are two analyses of SDS and the student movement. The first analysis, written by members of Princeton SDS, discusses relations with liberals and the distinction between moralistic stands on particular issues and a radical analysis of society. The authors doubt that the student movement will actually be able to deny the government use of the university's resources, but they see student protest as a valid means of spreading radical consciousness.

In the second analysis, Eric Mann deals with several tactical and organizational problems ranging from internal democracy to the development of "parallel institutions." Mann sets out a long-range strategy of "permanent resistance" involving both confrontation and negotiation with the university. Mann's views reflected the dominant mood in SDS immediately prior to the Columbia rebellion. It was this outlook which the SDS leadership at Columbia, including Mark Rudd, rejected during the spring 1968 strike there.

From an article by Todd Gitlin, a founder of SDS, in New Left Notes, *March 20, 1967.*

Resistance and the Movement

. . . It seems that SDS people are caught in a serious tension: on the one hand, they want to do something about the war and the garrison state; on the other, they have a commitment toward transforming the institution at hand, the university. It might make sense, then, for SDS to consider a strategy that joins the two concerns.

The natural synthesis would be a national movement to expel the military from the campus. Local movements in this direction would continue, but self-consciously in the context of a national objective. SDS would announce that it is absurd to talk about a free university as long as militarism is linked to learning; through direct action, research and education, locally and nationally, chapters would take on the task of depriving the military of every shred of legitimacy on the campus. They would engage faculty as well as students in a here-and-now confrontation between our vision(s) of education and the obscenity of Pentagon contracts and recruitment. Needless to say, questions of student control and the uses of the university would flow directly out of such a strategy; so would larger questions of the functions of learning in a repressive society.

There would be several advantages to posing this as a national strategy. First, chapters at different levels of solidity and commitment could all identify with the same momentum, could gain strength from a knowledge that success in one place had national importance. Second, a national campaign could generate concerted activity on campuses hitherto untouched by more diffuse activity. Third, by naming national targets, the campaign could win victories more resonant in proportion to the amount of work put into them. (In other words, a whole national military program could be expelled more easily than could the sum of its parts; just as, say, national NSA was punctured without much more work than it would have taken to puncture a few campus student governments.) Without succumbing to a kind of centralist mystique, neither should we ignore the fact that the dominant institutions are indeed centralized and must be treated as such.

It would not be farfetched to envision tangible victories at the national level. Take, for example, the Pentagon's unpublicized Project THEMIS, "A Program to Strengthen the Nation's Academic Institutions," announced in January. . . . THEMIS begins by recognizing that military contracts have been overly concentrated in a relatively small number of universities, and proposes to correct the imbalance by funding new "centers of experience" on "no more than 50" new campuses just within its first year. One criterion for eligibility is "The willingness of the college or university to assist in (a) coupling the output of the research program to the potential users of such knowledge by publishing suitable reports, data, and handbooks; (b) providing occasional advisory assistance to the Department of Defense and its agencies; and (c) participating in joint seminars and symposia." The attempt, clearly, is fully to penetrate every corner of the academic world, to hedge the military-intellectual complex against future instabilities. Because of the insistance on "coupling mechanisms," there can be no pretense that the money will come without strings.

I cite THEMIS as a possible first target because it has not yet been set into operation and therefore could possibly be stopped in its tracks by a concerted national campaign. . . . Clearly a victory over something like THEMIS could launch the total campaign in a big way.

This is not to say that the Pentagon could not survive and conduct wars without Project THEMIS. The point is rather that such a marginal victory could impart a certain momentum then applicable to steadily more important objectives. (The campaign could be thought of as a sustained rollback, over a period of time, perhaps with a tentative time table.) Simply to demonstrate to ourselves that we can have a tangible effect on a national abomination would be a major victory for our own morale, and hence for our future possibilities as a resistance facing outward.

Article by Carl Davidson, in New Left Notes, *November 13, 1967.*

Toward Institutional Resistance

The recent confrontations on our campuses between radical students and recruiters from the military and the war industries demonstrate the beginning of a new phase of struggle within the anti-war movement. The resistance being offered campus officials and civil police by radical students is almost without precedent in the history of the American university. As radicals, we unequivocally celebrate the recent events at the Universities of Wisconsin and Illinois, and at Brooklyn and Oberlin Colleges. But celebration is not enough. We must critically evaluate the present conflicts in order to draw lessons for the future.

The current battles are not without a history, however young the movement might seem. The first student protests against the Vietnam war go back to 1963. Beginning in the fall of 1964, the teach-in movement swept across American campuses for almost two years. Hundreds of thousands in the academic community turned against the government's policy in Southeast Asia. On almost every campus a dissident and active minority took root and grew. After an initial showing of 25,000 at the SDS April 17, 1965 March on Washington, a primarily campus-based anti-war movement turned out over 200,000 demonstrators in nearly 150 cities for the fall 1965 International Days of Protest.

Before the spring of 1966, the campus was seen primarily as a haven and recruiting ground for the anti-war movement, with periodic public demonstrations and teach-ins continuing to be our principal tactics. During this period, there were only a handful of sporadic leaflettings and picketings of CIA and Marine Corps recruiters on campus. The issue of university complicity with the war was not raised until April and May of 1966. During that time, shortly after major escalations of the war, the student movement had been developing a program of opposition to the draft. Concurrently, the Selective Service System initiated requirements for the ranking of male students by their grade averages and scores on a National SSS exam, to be given on 1200 campuses in May 1966. SDS attacked the exam, the draft, 2S deferments, the war, and, most importantly, university complicity with the war by ranking male students and holding the Selective Service exams. Demonstrations again swept the campuses. Thousands of students sat-in and hundreds were arrested at the University of Chicago, Roosevelt, Buffalo, Brooklyn College, University of Wisconsin, Cornell, Stanford, and CCNY. The government eventually abolished class rank and the tests, probably as a result of the sit-ins and the threat of more to come.

However, the issue of university complicity with the war remained in the consciousness of the student movement. Already alienated from college administrations as a result of the free speech and *in loco parentis* fights of 1964 and 1965, the radical student movement began a deeper probe of the university's connections with the military. In the winter of 1966 the University of Pennsylvania students gained nationwide publicity for uncovering chemical and bacteriological war research for Vietnam on their campus. *Ramparts* magazine had already exposed Michigan State University's cooperation with the CIA in developing Diem's police state. Several SDS chapters had picketed and protested against military recruiters on campus. The first major confrontation occurred at Berkeley, early in December of 1966. SDS members on the campus attempted to set up an anti-draft table next to a Navy recruiting table in the student union. The administration called in the police and a massive sit-in began. To break the sit-in, over 100 police were used. Nine students were arrested and scores were injured. Over 10,000 students rallied and formulated the demands for a strike. Five days later, the strike was broken, although it had been 70% effective in the first two days.

While the students might have lost the battle of Berkeley, the event sparked the beginning of a series of similar conflicts across the country. From January to June, for the remainder of the school year, demonstrations and sit-ins against the presence on campus of recruiters from the military and related institutions were commonplace. Columbia University, Iowa State, and the University of Wisconsin saw major sit-ins against CIA recruiters. Beginning in January at Brown University, recruiters from Dow Chemical Company, manufacturers of napalm, were confronted on several dozen campuses. Major anti-Dow sit-ins occurred at the University of Wisconsin, San Fernando Valley State, UCLA, and Claremont College. At Claremont, students not only drove the Dow recruiter off campus, but literally chased him out of town. In April 1967, Columbia University SDS organized a massive and significant confrontation with Marine recruiters, with 800 students almost physically removing the Marines from campus, while fighting off violent attacks from a smaller group of 200 right-wing students.

Finally, during the two days before the Spring Mobilization, SDS at the New School for Social Research organized an 80% effective strike against the war. While the New School Strike was a symbolic action without any specific demands of the college administration, it was an important event, indicating to the student movement that student strikes were a viable strategy.

The most interesting aspect of the scores of similar confrontations between radical students and recruiters from Dow, the CIA, and the military is that the events were unplanned and unconnected on the national level. Furthermore, they received relatively little coverage in the national news media. It seems that SDS's weekly newspaper, *New Left Notes,* deserves most of the credit for spreading the actions, since it covered the first actions against Dow and the military in detail. SDS chapters probably picked up on the strategy from there, and followed with similar actions on their local campuses. While the SDS national staff certainly approved of and encouraged the confrontations, the major part of its time and resources during that period were spent developing a draft resistance program and organizing regional educational conferences. The idea of organizing a national movement to expel the military from the campus was never suggested as an SDS national program until late March of 1967 in an article in *New Left Notes* by Todd Gitlin. The strategy formally became a major SDS national program at the June 1967 National Convention in Ann Arbor, Michigan.

In the time between the confrontations ending with spring semester of 1967 and the present struggles this fall, the radical student movement has gone through several significant changes. To better understand both the actions of our past activities as well as the direction of our present and future struggles on the campus, we must consider those developments.

First of all, we have grown. The Vietnam war continues filling our ranks with fresh recruits. Not only has the left grown, but all sectors of the population have become increasingly dissatisfied with the war, especially the campus community. In addition to building our numerical strength, the war has constantly and consistently pushed us to the left politically, strategically and tactically. Who among us today would argue that America is not an imperialist power? Less than a year ago, only the "crazy left sectarians" used that language. Now even clergymen talk about imperialism. Draft resistance activity is commonplace. Less than two years ago, SDS went through a major political crisis over simply printing a *proposal* for anti-draft activity. We no longer talk about moving from protest to resistance. The resistance has already begun.

Apart from the war, the black ghetto rebellions this summer fundamentally altered the political reality of white America, including the white left. The black liberation movement has replaced the civil rights and anti-poverty movements, revealing the utter bankruptcy of corporate liberalism's cooptive programs. The events of this summer marked not only the possibility, but the beginning of the second American revolution. This second factor has made more important than ever the organizing of white poor and working-class communities by the white radicals. SDS is beginning a response to this situation which includes a major refocusing of draft resistance work away from the student community and into poor and working-class communities.

Thirdly, in the past few months, SDS people have had to deal with an increasing repression, often violent, from the state and its supporters. Some of us have fared better than others, but no one goes limp anymore, or meekly to jail. Police violence does not go unanswered. Sit-ins are no longer symbolic, but strategic: to protect people or hold positions, rather than to allow oneself to be passively stepped over or carted off. The implications of this change, asserting itself for the first time nationally on the Pentagon steps October 21st, are more important than one might assume. For instance, while the anti-recruiting sit-ins last spring were primarily acts of moral witness and political protest, an increasing number of the sit-ins this fall displayed the quality of tactical political resistance. Their purpose was the disruption and obstruction of certain events and actions *by whatever means necessary*. Politically, the occurrence of this kind of activity implies the prior dissolution of whatever legitimacy and authority the institutions being resisted may have formerly had. This exceedingly important process of desanctification points to the weakening of the existing institutions of power as well as the growing revolutionary potential of those forces opposing that power.

The final factor we should take into account has been the development over the past six months of an analysis and strategy for institutional resistance. Near the end of 1966, SDS emerged from a dormant and disconnected summer with a mood and rhetoric of resistance. By the beginning of 1967, that rhetoric had little substantive content, except for an audacious but unimplemented draft resistance program. When the present school year started, we seemed to be somewhat better off. We had an analysis and strategy, at least in part. We had begun the task of developing a politics of anti-imperialism within a growing anti-war movement. We developed an analysis of the university as a "knowledge factory" adjunct to the multinational corporations of American capitalism. Our factories had the task of supplying an expanding but orderly flow of two valuable and strategic commodities into American business, government, and military institutions—manpower and intelligence. During the summer, our research into the penetration and use of the university by military and paramilitary operations revealed extensive connections with organizations like Project Themis, IDA, TRICAT, RAND, Project Agile, and CRESS, to name a few. All of these had, in one way or another, commandeered the work and energy of our schools and had put our resources to the ends of the present and future oppression and domination of the people of the world, both in Vietnam and in our urban ghettos. We found our own unfreedom in the face of those IBM bureaucracies tied to the oppression of people everywhere.

SDS had always urged powerless people to take power in those institutions affecting their daily lives. We now fully understood the impossibility of freedom in the university so long as it remained tied to the interests of America's corporate and military ruling elite. Secondly, we saw the possibility of engaging in a common struggle with the liberation movements of the world by confronting the on-campus sector of the same military apparatus oppressing them. Our strategy became clear: the disruption, dislocation and destruction of the military's access to the manpower, intelligence, or resources of our universities. Our tactics: a varied series of local confrontations with campus military and paramilitary operations, hopefully escalating into student strikes, culminating in a national student strike, in the spring of 1968 against the military's presence on campus and against the war in Vietnam. This was by no means seen as our only program, even by the campus. But it was to be a major effort and experiment in a strategy of institutional resistance.

Thus far, SDS has confronted a moderate range of military and counterinsurgency operations on campus. The work of these operations falls into three general areas: (1) recruiting, (2) research and development or R&D, and (3) classroom training. In the area of recruiting, we have confronted, at a variety of levels, the Army, Navy, Marines, Air Force, CIA, Dow Chemical, Peace Corps, Vista, and ROTC. Concerning research, we have had little experience, the only major exceptions being the discontinuance of a CBW project called "Spicerack" at the University of Pennsylvania and the temporary disruption of IDA offices at Princeton University. In the classroom, we have disrupted or otherwise rendered temporarily disfunctional a range of ROTC training sessions on several campuses, as well as regular foreign policy courses following the government line. One imaginative confrontation in this area was with a TRICAT (Triennial Civil Affairs Training, Army Reserve) counterinsurgency seminar on Greece at the University of Florida. Several dozen SDS pickets, complete with sound truck, calling themselves the Peoples Liberation Army made a surprise appearance at the Army's Saturday morning COIN lectures. After surrounding the building, they quickly leafletted the classes, gave short speeches over their PA system, planted an insurgent flag on top of the building and disappeared. Other confrontations involved a major resistance to and defeat of the ranking and testing process of the SSS and several successful occasions of resisting HUAC's overt attempts at gathering campus information on radical students.

The tactics we have developed thus far cover a wide range, beginning with mild dissent and protest and reaching to forceful resistance. The selection of tactics naturally depends on one's strength relative to a particular opponent within the limits of the current political situation. In general, we have been underestimating our own strength and overestimating the enemy. The following list attempts to present a general outline of the tactics we have used and developed in the last two years of confrontation:

1) individual vocal dissension, questions, and speeches at recruiting areas.

2) attending, officially or unofficially, training classes and "teaching-in," either on a one-shot basis or for the duration of the course.

3) leafletting training classes with counter-information, counter-readings, and counter-exams and/or holding counter-classes.

4) leafletting recruiting areas and research sites.

5) exposing secret research and/or exposing clandestine connections of open research, recruiting, or training institutes in campus and national news media.

6) making appointments with recruiters in order to debate, harass, and/or take up their time.

7) obtaining favorable resolutions against current and future recruiting, research and/or training from student governments, faculty senates, and other groups.

8) placing "war crimes" and other dramatic posters at recruiting sites or training classrooms.

9) setting up counter tables next to recruiting tables or training classrooms.

10) picketing recruiting areas or training classrooms.

11) staging "guerrilla theater" with death-masks, posters, props and pictures in recruiting areas and training classrooms.

12) holding teach-ins before, during and after recruiting, training, or research work.

13) holding "war crimes trials" for recruiters, trainees, and researchers.

14) holding a "guerrilla siege" of buildings(s) during counterinsurgency classes.

15) holding speaking forums, questionings, and rallies drawing sufficient numbers into recruiting or training areas in order to indirectly stop or disrupt the recruiting or training process.

16) holding non-obstructive sit-ins at recruiting sites, leaving a pathway cleared for recruitees.

17) holding obstructive sit-ins at recruiting sites to prevent recruiting:

a) passive: recruitee or others can pass if they use force.

b) active: recruitee or others using force to pass will be met with counter-force by those sitting-in.

18) holding obstructive or non-obstructive sit-ins at administration offices to bring pressure for the cancellation of recruiting, training, or research.

19) holding obstructive sit-ins around automobiles and/or campus entrances to prevent recruiters and/or police cars or paddy wagons containing arrested students from leaving.

20) tipping over recruiting tables and/or seizing recruiting literature.

21) removing recruiters and/or police from campus by force or threat of force.

22) organizing a student strike until administrators stop the activity of certain recruiters, researchers, training classes, police action, or their own reprisals.

Naturally, this list is not meant to be inclusive of all our tactics, only the most common. Also, there are no set formulas for deciding which tactics to use in any given situation. However, there are a few guidelines to keep in mind. First, and most important, don't become *isolated* by using tactics likely to divide the participants in the action from their present and *potential* constituency. But even our potential constituents are limited, and we shouldn't try to please everyone. The problem is not whether or not one makes enemies, but whether or not one has the right people for enemies.

Secondly, the tactics of the resistance struggle should result in two complementary goals: 1) the weakening of the resisted dominant institution and 2) developing a consciousness of power among those resisting the dominant institutions. Towards this end, we shouldn't be afraid to proclaim a victory when we're ahead; and then retreating, rather than allowing a resistance struggle to degenerate into a symbolic protest and defeat. A perfect example of this situation was the Pentagon siege on Oct. 21st. The high point and victory of the resistance struggle occurred near dusk, after we had broken military lines, occupied *their territory,* entered the Pentagon, and held our ground until the point where two of their soldiers came over to us. At that point, we should have declared a victory and marched away; rather than sitting there, hour after hour, in slowly weakening and decreasing numbers, waiting for our final symbolic defeat.

A final guideline, a corollary of the first, is that a resistance must grow both in numbers, and in depth of commitment, if it is to survive and eventually win. Most important in this area is political education, for both ourselves and our potential constituency. For instance, *we* may know about the CIA, but what about the rest of the campus? And the surrounding non-academic community? Before we use tactics like obstructive sit-ins, we must be careful to carry out extensive educational work, such as speeches, leaflets, rallies, or teach-ins, both on and off the campus. . . .

My next criticism deals with those anti-military protests on campus that have contained their objections to the work of the war machine within the limits of academic policy. While it is true that, say, secret research is poor academic policy, we are not opposed to it because of its cluttering up academia, but because it is directly a part of the apparatus dominating and oppressing most of the world's people. To limit our opposition to recruiting and research because "they are disruptive of the academic and educational atmosphere" is to enclose ourselves within the elitist ivory tower academias of the past centuries. We are interested in building a movement of ordinary people, rather than one of academics still swayed by such arguments.

A third question, rather than criticism, we have been forced to deal with by recent events is the issue of civil liberties. Objection after objection has been made that by obstructing recruiters, we have been denying others—the recruiters and those who wish to see him—the right of free speech and assembly. In a sense, this is true. As I mentioned earlier, the institutions our resistance has desanctified and delegitimatized, as a result of our action *against their oppression of others,* have lost all authority and, hence, all respect. As such, they have only raw, coercive power. Since they are without legitimacy in our eyes, they are without rights. Insofar as individuals, such as recruiters, continue to remain in association with those institutions, they run the risk of being given the same treatment. Most people agree with this position *in principle.* There are very few who would argue that we should not stop, rather than debate, individuals who might have recruited for the staff needed to operate Hitler's death camps. The question we are asked to answer, rather, is by what criteria do we determine whether or not an institution or individual has lost their legitimacy. There are two kinds of answers, one within bourgeois thought, the other without. For the first, we can assert the Nuremberg decisions and other past criteria of war crimes as the criteria by which we, in conscience, decide whether or not an institution and individuals associated with that institution have lost their legitimacy and their rights. Our second answer rests in a revolutionary critique of the institutions and society we are trying to destroy. Our critique argues that the social order we are rebelling against is totalitarian, manipulative, repressive and anti-democratic. Furthermore, within this order of domination, to respect and operate within the realm of bourgeois civil liberties is to remain enslaved, since the legal apparatus is designed to sustain the dominant order, containing potential forces for change within its pre-established and ultimately castrating confines. As a result, it is the duty of a revolutionary not only to be intolerant of, but to actually suppress the anti-democratic activities of the dominant order.

There are other answers as well as these two. One is that the recruiters haven't come to debate, only to recruit; hence free speech is not the issue. Most recruiters will help you out on this one by refusing a public debate. After he refuses, we can make the point that he decided himself that free speech wasn't the issue. No matter what they say, however, we are bound to find much opposition on this issue. Which is often good, since it raises substantive questions that work toward the deobfuscation of the reality of American power.

While it remains an important strategy, institutional resistance to the military presence on campus is not a panacea for revolutionary change in the United States. It is not even a complete strategy for an anti-war movement, but only one facet. However, it seems to contain within it, not only significant lessons and possibilities for the student movement, but also ideas that might be central to the development of analysis, strategy, and tactics for other battlefronts within the American Leviathan as well.

Resolution of the SDS National Council, December 1967, presented by Naomi Jaffe, John Fuerst, and Bob Gottlieb.

Program for a Spring Offensive

(A) A national program should provide a broad political framework which responds to the felt needs of chapters for political coherence and strategic direction. Within this framework, chapters develop tactics based on analysis of their own specific situation and in response to their own local needs.

(B) Chapters feel the need to break out of political isolation, to make our politics understandable and relevant to other students and non-students. To do this, we have to organize around their needs and interests, but to select those issues which make it clear that those needs and interests are part of a broad radical struggle.

(C) Thus student issues should be raised in a way which shows that the form of our education in the university is related to its function of channeling manpower into the corporate structure of society. Education over which we have no control prepares us for jobs over which we have no control.

(D) We don't attack dorm rules simply in order to relate to students, but we attack them as a form of socialization of women into subordinate roles in society.

(E) We don't attack Dow simply because it recruits on campus, but we use Dow to expose the university's function as a training ground for the repressive institutions of American society. We don't attack university complicity with the war, but the university as an integral part of the corporate structure which necessitates and wages imperialist wars.

(F) The same strategy applies to the formation of links with non-students: We should choose issues which demonstrate the links between immediate needs and anti-imperialism. Specific ways in which people are being fucked by the war, such as the draft and urban deterioration are obvious opportunities in radical action.

(G) In forming links with non-students, a further criterion is to choose issues which establish organic connections between students and other groups—issues which identify a common source of oppression.

(H) At Columbia, the university is using a public park in a ghetto area to build a huge gymnasium. In Chicago, the university profited from urban renewal which destroyed the housing of graduate students and black ghetto residents. In Boston and New York students and other subway riders pay high fares, and transit workers are payed low wages, while banks and large bondholders reap tax-free profits from the public transit systems.

(I) Leafletting at factory gates is the sort of mechanical approach we should avoid. It produces no real contact. Popular fronts based on narrowly defined economic issues force us to hide our politics instead of sharing them.

(J) Universities are factories producing technical, professional, and service workers. We can relate to these workers on issues coming from their powerlessness and alienation. We can reach them because we are being trained to become them.

(K) The draft cuts through the fragmentation that divides students from non-students. The privileged status implied by the student deferment is being eroded by the new draft law. The military and university are parallel institutions. Whether the 2-S forces students to remain in school and become technicians or the draft forces them to become soldiers, both coerce individuals into the roles required to maintain a repressive system.

(L) Local issues should be explicitly related to a radical context. A nationally linked program can and should reinforce and make visible the anti-imperialist content of local struggles and act as a catalyst in areas and groups otherwise beyond our reach.

(M) The links we want to build are those which really unite fragmented groups because we experience similar problems and similar sources of oppression. These links have to be developed organically, not mechanically or on paper or in rhetoric about the "working class" but in terms of our politics and chapter programs.

Implementation:

1) A period of action would extend over a ten-day period in April to allow chapters to carry out a schedule of educational programs, joint actions and demonstrations aimed at a variety of institutions related to the issues that have given urgency to the question of a national program. The specific choice of date can include different spans of ten days in April which each region can decide in terms of their own needs.

2) Local and regional chapters should choose actions for the national program that come out of their own needs.

3) Chapters should begin to plan their work, their strategy, for the coming semester as soon as possible and submit requests to the NO [National Organization] for materials needed, travellers desired, and other assistance required to implement their local programs.

4) The NO will make as one of its major priorities in the coming months the production of materials on a series of topics relevant to the work of local chapters. The pamphlets should be short and analytic and suited for use in a wide variety of situations. (Examples of topics are imperialism, draft, racism, university and manpower channeling, electoral politics.)

From the counterproposal at the same SDS National Council meeting, December 1967, supported by members of the Progressive Labor Party, and others.

"Base-building"

. . . The concept of "resistance" with no strategy for victory is just another version of the pacifist, moral witness concept. We are for sharpening the struggle with US imperialism, but only on our own grounds—where we come out stronger both ideologically and numerically, and closer to the working class, not fighting it. The whole concept of the present string of "resistance" demonstrations must lead to a series of tactical defeats. Our weakness is not one of improving our "military tactics", but one of strategically breaking out of our isolation from the majority of both students and workers.

The many struggles against university complicity which have taken place during the last 3 months underscore these points. Where SDS chapters have applied a base-building approach, their confrontations have strengthened and broadened anti-imperialist forces. Where they have rushed headlong into super-militant demonstrations or sit-ins, without trying to win over or neutralize the masses of students, they have weakened and isolated themselves. In fact the largest, most militant, and most victorious struggles of recent months, such as that of Brooklyn College, have grown out of careful base-building work.

Our strategy shouldn't be based on a cynical outlook toward the vast majority of the American people. . . . The "resistance" outlook holds . . . that the working class is apathetic, bought off, and reactionary, but . . . argues that if a small minority takes super-militant action the workers will follow their lead, even though we have made no attempts to reach them with our political ideas.

A winning strategy must have two aspects:

1) We hold that US imperialism hurts most students, both intellectually and materially. Therefore we should not aim at a minority student movement, but at one which encompasses the majority of the campus. We should build a mass anti-imperialist student movement.

2) We further hold that the central force in defeating US imperialism is the working class, both black and white, whose interests are fundamentally opposed to imperialism. Students will play a very important role in crushing imperialism. Building strong ties between workers and students is absolutely essential for victory. This should not be done only by students becoming workers, but by building an alliance between them. . . .

A) . . . for the coming term. . . . Our primary focus should be an attempt to defeat the open use of the university for the War. . . . During one week in mid-spring, this organizing should come to a head with sharp, campus-based struggles throughout the nation, relating to the organizing needs of each chapter, including student strikes wherever possible. The national character of these actions creates the possibility that universities may be forced to retreat, giving us victories in some places and laying the basis for future actions in others.

To prepare for these struggles, we should use this period to broaden our influence among students. We should turn classrooms into forums to debate the universities' complicity with the War, and we should participate in and raise anti-imperialist ideas within student struggles on other issues in order to win over those not yet committed to opposition to the Vietnam war.

Article by Richard P. Fried, Jerome R. Hoffman, James J. Tarlau, Princeton SDS members, in New Left Notes, *February 5, 1968.*

Potentialities and Limitations of the Student Movement: 1967-68

Last year, in response to Greg Calvert's article on the shift in SDS from protest to resistance, Todd Gitlin noted that a campaign to expel the military from the campus would join revulsion against the War with the drive to reform the university. In such a way, SDS could link strictly on-campus issues with a larger and more significant political movement off-campus.

In fact, this type of campaign, as suggested by Gitlin, has occurred more than once in recent months. Yet, although there is a greater awareness among radicals that the student movement, by itself, cannot be the only white radical group in motion, SDS remains contained within the university community, isolated from the insurgencies in the urban ghettos and in the labor unions. We find ourselves largely without support from any organized group off-campus.

Last June the SDS National Convention decided to spend this year building an anti-war student resistance movement. This decision derived from the belated discovery that mass mobilizations and marches—whether in New York or Washington—do little to slow down the war machine. Emphasis has consequently shifted to the slow dismantling of the military complex at its roots, one of which is the university. Precisely because it is the location of the anti-war movement's social base and political strength, it is open to attack.

Although only first impressions can be entertained, it may be worthwhile to discuss several aspects of this campus phenomenon. The campus movement consists primarily of three distinct though inter-related programs: draft resistance, anti-recruiting protests, and campaigns against university war research. It is with the last two that we intend to deal specifically, because such an approach will enable us to derive relevant general impressions about the campus movement as a whole.

Two types of politics

In examining the student movement, it is important to understand the various political positions supporting the current campaigns against secret war research and recruiting. Though quite intricate, and never completely separated, these types of politics form two rather distinct modes of thought and action which embody serious differences and have ultimately profound consequences for the movement. In order to attain greater clarity in describing and analyzing them and to avoid the prejudicial reactions that unavoidably accompany familiar labels, we will arbitrarily call them types "A" and "B". After having described each separately, we will be able to make judgments about what is appropriate to "radicals" and what is not. Of course, in virtually every SDS chapter, tendencies toward both types exist and often the individuals involved are unable to discern the distinctions between them. This is what makes this critique necessary, for it is only by understanding these very distinctions that we can move on-campus programs in directions that are meaningful in a larger context.

In the first type of politics ("A"), its proponents act to define themselves by taking a specific position on specific moral issues. They may be characterized in that they see the War as the primary target for the movement, and that they do not have any strategy for social change which would not only seek to stop the War but would also work for a permanent transfer of power away from those elites guiding America's imperialist policies. Though the advocates of this type of approach admit that building a movement for radical social change is important, they say that it deserves secondary consideration either because the War, as the greatest evil, must be stopped first or because any other major issue may be divisive for the anti-war coalition. What is implicit in this position is the belief that the War is a tragic miscalculation, an aberration of the government.

This leads to the view that campaigns against war research and recruitment are important as effective protests against the War and in helping to fight the encroachments of the military-industrial complex on the university. From this perspective comes a demi-strategy for changing the university, or at least parts of it. The university, here, consists of a community of interests (and perhaps scholars) which would act in pursuit of a common interest were that view articulated. The common interest is seen as the preservation of the university for open scholarship which is bound only by the most minimal restrictions. In our case, the university should not, as a corporate body, be a party to any agreement which facilitates secret research. As shall be noted later, this minimum definition of the university's role as an institution of critical intelligence leaves much to the discretion of the individual faculty member, and thus, ultimately, to the power of a few external institutions which have the necessary funds for research. Consequently, the primary objective for the anti-war "A"-type activist is the termination of all secret contractual ties between the university and the military.

To this we may counterpose "B"-type politics. It is probably fair to say that this brand of politics is practiced by very few of us because, by its very nature, it demands that we transcend the difficult but inevitable boundary between symbolic and effective action. Its general perspective is that the university is relevant to us not in isolation but as it relates to other institutions in society. The university exists, as it is, in a complex field of social forces in which it finds itself dependent upon certain elites which utilize it for very specific ends. As such, the ability of SDS to achieve significant changes within the university or in the university's relations with society may be impossible without a political movement based upon groups located elsewhere in the American social structure. Of course, we may be able to wrest certain immediate gains of a narrow scope from a university administration, but such advances will probably not alter the primary role of the university in society, and thus not allow real changes in the educational conditions of most students, or in the function of the university as it is related to the government and military. In the interim, before the creation of a mass political movement, "B"-type politics strives to impart to individual students what is generally referred to as a radicalized consciousness, which is essentially an awareness of their role in society, of the real nature of their condition, and of their collective potential in a truly liberated society.

"B"-type politics views campaigns against war research and recruitment in terms of their effectiveness in enabling students to see the actual role of the university in society. Its primary objective is to make explicit the university's integral role in a society controlled by a highly differentiated, polyelite power complex which furthers its ends by supporting abroad and at home interventionist policies serving to suppress any manifestations of discontent which may have the potential for general liberation. With this new awareness will hopefully come the vision of what a free university in a liberated society might be; indeed, a large part of "B" politics involves the necessary model-building which points the way for radical change. Consequently, this analysis assumes that for democratic control in the university to be meaningful the general society must be substantially changed.

The proponents of "A"-type politics measure success by the number of "victories" that are won. "B"-type politics, however, weighs the value of campaigns waged on campuses by their success in building a movement of students with a radical analysis of society and a strategy for changing it. While some "victories" can certainly be important in building such a campus movement, others may not. With the current high degree of "mobilization" in the student community, almost any activist can generate sufficient interest for a protest or demonstration which, however ineptly executed, usually manifests a greater degree of militancy than was evident anywhere only several years ago. Yet student activism is becoming increasingly institutionalized. Its capacity for new assaults on the status quo is not significantly increasing. Despite the rhetoric of resistance, there has, up to now, been no qualitative shift in our activity. What is badly needed is a set of criteria which contain guidelines for activities that can build a radical student movement.

At this point we must recognize that SDS should be aiming at "B"-type politics, and we may even allow ourselves to denote this as radical politics. Moreover, keeping in mind what we have already said about it, we can begin to construct guidelines for meaningful political action. To this end, we may observe that not every demonstration is to be desired, nor are all protests equally valuable; success, we would claim, is linked to any activity which significantly furthers the development of a student movement having as its conscious goal the changing of this entire society. Should this general definition be accepted, we will then be forced to reach the somewhat disappointing (for sentimentalists) conclusion that many of the "victories" achieved recently on many campuses have not been at all "successful"; some have, in fact, actually been damaging.

Significance of the current campaigns

In light of the descriptive dichotomy between "A"- and "B"-type politics, most of the recent campaigns (related to recruiting and war research) must be classified as "A"-type, that is, grounded on moral objections and taking their strategy from that position. We notice that the CIA has begun to recruit off-campus, and though there are stories that Dow is worried about the demonstrations, there is no indication that it is having any trouble in recruiting able scientists. The implication is that the net effect of the demonstrations against military-oriented recruiters, particularly Dow and the CIA, has been, at best, to force them into town instead of recruiting directly on campus. More often, not even this minimal "achievement" has resulted, and the operations of these organizations have not been affected in any degree at all. So what we have is non-radical logic and non-radical effect: this war is seen as immoral, and thus the university should be no part of it; the recruiters, because they serve a part of the war machine, are likewise immoral; hence they ought to be excluded from the university, a citadel of purity. For all the militant rhetoric and revolutionary slogans, the substance of the campaigns is politically minimal, as we can safely agree that radicalism does not generate demands as a collective personal catharsis.

The campaigns against war research are somewhat more deceptive. Gabriel Kolko, who seemingly has become the leading authority on war research at universities, recites "victories" every month in the Nation. The list continually grows longer: the University of Pennsylvania's chemical warfare research contract, the Cornell Aeronautics Lab, the University of Minnesota, Stanford, Columbia's Electronics Research Lab, and now, maybe, even Princeton and IDA. What are we to make of this?

Kolko has stated that the "achievements" at universities in opposing war research have occurred because of an undefeatable coalition of the anti-war forces which are attempting to stop the war machine and those liberals who wish the university to remain free from classified research because it is contrary to "the goals of a liberal institution." The coalition, in effect, consists of establishment liberals who are lodged in the university-faculty apparatus and have not yet completely surrendered their consciences to the status quo, and insurgent students who engage in "A"-type politics to satisfy their revulsion against this war. Against such a coalition, which demands so little, the administration invariably yields after making sure that nothing significant to the functioning of the university's primary operations is given up. Yet another "victory" is added to the list.

But, of course, we should analyze these "victories" more closely. While the Department of Defense was inconvenienced by the Penn affair, it did not take long to find another manufacturer to do chemical-biological research. Cornell and Columbia cut all institutional ties with the two DOD research labs, thus leaving them relatively more immune to any further student protests against informal collusion. Stanford, Minnesota and NYU continue to accept classified research, though in lessened amounts.

We have even scored such a victory at Princeton. As a result of the arrest of thirty-one students, and numerous open and closed faculty meetings, a committee of the faculty will probably recommend to the Board of Trustees that Princeton withdraw its sponsorship from the Institute for Defense Analyses. Another victory: the important decisions were made solely by the administration and the faculty without any meaningful participation by the students, the legitimacy and structural integrity of the university apparatus remains unimpaired and, ironically, perhaps stronger for adopting the content and rhetoric of the anti-war reformists. In fact, this was a victory which accomplished nothing but increasing the prestige of SDS. We have arrived as an accepted part of the student political culture. But nothing of real substance resulted; witness that one of the most convincing arguments for Princeton's severing all institutional connections with IDA was that this would materially affect neither IDA nor Princeton. . . .

From a series of three articles by Eric Mann, SDS leader, in New Left Notes, *March 1969.*

Appraisal and Perspectives

Radicals have traditionally been plagued by the dilemma of having a different set of priorities and ultimate goals than the people they are trying to organize. Besides the obvious challenges to democracy and honesty that such a situation creates, it also raises some profound technical problems. Recent SDS history reflects a long-standing conflict among radicals—the battle of the "hards" and the "softs."

The "hards" are very concerned with maintaining an ideological and stylistic purity, believe that co-optation is the major threat to the Left, and often advocate measures considerably to the Left of their constituency. They argue that the role of a radical is to project challenging programs and analyses that "radicalize" people's thoughts and actions. The traditional pitfall of the "hards" has been projecting programs and tactics that are irrelevant or harmful to the constituency they are trying to organize. By trying to avoid co-optation they often isolate themselves from struggles which the "masses" think are important, such as large peace demonstrations, elections, and poverty programs.

The "softs" argue that a radical must get involved with people's immediate concerns and relate to the existing institutions in the society that affect people's lives. They see the major threat to the Left as isolation. In practice, the "softs" actually like American society more than they let on. But they often have a better understanding of the people than the "hards" (particularly because most Americans are more like the "softs"). They find it difficult to maintain a clear radical position in their day-to-day politics. They believe in winning reforms as both important in themselves and as stepping stones to building a radical movement, but have great difficulty in developing a strategy to effect the latter. They often become very defensive about being "outflanked on the Left," and develop an analysis of "objective conditions" that precludes radical action. "Personally, I think it's a great idea; but the people aren't ready for it now."

Fortunately, these stereotypes have less relevance to the present situation in SDS. The factions and stereotypes exist, but they are less sharply drawn. Although not immune to sectarianism, SDS also has the benefit of a vital and critical membership that is in touch with its constituency and can inject needed doses of reality into doctrinal arguments. This sense of reality will be necessary to help synthesize the strong points of both tendencies into a program of Permanent Resistance. . . .

I

An article by Greg Calvert entitled "Participatory Democracy, Collective Leadership, and Political Responsibility" (*New Left Notes,* December 18, 1967) has many frightening implications. The article is frightening, not because of the specific organizational suggestions made, which are reasonable and well overdue, but because of the analysis offered to justify these proposed reforms. Greg begins by giving a sympathetic history of the importance of participatory democracy, but then criticizes the concept as not being applicable to present-day conditions. Calvert states: "The primary contradiction in SDS involves the conflict between the notion of participatory democracy as a vision for the good society and its ineffectiveness as a style and structure for serious radical work." In fact, however, the specific organizational reforms he proposes—elected steering committees taking programmatic initiative, work-study groups analyzing, criticizing, and offering alternatives—are already in effect in some of our better chapters and are quite compatible with the idea of participatory democracy. I don't remember ever hearing that participatory democracy doesn't allow for the delegation of responsibility. What is strange, therefore, is the way Greg attempts to justify some reforms which don't contradict participatory democracy, but are aimed at making it work. Basically, Greg argues that participatory democracy is a "Marxian vision of post-scarcity communism" and not a working model for a present-day radical movement. If this argument is accepted, then radicals can have no criteria for combatting the development of an undemocratic and authoritarian radical organization. It will probably take a revolution to make participatory democracy real for all Americans. But the development and expansion of a democratic, radical organization in America is clearly possible right now. SDS has many problems, one of which is the inadequacy of its internal decision-making institutions; but the basic nature of the organization is democratic, and that nature is quite compatible with present-day political conditions.

While stating that participatory democracy is ineffective as a style and structure for radical work, Greg doesn't advance any specific arguments to justify his assertion. Two major arguments, however, have been advanced by others to justify this position, and should be discussed.

A psychological explanation argues that a radical organization can't be democratic until its people are freed from the contradictions of capitalist social relations. But this is just a cop-out. One of the key tasks of our movement is to liberate people by offering them alternatives. Many of those alternatives will have to be developed within the present economic structure, and if one argues that all alternatives must wait until after capitalism is done away with, then we offer people no hope or model for the type of society we believe in. With regard to internal democracy, present-day capitalism clearly debilitates people—including Movement people—and makes the building of a democratic and efficient radical organization difficult. But although capitalist society can be used as explanation for the difficulties of building such a movement, it shouldn't be used as an excuse for authoritarian measures.

A second argument advanced as to why participatory democracy can't work is that under the present system repression will force us to develop a tightly disciplined cadre organization. This argument is weak in that despite the existence of genuine attempts at political reprisal, the basic response of the Government right now seems much more in the nature of harassment than of repression. In the face of this harassment our best response seems to be the development of a broad-based radical movement, not a cadre organization. Historically, radicals have used the spectre of repression to retreat into "underground" activity that often wasn't justified by the actual political situation, and which served as an excuse to avoid the hard, tedious local organizing work that was necessary. There may very well come a time when some of our democratic options may be limited by government repression, but such a situation clearly does not obtain at present. Since present political conditions offer tremendous possibilities for open organizing and increasing both the democracy and the efficiency of SDS, articles that imply that the Government's basic response to us is one of repression are misleading and harmful. There is need for a great deal of discussion among chapter people, at NCs, in *New Left Notes,* and so forth about the possibilities of maintaining and even increasing internal democracy in the event of actual government repression. We should turn our attention to developing specific organizational responses to repression that will avoid the need for increased elitism in times of crisis.

II

Style, semantics, and political isolation

A dominant mood in SDS is one of revolutionary posturing coexisting with tremendous insecurity about playing such a role. . . . It is one thing to advise student radicals to go into cities, develop political and social communities that will protect them from co-optation and intimidation, and actively challenge the society in their job situation and in their neighborhood; and it is quite another to urge students to become "urban guerrillas." The worst result of this kind of talk isn't that it alienates people, but rather that people don't take it seriously. . . . Even the most dedicated SDS people who have been off campus for less than a month must laugh among themselves at the inappropriateness of the phrase "urban guerrilla" to describe the role they must play. A committed radical, sure. But an urban guerrilla? . . .

Right now political conditions on the campuses are very favorable to greatly increasing the size and political impact of our organization. In the context of this evaluation of SDS and the great political possibilities open to us, let's examine a program of Permanent Resistance.

The concept of resistance is an essential part of our politics, but in the past it has often been defined too narrowly. The actual programmatic results of the resistance rhetoric have given the impression that resistance means militant anti-war demonstrations—which in practice involved physical confrontations between unarmed students and the coercive arms of the ruling class: the police and the Army. Although there are certain situations in which such confrontations are politically valuable, resistance shouldn't be defined as a series of sporadic, militant demonstrations. It should be a total political style involving continuous resistance to the institutions and policies of corporate capitalism.

A program of Permanent Resistance means that SDS chapters should change their role from campus protest groups to radical community organizations that act as a de facto government for a growing number of students. Programmatically this means developing programs and raising issues that deal with a wide variety of student needs, while also injecting radical content into those campaigns to avoid becoming an apolitical service organization. Organizationally, that means raising our politics in every constituency and every relevant institution on the campus.

We should run our own candidates for student governing bodies—not merely to expose those bodies as worthless, but to advance specific proposals for how we would change the structure of student government to make it an effective instrument of student power, and the programs we would institute to deal with student grievances. Similarly, there will be increasing opportunities for SDS people to serve on student-faculty committees set up to study and recommend solutions for particular problems. Standing on the outside, putting out literature saying the committees are designed to mislead the students and avoid dealing with the real issues is not enough. Nor is our job to sit on such committees and try to obstruct their functioning. Instead, we should clearly publicize the political program that SDS plans to fight for on such a committee, and work to develop support for that position on the campus.

In some situations, by taking the programmatic initiative and developing alliances with liberal student-government types and liberal faculty members, we can win our demands. Winning political victories by aggressively pushing a clear political program and developing constituency support for it helps to build a radical movement. If we aren't satisfied with the recommendations of the committee—which will more often than not be the case—we can go back to the "streets" with the possibility of greater student support.

The theory isn't very unique. It is based on the assumption that many students want to give existing institutions "a chance to prove themselves," and are put off by radicals who reject them out of hand. Radicals who expect to build a political movement on the assumption that the response of corporate-liberal university administrators will be blanket opposition to student demands will often find themselves in the embarrassing position of predicting administration intransigence and letting the liberals get credit for ultimate concessions that the radicals were instrumental in eliciting.

Confrontation and negotiation will be the dominant political style in the immediate future, and there is a great need to develop regional meetings, specific case histories of chapter confrontations with university authorities, and detailed articles in *New Left Notes* to discuss the problems and techniques of maintaining and even increasing student support while the drawn-out parliamentary infighting takes place. Whenever possible, we should advance our own institutional suggestions for dealing with the issues we raise —for example public hearings in front of the student body rather than committee meetings which, even if they're open to the students, won't attract much attention since outsiders can't participate.

Total Resistance should include raising structural and content criticisms of every course we attend. We should occasionally interrupt lectures to question specific statements by faculty members, and ask for opportunities for alternative positions to be advanced. This approach helps make students aware that a professor is not an objective purveyor of "knowledge," but, like us, is a person who, given a variety of conflicting sources and contradictory factual information, will make his decisions about which sources he trusts on the basis of his values, and will select the most "important" facts on the basis of his analysis.

. . . Since we are not in power, we often assume an aggressive, hostile style in many of our actions. While this is necessary at times, it often creates the impression that radicals are humorless, even insensitive people. Our close friends, most of whom are politically active themselves, don't share this characterization; but many students come to believe that anger is the only defining quality of radicalism. It is important for us to develop parallel institutions—not as a means of avoiding dealing with the powerful institutions of society, but to give our constituency a tangible idea of the different human values we hold as radicals. In this way we can best explain that our aggressiveness and anger are caused by a hatred of capitalism, precisely because capitalism thwarts the realization of those values. SDS guerrilla theaters; coffee houses that serve good, cheap food and provide a hospitable meeting place; co-operative stores; laundries; and film centers can attract students who may not be ready to join or demonstrate or even attend our meetings.

Clearly, parallel institutions are not the solution to changing the institutions of corporate America by circumventing them. The major changes will have to take place by political organizing within and against those institutions. But parallel institutions can help build a radical movement—both by providing tangible examples of our politics and by pointing out the limitations of trying to build human institutions within a capitalist society.

A program of Permanent Resistance involves developing a radical movement that is deeply rooted in its constituency—rather than an unhealthy self-imposed graft on the student body. In this sense it is an attempt to develop an approach to politics that draws on the experience of the Chinese and Vietnamese guerrilla movements—not by mimicking their vocabulary and tactics—but by trying to understand the organic nature of their politics. A program of Permanent Resistance can't afford to abandon issues like dormitory hours as "reformist," when to hundreds of thousands of women students the issue is of great personal importance. We can't afford to develop a vocabulary that makes it difficult to communicate with our constituency—a vocabulary which implicitly says "stay out" to the uninitiated. Although necessarily critical of institutions such as fraternities and ROTC, we can't afford to write off large constituencies such as "fraternity men" and "ROTC types" if we are serious about becoming a majority movement on the campus.

III

Raising a radical political analysis

The most effective radical analysis should have four elements: critique, causation, immediate alternative, and ideal alternative.

1) Critique: This is easiest. It involves showing dissatisfied students that dorm hours, the grading system, the psychiatric clinic, course requirements, ROTC, and the "reading and regurgitating" syndrome are not a coincidental set of maladies, but are parts of an institutional pattern. The creation of an awareness that "the whole system is shit" can be facilitated by the work of a radical organizer, but is ultimately dependent on the feelings of the people he is trying to organize. There is little to be gained in trying to convince a satisfied student that the system is rotten. Our job is to give a focus to the unhappiness which many students do feel—an unhappiness which many of them blame on their own inadequacy until they are given an alternative explanation.

2) Causation: This involves showing students that the aliena-

tion they feel is not simply a product of a generation gap, or a "communication problem" between students and administration; it is a product of the conflict between the priorities of a university in a corporate capitalist system and the human potentialities of the people who must serve that system. Exposing the manpower-channeling functions of the university and its institutional and inter-personal links with the corporate, military, and governmental elites can be aided by actions such as the recent Dow and CIA protests which give specific focus to our general analysis. . . .

There is a great need for serious analytical work to better understand the specific inter-relationships between the corporate elite and the university system. This understanding can come through more SDS people applying themselves to power-structure research, and the continued confrontation with the university which, besides winning immediate victories and building our movement, will help expose particular institutional inter-relationships. With regard to the example of corporate concern for the maintenance of restrictive dorm hours, I think our research and experience will show that while the corporate elite is vitally concerned with the manpower channeling functions of the university, it is often careful not to interfere in the specific details of how the university operates. Many sophisticated corporate types are convinced that Benningtons and San Francisco States are ultimately more compatible with their needs than the "conventional" schools.

3) Immediate alternatives: One of the cliched criticisms of the Left—one which, unfortunately, is often accurate—is that we don't offer people alternatives. In some situations this has been a result of unimaginative leadership, but more often it reflects our ambivalence toward improving a society toward which we feel contempt. Many of us fear that rather than fundamentally changing America the Left will serve as the social movement that allows corporate capitalism to rationalize itself, and in doing so will lose most of its members, whose immediate and most pressing grievances will be satisfied. While this certainly is a possibility, the alternative—hoping or even working for things to get worse so they can get better—isn't worth serious consideration. Our best hope is to create a movement of people who know why they're fighting. The problem of "selling out" is in some ways less pressing in a middle-class movement, because most of the people we are organizing have grown up partaking of "the fruits of the system" and

have discovered that while a little fruit is a good thing, a constant diet of it can give you a bad case of diarrhea. Our immediate alternatives on campus issues should aim to win victories and put us in a position from which to push for further changes. There is a great need for educational material, produced by regional or national structures, that draws on chapter experience in dealing with the problems of raising immediate demands. For example, what are some specific radical alternatives to large lectures besides seminars which only repeat the same process on a more personal scale? What are our specific alternatives to campus disciplinary bodies, the grading system, hiring and firing procedures for faculty members, corporate financial control of many universities, tuition raises, and required courses?

Despite the need for greater tactical imagination, our major problem in offering alternatives is the lack of an adult radical movement. Despite the necessity of raising a critique of the many debilitating aspects of university life, the worst part of university life is that it is just the beginning of a life without power or integrity. The central issue of university life—the manpower channeling function of the university—is one which the Left is organizationally incapable of dealing with right now. Many students see the campus Left as "utopian" because it can't answer their question: "What am I supposed to do with my life?" We are asking students to take risks when they get out of school, but we don't have a political organization to protect our people and to convert people's courageous acts into effective organizing work. We can't seriously expect to tell engineering students to refuse to make weapons for the Army or to demand that their fellow employees have a say about the projects they work on if we aren't organizing engineers, and if we don't have committed radicals with engineering degrees who are willing to get jobs in selected corporations and take the initiative. Similarly, we have nothing to offer prospective doctors, teachers, social workers, lawyers, management trainees, chemists—in short, anyone who isn't a student. This is hardly the fault of SDS. It's hard enough to build a vital student movement without also having to worry about initiating an adult organization as well. . . . But I think that some of the ultra-revolutionary posturing in our movement reflects a widespread fear among radical students that their parents' cynical dismissal of student protest as a last fling before a lifetime of submission may be accurate. The success of our assault on manpower channeling (and our assault on our parents' critique) is dependent on the development of a political organization that can offer some protection from intimidation, co-optation, and irrelevancy to former student radicals who will be working and organizing in the schools, factories, social agencies, and large corporate and government bureaucracies.

4) Ideals: Projecting ideal solutions without offering students a workable alternative to immediate problems can lead to isolation from our constituency. But stressing "practical" solutions without pointing out the limitations of such solutions can encourage a political consciousness that deals with all questions within the assumptions and institutional limitations of corporate capitalism. For example, while agreeing with many liberals that classified research shouldn't be conducted on campus, we shouldn't limit our analysis to a statement that the university should be protected from the incursion of government priorities. In a society in which the political and economic institutions were under broad popular control the universities should serve the priorities of the government. Thus, our opposition to government interference with the functioning of the university is not based on the ideal of the university as an "ivory tower." Our ideal is a democratically-run society in which the university is one of many useful and liberating institutions—not a haven for an elite that considers itself above the rest of the society. . . .

The final element in a coherent radical perspective is our choice of issues. At this point in history, however, there are very few issues which clearly are the property of the radicals. Two of the most controversial issues—draft resistance and drugs—are defined as "radical" by most of the people in the country, but within the definitions of the Movement have been raised by both liberals and radicals. The fact that most people confuse liberals and radicals today is sometimes a reflection of the inability of radicals to clearly communicate their politics to the public, but also reflects the fact that at times the differences just aren't that significant. An important distinction should be made between liberals who disagree with our actions and liberals who disagree with our analysis. The first group are often tactical allies in certain situations, but should also be the object of political criticism. It makes sense to use the term "liberal" in a derogatory way when we are talking about Humphrey, Reuther, Rustin, and their ilk working behind the scenes to stifle the MFDP challenge at Atlantic City; it makes sense when we criticize McCarthy for his terrible positions on domestic issues and his refusal to support a program of immediate withdrawal; it makes sense when we criticize campus liberals for secretly meeting with administration people while claiming they speak for a constituency they don't represent; and it makes sense when a campus group consistently opposes our tactics and program. But if a student on campus gives up his 2-S, is in the front lines of militant demonstrations, is liberated from the "pleasing the professor" bag, but also believes that if President Kennedy were alive the War would be ended—that person may be correctly defined as a liberal, but he's also a pretty groovy person.

Our dealings with humanitarian liberals should reflect an awareness that people's politics are subject to great change, especially during college. Many dedicated liberals will be future radicals, and many of our scholarly brethren who agree with our analysis of corporate capitalism but oppose every specific action as "inopportune, impolitic, and precipitous" may someday be drafting faculty resolutions condemning student demonstrators. If our analysis of the country is correct it will be borne out by events. Students whose involvement in the Movement is based on a hatred of oppression will more often than not abandon their liberal perspective because it just doesn't explain how this country works. That process, however, will hardly be facilitated by a sectarianism that places a greater value on anti-imperialist rhetoric than on commitment and action. It can be facilitated by radicals taking the programmatic initiative on a wide variety of issues that concern our student constituency.

POSTSCRIPT TO "APPRAISAL AND PERSPECTIVES"

The editors received the following reply from Eric Mann when they asked him for approval to reprint the preceding article:

"I agree to let you use the piece you requested. Reading my own work in historical perspective is difficult. All work of that period was severely limited by the widespread low level of consciousness among the SDS leadership—a product of the undeveloped contradictions of white middle-class life that have subsequently sharpened considerably. But at every historical juncture some people—despite the limits of their material surroundings—are more correct than others. I was clearly much more wrong than the leadership I attempted to challenge. The thrust of those articles is essentially a reaction to the sectarianism and posturing of the period—but more importantly was the threatened reaction of an anti-communist who sensed the stakes were getting greater, didn't believe a revolution was possible, and was feeling increasingly uncomfortable with the communist direction SDS was taking.

"I don't feel badly on a personal level, to have something printed with which I virtually totally disagree. The movement has clearly survived my article. The article is important both because it represented a significant—probably majority—rank and file sentiment and because it reflected the strengths and weakness of the best anti-communist leadership at the time (Mike James, Oglesby, me) a 'common sense' approach to problems, that is, unsystematic individual perception of events . . .

"I am now a communist, a Weatherman, and a political prisoner, serving a two-year sentence for participating in a militant attack on Harvard's Center for International Affairs—a government financed research operation specializing in counter-insurgency work. . . .

"I am happy you are printing the Weatherman paper. Even with the shortcomings of its style, hasty preparation, and political errors it is the basis of my life and the key to a successful white revolutionary movement in Amerika."

Deer Island Prison
July 11, 1970

CHAPTER 7

The Columbia Revolt: The Tensions of Alliances

The revolt at Columbia that began April 23, 1968, was one of the most spectacular student rebellions of the sixties. It was also a critical experience for the radical movement, and was followed by major shifts in its strategy. In this section, participants in the Columbia strike, representing different perspectives within the movement, present their analyses of the events.

Tom Hayden, one of the founders of SDS and principal author of its first important manifesto, "The Port Huron Statement," led one contingent of protesters in Columbia's Mathematics Hall. Echoing Che Guevara's call for "two, three, many Vietnams," Hayden issued his own call after the strike for "two, three, many Columbias." Hayden contended that the Columbia strike had opened a new tactical and political stage in the resistance movement. Students, he said, were no longer interested in just winning new privileges and power for themselves; they wanted to be included in the decision-making processes "only if their inclusion is a step toward transforming the university."

In building a mass strike at Columbia, SDS attracted a considerable number of students who saw increased student participation in university decisions as a means of transforming society. After the police had busted the five Columbia buildings under occupation on April 30, these "moderates" joined the SDS leadership in an expanded Strike Coordinating Committee. Two weeks later, however, they split off and formed their own group, Students for a Restructured University (SRU).

Following Hayden's article is a speech given by the chairman of SRU, John Thoms, explaining his group's decision to break away from SDS. While referring to the SDS leaders as his "mentors," Thoms stated that the two groups could not agree on the possibilities for change within the university. Whereas SDS contended that the university could not be free in an unfree society, SRU believed that "a free university can be the vanguard of a free society." Furthermore, Thoms indicated, the liberals were uneasy about the rhetoric of SDS, "with its categorical rigor, its moral black and whites . . . its startling catchwords." "We are, after all, members of a community of scholars," Thoms declared. He concluded that the sovereignty of the university belonged to students and faculty and that the radicals should devote themselves to restructuring the university's policy-making structures.

In an extended analysis of the strike written several months after the events, another SRU member, Rusti Eisenberg, saw serious objections to SDS's actions. The SDS leaders, she stated, while pretending to serve as representatives for the students who occupied the buildings, actually behaved as a cadre and ignored the students' wishes. "Students cannot long be expected to revolt against a power structure merely for the purpose of substituting student despots for grown-up despots." She took exception, on ethical and strategic grounds, to SDS's efforts to maneuver students into situations where they would be radicalized, noting that pushing students into radical actions would not necessarily make them radicals. "Radical action without radical perception," she stated, "is intrinsically short-term." Eisenberg also objected to the sanctification of the strike's six demands; they were symbolic, she noted, not substantive. And she disagreed with the tendency in SDS, after the strike, to reject demands simply because they were reformist. She pointed out that all demands short of revolution itself call for reforms.

In an article that appeared almost a year after the Columbia strike, SDS chairman Mark Rudd laid out the new directions that the events set for his faction of the organization. Rudd contended that the success of the strike disproved the views of those in SDS (the praxis axis) who favored accommodating liberals to win mass support. The real danger was not that SDS might overextend itself, Rudd maintained, but that it might water down its radical politics. Rudd naturally rejected restructuring. "Whatever 'good' function the university serves is what the radical students can cull from its bones—especially the creation and expansion of a revolutionary movement. The university should be used as a place from which to launch radical struggles—anything less now constitutes a passive capitulation to reformism, whatever the intentions of the radicals involved."

Rudd believed that his decision to broaden the strike committee by welcoming liberal students after the bust was a mistake, although it did prevent the liberals from organizing their own separate group for two weeks. However, in the eyes of the SDS Labor Committee, a faction which was expelled several months after the strike by Columbia SDS, the alliance with liberals was a move in the right direction. According to a restrospective analysis of the spring rebellion by the Labor Committee, the strike was ruined because of SDS's failure to move outward and draw in new people. The Labor Committee contended that if SDS had mobilized its adherents to support New York's garment workers, for example, it could have precipitated a strike in the clothing industry and maintained the momentum of its own movement. The views of the Labor Committee are an interesting footnote to the strike. It was one of their leaders who, on the night of April 22, the eve of the uprising, presented the program for the next day's offensive; it was another of its leaders who made the decision on April 24 to stay in Low Library, Columbia's administration building, when most others in SDS, including Rudd, temporarily fled.

Article by Tom Hayden, a founder of SDS, in Ramparts, *June 15, 1968.*

Two, Three, Many Columbias

The goal written on the university walls was "Create two, three, many Columbias"; it meant expand the strike so that the U.S.

must either change or send its troops to occupy American campuses.

At this point the goal seems realistic; an explosive mix is present on dozens of campuses where demands for attention to student views are being disregarded by university administrators.

The American student movement has continued to swell for nearly a decade: during the semi-peace of the early '60s as well as during Vietnam; during the token liberalism of John Kennedy as well as during the bankrupt racism of Lyndon Johnson. Students have responded most directly to the black movement of the '60s: from Mississippi Summer to the Free Speech Movement; from "Black Power" to "Student Power"; from the seizure of Howard University to the seizure of Hamilton Hall. As the racial crisis deepens so will the campus crisis. But the student protest is not just an offshoot of the black protest—it is based on authentic opposition to the middle-class world of manipulation, channeling and careerism. The students are in opposition to the fundamental institutions of society.

The students' protest constantly escalates by building on its achievements and legends. The issues being considered by seventeen-year-old freshmen at Columbia University would not have been within the imagination of most "veteran" student activists five years ago.

Columbia opened a new tactical stage in the resistance movement which began last fall: from the overnight occupation of buildings to permanent occupation; from mill-ins to the creation of revolutionary committees; from symbolic civil disobedience to barricaded resistance. Not only are these tactics already being duplicated on other campuses, but they are sure to be surpassed by even more militant tactics. In the future it is conceivable that students will threaten destruction of buildings as a last deterrent to police attacks. Many of the tactics learned can also be applied in smaller hit-and-run operations between strikes: raids on the offices of professors doing weapons research could win substantial support among students while making the university more blatantly repressive.

In the buildings occupied at Columbia, the students created what they called a "new society" or "liberated area" or "commune," a society in which decent values would be lived out even though university officials might cut short the communes through use of police. The students had fun, they sang and danced and wisecracked, but there was continual tension. There was no question of their constant awareness of the seriousness of their acts. Though there were a few violent arguments about tactics, the discourse was more in the form of endless meetings convened to explore the outside political situation, defense tactics, maintenance and morale problems within the group. Debating and then determining what leaders should do were alternatives to the remote and authoritarian decision-making of Columbia's trustees.

The Columbia strike represented more than a new tactical movement, however. There was a political message as well. The striking students were not holding onto a narrow conception of students as a privileged class asking for inclusion in the university as it now exists. This kind of demand could easily be met by administrators by opening minor opportunities for "student rights" while cracking down on campus radicals. The Columbia students were instead taking an internationalist and revolutionary view of themselves in opposition to the imperialism of the very institutions in which they have been groomed and educated. They did not even want to be included in the decision-making circles of the military-industrial complex that runs Columbia: *they want to be included only if their inclusion is a step toward transforming the university.* They want a new and independent university standing against the mainstream of American society, or they want no university at all. They are, in Fidel Castro's words, "guerrillas in the field of culture."

How many other schools can be considered ripe for such confrontations? The question is hard to answer, but it is clear that the demands of black students for cultural recognition rather than paternalistic tolerance, and radical white students' awareness of the sinister paramilitary activities carried on in secret by the faculty on many campuses, are hardly confined to Columbia. Columbia's problem is the American problem in miniature—the inability to provide answers to widespread social needs and the use of the military to protect the authorities against the people. This process can only lead to greater unity in the movement.

Support from outside the university communities can be counted on in many large cities. A crisis is foreseeable that would be too massive for police to handle. It can happen; whether or not it will be necessary is a question which only time will answer. What is certain is that we are moving toward power—the power to stop the machine if it cannot be made to serve humane ends.

American educators are fond of telling their students that barricades are part of the romantic past, that social change today can only come about through the processes of negotiation. But the students at Columbia discovered that barricades are only the beginning of what they call "bringing the war home."

Speech given at Columbia by John Thoms, chairman of Students for a Restructured University, Columbia University, May 16, 1968.

Remaking a Community

The physical symbols of the strike have been absent for several days now. The arrogant uncertainty of the policemen who held our campus, the even more uncertain picket lines, the barricades at either end of College Walk—all are gone. Yet the strike continues. Perhaps those external manifestations were never as important as they seemed. Perhaps, since our brutal night of truth, the strike has been preeminently a mode of consciousness, a state of mind. But this central consciousness has been split almost from the beginning, just as the Strike Coordinating Committee has been split between the so-called "moderates" and "radicals." We have worked together in a tender and tense coalition in order to demonstrate our fundamental unity in support of those who went into the buildings and the political demands for which they fought. This evening twenty-two delegates to SCC, representing constituencies of about fifteen hundred students, formally severed ties with that body and reconstituted themselves as a new group called Students for a Restructured University. Let no hasty functionary at Low Library or overzealous agent of Sulzberger's *Times* smile at the news. The strike is not broken. Those of us who left have not broken faith with our mentors in SDS. We continue to feel a deep gratitude to the original strikers for their role in awakening us to the political realities of our common situation and we remain in admiration of the efficiency and effectiveness of the dedicated team at Strike Central. But we have reached a point now where we must require of ourselves an affirmation of our own distinct identity, our own distinct concerns.

Although the SCC has been consistently united behind the demands of the May 3 resolution—notably the demand for amnesty—there has existed a concurrent division over questions of emphasis and style. SDS has continually emphasized the necessity for viewing our political demands within a national political context; thus the political education of the community at large has assumed for them the highest priority. Their reiterated assertion has been that a free university is impossible in an unfree society. We, on the other hand, while recognizing the force of this analysis, have nevertheless been concerned with the wresting from the present upheaval some constructive rebuilding of our immediate context. Briefly, we believe that a free university can be the vanguard of a free society. We cannot view with equanimity the prospect of an indefinite future of polarization and unrest, while awaiting the total political awakening of the total society. We want amelioration of our condition, and we want it now.

Some of us have also felt uneasy with much of the rhetoric emanating from Strike Central, with its categorical rigor, its moral blacks and whites, its typical reliance upon generalizations. This kind of diction, with its startling catchwords—"racist imperialism," "capitalist corporate structure"—is, we believe, unsuited to the discourse of a university. We have constantly pressed for a language of reason and understanding, a tool for clarity and communication not only with our allies but also with those who yet misinterpret and mistrust us. We are, after all, members of a community of scholars. Ours is a deeply flawed one, scarred with old lies and new breaches of faith.

Nevertheless the ideal remains in our minds, and before this year's end we wish to speak to that ideal. We appeal to you now to strengthen our voice. We are not on strike, nor have we ever been on strike, merely to achieve an advisory role within the present university structure. We believe that the sovereignty of a university lies with the students and faculty, and that all power must derive from them. We are convinced that it is necessary for students to formulate their own restructuring proposals, unadulterated by the sway of other interest groups. We hope that our efforts will help to lay the groundwork for a new community which will not be subject to such another breakdown in the social structure.

I confess myself to be deeply excited by the hidden promises inherent in our situation: to speak truth to those to whom we have been for so long merely polite; to claim our rightful share in shaping the context and content of our own education; to insist that we be listened to when we have something to say. Students are human beings. So, I understand, are professors. Human beings gathered together in the same room would do well to pay attention to one another.

Article by Rusti Eisenberg, a student member of the Strike Steering Committee, in Ripsaw, *a journal of the Graduate Student Union, Columbia, December 1968.*

The Strike: A Critical Reappraisal

Superficially it appears that the Left won a great victory at Columbia last spring. Clearly, the protest on Morningside Heights was the most sustained, the most dramatic, the most far-reaching of its kind at an American campus. Educational institutions, like other major institutions in this country, carry an aura of invulnerability, and it is no insubstantial thing to demonstrate that their operations can be brought to a grinding halt. Yet the immediate effect of this accomplishment has been to foreclose realistic discussion of two critical problems: 1) the relationship of Strike Central's strategy to the apparent success of the movement, and 2) the implication of the Columbia action for fundamental radical goals.

I. STRATEGY

Students for a Democratic Society was the only group on campus last year which consistently raised the important issues at Columbia, conducting a continual educational effort about the University's complicity in the Vietnam war and its larger involvement with the critical institutions in our society. Students for a Democratic Society was the only group which consistently seized the initiative, attempting to involve students in action around these issues. Without the impetus of S.D.S., Cit Council and the Afro-American Society, it is likely that last spring there would have been no sit-in, no strike, no revolt. But in analyzing the events that followed the crucial first steps, it is important to remember several significant points about Columbia. In addition to the fact that there has been an incredibly restive mood among students nationally, a growing willingness to confront authority any place, any time, Columbia as an institution has been peculiarly rife with dissatisfaction—much of the dissatisfaction only tangentially related to radical perspectives. Columbia is after all a school of declining reputation and academic quality. Students in the college,

Graduate Faculties and other important sectors of the University often find their lives here frustrating, boring, and unpleasant. Courses are large, departmental relations impersonal, programs of study anachronistic and limiting. Student life is diffuse, and Columbia affords relatively little opportunity for students to meet and establish real relations with one another. Columbia is a school where even students have colleagues instead of friends.

The fundamental point is simply that Columbia last spring had tremendous explosive potential. Almost any incident could have precipitated the explosion and almost any strategy could have sustained it. There were very few people on campus who did not have good solid personal as well as political reasons for wanting to strike a blow at Columbia. Columbia's internal weakness was enhanced by the presence of an unusually incompetent and inept administration, one so totally benighted and out of touch with opinion on the campus that it did not see fit to field the standard techniques of cooptation, which are part of the normal arsenal of "establishments" which expect to stay established.

Given these ingredients it is hardly clear that Strike Central ought to rush to congratulate itself on the closing of Columbia last spring. Rather, it is time to stop regarding the closing of Columbia as a vindication of the Left's strategy. This year it is likely that the ground will be less fertile. Andrew Cordier appears a more formidable adversary than Grayson Kirk. Students are tired. Strategic errors will be more costly. Strategic errors that duplicate those of last spring could be disastrous. There is a pressing need for reappraisal.

It seems apparent, at least in retrospect, that a substantial segment of S.D.S. attempted to function as a cadre during last spring's confrontation. It is hard to indicate all the components of this approach but certainly the most important was the commitment to vanguard action. The cadre was to stay ahead of the movement. Its task was to seize initiative even during the crisis, thus setting the terms of a conflict, to which others—allies as well as opponents—would have to respond.

On one level such an approach is unassailable. Any group has the right to act on the basis of its own consciousness, to shift the conditions of struggle, attempting to induce others to adopt positively to the evolving situation. Had S.D.S. members continued to make clear, during the occupation of the buildings, that indeed they did conceive of themselves in this light, that they intended to act according to the dictates of their own critique, and that they would be politically responsible to no one, their strategy would have been morally impeccable. With full clarity as to how S.D.S. members were committed to behave, those who were not in total agreement with S.D.S. policy would have been free to make clear and rational determinations of how far they were personally willing to go along with particular courses of action.

A cadre operation is different from a "united front" and such a distinction ought properly to have remained explicit. Unfortunately, out of a kind of opportunism, and also as a consequence of honest confusion, S.D.S. members did not make this distinction explicit. The consequence in terms of the functioning of the Steering Committee were disastrous.

After the first night of the occupation of the buildings, the people inside the buildings elected representatives to a central steering committee which met continuously in Ferris Booth Hall. *People did not believe they were electing a cadre. They thought they were choosing a representative body.* The Steering Committee was composed largely of S.D.S. members, and its decisions clearly revealed an S.D.S. orientation. This was true for two rather obvious and straightforward reasons. S.D.S. assumed the lion's share of responsibility for the more bureaucratic tasks of the movement, and those involved in these day-to-day activities, while not official representatives, were often present at Steering Committee meetings, frequently setting the focus, tone, and direction of the discussion. In addition, since people in the buildings didn't know each other very well, they commonly elected S.D.S. members as representatives, for they were generally more visible, articulate, and experienced than anybody else.

The objection is not that seven, eight or nine members of the Steering Committee were members of S.D.S. It would not have mattered if it was a completely S.D.S. body. What did matter was that the S.D.S. people did not for the most part regard themselves as representatives of a constitutency; they continued to think of themselves as part of a cadre. Consequently it was quite common for members of the Steering Committee to cast votes that clearly violated the mandate from their own building. Furthermore when representatives went back to their constituency they tended to report the *votes* of representatives from other buildings, thereby conveying a misleading impression as to the sentiment of the people inside the buildings. The result was a growing paranoia. People began to distrust each other, they felt unconfident of their information, and uncertain as to whose contradictory story was to be believed. Most seriously, they began to feel impotent and fearful.

This situation raises fairly obvious ethical as well as political issues. An elementary sense of fair play would seem to indicate that if people do not intend to act as representatives, if they prefer to function in cadre arrangements, then they should act openly, refusing to serve as representatives in order to permit those who do want representation to get it. Similarly, if a group participating in a political action wishes to retain a free hand (and a cadre by definition requires a free hand), then it must be willing to sacrifice the right to demand that others observe rules of solidarity. Solidarity presupposes a democratic structure in which *all* agree to adhere to the decisions of the full group.

The political issues are equally serious. Clearly one of the main objectives of the Columbia action was the *radicalization of new students.* This objective was in many respects even more important than the achievement of specific demands. There are many ways to radicalize people—no doubt the most important is to create consciousness, by bringing people to clearer perceptions about the nature of the social structure of which they are a part. But in America it is one of the great liabilities of the Left, that while many students are extremely sensitive to the negative aspects of contemporary society, they have little in the way of positive vision which can sustain on-going revolutionary activity. That is why the quality of the revolutionary movement *itself* takes on a very special importance. By experimenting with new forms of organization within the movement, it becomes possible for the membership to develop new perspectives and new conviction about the feasibility of creating a decent and humane social order. It is difficult for people to sustain revolutionary élan when they feel irrelevant and impotent within the revolutionary movement itself, when they experience their own movement as a miniature replication of the society they oppose. Students cannot long be expected to revolt against a power structure merely for the purpose of substituting student despots for grown-up despots.

In short, the absence of genuine democracy within the strike movement itself was dysfunctional because it was demoralizing. Only the timely intervention of the New York Police Department stemmed an inner erosion which might ultimately have destroyed some of the communes.

This still leaves the larger questions of if and when cadre action is appropriate. Unfortunately the very word cadre becomes so thrilling to some that at the mere use of the word all critical faculties are dissipated. It is a positive development that the Left has begun to perceive the uses of cadre action. Such action is particularly desirable in the context of American society precisely because it wears such a deceptive mask. It has been amply demonstrated that the essential character of the system stands revealed only when provoked, that to know the quality of American society is to challenge it, that to uncover its fundamental weakness is to battle it. Such events cannot wait on parliamentary democracy. But to recognize the importance of cadre action as an essential component of a radical strategy, is not the same as saying it is appropriate or desirable on all occasions. Indeed if cadres are to be a significant and useful part of the movement, it will be in part because the Left has a fully developed concept of when a cadre action is not appropriate.

This is not an easy problem to deal with, particularly in the abstract, but certain basic concepts should be adhered to:

1) A cadre should not take action when it imperils the safety and well-being of people who are not fully in accord with the action. In its simplest form this means that people in a demonstration ought not to provoke police into a confrontation if most of the people do not wish to get clubbed over the head. But the more complicated example, relevant to the Columbia situation, is that it is not the place of a cadre to decide that other people ought to get arrested. The cadre is free to make this decision for itself, but it is politically disastrous for the cadre to attempt to use its action as a kind of *moral coercion* over others to take similar action. It is one thing for someone to say "My friends and I will take this action for the following reasons . . . For the same reasons we think you should too." It is quite another to use the argument, "I am going to lay my body on the line; if you don't join me *I* will be in greater peril."

2) A cadre does not take action when it imperils the maintenance of a large mass-based movement. The main advantage of a cadre is that it retains a free hand in creating and shaping contexts for action. Its chief disadvantage is that in retaining the free hand it must sacrifice its influence over a movement by impairing solidarity. In the long run, sustained cadre action threatens the unity of a movement for the simple reason that the unwillingness of the cadre to be bound by the sentiments of the larger group is ulti-

mately license for every faction to feel itself under no obligation to the group. Ultimately the movement unravels.

Finally it is relevant here to discount an assumption which had never been articulated but which had a great deal to do with the way Strike Central operated last spring. The assumption is that the way to radicalize people is to force them into a situation where they must take militant action. This is a myth which is most dangerous and counter-productive. Radical action *without* radical perception is intrinsically short-term and produces just exactly the sort of people who one day tell their children, "I was idealistic like you once. I've been through it all . . . but Henry, be realistic!" It is not hard to catch people up in a tide where they find themselves taking action which would have been out of the question two weeks ago. But unless they really feel in their inner being that such action has genuine importance and a strategic meaning that transcends a temporary fit of perversity, such people will very quickly become passive, precisely because they have taken the big action and in a sober moment of reflection cannot satisfactorily answer the question, "Was it worth it?"

We know that last spring students at Columbia were moved to militant action. But was this an ephemeral phenomenon or did it imply a genuine deepening of radical consciousness? Certainly it is now fashionable for people to wander about explaining how "radicalized" they are. Yet it is important to put this in context. Television has, after all, created the image of "the new Columbia Man"—bearded, zealous, disillusioned, militant. While this role retains its peculiar in-group charm, it would seem prudent to retain at least a healthy skepticism. Nobody, not even the august Bureau of Applied Social Research, has as yet a clear view of what real change has taken place in people's political perspective as a result of the strike. But minimally one should raise the question of whether the Left's articulation of goals and demands was of such a nature as to contribute to mass consciousness or to befuddle it.

II. THE DEMANDS*

There was nothing quite so ludicrous during the strike as the sanctity of the "Six Demands." They assumed a sort of celestial

* For the original text of the demands, see p. 486.

magnificence which made rational discourse out of the question. One Tuesday afternoon six rather innocuous points were thrown together into a program. Curiously, people began to act as if the vast tradition of radical and revolutionary thought had found their ultimate expression. To be radical was to believe in the "Six Demands." The true dividing line of liberals and radicals came on the issue of whether one supported the "Six Demands."

But this dividing line was entirely arbitrary and nonsensical. Certainly there was nothing about the six demands that a liberal could not support. They were minimal in substance. Had David Truman adopted them all immediately, they would not have had even the slightest effect on racism and imperialism. Nor was it the case that amnesty would have meant the University's capitulation. Amnesty would only have meant that the Administration was strengthening its tactical hand by a posture of leniency and moderation, which would insure it wider support for repression should outbreaks occur a second time. The domino theory is a theory erected by nitwits—it is no more applicable to Columbia University than it is to Southeast Asia. There is nothing cataclysmic about an initial tactical retreat. So long as it is not a rout, it often frees the opposition to come back and fight with fuller force another day. It happened to be the case that the Columbia Administration was sufficiently rigid as to have a kind of compulsive horror of giving an inch, but that was simply a further reflection of its general incompetence on the field of political battle. Because Grayson Kirk was foolish enough to believe that amnesty constituted a mortal blow to the interests of Columbia, the Left came to believe it too. Only it wasn't true. Amnesty could quite easily have been turned to a moral victory for the administration, vindicating its "essential fairmindedness," etc.

Fundamentally all of the demands were symbolic rather than substantive. The removal of Kirk and Burden from the IDA Board would not have affected to the slightest degree the continuation of defense department research, nor could it have had a real impact on defense research even at Columbia. Similarly the gym assumed importance as a symbol of exploitation of the Harlem community—the cessation of its construction had no potential for altering the essential relations that obtained between Columbia and the ghetto.

It is certainly fair to add here, that the Strike leadership basically understood that these demands were symbolic. Indeed, it was always Strike Central's real position that substantive change could only emerge as a consequence of revolution—that the demands were merely levers in a revolutionary struggle. Yet even with this kind of perception of the "instrumental" character of the demands, the question should be raised as to whether it was wise to use *symbolic* demands as the focal point of the movement.

Assuming again that a major goal of the movement was the raising of radical consciousness among ever increasing number of students, there is grave doubt as to whether the demands supported this aim. Primarily this is because the constant glorification of the "Six Demands" endowed them with an importance that they simply did not have. Educational efforts ought to have been directed not at proving to students how meaningful would be cessation of construction on the gym and termination of Kirk and Burden's relationship to IDA, but rather at underscoring just how insignificant they were in the context of a larger struggle against the social forces they embodied. With the six demands as the beginning and end of all agitation last spring, it was impossible to place these things in their proper perspective.

The demand for amnesty was particularly misleading, but for somewhat different reasons. It became clear early in the strike that amnesty was the pivotal, central issue. This was true primarily because of all the demands, it was the least palatable to the faculty and administration. Yet there is real question as to the educational value of waging a broad, powerful, and intense struggle over the issue of amnesty for the people in the struggle.

Strike Central saw amnesty as important because it embodied an affirmation of the illegitimacy of the administration's authority. Yet most of the campus never perceived the matter in this way. For the large number of students at Columbia the demand for amnesty concerned nothing more profound than an insistence that people not be punished. Demands ought at least to have the virtue of clarity. If their meaning remains obscure, they lose their value. This consideration alone ought to have raised questions as to whether amnesty was a desirable rallying point for the movement.

But there is a deeper issue. Amnesty only had theoretical meaning as part of a larger claim that the Administration and Trustees were illegitimate. This is altogether reasonable. But implicit in this position was a commitment to an alteration of power relations within the University—in other words, University re-structure. As part of a thrust towards student power the demand for amnesty made sense. But Strike Central had little interest in student power and for this reason the demand for amnesty made little sense.

It is useful to consider Strike Central's approach to University restructure. This position was rather complicated but not unintelligent. Essentially the argument was that given the context of the larger society, University restructure could not in any way qualitatively alter the nature of the institution either in its internal relationships or its external ones. Therefore University restructure was a dangerous ploy which, while offering no genuine hope of redress, could mislead people into believing that important concessions had been made. In other words, restructure would only serve to split the movement, serving as the critical cover for massive cooptation.

While all of this may well be true, it should be clear that the argument had equal validity with respect to the IDA, gym, and disciplinary demands. Short of a revolution, the granting of any of these demands would not substantively affect deep-running policies and would create the illusion of victory.

What conclusions can we draw? Is it the case the only safe demand to make is one calling for total revolution? Obviously this is less than satisfactory. Rather the first conclusion ought to be that *no* demand should be rejected simply because its underlying character is reformist. It ought to be evident that any demand short of revolution is essentially reformist. Other criteria for selection of demands would be more illuminating. A radical movement ought to put forth demands which can be made to seem reasonable and humanly desirable to a large number of people and which carry with them real and not merely symbolic content. In other words instead of simply calling for the removal of Kirk and Burden from the IDA board, the movement should center its efforts on the demand to an end to Defense Department research at Columbia. Instead of calling simply for an end to construction of the gym, the movement should address itself to the substance of University expansion.

As the movement struggles for these substantive demands, it is to be assumed that University resistance will stiffen, revealing ever more clearly the institution's inner imperatives. In consequence, it can reasonably be expected that radical consciousness will increase as growing numbers of students find themselves embroiled in an ever escalating conflict over issues that they genuinely believe have real importance and meaning.

III. PRIORITIES

Curiously, despite the rhetoric of last spring, despite all the attacks on Columbia as a citadel of racism and imperialism, there was a strong strain of opinion within Strike Central to the effect that Columbia didn't really matter at all. The primary object of the movement was to use the dissatisfactions with Columbia as a way of radicalizing student opinion and sensitizing it to the fundamental forces at work in the larger society. While it has remained unclear as to what radicalized students are supposed to do once they have been radicalized, there is a strong undercurrent of feeling that they should somehow involve themselves in struggles outside the campus. The critical fronts for battle appear to be elsewhere—in ghettos, factories, at the Pentagon.

It is time that the Left seriously re-examined the question of what it actually wants to get out of these battles on university campuses. And it is time that the Left begin to regard the university campus as something more than a recruiting ground for new leftists. This is as good an occasion as any for us to start believing our own rhetoric. The grim reality is that university campuses matter a great deal—they are not only critical socializing agencies, they also form a very important link in processes which perpetuate oppressive structures both in this country and abroad.

Oddly enough, it really appears to be the case that knowledge is power. Knowledge builds weapons. Knowledge enables the U.S. government to maintain and strengthen the Empire. Knowledge is a source of new methods of social control. Knowledge aids in the suppression of ghetto discontent and abets the gradual "moronization" of the American working class. Increasingly the very functioning of our society depends on the production of highly trained personnel and on the expansion of intellectual vistas. For this reason, universities are themselves a crucial arena of struggle.

Minimally, there is an important educational job for the Left to do. Young people coming out of the universities are the possessors of a very marketable commodity—their own intellectual equipment. They carry with them a very grave responsibility for its use. It is part of the responsibility of the Left to create a climate of opinion in which an increasing number of scholars will refuse to put their intellect to work for anti-human purposes.

Furthermore, because universities are centers of important government research, they are centers which must be vigorously attacked. It is part of our task to drive this research out of the universities. It is part of our task to sabotage the university's efforts towards molding personnel to fit comfortably into government and corporate slots. It is part of our task to make universities genuine centers of independent and critical thought, directed toward human ends.

This struggle should be undertaken seriously and in good faith. It is unlikely that Columbia as an institution can sustain such an enterprise. But if the American university cannot survive without its defense contracts, if it cannot survive except as poor relation in a mesh of connections to larger and unacceptable social forces, then it does not deserve to survive at all.

But the reality is that we have not yet put the University to a serious test. We should do so. In a genuine battle for University disengagement, we will find many allies, both students and faculty. We shall not need to create symbols and cadres to make them radical.

Article by Columbia strike leader Mark Rudd in Movement, *March 1969.*

Columbia

Before and during the Columbia rebellion, the SDS chapter faced situations very similar to those encountered by other chapters around the country. Questions of militancy vs. isolating yourself from the base, questions of relating to a black students' movement, questions of student power vs. a radical position on the university, questions of how to work as a radical within mass political situations, all came to the forefront in our experience at Columbia. They also became the key questions at places like Brooklyn College, Kent State in Ohio, San Francisco State, Brandeis and literally hundreds of other campuses where the movement is at various stages of building itself.

From April, 1967 to March, 1968, the SDS chapter had been led by a group of people who tended to stress "organizing" and "base-building" above action and "confrontation." Though possessing a "Marxist" analysis, they believed that the way support is gained is by going out to people and talking to them about our analysis. Various pieties about the necessity to build the base before you take action, and the dangers of isolating yourself from the base were incessantly pronounced in the name of the "Marxist analysis." The word "politics" was used as a bludgeon with which to beat unruly upstarts into place and to maintain control over the chapter. One example will illustrate this point.

In early March, at a meeting of the SDS Draft Committee, the question of what to do when the head of the Selective Service System for New York City came to speak at Columbia came up. Someone suggested that SDS greet the Colonel by attacking him physically—which would clearly define the fact that we consider him to be an enemy. The idea was defeated by a vote of 30–1 after the old leadership of the chapter argued that an attack on the Colonel would be "terrorist, apolitical and silly," and especially would not communicate anything to anyone (since the action had "no political content"). It was decided that the draft committee would be present at the speech to "ask probing questions."

Several SDS members and non-members then organized clandestinely the attack on the Colonel. In the middle of his speech a mini-demonstration appeared in the back of the room with a fife and drum, flags, machine guns, and noise-makers. As attention went to the back, a person in the front row stood up and placed a lemon-meringue pie in the Colonel's face.* Everyone split.

Only two groups on campus did not dig what became known as the "pie incident." First was the administration of Columbia University. Second was the old leadership of Columbia SDS, which disapproved because the action was terroristic and apolitical and would jeopardize our base on campus.

Meanwhile almost everyone on campus thought this was the best thing SDS had ever done (though we disavowed any part in it and said it was the NY Knickerboppers who had done the job). People understood the symbolism in the attack and identified with it because of their own desires, often latent, to strike back at the draft and the government. This was in symbolic miniature form, the same dynamic of militant action by a vanguard and then mass identification which worked so well during the rebellion a month later.

* This was none other than Rudd himself. Eds.

In a criticism session held after the pie incident, members of the chapter began to learn the difference between the verbal "base-building," non-struggle approach of the old leadership (now called the "Praxis Axis" after the supplement to *New Left Notes* edited by Bob Gottlieb and Dave Gilbert, of whom many of the old leadership were self-styled followers) and the aggressive approach of those who saw the primacy of developing a movement based on struggle. This latter group, centered around myself and John Jacobs, as well as others in and out of SDS, came to be known as the "Action Faction" due to the never-ending search for symmetry.

Subsequent to the ascendancy of the ideas of the Action Faction the chapter began engaging in more and more militant confrontations—an illegal demonstration on March 27 against IDA, in which we chased two Vice Presidents around the campus; the disruption of a memorial service for Martin Luther King in order to expose the fact that while Kirk and Truman were eulogizing King, their university was completely racist toward the community and toward its employees.

This prominence of militancy and the aggressive approach should not be interpreted as a victory for the action side of the action vs. base-building dichotomy. In fact, action and education (verbal and otherwise) are completely united, two aspects of the same thing (call it "base-building," "organizing," "building the movement," whatever you like). A leaflet or dorm-canvassing is no less radical activity than seizing a building—in fact both are necessary.

At Columbia we had a four-year history of agitation and education involving forms of activity from seminars and open forums on IDA to confrontations over NROTC and military recruiting. All went into developing the mass consciousness that was responsible for the Columbia rebellion. The point is that we had to develop the willingness to take action, vanguard action, before the tremendous potential of the "base" could be released. In addition, the vanguard action also acted as education for many people not yet convinced. The radical analysis never got such a hearing, and a sympathetic one, as during the rebellion.

There are no sure ways to know when the base is ready to move. Many militant actions which expose the participants will result only in an educational point entering the consciousness of the people, without developing mass support. An example of this is the sit-in against the CIA which took place at Columbia in February, 1967, involving only 18 people. This seemingly isolated action (even the SDS chapter did not participate) helped ready people for the direct action to come one year later by making a first penetration into students' minds that direct action is both possible and desirable. . . .

We had no way of knowing whether the base was ready at Columbia; in fact, neither SDS nor the masses of students actually were ready; we were spurred on by a tremendous push from history, if you will, embodied in the militant black students at Columbia.

Before April 23, the Students' Afro-American Society and Columbia SDS had never joined together in a joint action or even held much cross-group communication. SAS had been mostly a cultural or social organization, in part reflecting the class background of its members (SDS's position on campus likewise reflected its members' middle-class background—the tendency toward over-verbalization instead of action, the reliance on militant, pure, revolutionary rhetoric instead of linking up with people).

It was only with the death of Martin Luther King that SDS began to make political demands—though still mostly about the situation of black students at Columbia. Another important factor in the growing militancy of SDS was the struggle of the Harlem community against Columbia's gym in the form of demonstrations, rallies, and a statement by H. Rap Brown that the gym should be burned down if it somehow was built.

The pivotal event of the strike, however, was the black students' decision to barricade Hamilton Hall the night after the joint occupation began. In this decision, the blacks defined themselves politically as members of the Harlem community and the black nation who would fight Columbia's racism to the end. It was also this action that gave the whites a model for militancy and, on a broader scale, forced the whites to wake up to the real world outside themselves.

At the time that the black students in Hamilton Hall announced they were going to barricade the building, SDS's goal was the same as it has always been—to radicalize and politicize the mass of white students at Columbia and to create a radical political force of students. This self-definition, however, led to the conclusion that we did not want to risk alienating the mass of other white students by confronting them, say, from behind a barricade. Part of our decision not to barricade must also be seen as a remnant of the earlier timid and non-struggle attitudes so common in the chapter.

The blacks, for their part, had decided that they would make a stand alone, as a self-conscious black group. This decision was also prompted undoubtedly by the lack of militancy on the part of the whites in Hamilton and especially our lack of discipline and organization.

After leaving Hamilton, a change came over the mass of white students, in and out of SDS. People stayed in Low Library "because we can't abandon the blacks." Not only did people see the model for militancy in the black occupation of Hamilton, but they also began to perceive reality—a world outside themselves—and the necessity to fight, to struggle for liberation, because of the situation in that world.

It was the action of the black students at Columbia—a group outside the individual fragmented "middle class" students at Columbia—that woke up these students to the fact that there is a world of suffering, brutalized, exploited people, and that these people are a force willing to fight for freedom. Especially important to this realization was the power of Harlem, both manifest and dormant. Now the liberal universe—the isolated self—was shattered, and the mass occupation started by a handful of whites, the 23 who stayed in Low, grew to be the natural response of well over 1,000 people who wanted to fight back against the oppression of blacks, Vietnamese and themselves.

From another point of view, the militancy of the SDS whites forced others to reconsider their position and eventually to join the occupation. But the SDS occupation itself hinged on that of the blacks, and the overwhelming presence of the black students and Harlem itself forced us to keep the image of the real world clear and bright in our minds. Because of the blacks, we recognized the immediacy and necessity of the struggle: Vietnam is far away, unfortunately, for most people, and our own pain has become diffuse and dull.

This point about the example and vanguard role of whites vis-à-vis other whites must also be stressed. When neutral or liberal or even right-wing students see other students, very much like themselves, risking careers, imprisonment, and physical safety, they begin to question the political reasons for which the vanguard is acting and, concomitantly, their own position. Here, education and propaganda are essential to get out to people the issues, and also the rationale for action. At no time is "organizing" or "talk" more important as before, during and after militant action.

This is not to deny the importance of black militancy, but only to emphasize the complex and dialectical relationships existing between blacks, white militants, and "the base." In struggle after struggle on campuses and in shops, the blacks have been taking the initial and even vanguard role. San Francisco State, where the direction and militancy of the struggle has been given by the Black Students' Union and the Third World Liberation Front, is the best example of the most oppressed taking the vanguard.

Kent State in Ohio, Brandeis, the high school students' strike in New York City, and numerous other cases, similarly show the importance of black vanguards. This is not an empirical fact peculiar only to schools, but in shops and in the army, too, blacks have been taking the lead and whites following—e.g., the Dodge Revolutionary Union Movement, which gave rise to a white insurgent caucus in the UAW and the Fort Hood 43.

The implication of the primacy of the black movement is not that whites should sit back and wait for blacks to make the revolution. It is, rather, that we should study and understand the roots, necessity of, and strategy of the black liberation movement in order to understand how our movement should go.

At Columbia our understanding of the dynamics at work was at best intuitive: we knew that whites and blacks had to organize their own, but we didn't know how this worked in practice—separate tactics, separate organization. At some schools, such as Kent and San Francisco State, the white militants did as well or better than we to the extent that they were conscious of their own role in relation to black militants.

This question "in relation to" has at least two clearly different pitfalls. First, because of the intensive and all-pervading racism in the United States, white radicals are sometimes unwilling to follow black leadership. This was the situation during the recent UFT boycott of the New York City schools over the issue of community control. Both Progressive Labor Party and their arch-enemy, the Labor Committee, manifested their racism by refusing to support community control on the grounds that it was a cooptive plan designed by the ruling class to split the working class (both racist teachers and black parents are "workers" primarily, according to PLP). Neither grouplet saw the class nature of a *united* black community fighting for better schools against the racist ruling-class school board and racist teachers' union.

The implication of this blindspot on the part of PLP is that blacks are too stupid to figure out when community control turns into cooptation, and therefore, they should follow the dogmatic and unreal line of PLP: black parents and white teachers unite to fight for better education (a position which ignores both the racism of the white teachers and the fact that blacks already are fighting for better schools). SDS, because of its internal factional warfare, lost numerous opportunities to support the black struggle and also to begin educating the white community about its own racism, both of which are absolutely necessary.

The second pitfall "in relation to" the black movement is a passivity based on the opposite side of the traditional white leadership syndrome. Blacks are often unwilling to take the leadership or vanguard position in a struggle, having had white leadership thrust on them for so long, or else feeling isolated (as they, in fact, are at many white schools), or else having assimilated traditional middle-class values of success. (This latter point is both the most common and the most complex. For a fuller discussion of this phenomenon, see James Forman's new book, *Sammy Younge, Jr.*) White radicals at many places feel that blacks must initiate anti-racism struggles, and that they will follow in support. The origin of this feeling is both the desire to see blacks taking leadership positions, a good thing, and also the attitude that racism is a "black problem" and cannot be raised legitimately by whites as a "white issue."

Racism must become a conscious "white problem," and must be fought at every point. This was our belief at Columbia, when Columbia SDS took independent action against the Administration for its racism by disrupting the Martin Luther King Memorial service. The black students did not take part in this disruption, but the disruption did help shock SAS into action, along with other factors, especially the demonstrations of the Harlem community against Columbia.

Similarly, at Kent State in Ohio, the demonstrations against the Oakland Pig Department recruiters, as anti-racist demonstrations, were initiated by the white SDS chapter and picked up by the black students. At both Kent and Columbia, the black students then went on to take dominant and even decisive roles.

At school after school, white radicals are waiting for black students to take the lead. Since racism must be combatted, they are in error in not taking the initiative, giving both black students and the mass of whites the impetus to carry the struggle forward. They must also, however, know when to follow the lead of blacks, and when to work parallel. At Columbia, inadvertently sometimes, we did all three.

STUDENT POWER

One of the things we learned at Columbia is the old SDS dictum, "People have to be organized around the issues that affect their lives" is really true. Not in the way it has always been meant, i.e., student interest type demands like dorm rules, bookstores, decisions over tenure, etc., but in the broadest, most political sense. That is to say, that racism and imperialism really are issues that affect people's lives. And it was these things that people moved on, not dorm rules, or democratizing university governance or any of that bullshit.

The general public, and the movement in more subtle ways, has been subjected to a barrage of propaganda trying to show conclusively that the rebellion at Columbia (as well as other rebellions) was due to campus unrest over archaic administrative procedures, lack of democracy in decision-making, and, above all, an immense failure of communication among students, faculty and administration. It is unnecessary to document this beyond referring the reader to any article about Columbia in *Time* magazine.

In general, the Left itself has understood the primacy of revolutionary anti-imperialist politics present in the core of the rebellion, but few have had access to our arguments concerning student power and "restructuring" of the university, and thus many have believed either 1) We admitted the necessity for reform and at least partially worked toward it; or 2) The failure of the movement this fall was due to the failure of Columbia SDS to respond to the mass movement for restructure and reform. In other words, we were coopted by the new liberal administration and Students for a Restructured University. Neither is the case.

Every militant in the buildings knew that he was there because of his opposition to racism and imperialism and the capitalist system that needs to exploit and oppress human beings from Vietnam to Harlem to Columbia. It was no accident that we hung up pictures of Karl Marx and Malcolm X and Che Guevara and flew red flags from the tops of two buildings. But there was some confusion over our position toward the university itself.

We were engaged in a struggle that had implications far beyond the boundaries of the campus on Morningside Heights—and, in fact, our interest was there, outside the university. We did want to stop the university's exploitative, racist and pro-imperialist policies, but what more? This unsurety over program toward the university reflected a political confusion that only became solved as the radicals discussed more among themselves and were faced with a greater number of self-appointed liberal reformers who wanted to "save the university."

Given that the capitalist university serves the function of production of technology, ideology, and personnel for business, government, and military (we had hit at these functions in our exposure of IDA and expansion), the question of "saving" the university implies capitulation to the liberal mythology about free and open inquiry at a university and its value-neutrality.

Whatever "good" function the university serves is what the radical students can cull from its bones—especially the creation and expansion of a revolutionary movement. The university should be used as a place from which to launch radical struggles—anything less now constitutes a passive capitulation to reformism, whatever the intention of the radicals involved.

This position on the university leads to a clear position on "restructuring." It is irrelevant. Tremendous pressure on the coalition strike committee was brought by liberals who proclaimed the creation of a "new, just, democratic Columbia University" as their goal. Professing revolution as another one of their goals, they saw reform of the university as one of the many "steps" toward revolution. Behind this conception, of course, was the traditional liberal view of reform of institutions, one by one, which would through evolution lead to enough humanistic reform, somehow called revolution. Also present was a healthy fear of both the personal and social effects of struggle.

Demands about democratizing the university are *procedural*—from which of necessity would be empty and easily coopted by an extraordinarily powerful ruling class and its representatives, the Board of Trustees and Administration. What we are after is *sub-*

stantive change—such as was embodied in the six demands, and especially the demands on IDA and the gym. This is where our fight for power is located. How can any reforms in procedure ever mean power to change the university's exploitative function if we can't even win our direct demands on that function now? For radicals who were somewhat confused, we added, one of our main goals is the building of a radical movement that can engage in fights, that can struggle against capitalism and expose it and its institutions to more and more people and also gain support. Will our fighting over some petty little tri- or bipartite committees do this? Or will we just be coopted into some silly little liberal game, deflecting the focus of our movement and depoliticizing it?

Eric Mann in his *Our Generation/Movement* article, criticizes the strike position on student power by saying, "leaving the issue of student power to the liberals is a bad mistake." According to Eric, there is a "radical position on student power," though it never gets explained beyond some vague phrasing of "structural changes within the context of the (radical) critique (of the university)." What are these radical structural demands? What will they accomplish?

According to Eric, there are *two valid* categories of issues: 1) Off-campus type issues, such as embodied in the IDA and gym demands. 2) On-campus reform issues, which Columbia SDS left to the liberals. "Building alliances with off-campus groups is an important task for the radical student movement," but this second type is also important. Much work was done by ad hoc liberal-radical groups on departmental reform, but ultimately, the political content of this work was null in terms of building a revolutionary movement.

The validity of campus reform issues implies an understanding of the tasks of a student movement which is different from ours at Columbia and also that of the most advanced elements of nationwide SDS. We see the goal of the student movement not as the creation of an eventual power base, involving all students around all their concerns, radical and otherwise, which is a very old conception of what we're up to, but rather, building a radical force which raises issues for other constituencies—young people, workers, others—which will eventually be picked up on to create a broader, solider revolutionary movement.

Since the working class will be the agency of change, it is these people who must be addressed by any action initiated by students. This is very different from "creating alliances." It means the entire content of our movement must be radical—i.e., anti-imperialist, and anti-capitalist—not concerned with the parochial, privileged needs of students. This use of the student movement as a critical force is exactly what began to happen at Columbia—no power base was carved out; rather, good, solid radical issues were raised for the community, the city, and, in fact, the entire nation. To the extent that our issues lacked a focus and a target outside students, they were not consciously "revolutionary."

The reason we went so far with "restructuring" demands (after the Trustees had already called for a student committee on restructuring) was both because of a certain amount of confusion along the lines of Eric's thinking described above, and because we misread the extent of the liberal base on campus for "student power," very much as Eric Mann does. Self-proclaimed liberal "leaders" kept coming to the strike committee saying that their constituencies wanted restructuring and the strike committee was going to lose their support if it wasn't granted. Throughout the summer we considered the arch-liberal Students for a Restructured University to be the main competition to the radical movement on campus. But we were totally mistaken.

After people have been exposed even peripherally to a movement that fights for meaningful goals—an end to racism, an end to exploitation—the creation of a better world, how can they go back to their old liberal ideas about reform of institutions? We had underestimated the relevance of the radical movement at Columbia, and how deeply it undercut all the liberal sops.

This fall, the fifteen student, faculty, administration and trustee committees on restructuring held hearings on plans to reform Columbia. Out of a university of 17,000, 40 people showed up. Columbia College, the undergraduate liberal arts division, held elections for candidates to various restructuring committees. Out of a student body of 2,600, 240 voted. Don't blame the turnout on apathy—15% of the College was busted in the demonstration last spring. The answer is clear—"restructuring" is not only irrelevant to radicals, it's irrelevant to everyone.

Analysts of the New Left, both in and out of the movement, are fond of saying that Columbia SDS failed to revive the strike because of Administration cooptation. Randy Furst, in a celebrated mis-article in the *Guardian* wrote, "Strike fizzles as liberals take over." James P. O'Brien, writing an all-inclusive history of the

New Left, makes this authoritative remark, "The SDS chapter has been baffled by a liberal new president and by a proliferation of student proposals for structural changes in the University that have little relevance to the questions (still raised by SDS) of the University's relationship to society." And Eric Mann, in his article, warns of the SRU/liberal/cooptation threat.

Don't our comrades realize that this position that the movement was coopted is exactly the position of the *New York Times* in what it hopes is the obituary for the New Left? It is a liberal position which denies the integrity of our original struggle, saying that the radicals who were interested in real issues were only a tiny minority in the strike, and the other thousands were just protesting the lack of communication and democracy in a great, but archaic university. Of all possible reasons for the failure of the strike to revive, this one of liberal cooptation is the least important.

There are many reasons why the movement waned this fall, an analysis of which should be done separately when enough people have discussed the subject. Included in this discussion should be the effects of the baseless Liberation School, the repression playing on fear of further arrest and being thrown out of school, the escalation in rhetoric by SDS, the rise of an elite leadership in SDS, the insane sectarian faction fighting forced on the chapter, first by the Labor Committee sectarians, and then by Progressive Labor Party members who moved into Columbia (there was one member over the summer), and most of all, the failure of many students to see where the whole movement is going, how a revolution will be made, and what are the life-alternatives for people within the movement. These are questions which the movement itself is only now in the process of answering.

FAILURE OF MASS POLITICS

After the police bust which cleared over 1,000 people from five buildings, the rebellion faced a critical turning point. The mass of students, faculty, community people and others demanded spontaneously a strike against classes, shutting down the university. But the political basis for this strike—its demands, tactics and organization were still unclear. Radicals wanted the strike to maintain the original six demands, as a means of keeping the political focus on racism and imperialism, while liberals pushed for as broad a strike as possible—"You've got a good thing here, don't blow it, everyone's with you, but don't force your politics onto people" was a typical liberal remark.

The real danger despite the chorus of liberal warnings, was in watering down the politics and the tactics of the strike. This the radical strike committee knew (this was the same strike committee that had been established during the liberation of the buildings, with two representatives from each building), and yet the result of the expansion of the strike committee, even with the politics of the six demands, was the eventual weakening and loss of mass base which occurred in the weeks after the bust.

In brief, the story of the expansion of the strike committee is as follows. The original committee called for a mass meeting for Wednesday night, the day following the bust. This meeting was attended by over 1,300 people, all vigorously anti-administration, and most of whom were ready to follow radical leadership. At that meeting, the strike committee proposed a two-part resolution:

1) Expand the strike committee to include representatives of any new constituency groups to form on the basis of 1 representative to 70 members. Groups could join if they supported the original six demands.

2) Restart the university under our own auspices by running liberated courses, and eventually establishing a provisional administration.

Debate centered around the question of requirements for joining the strike committee: the radicals thought it was absolutely necessary in order to maintain some political coherence, while the liberals, centered around the graduate-faculties student council grouping, wanted, as usual, the broadest base possible and no requirements. . . . Through a misunderstanding, I capitulated the strike committee position to the liberal one, establishing an apolitical strike committee.

This error in itself did not have to be fatal; nor was it, since the radicals did go out and organize like hell the next day, both in the constituent groups which were being formed and in the new strike committee itself. The new committee passed almost unanimously the six demands, plus a seventh on being able to participate in restructuring, so it looked to us (the radicals) that we had "reinjected" politics back into the committee. One good aspect of the error, which should not be underestimated, was that the liberals were prevented from organizing themselves into an opposition for two whole weeks. They had had plans to walk out of the original meeting described above and form a rump strike committee, but those plans were blocked by my "cooptation."

The failure to deepen and expand the radical base which had formed during the occupation of the buildings, however, lay at the root of our problems. Instead of maintaining the communes as the bodies with effective power, they became only the left wing which sent delegates to a coalition strike committee organized much like a student council. Not only political sharpness, but also the militancy which defined our strike by struggle was lost.

The people in the buildings had fought. Many were new to the radical movement, many were just learning—this was a time of openness, of new experiences and life-situations. If ever the phrase "practice outran theory" was true, this was such a time. People seizing buildings, yelling "Up Against the Wall, Motherfucker," fighting cops, committing their lives and careers to a movement for liberation—this was all new and unexplained in political terms. During the liberation of the buildings, too, the frantic pace had kept discussion on too much of a tactical level (should we barricade? should we negotiate with the cops?), often focused away from the broader questions that would tell people why, where this is all going, how it fits into a broader, world-wide struggle.

After the bust, there was more time, yet two important factors relating to the formation of the coalition strike committee intervened: 1) The communes were kept together, but their function became more and more a combination veterans' organization and discussion group rather than power source. In the buildings the knowledge that political decisions had to be made, and no one else would do it, held the discussions together. Now, through a system of representative democracy, and also the sharing of power with liberal groups, people in communes, feeling powerless, said, "so what?". The communes should have been given effective power. 2) The radical leadership was kept occupied in the nightly torture session called "Strike Coordinating Committee Meetings." This was totally wasted time since the Strike Committee, instead of being a source of strength for the strike, was really the weakest element. Vis-à-vis the needs of the radical constituency, the strike committee kept the leadership tied up instead of free to talk with and "organize" the real base, working with the people, the real power.

This denial of power to the militants and reliance on the coalition strike committee resulted in the lack of militancy which sealed the fate of the strike and kept it from becoming a struggle as intense and drawn out as San Francisco State.

There were many of our number who saw the mistake, but their counsel, "escalate at all points," certainly the wisest strategy in a struggle where radical politics have the upper hand and the initiative, went ignored.

How does a mass radical movement involve greater and greater numbers in decision-making? How does it maintain its radical politics when faced with demands for coalition? These problems are still unanswered, though the experiences of Columbia and San Francisco State do help provide some ideas.

SIGNIFICANCE OF THE COLUMBIA UPRISING

In these notes I've tended to emphasize the errors we made in order to communicate some of the lessons learned during what was for all of us the most intense political experience of our lives.

The failure to establish mass, militant, long-term radical politics has at least in part been answered by the experience of San Francisco State and other schools, Martin Nicolaus writing in the *Movement* has also pointed out that the TWLF/BSU movement at State has allowed no leader/symbol/star figures to emerge through the mass media.

The confusion over the radical position on the university, and the function of a student movement in building a revolutionary movement has begun to be cleared up by the Revolutionary Youth Movement proposal passed at the SDS National Council meeting held at Ann Arbor, Christmas 1968.* The ideas in this resolution have not been completely clarified in SDS, but the departure from both student-movement-in-itself and also worker-student alliance politics is clear to most. This proposal is, in a sense, the ideological successor to Columbia.

The victories of the Columbia struggle, however, were great. It was the most sustained and most intense radical campus struggle up to that time, around the clearest politics.

* See below, pp. 216–21.

Nationwide, Columbia and Chicago provided the models for militancy and energy which attracted masses of students after the total failure of conventional politics this summer and fall. The content of that politics, too, the compromise and reformism of McCarthyism, were juxtaposed to the thoroughgoing analysis of the left on imperialism, racism, poverty, the class nature of the society. All this was highlighted by Columbia.

At Columbia, our two principal demands, the ending of construction on the gym in Morningside Park, and the formal severing of ties with the Institute for Defense Analyses, were, in fact, met. This laid the basis for broadening the demands this fall to ending all defense and government research and stopping all university expansion into the community.

Perhaps the most important result of the rebellion, in terms of long-term strategy for the movement, was the creation of new alliances with student, non-student, community and working class groups throughout the city. A chapter that had been mostly inward-looking and campus-oriented suddenly opened up and began to realize the tremendous importance of the various types of hook-ups—support, tactical alliance, coalition—which would broaden the radical movement beyond its white "middle class" student base.

First of all was the tactical alliance with the black students in Hamilton Hall, sometimes close, sometimes more distant, but always working parallel toward the same goal. This was described at the beginning of this article, but it's worthwhile reiterating the tremendous importance of the experience as a model for the different types of relationships possible with militant black students.

Backing up the black students as a source of power, and to some extent behind the whites as well, was the Harlem community, sometimes mobilized, sometimes lying in wait. This force proved not only the greatest single deterrent to a police bust, but also provided *all* demonstrating students with support in the form of mass rallies and demonstrations, manpower, money, food donations and morale boosting. Black high school students sparked the militants in Fayerweather Hall, then returned to their own schools and within two weeks had created the most militant high school anti-racist strikes New York City has seen in recent times. A Strike Committee member spoke at a rally at 7th Avenue and 125th Street in Central Harlem, the first white person to do so in anyone's memory. After the rebellion, the relationship between N.Y. SDS and N.Y. Black Panther Party has grown increasingly close.

As a result of the liberation of the buildings, anti-Columbia organizing activity in the mostly white Morningside Heights neighborhood revived to an all-time high. The Community Action Committee, organized completely by community residents, provided support to the students in the form of demonstrations and even a rent-strike of tenants in Columbia's tenements. On May 14, the CAC liberated an apartment in a tenement on 114th Street in an effort to dramatize the decimation of the community by Columbia's racist expansionist policies. The CAC led numerous actions over the summer, all working closely with students at the Liberation School.

As a direct result of the strike, cafeteria workers, mostly Spanish-speaking, ended their 30-year battle with Columbia, one of the most repressive employers in the city, with the formation of a local of Local 1199 of the Drug and Hospital Workers' Union, one of the few anti-war unions in New York City. Student organizers, all SDS members, did most of the work for Local 1199, and red-baiting by the bosses was effectively turned against Columbia since the workers knew the students would be on their side if the union was denied.

More general off-campus results of the uprising, though important, are hard to estimate. Despite the distortions of the press, many people began to see that students are willing to fight militantly for good goals—ending racism, ending the war. Though no mass or general strike erupted in the nation around our demands, we feel the Columbia rebellion helped break down the antagonism of working people toward students fighting only for their own privilege (at least where the truth got through).

Internal changes in the chapter took the form of the wealth of experience absorbed by hundreds of individuals. It is almost a truism at this point to cite the incredible changes in consciousness that took place through the action ("Revolution is the best education for honorable men"—Che). The rebellion trained new leaders, some of whom have left Columbia to provide other local movements with leadership. From my travels around the country, I've seen that the level of political discussion at Columbia is as high or higher than anywhere in the country, including the radical "center" in the Bay Area. Though the number of militants active in the chapter is only slightly greater than last year, a terrible failing attributable to reasons cited above, a chapter member with many years' experience recently commented that the entire undergraduate school and most of the graduate students look to SDS for political leadership, and, most important, see SDS as acting in their interest. This is perhaps the only campus in the country where the SDS chapter can call the whole school its "base."

Our strength was greatest at the time of our greatest militancy. It was also the time that we resolved to fight—to disregard all the liberal Cassandras warning us of the horrors of the police bust and the right-wing reaction. In a sense it was a time when we overcame our own middle-class timidity and fear of violence. We, of course, were following the lead of the blacks, but we were also forging new paths where elite white students had never been before. At that time nothing could defeat us, not the police, not the jocks, not the liberal faculty, so treacherous and yet so important, only our own (we found out later) weakness and bad political judgment. The liberal world was paralyzed; radicals had a vision of what victory seems like.

Of course we made mistakes, dozens of them. At the lowest points, feeling that the movement itself had erred in irreconcilable ways (such as leaving Hamilton Hall, which we at that time did not understand as inevitable and even a source of strength), we found the strength to go on in the knowledge that somehow history was carrying us forward. Also important was the observation that after making 43 mistakes, 44 wouldn't make any difference, so we threw ourselves into the next crisis.

Above all, we learned almost accidentally the great truth stated by Chairman Mao Tse-tung, "Dare to struggle, dare to win."

From a leaflet by the Columbia branch of the N.Y. SDS Labor Committee (a group expelled from Columbia SDS), January 22, 1969.

How the Anarchists Destroyed the Columbia Strike

At the high point of the Columbia upsurge, in early May of 1968, the Strike Steering Committee was a growing organization representing about 6000 Columbia students, faculty members, campus employees, Harlem and Morningside Heights tenants, and insurgent groups of Manhattan high school students. Today, seven months later, the strike forces have been dispersed and the former heroic strike committee reduced to a tiny, discredited, anarchist-ridden relic, the Columbia SDS chapter.

This decline is only partly the result of unavoidable objective "factors." Once the campus movement reached a certain point of maximum mobilization, the limited scope and potential of a student struggle as such would be reflected. At that juncture the size and intensity of the campus movement would consequently wane. We must grant, in part, that no SDS leadership, however superbly gifted, could have prevented such an ebb in the campus movement itself.

Despite such inevitable contractions in the campus movement, Columbia SDS, under competent political leadership, should have come out of the summer as a chapter of several hundred members, an always potentially "dangerous" organization enjoying the reluctant admiration of even its bitterest opponents. Instead, a summer-fall leadership, composed mainly of student anarchists, has alienated nearly all serious potential socialists on campus, degrading the SDS chapter into a trade association for political clowns. . . .

The timing of the SDS "Spring Offensive" and the Columbia-Harlem alliance were the results of a conscious assessment by certain left-wing SDS leaders. The basis for the Columbia strike was not a set of issues isolated to the campus. Key to the strike was the social eruption triggered by the assassination of Rev. Martin Luther King. Those left-wing SDS leaders who drew up the "Spring Offensive" proposal judged that the accumulated social potential for a campus explosion could be programmatically and physically linked to a coinciding explosive potential within the adjacent ghetto.

It should be stressed, in this connection, that the apparent tactical vacillations of the Columbia Administration and New York City Hall during the critical early stages of the strike were caused by fears of the black militant-student alliance among the enemy's leaders and advisors.

The second great victory of the spring strike was also the product of left-wing SDS leadership's deliberations. This included the Tony Papert motion to constitute the enlarged, open-ended Strike Committee, the policy supported by Mark Rudd up to the point that he broke off his collaboration with Papert and other leading Labor Committee members in early June. The motion to include campus employees, faculty members, Columbia tenants and other strike allies in the new Strike Committee was the basis for the moral capital of the strike through the rest of the spring and a conception advanced from the theoretical standpoint of Marx's "class for itself."

This special social form, the enlarged strike committee, was much more than a "structure" for democratic representation of various strike-supporting groups. Such open-ended integrated associations are indispensable if an upsurge occurring in one locale is not to die of its own isolation. Political strikes, of which the Columbia strike is one example, are easily defeated unless they spread beyond local struggles, unless initial local strikes become transformed into the struggle of an expanding "general strike" organization representing the common political interests of the broadest possible alliance of the ruled.

The effectiveness of the "general strike" committee as a tactical weapon depends upon the most fundamental principles of sociology. That is that individuals define their own identity, their morality, their world outlook in terms of those special groups of which they regard themselves members, or, of which they aspire to become members.

In order to conduct effective political struggles, to marshal the moral qualifications required of the combatants, it is indispensable to effect certain qualitative moral and intellectual changes in the ranks of our own forces. This means to get individuals out of the each-group-for-itself world outlook—students as students, trade unionists as local interest groups, black militants as merely black nationalists, etc. All such forms of capitalist ideology, from "student power" movements to "black local control" are residues of intellectual and moral garbage which must be superseded if the struggle is to have the internal qualifications for victory.

The notion of the open-ended strike committee, extending from campus to ever broader off-campus forces, from campus struggles to ever broader off-campus struggles, is not only a tactical instrument, but a way of qualitatively changing the participants. By bringing diverse groups of potential allies together in a common political struggle, we change their relationship to one another in a fundamental way, and by changing their relationships to one another, we change the individuals themselves—students, workers, black militants *begin* to become real human beings for the first time in their lives.

It was the changed form of organization, both in the communes and in the strike committee, which briefly changed so many students and other strikers in early May, which made many students briefly almost real human beings. This social process provided the basis for the moral and political strength of the strike during early May.

Tactically, the campus strikers could not possibly hold the ground taken temporarily on Morningside Heights unless the force of a united and growing strike organization spread throughout the city to include housing struggles, trade union struggles, high school student strikes. The momentary, tenuous grasp on true humanity attained by so many strikers would be lost unless these strikers could be brought into more active engagement with substantial off-campus forces.

For example, if it had been possible to mobilize a major portion of the 6000 strike supporters into the New York City garment center, during May, against poverty working conditions and wages there, the full and growing force of the Columbia movement could have triggered a general strike of 250,000 workers in that industry—and echoes in other industries—within a relatively brief period. That we did not accomplish that nor organize the beginnings of a city-wide rent strike does not signify that we lacked the objective potential to spread our spring movement in that way. Our shortcomings were subjective: the campus forces and their active allies were too politically "green," lacked the matured subjective qualifications to envisage and boldly undertake such otherwise obvious steps outward. . . .

So, beginning in mid-May, the strike movement began to ebb—in what Marxian sociologists would regard as a lawful way. The first conspicuous reflection of that turn was the success of certain CIA-type agents in splitting the campus wing of the Strike Committee—creating the Ford Foundation's Students for a Restructured University, a classic application of CIA techniques to the Columbia situation. This split was not the result of the cleverness of the "CIA" agents involved, but the result of the opportunity created for "CIA" intervention by the combined ebb of the movement and its lack of subjective preparation.

CHAPTER 8

Beyond the University

After the spring of 1968, the emphasis in SDS on building a student movement began to recede. Although SDS continued to lead protests on various campuses, it came to define itself less as a student organization and more as the nucleus of a revolutionary movement. Within SDS, the primary debates now concerned the organization's relations with the working class, with Blacks, and with youths.

It was not as though SDS had suddenly undergone a metamorphosis. In the days of student syndicalism and institutional resistance, most SDS leaders also saw revolution as their goal, but they limited their immediate programs because they thought less was feasible. The Columbia strike and the other events of 1968 did not change their minds about American society; they expanded their perception of what actions might succeed.

The documents in this section were nearly all written between the summer of 1968 and the spring of 1969. This period was marked by bitter factional strife within SDS, increasing emphasis on the issue of racism, declining interest in the university, and considerable disenchantment over the tendencies toward rigidity and dogmatism within the organization.

The question of how to relate to the working class produced a split within Columbia SDS in the fall of 1968. The SDS Labor Committee maintained that radicals should devote their efforts to organizing the working class around their economic problems. In a paper entitled "What is to be done?" presented at a meeting of Columbia SDS in September 1968, Mark Rudd and the majority of the SDS leadership admitted the need for reaching out beyond students. But they argued that the most effective way to reach workers would be for students to continue developing their movement so that they might provide other groups with an example of revolutionary struggle. By fighting for their own interests, students would "set in motion" workers and Blacks. This theory of "exemplary action" allowed SDS to continue acting as a student movement. But by emphasizing the necessity of working-class support, SDS took its first step away from the university since its return there in 1966.

"What is to be done?" contained many of the ideas that eventually became part of the Revolutionary Youth Movement position in SDS. Particularly interesting was Rudd's belief, derived from Herbert Marcuse, that the economic demands of American workers could never become the basis for revolutionary activity: "Capitalism can grant all or most of labor's economic demands—it's been doing it for years—including, now, the demands of blacks. But that does not mean that the totality of oppression does not increase or that workers in third world countries are not exploited even more."

Several months after the Columbia SDS 1968 fall offensive had failed, a critique of the kind of strategy Rudd had advocated appeared in the *Young Socialist,* a magazine of the Trotskyist Young Socialist Alliance (YSA). YSA attacked SDS on several grounds: the "exemplary action" or "spark" theory, the failure to form a united front with other left-wing groups, the multiplication of demands, and the denigration of any struggle for reform.

SDS's lack of interest in winning campus reforms is evident in "Shut down the universities," a leaflet written by Chicago SDS leader Les Coleman and circulated during the Democratic Convention in August 1968. Coleman, later a Weatherman, indicted universities on various counts and concluded that radicals must close the schools "because they are the institutions which aid in the regimentation and oppression of our people."

Writing a column on "campus strategy" in the *Guardian* in December 1968, Carl Davidson took a different position on the university, consistent with his earlier views. Endorsing the idea of the "critical university" popularized by German SDS, he suggested that radical organizers work "within the ongoing courses of the university . . . challenging bourgeois intellectual hegemony with an anti-capitalist critique . . . recruiting sympathetic students from the class . . . [opposing] grades and competitive exams and term papers."

The rationale for the creation of a youth movement, as opposed to a student movement, manifested itself as early as the 1968 Columbia strike in a leaflet by one of the few members of SDS who at that time publicly called himself a communist, John Jacobs (known as JJ). What caught attention at the time the leaflet was written was JJ's open advocacy of terrorist tactics to shut down Columbia. Particularly relevant here, however, is JJ's analysis of the "coming American revolution." "Even though revolution is in the interests of the majority of people within the American economic empire, nevertheless, within the territorial U.S. the majority of people are materially a privileged group. Still, the need of the system to regiment and pervert people's lives is so great, that many youths will revolt against being the well-fed-but-spiritually-castrated cogs in the oppression machine." That succinctly summarized the logic of forming a revolutionary organization whose focus would not be the American working class, but youth.

In December 1968, SDS national secretary Mike Klonsky put forth a proposal for a new "Revolutionary Youth Movement." Klonsky suggested that as a means of reaching the working class, SDS begin organizing working-class youth. Students, he said, should fight for their class interests, not their particular interests as students. He recommended, therefore, that campus protests be mobilized at working-class colleges, community colleges, and technical schools. This desire to shift away from the elite liberal arts universities had previously been the aim of SDS in 1967, when it talked of radicalizing the "new working class."

Opposition to the Revolutionary Youth Movement (RYM) faction emanated principally from adherents of the Progressive Labor Party (PLP), who called on SDS to form a "worker-student alliance." Their counter-program, "Fight racism; build a worker-student alliance; smash imperialism," denied that students were workers. The major difference between RYM and PLP, however, centered around relations with Blacks. In March 1969, a few months after the "Fight racism" proposal had been passed by national SDS, the RYM faction mustered a majority at a national council meeting and repudiated the PLP-supported statement because of its condemnation of nationalism and its "refusal to recognize the colonial oppression of blacks in this country."

The continuing fight among SDS factions over control of the organization and the "correct line" alienated many of SDS's early supporters. Among them was Staughton Lynd, who wrote sadly to *New Left Notes* that "present SDS practice appears to me indistinguishable from that of the Old Left sects in the days of my youth." Another letter from David Doggett, a drop-out from the SDS-affiliated Southern Students Organizing Committee, denounced the pervasive use of "inapplicable, abstract, European Marxist theory." Doggett, a member of a commune, scored all the machinations of SDS leaders and concluded, "Fuck the leaders and their 'correct line.' Power to the people—the tribal youth of the world."

Position paper presented at a meeting of Columbia SDS, September 12, 1968, written by Mark Rudd, Rob Roth, Jeff Sokolow, Lew Cole, et al.

What Is to Be Done?

BEYOND STUDENTS:

It is now a truism, and nothing more, to say that a revolution must be made by more than just students. But what is the role of students in setting in motion other classes, including labor, in a revolutionary struggle?

There is much evidence that other groups in the society are also "in motion" around the issues of racism, imperialism, and social control. That is because these are the main crises—i.e., these are the main manifestations of contradictions in capitalism itself. What is the evidence?

On the right we are faced with the Wallace campaign, which has deep worker support; if what Wallace says is any indication of why he is supported by white workers, it is not because he articulates for them economic demands which they feel: it is, rather, a response to racism, and social manipulation by centralized bureaucracies—i.e., big government, big business, large foundations, and trade unions. Such social manipulation is a necessary resolution of contradictions within monopoly capitalism. On the left, we find workers striking and organizing for other than economic reasons: in Detroit a black caucus of automobile workers won substantial white rank and file support for a wildcat strike against the company's investing in South Africa. Local 1199 and District 65 increasingly bring into their organizing campaigns the issues of racism, the draft, workers' control over their own lives, and the war in Vietnam. In Chicago, during the convention, a wildcat strike timed to be simultaneous with the convention was called by black and young white workers over reshaping and control of the racist trade union bureaucracies.

It is obvious that various segments of the working class are already in motion around issues that will become revolutionary. It is not for SDS or for the Labor Committee to put themselves forward as a quasi-vanguard party of the working class. "There is no such thing as a self-bestowed vanguard of the masses. The masses choose their own leaders."—Inti Pareto, leader of guerillas in Bolivia. The Labor Committee does not recognize the spontaneous movements of workers as outlined above.

To say that a problem is economic in origin, is not to say how people are oppressed. The Labor Committee's view of the world is highly mechanical: falling rate of profit crisis in underproduction, attack by the government and ruling class on workers' standard of living which a revolutionary program should counterattack. We say that the crisis manifests itself in much more than economic ways, and that we should attack these.

Our development of the issues of racism, imperialism, and social control is a response to the total nature of oppression in the society (both felt and unfelt), war, the draft, racism, closed-off opportunities, alienated labor, meaningless work, and the perpetuation of domination, economic waste amid economic poverty, high taxes, bad schools and housing, rotten class institutions like Columbia and the New York hospitals, etc.

The Labor Committee, on the other hand, wants us to apply a formula about an economic crisis and its economic manifestations to deal with this totality: theirs is a one-dimensional, mechanistic, vulgar-Marxist view of how to make a revolution.

The capitalist system is a *system* because it is not one-dimensional. Revolutionary consciousness is consciousness of the totality of oppression and not just its economic manifestations. The Labor Committee believes, as is manifest in its program, that workers can be organized around a $100/week minimum wage. That's true. Labor unions have been doing that kind of organizing for years. Where is the revolutionary aspect of $100/week? Cafeteria workers at Columbia have already won that.

There is a difference between economist demands, such as the Labor Committee's, and revolutionary demands which develop consciousness of the totality of capitalism—more than just economic attacks. Capitalism can grant all or most of labor's economic demands—it's been doing it for years—including, now, the demands of blacks. But that does not mean that the totality of oppression does not increase or that workers in Third World countries are not exploited even more. We need to develop a revolutionary perspective, not a one-dimensional economist perspective.

WHERE DO WE GO FROM HERE:

Our experiences of the spring and our understanding of the crises in capitalism should tell us. Students can and will take strong, exemplary actions around the issues that affect them and everyone else. We should continue even stronger what we began for two reasons:

1) It will develop people's understanding of the total nature of oppression—by involving them in struggle against this particular class institution.

2) It will provide an example for other groups—high school students, blacks, workers—to struggle against their institutions, schools, ghettos, labor unions, bosses, draft boards—all the forms of domination which oppress people. Our challenging the power of our rulers will show people it can be done—just as the struggle of French students showed workers they could fight for their needs.

> "THE STUDENT MOVEMENT IS PART OF THE WHOLE PEOPLE'S MOVEMENT. THE UPSURGE OF THE STUDENT MOVEMENT WILL INEVITABLY PROMOTE AN UPSURGE OF THE WHOLE PEOPLE'S MOVEMENT."
>
> —Chairman Mao

SUMMARY:

Major disagreement with the Labor Committee:

1) Students are neither a revolutionary class within themselves, or simply revolutionary intellectuals, as the Labor Committee

would make them; they are a social group whose needs can only be satisfied by a social revolution made in conjunction with other social groups. They can and will act, as students, and set other groups in motion.

2) The totality of oppression—the issues people are concerned with—are more than just economic needs. Further, to put forward only an economic program "for the workers" is to reinforce trade union consciousness, not a revolutionary program. The Labor Committee's view of the world is totally one-dimensional and mechanical.

3) The task of the student movement is to listen to voices of protest that *do* exist in the working class and to try to act in alliance with these movements of workers wherever they exist. But it is not our intention to impose from the top, from the outside a "program" to "lead the masses." That method of organizing only shows contempt for people's struggles and for their own ability to choose their own leaders and their own demands. It is only through their own struggles that people come to revolutionary consciousness and not through the isolated formulations of the self-proclaimed "thinkers" of the movement, the Labor Committee.

4) Writing down a "socialist program," standing on street corners with leaflets, occasionally holding a meeting, or attempting to instigate walk-outs, marches, and the mass strike will not lead to revolutionary consciousness on the part of anyone. If the Labor Committee program wins, we will be leafleting garment workers, four million subway riders, anyone we can leaflet, and hopefully leading a mass strike of angry workers armed with the correct leaflet. Also, as an afterthought, we will see that SDS consists of fifteen people and our movement is dead.

OUR PROGRAM:

Develop the student movement around the major issues of imperialism, racism, and social control. Make as many contacts and ties with other groups as possible, but don't give them their program. Show directions and potential for struggle through our example.

DEMANDS:

We should attack the institution in which we are to expose its class nature. Columbia University is a can of worms whose lid we have only just begun to pry off. Demands should be around the three main themes of the original six demands, only broadened:

1) *End all racist expansion.*
   a) No gym.
   b) No more expansion at all.
   c) All vacant apts. in Morningside Heights should be renovated and turned into low-income housing.
   d) The Piers' Project should be converted into low-income housing.
   e) All emptied university buildings vacated as a result of demand (2) below should similarly be turned into low-income housing as indemnity to the community.
2) *End all support for American imperialism.*
   a) End all ties to IDA.
   b) End NROTC.
   c) End all military, paramilitary, and CIA research.
   d) Close down the School of International Affairs (CIA Hall). The new building should be turned over to the community for housing.
3) *Amnesty.*
   a) Total amnesty. No bullshit.
   b) No university cooperation with the city Red Squad, FBI, CIA.

The amnesty demand is essential because it 1) cuts through the cooptative junk the administration has been giving us: all the reform committees, faculty, etc., etc. Fights very skillful pacification tactics of [President] Cordier; 2) demonstrates the lengths the ruling class will go to hold onto its university. Exposes the trustees; 3) fights repression of our movement. . . .

From an article by Tony Thomas, a member of the Young Socialist Alliance, a Trotskyist student organization, in Young Socialist, *June 1969.*

The Student Revolt: An Analysis

A series of errors has cropped up within the struggle, errors that have led to defeats. The principal one is the ultraleft tendency to substitute the consciousness and actions of a political vanguard for the consciousness and actions of the masses of students. This short-sighted view fails to understand that the ramifications of the contradictions of the imperialist university go beyond the small handful of organized radicals. The result of this trend of thought is adventurist acts in line with the so-called "spark" theory, elitist and sectarian organizational concepts, and a catch-all piling up of demands that diffuses the struggle. . . .

According to the "spark" theory, all that is needed for a successful struggle is a bold act on the part of a small group, regardless of the political situation and the consciousness of the masses of students. Somehow such an act is supposed to instantly mobilize and organize the masses of students, or else by sheer audacity overwhelm the power of the bourgeois state and university, and lead to instant victories.

The "spark" theory attempts to "get rich quick" by avoiding the most important political question—the consciousness and organization of the masses for struggle. The vanguard aims at building a mass movement because this is the only way a revolutionary victory can be won, whether in a campus struggle or in a revolution itself. Serious revolutionaries utilize every chance to organize the broadest possible section of people, not only to spread the heightening of consciousness, but also because this is the only way the power of the ruling class can be set back. They have the guns, but we have the numbers.

One other problem of this ultraleftism in the campus struggles is closely related to the "spark" theory. This is the tendency to reject democratically organized united fronts for elitist and sectarian forms of organization.

The best and most effective way to organize for struggle is through a united front, that is, a coalition of all groups and individuals who are willing to struggle around the agreed-upon demands. Within such a formation, all decisions should be made through open and democratic discussions, including the election of leadership which should try to represent the various points of view. There are several important reasons for this: 1) Only through democratic and open discussion can the highest possible understanding of the issues and appropriate tactics be developed among *all* those involved in the struggle; 2) Only by such discussion can the leadership find out whether the actions are supported by the rank and file; 3) Only through democratic functioning can new policies, tactics and leadership be developed to replace old ones that have shown themselves to be inadequate. The more prolonged, the wider, the sharper the struggle, the more important is the maintenance of democratically organized united fronts for broadening the struggle and adjusting the leadership and strategy to the objective needs of the struggle.

Ultraleftists oppose sectarian and elitist forms to this conception. This is especially true of SDS. They say that their political organization should hold a monopoly of the leadership of the struggle instead of uniting with all who are prepared to struggle. They also attempt to impose their program on all other issues whether or not it is relevant to coalitions or united fronts. They furthermore tend to act outside of the control of these united fronts. They seek to build their organization before advancing the struggle and as a result wind up setting the struggle back and isolating their group from the broadest sections of militants.

There is also a tendency among such groups and among a few Third World student groups to organize themselves in an undemocratic fashion. This was especially true in the CCNY struggle. The demands and tactics are handed down from the top. The organizations are divided into small cell groups. Negotiations are carried on between the leaders and the administration, while the masses are kept in the dark. The result is that the rank and file does not understand the political axis of the struggle, many tactics with which the leaders may not agree are not implemented, suspicion develops between the rank and file and the leaders, new leaders and policies do not come forward when old ones fail, and eventually the struggle dissipates.

A third expression of this substitution is the attempt to add catch-all demands to the basic issues of the struggle. This usually takes the form of either insisting on an anti-imperialist consciousness as a prerequisite for struggle, or of a feeling that demands that can be met are reformist or counterrevolutionary.

SDSers often make *verbal support* to an anti-imperialist position rather than readiness to struggle against the imperialist war, the imperialist university or the imperialist state a precondition for struggle, or even a central demand. This approach actually hinders the real anti-imperialist struggle. The contradictions of the university, the war, the oppression of Third World peoples are the outgrowth of the imperialist nature of society. Anyone who really understands imperialism should understand that those who struggle against imperialism in its concrete forms are carrying out anti-imperialist struggle. This insistence upon verbal anti-imperialism hinders the development of real anti-imperialist consciousness among the broad mass of students because real anti-imperialist consciousness flows from real struggle against real imperialism, not from verbalism.

The addition of irrelevant demands and issues to the struggle only serves as an obstacle to winning its objectives. This is often the result of an attempt by one group to impose its full program on the others and can only needlessly split the movement by diverting its focus away from the central issues.

The idea that demands that can be met (that is, won) are bad demands is incorrect and simplistic. Revolutionary movements are built from victories, not defeats. Struggles for demands that can be met (that is, reforms) are not "reformist" if they teach the masses how to struggle in an independent, anticapitalist fashion. By fighting for reforms in a revolutionary way, revolutionaries can reach the vast majority of students who have not yet reached revolutionary consciousness. Moreover, refusing to fight for reforms leaves the leadership of these struggles to the real reformists.

Leaflet by Les Coleman of SDS, August 1968, distributed in Chicago.

Shut Down the Universities

We ain't gonna work on Maggie's farm no more!

Make it clear. We are taking our stand against universities. We have talked long enough about getting more of a voice in the university—getting student-faculty-administration groups that discuss admissions, and social regimentation as with dorm rules, and curriculum—and we still have no real power. We talked about student power a lot, the way some of us talked about political power a few years ago: If we could just mobilize our people, we said, inside the liberal elements of the Democratic Party, we could bring the liberals to vocalize our demands and win some gains from the Government, which now serves only the interests of the big corporations and militarists.

We have found out we can't change the political party or the university; we can't get control. (What changes were made at Columbia in response to the vast majority protest of the students who go there?) And if we can't change them, if we can't get any meaningful control, we don't want positions of "power" in them. Why do we want "power" to shoot the gun or ring up the corporate cash register when we don't want the gun shot or the register rung? Forget it!

WE INDICT THE UNIVERSITIES . . .

We indict the universities—at the courts of human justice, not the courts that have indicted a thousand of our brothers and sisters at Columbia and many others in other cities. We indict them first because they directly participate in research and training for the Military, the Military which is used against movements of exploited people's liberation throughout the world and right here in the black colonies of this country. It may even be used against us —very soon. We have already been maced, and perhaps new kinds of "peace" gas developed right here at the University of Chicago will be used against those concerned people who have come to protest the Democratic Convention. And it is not just a few universities that do this research.

We indict the universities because they function primarily to train young people for technical and managerial jobs in the big corporations. The way we see it, those corporations are the source of poverty and stupid long-hour jobs because of their calculated mis-management of the productive resources of America. Those same corporations are the source of America's holy war against movements of national liberation because they want their foreign-investment empire well protected. Forget it! We don't wanna work on Maggie's Farm no more. Shut it down!

Finally we indict the universities, the community colleges, and the high schools—especially the high schools—for their mis-education and ideological and social imprisonment of our people. We understand that an educational system functions to maintain the values of the society (the values that maintain the society itself). But they are not our values, brothers and sisters. And it's ours against theirs.

WE STAND . . .

We stand for dignity, self-realization, a real living consciousness of other people's needs of survival and dignity, and a life based on community.

They stand for entrepreneurial relationships between people, having an edge on other human beings, stupid individualism, and racism.

We don't stand for imperialist wars.

They do.

We stand for building together to free men and women of the chains of necessity—of long and meaningless hours of alienated work.

They stand for using the productive resources of this country to increase the profit and social and economic control of a small class.

They enforce their values through courses in history, social science, government, and literature, and through the loads of stupid social rules that make young men and women feel like foolish kids—controlled and powerless. Are you with them or with us?

They say we have no program. But we do. Everywhere men and women are refusing to live their lives out in the midst and in support of this corruption—blue- and white-collar working people, university students, high-school students, people contained in ghettos. Everywhere we are helping to work out organizations and forms to gain power of the people in their cause: our cause.

At the schools we are rejecting the false privileges—the stupid privileges—they have offered, and we are seeing that our struggle is one with the people of the world. Our struggle of liberation is to become more and more human by fighting with and for the people—for their and our self-determination.

Our tactic must be, therefore, organizing people to shut the schools down, because they are the institutions which aid in the regimentation and oppression of our people. This will take time. The going is slow. But we will break ourselves and others out. We will refuse to be used by the institutions we have indicated. As we break out, we understand that more and more we are simply political prisoners of a small class that have state power and institutional power on their side. As we challenge the bars of education and discipline, they become bars of pigs and guns—at Columbia and many other places. And we know what we have to do. FREE THE POLITICAL PRISONERS, SHUT THE JAILS DOWN! Join in the youth revolution, the beginning of the end of capitalism and its cultural jails.

Are you with us—or with them?

Article by Carl Davidson in the Guardian, *December 21, 1968.*

The Critical University

The radical student movement has been unable to offer ordinary students an adequate revolutionary critique of the entire capitalist content of their university education. This should not be difficult to understand. The new left itself has yet to develop a full anti-capitalist consciousness within its own ranks. This phase has only begun.

Because of the Vietnam war, the movement acquired an analysis of how the system operates externally (anti-imperialism) before coming to grips with its internal functions (anti-capitalism). Most campus activists can explain the military's use of the social sciences in repressing liberation movements abroad far more easily than they can describe a basic economic textbook's role in obfuscating the workings of the capitalist system at home.

Since the new left has reached the point of becoming a mass movement on many campuses, it has become increasingly important to overcome this weakness. However bored and alienated most students may be, their lives are still centered around the classroom. Unless political struggles are initiated against the capitalist content of their courses, the work of the new left will remain, in their eyes, another extra-curricular activity, along with intramural sports and the boating and outing club.

The critical university program directly confronts the problem of initiating political struggle within the training-indoctrination sector of the university—the classroom. As one part of a general strategy, however, the program must be seen as secondary, playing a supplemental role to the primary task of this period—mass action against those aspects of the university which can unite students and oppressed constituencies beyond the campus in anti-racist and anti-imperialist struggles. Unless the work of the critical university occurs in this context, its effect will degenerate into an impotent, distracting intellectualism.

The critical university is quite different from the "free university." Rather than withdrawing from the classrooms, the organizers are firmly implanted within the ongoing courses of the university, especially in the large, poorly-taught, introductory courses.

It starts small, with as little as one organizer to a class. The first phase of the organizer's work is challenging bourgeois intellectual hegemony with an anti-capitalist critique of the day-to-day content of lectures, texts and course materials. This should be done verbally, as well as by distributing leaflets and pamphlets before and after class.

After this initial agitation (which continues throughout the course), the second phase of the organizer's work is directed at recruiting sympathetic students from the class into a caucus. They meet before and after class to evaluate their work, develop new critical materials and better critical theory against the course content, plan longer-range classroom confrontations, and, over time, expand their size.

This classroom caucus study group, along with similar groups in other classes, makes up the core of the critical university as a whole.

The third phase of the organizer's work should begin only after the caucus has broken capitalist hegemony over the content of the course. This occurs when a majority or even a significant minority of the class generally respects and accepts, though not in every detail, the critique of the course content offered by the caucus. At this point, the group can move to confront the capitalist forms imposed on the class—grades and competitive exams and term papers.

One method of destroying the privatization imposed by bourgeois education is to destroy the secrecy of grades and exams. Immediately after tests are passed out during exam periods, members of the caucus could begin reading the exams aloud, openly criticizing the questions and discussing whatever answers they think are best. All members of the class would be urged to join in the dialogue.

If the teacher objects, the organizers should simply inform him that their main interest is acquiring a critical education, and not competing for favors from him. They could further explain their belief that 10 so-called "C" students working together can learn better and more than 10 "A" students working alone. Finally, he should be urged to join the discussion, if he is authentically interested in evaluating the class's work. From this point, all sorts of interesting struggles can occur.

Proposal to Columbia strikers by John Jacobs, SDS member, early May 1968.

Beginning to Bring the War Home

Strike Strategy: Begin Round Two

The great bust of the Columbia rebellion has been anything but the political defeat which the liberals and the faculty had projected. The "intransigence" of the central committee, based on the belief that the six strike demands were popular and could be won—even if we were busted—has been proven to be an accurate political assessment. When we say that the University will not open this spring without granting *all* of the demands, perhaps this time those who mainly want normalcy will believe us; and join in getting those demands, rather than spending their time trying to convince us to be "reasonable" and give up.

The active strategy of the strike committee, to continue escalating until our determination *was* clearly proven to the liberals, has also proven sound. Such an active strategy exposes the contradiction in the thinking of the liberals: they want change, but are unwilling to struggle when necessary to get it. That they "support your moral position and your demands but can't accept your tactics at this time." This does not come from them believing that the liberal tactics of pleading with the ruling class will win it instead. Rather, they don't understand where *our* strength will come from; they don't understand class antagonisms and the dynamic of revolution.

Communism in Action

700 people who were part of the building communes know better. Our strength to win will come from electrifying people's resentment against the corrupt, sterile quality of life under the old society, and releasing their creative, human energies and emotions toward building the new. The new society, whether in liberated territory or just among liberated people, is founded on two principles: brotherhood and love among ourselves and class war with the enemy. The bonds are real because we are struggling together for something real, rather than being sucked down by the compet-

itive psychological swamp of the old world; it is because of this solidarity that we can win the war, against an enemy who, whatever his material strength, must rely on mercenaries and perverted fools to fight his battles.

By Any Means Necessary

If we will close Columbia until the strike demands are met, charges are dropped, and Kirk and the trustees resign, then, tactically, how? No university has ever been successfully run under martial law. If they try to reopen, strike, and don't allow scabbing. Block classroom buildings. If they call the cops to keep the buildings open, disrupt classes. Since they will conduct reprisals, use hit-and-run tactics. It's no big thing for ten people to get together and wreck one of the enemy's precious offices. Further, if all such above-ground tactics are suppressed, it is predictable that individual acts of terrorism will be plentiful and varied.

But the largest task we face is to consolidate the thousands of students and non-students who participated in and understand the struggle into a solid political force, which can draw to it more of the thousands of students who have begun to be drawn into the struggle. It is this solid movement of several hundred—and not their less radical following—which in the long run will make it politically unfeasible for the University to try to open. The basis for this consolidated political force is certainly there, and to tighten it some on an organizational footing is by no means an impossible task. The reconvening of the building communes is the crucial first step in this work but there's much to be done from here. Solid political organization growing out of the experience of this struggle would be a political breakthrough second only to the rebellion itself.

This Is Only the Beginning

Finally, what long-range perspective is worthy of this rebellion? Obviously, the question is not *whether* to work for revolution—armed, communist revolution—in America, but how, and what form it will take. First, any real revolution is a process of expanding human freedom: both freedom from material wants and also the freedom to rearrange society according to the kinds of lives people want to live. Certainly the government, university administration, and ruling class in general will deny this and slander us. But we have already been called "left-wing fascist anarchist nihilist hooligan gestapo," and how much worse could it be?

Where It's Coming Out Of

It bears remembering that the primary origin of our rebellion, and of the revolution to come, is the struggle against the oppression of U.S. internal and external colonialism. This means certain very specific things as to the form of the coming American revolution. Even though revolution is in the interests of the majority of people within the American economic empire, nevertheless, within the territorial U.S. the majority of people are materially a privileged group. Still, the need of the system to regiment and pervert people's lives is so great, that many youth will revolt against being the well-fed-but-spiritually-castrated cogs in the oppression machine. Thus the revolution will combine these two forces, those totally oppressed by colonialism, and the youth revolting against *their* noneconomic, but still very real, oppression. Both of these forces have of course been very crucial in our rebellion and thus we can begin to see how they can together win in the long run.

Education and Change

Throughout the last week, one of the most unfortunate slanders leveled against the rebels was that we lacked concern for education. On the contrary, education was our highest goal. Kirk, and many faculty, believe that Columbia is the greatest school. We, on the other hand, believe that *revolution* is the greatest school. In short, that at very least people learned in classes there all together in the last ten years. [*sic*]

The main thing was learned despite what years of brainwashing did to keep it from us—things can change. When we talk about revolution now some people still smirk—some learn slower than others. For those for whom it still hasn't sunk home, we will remind them again: when things change, they can change very fast, and there won't be very much role for mediators. You may be for what we want, or against it; but believe we mean it, and decide.

John Jacobs
member of the occupancy of Low and Mathematics

(The above views are not the official position of any group, and now represent only the views of myself.)

Resolution adopted by the SDS National Council, December 1968. Introduced by Mike Klonsky.

Toward a Revolutionary Youth Movement

". . . How should we judge whether a youth is revolutionary? . . . If today he integrates himself with the masses . . . then today he is a revolutionary? if tomorrow he ceases to do so or turns around to oppress the common people, then he becomes a non-revolutionary or a counter-revolutionary."

Mao Tse-tung

At this point in history, SDS is faced with its most crucial ideological decision, that of determining its direction with regards to the working class. At this time there must be a realization on the part of many in our movement that students alone cannot and will not be able to bring about the downfall of capitalism, the system which is at the root of man's oppression. Many of us are going to have to go through important changes, personally. As students, we have been indoctrinated with many racist and anti-working-class notions that in turn have produced racism and class-chauvinism in SDS and were responsible largely for the student-power focus which our movement has had for many years. Student power at this stage of our movement has to be seen as economism: that is, organizing people around a narrow definition of self-interest as opposed to class-interest. We are moving beyond this now, but that movement must be planned carefully and understood by all.

The fact that we saw ourselves as students as well as radicals, and accepted that classification of ourselves and many of the false privileges that went along with it (2-S deferment, promise of the "good life" upon graduation, etc.) was primarily responsible for the reactionary tendencies in SDS.

MAIN TASK

The main task now is to begin moving beyond the limitations of struggle placed upon a student movement. We must realize our potential to reach out to new constituencies both on and off campus and build SDS into a youth movement that is revolutionary.

The notion that we must remain simply "an anti-imperialist student organization" is no longer viable. The nature of our struggle is such that it necessitates an organization that is made up of youth and not just students, and that these youth become class conscious. This means that our struggles must be integrated into the struggles of working people.

One thing should be clear. This perspective doesn't see youth as a class or say that youth will make the revolution by itself. Neither does it say that youth are necessarily more oppressed than older people, simply that they are oppressed in different ways. There are contradictions that touch youth specifically. To understand why there is a need for a youth movement, first we must come to see how youth are oppressed.

OPPRESSION OF YOUTH

Youth around the world have the potential to become a critical force. A youth movement raises the issues about a society in which it will be forced to live. It takes issues to the working class. They do this because, in America, there exists an enormous contradiction around the integration of youth into the system. The period of pre-employment has been greatly extended due to the affluence of this highly-industrialized society and the lack of jobs.

Institutions like the schools, the military, the courts and the police all act to oppress youth in specific ways, as does the work place. The propaganda and socialization processes focused at youth act to channel young people into desired areas of the labor market as well as to socialize them to accept without rebellion the miserable quality of life in America both on and off the job.

The ruling class recognizes the critical potential of young people. This is why they developed so many organizational forms to contain them. Many young people have rejected the integration process that the schools are supposed to serve and have broken with and begun to struggle against the "establishment." This phenomenon has taken many forms, ranging from youth dropping out as a response to a dying capitalist culture, to young workers being forced out by industry that no longer has any room for the untrained, unskilled, and unorganized. Both the drop-out and the forced-out youth face the repressive nature of America's police, courts, and military, which act to physically and materially oppress them. The response from various strata of youth has been rebellion, from the buildings at Columbia to the movement in the streets of Chicago to Haight-Ashbury to the Watts uprising.

REVOLUTIONARY YOUTH

We must also understand what role a youth movement would have in the context of building a revolution. An organized class-conscious youth movement would serve basically four functions in building revolutionary struggle:

1) An organized revolutionary youth movement is itself a powerful force for revolutionary struggle. In other words, our struggle is the class struggle, as is the Vietnamese and the black liberation struggle. To call youth or even the student movement a section of the bourgeoisie which must simply support any struggle fought by working people is economism. The struggle of youth is as much a part of the class struggle as a union strike. We ally with workers by waging struggle against a common enemy, not by subjugating our movement patronizingly to every trade union battle. We also ally with the liberation struggle of those fighting against imperialism, recognizing that this is the true expression of the working class at its most conscious level.

2) Youth is a critical force which—through struggle—can expose war, racism, the exploitation of labor and the oppression of youth. We do this by putting forth our class analysis of capitalist institutions via propaganda and sharp actions. Exemplary actions of the youth movement lead to higher consciousness and struggle among other people.

3) Because we can organize—as a student movement—around those contradictions which affect youth specifically, we can organize young working people into our class-conscious anti-capitalist movement. These young workers will (a) strengthen the anti-capitalist movement among the work-force, (b) provide an or-

ganic link between the student movement and the movement of working people, and (c) add to the effect that we will have as a critical force on older working people today.

4) The expansion of the base of the youth movement to include young working people changes the character of our movement importantly: because it fights the tendency of our student movement to define itself in terms of "student interest" rather than class interest.

Because we see a revolutionary youth movement as an important part of building a full revolutionary working class movement we must shape our own strategy self-consciously now with a view to that youth movement. This means that, in addition to expanding our base to include more young working people, we must insure the class consciousness of our movement now, and we must attack the class nature of the schools we are organizing against.

RACISM

Building a class-conscious youth movement means fighting racism. SDS must see this fight as a primary task. Racism is a central contradiction in American society, since racism is an inherent part of capitalism and a primary tool used to exploit all working people. In order to fight racism, we must recognize that there is a struggle being fought right now for black liberation in America with which we must ally. This fight for black liberation is at once an anti-colonial struggle against racism and the racist imperialist power structure, as well as being part of the class struggle because black workers are among the most oppressed. It is through racism and its development into colonial oppression that black people are maintained as the most oppressed sector of the working class. Racism (white supremacy) ties white people to the state by splitting them from the most aggressive class struggle.

We must also fight racism within our own movement and among youth in general and make our loyalty to the black liberation struggle more solid. While recognizing that "black capitalism" is not a solution to the problem of racism, we must be careful not to dismiss the anti-colonial nature of the black liberation struggle by simply calling it bourgeois nationalism.

IMPLEMENTATION

The implementation part of this proposal should not be seen as a national program of action but rather as some suggested actions as well as some necessary actions to be taken if such a youth movement is to be built.

1. BUILD CLASS CONSCIOUSNESS IN THE STUDENT MOVEMENT IN THE DEVELOPMENT TOWARDS A REVOLUTIONARY YOUTH MOVEMENT

a. SDS organizers should direct the focus of their energies to organizing on campuses of working-class colleges, community schools, trade schools and technical schools as well as high schools and junior colleges.

b. Attacks should also focus on the *university as an arm of the corporations* that exploit and oppress workers. Corporations that exploit workers should be fought on campus. (Aside from producing napalm, Dow Chemical Co. has plants in 27 countries of the Third World and is among the largest international corporations.)

c. SDS should move towards the building of alliances with non-academic employees on the campus based on struggle against the common enemy, the university. SDS should view the university as a corporation that directly oppresses the working class.

d. SDS should move to "destudentize" other students by attacking the false privileges of the university—e.g., the 2-S deferment should be attacked on that basis.

e. Some of us should move into factories and shops as well as into working-class communities, to better understand the material oppression of industrial workers, as well as to eradicate prejudices against workers.

f. We should move into the liberation struggle now being fought inside the armed forces and take an active part. Up until now, we have paid only lip service to that struggle of mostly working-class youth.

g. Youth should be made to see their own struggle and the struggle of the Vietnamese against imperialism as the same struggle. The war must continue to be an important focus for SDS organizing.

h. We must join the fight against the class and racist nature of the public school system.

i. Drop-out and forced-out youth both should be encouraged to join our movement.

2. ATTACK ON INSTITUTIONAL RACISM

We must view the university as a racist and imperialist institution which acts to oppress the working class and is the brain center of repression against the liberation struggles at home and around the world. Programs should be developed which aggressively attack it as such and attempt to stop it from functioning in that manner. Targets should include:

a. Police institutes on the campus.

b. The real estate establishment. (The University of Chicago is among the largest slumlords in the city.)

c. Centers for counter-insurgency (both domestic and foreign) including research and planning centers and sociology and education schools which teach people racism so that they can help defeat the struggles of the blacks.

d. Racism in the classroom, especially in high schools where students are forced by law to sit and listen to racist and class-prejudiced distortions of history.

e. A fight should be waged for the admission of black students and brown students to help wage the fight against racism on the campus. Blacks are carrying on the most militant fights both on and off the campus, and more black admissions means a more militant campus movement. We must also expose the racist and class nature of admissions systems and the high school track system and demand that the schools be opened up to the community so that they too can struggle to stop its oppression.

Resolution adopted by SDS National Council, December 1968, introduced by Elena Dillon, Bob Broadhead, Sue Hano, and John Levin, all of San Francisco State College.

Fight Racism; Build a Worker-Student Alliance; Smash Imperialism

FIGHT RACISM IN THE UNIVERSITY

Over the last few years SDS has led struggles to expose the imperialist and class nature of the university and the need to build a worker-student alliance. We must at this point begin to consciously point out and struggle against one of the main aspects of bourgeois education, one of its most sacred tenets—the promotion of racism. For instance it is good business for Dudley Swim, an illustrious member of the California Board of Trustees of the State College System and Director of the Del Monte Corporation, to fight to keep education under the control of the ruling class—otherwise he and his cronies would be hard put to find Mexican laborers to work in their fields for $1.25 an hour, or apologists and enforcers of that system.

In the last two years Third World students have begun to wage the sharpest struggles to occur so far in the student movement against the racist nature of higher education. In the South, four black students have already been murdered by the cops (Orangeburg, S.C., T.S.U.). The lack of reaction to this on Northern campuses displayed a good deal of racism in the student movement. This racism is beginning to be defeated. Columbia and S.F. State mark the entry of Northern campuses into this struggle. We should be clear that the force which the ruling class is willing to employ to crush these struggles illustrates that they have no intention of giving in on this question peacefully. Dudley Swim and his friends have too many billions that depend on the preservation of racism.

If we are serious about allying with Third World students as well as workers in fighting racism, we should have no illusions about the nature of this fight. It will lead us into even sharper struggles against the class enemy than we have previously experienced.

RACISM IN THE MOVEMENT

If we are to take part in or lead any struggles against the racist nature of the university, we must first of all conduct a struggle around racist attitudes in the movement.

1) Racism and the building of the worker-student alliance. The vast majority of the non-white people in this country are part of the working class—the most exploited section of the working class. Non-white workers are in the vanguard of struggles against the bosses and the sell-out union leadership. We should be clear that the contempt of many students for the working class in general is in particular an attack on Third World workers as well. To refuse or fight against building an alliance with the working class around anti-racist politics is nothing but capitulation to imperialism.

2) The attitude that "racism is amorphous—white students can't relate to it." This argument denies the super-exploitation and oppression of Third World people and Third World students in particular. It shows no understanding of the basic way in which racism is used by the ruling class. Those who objected to organizing white students around fighting racism are the same people who are so quick to attack the white working class for not supporting the struggles of black workers. Most students eventually become part of the working class as teachers and social workers whose primary job is to develop and perpetuate racist and anti-working-class ideology. Not struggling around the question of racism means perpetuating racism.

There was very sharp struggle around these questions during the first weeks of the strike at S.F. State. People who put forth the position that white students can't relate to racism (leaders of the Experimental College and the anti-working-class forces within SDS) argued that we should add "white" demands to the 15 Third World Liberation Front demands. These people did not see that the anti-racist struggles were in the class interest of students and workers. The "white" demands they came out with reflected the lack of class outlook. They were very narrow student-power-type demands, i.e., campus autonomy, free speech, student control of courses, etc., which didn't attack the class nature of the university.

"STUDENTS ARE NIGGERS" RACIST IDEA

3) The non-class "cultural oppression" which leads to the racist formulation that "students are niggers too." How many white students have been shot down by the cops? How many white students face the problem of ghetto existence? Non-white people are super-exploited. They get the lowest wages, worst jobs, worst working and living conditions, and are part of the most oppressed class, the working class. Students also are oppressed (i.e., were fed racist, anti-working-class lies in the classroom, taught to be social workers who regulate poverty and oppression instead of helping people, etc.), but this oppression is not nearly as sharp as the oppression of non-white students and workers. Students also have some privileges (for instance, 2-S deferments).

There is an even more racist lie in the "student as nigger" formulation. Instead of seeing Third World people as the heart of the work force, and therefore in a position of tremendous strength, it sees them as powerless and alienated—like students. This is an insult to both black people and students. It is the same as the liberal-conservative lie, "they're all on welfare." It leads to advocating that students and black people "drop out" (impossible for working-class families) rather than struggle against their oppression.

4) Reverse chauvinism. Some people say that it is racist to criticize anything put forward by a black person, or at least by someone who claims to be a black militant. This patronizing attitude comes from not understanding that the class aspect of imperialist oppression is primary. It furthers nationalism, an ideology that the ruling class relies on to split the movement.

REVOLUTIONARY VIOLENCE

5) The role of revolutionary violence. One of the main tactics of the administration at State was to have their liberal front men express their undying support for demands of Third World students, but at the same time condemn their "violence." At State during one afternoon of clearing scabs out of classrooms a typewriter was thrown through a window. A picture of the broken window and typewriter resting in the bushes was reprinted in at least 20 West Coast newspapers as an example of the violence of "roving bands of non-white militants." This was part of an effort by the ruling class to deny the mass character of the revolutionary violence used by the students, and to equate it with "senseless" terrorist attacks by individuals. This attack on Third World students must be met head on by exposing the class nature of violence. The necessity of working people and particularly black people to use violence is a result of the violent and systematic oppression which the ruling class perpetuates every day. Revolutionary violence against the class enemy and its lackeys (college administrators) is the only way that class in the long run is going to be smashed. The role of white radicals is not to excuse or rationalize the sharpness with which the Third World students are willing to fight the administration but to build support for it, draw courage from it and participate in it. . . .

SPECIFIC PROPOSALS

1) Special Admissions. Struggles around admissions of Third World students are breaking out on campuses around the coun-

try. This is a setback for the ruling class and a step forward for the student movement. These struggles unite Third World and white students. They unite the student movement with Third World workers. And they have raised the movement to a higher level of mass militancy. The ruling class wants to co-opt these struggles by claiming that admitting more Third World students will end racism. Further, when they are forced to admit more Third World students they will try to use this to train more people to help oppress the Third World section of the working class, the people who pay for the university to begin with. This strategy is already backfiring as Third World students lead some of the sharpest campus struggles throughout the country and often immediately move to link their struggles to the Third World working class.

SDS, as well as radicals among the Third World students, must play a major role in these struggles if they are not to be co-opted. We have to point out that more college admissions cannot be a strategy to end racism, but is a tactic to sharpen the attack on capitalism. We have to fight around the class content of our education. For example, courses should be taught on working-class history, the real story of U.S. Imperialism. These should include demands for courses on the history of the non-white section of the working class in particular—the super-exploitation of non-white workers in erecting the bloody edifice of U.S. Imperialism. We have to attack one of the major "sociological" functions of the university: to provide trained personnel for a variety of ghetto cooling-off projects, including schooling, policing, and (lack of) housing. We have to fight against racist institutions on campus such as ROTC.

2) Urban Removal. Many universities (Columbia, Chicago) are trying to expand their campuses into the surrounding ghettos. This means the eviction of Third World working-class families. Black, brown and white students should ally with the working-class communities to stop these evictions against their common enemy the administration.

3) Support Strikes. Part of the overall strategy for a worker-student alliance is to fight racism by supporting the on-the-job struggles of the Third World workers, including campus workers. This means interjecting anti-racist ideology into the struggles of all workers.

4) Support of ghetto rebellions. This means winning students to seeing the need to support the sharp struggles of black and

other non-white workers, as opposed to the band-aid running and helpful tactical hints to the black masses put forward in new-left publications. We must build this support around seeing the right to use "whatever means necessary" to fight the daily violent oppression used by the ruling class against the people. It is good to build for substantial mass actions at City Hall, National Guard armories, etc., in the event of ghetto rebellions. Mass action, as opposed to individual terrorism, is important. We are trying to build support on a class basis among the people for these rebellions, pointing out that black and white workers and students will have to take part in armed struggle to defeat imperialism.

5) High Schools. The alliance with high-school students was an important element at SF State: The H.S. students supported the strike and raised their own demands. Anti-racism is vital in building the student movement.

6) Take the initiative in education on racism. It is the responsibility of white radicals, not black students, to fight racist attitudes among white students. One thing we used successfully during the strike was classroom education—going into classes and speaking on questions of racism in the university and other questions relating to the strike. We should also be clear that racism is a principled question, and that it will destroy the movement unless it is fought and defeated.

7) The movement must involve working people or it will be isolated and doomed. Campus struggles must be related and tied to working-class struggles. Active support should be given to local strikes; students should keep in close touch with rank-and-file union caucuses and individuals previously contacted; community support and involvement should be sought for SDS activities. Only when the student movement is united with the masses of working people in this country will we be on the way to crushing the imperialist system.

From a resolution entitled "The Black Panther Party: toward the liberation of the colony," that was presented by Ed Jennings and adopted by the SDS National Council in March 1969.

Repudiation of "Fight Racism"

The sharpest struggles in the world today are those of the oppressed nations against imperialism and for national liberation.

Within this country the sharpest struggle is that of the black colony for its liberation; it is a struggle which by its very nature is anti-imperialist and increasingly anti-capitalist. The demand for self-determination for the black colony—a demand which arises from the most oppressed elements within the black community—is anti-imperialist and anti-capitalist insofar as it challenges the power of the ruling class. Furthermore the black liberation movement consciously identifies with and expresses solidarity with the liberation struggles of other oppressed peoples. . . .

The fundamental reason for the success of the Black Panther Party is that it has a correct analysis of American society. They see clearly the colonial status of blacks and the dual oppression from which they suffer; national oppression as a people and class exploitation as a super-exploited part of the working class. The demand for self-determination becomes the most basic demand of the oppressed colony. And nationalism becomes a necessary and effective means for organizing the black community and forging unity against the oppressor.

We must be very clear about the nature of nationalism. If the principal contradiction in the world today is that of the oppressed nations against imperialism, then support for these revolutionary national movements becomes the most important criterion for dividing revolutionaries from counter-revolutionaries (and revisionists). To say that "in the name of nationalism, the bourgeoisie of all nations do their reactionary and dirty work" is to obscure the reality that in the name of national liberation the workers and peasants of all oppressed nations will struggle against and defeat imperialism. To say that "all nationalism is reactionary" is objectively to ally with imperialism in opposition to the struggles of the oppressed nations. . . .

—This resolution should be seen as a formal repudiation of the resolution—"Smash Racism: Build a Worker-Student Alliance"—which was passed at the December NC. This previous resolution with its refusal to recognize the colonial oppression of blacks in this country, its statement that nationalism is "the main ideological weapon of the ruling class" within the black liberation movement, and its inability to distinguish between revolutionary and reactionary nationalism is at best non-revolutionary. SDS must not be on record as supporting any resolution which considers revolutionary nationalism—the main factor which ties all oppressed nations together in their fight against imperialism—as a "weapon of the ruling class." Anything less than complete repudiation of this previous resolution is a cop-out on the support and solidarity which we must give to the world-wide movement of oppressed peoples for national liberation.

Letter to the editor of New Left Notes *from Staughton Lynd, published February 5, 1969.*

Factionalism

The editor of NLN has asked me to compress to one-third its original length a letter I wrote six weeks ago protesting the spirit of factionalism which has developed in SDS. Briefly, then:

I have the gravest doubt whether the doctrinal in-fighting which presently fills the pages of NLN and the agendas of SDS meetings accurately reflects the concerns of the majority of rank-and-file members of SDS. I also question to what extent any of those rhetorically speaking in the name of the working class have been mandated by a working-class constituency to uphold a particular position, or even, in most cases, have day-to-day contact with working people.

Let me be as precise as possible about the difference I perceive between the organizational style which used to be characteristic of the New Left, and that now dominant in SDS.

Suppose that there is a general sense in the Movement that certain problems need to be confronted: for example, that students need to become familiar with the daily experiences of factory workers or that a strategy must be developed to resist repression.

In the early days of SNCC and SDS, the method of approaching such problems was to encourage individuals and groups to experiment. It was understood that, the problems being extremely difficult, most of the experiments would fail. Still it was felt that all attempts to, say, build a voter registration movement in a predominantly-black community in the rural South would add to the collective experience. A failure might be as fruitful as a success in pointing the way to next steps. At its best, "doing your own thing" was not a device for avoiding collective decision-making, but for acquiring experience on the basis of which decisions might more realistically be made.

Along with this approach to organizing went an insistence that no resolutions should be proposed at meetings which could not be implemented by the participants themselves.

In contrast, present SDS practice appears to me indistinguishable from that of the Old Left sects in the days of my youth. Caucuses form, meet secretly, and circulate position papers. Finally, amidst much mutual denunciation, there is a vote. Whatever factional position gets most votes becomes "the correct political perspective for the coming period."

Not only is it the case that debate rages about matters with which most of the debaters have no experience, but time and energy which might remedy that deficiency go toward contesting control of organizations, seizing offices, and other paper victories.

These two styles of organizing might be compared to two ways of traveling through strange country. For the Old Left (and for SDS today) it seemed essential not to set out until one had agreed on a road map, based on theoretical analysis. The New Left tended to believe that the most exhaustive theoretical analysis would still leave many things, perhaps key contours of the countryside, in doubt. Hence the important thing was to turn one's face in the right direction and begin the journey.

My immediate concern is the climate of human relationships within the Movement which the polemical spirit of the Old Left creates. Consider Bernardine Dohrn's attack on the Texas anti-repression conference organized by Greg Calvert and others in NLN for Dec. 18. Now it happens that I am not (to adopt the vocabulary which is just around the corner) a Calvertite. I agree with Bernardine Dohrn that a New Working Class perspective is often "used as a rationalization for continuing academic, professional bourgeois lives." But I have the profoundest respect for anyone in the Movement who undertakes to organize against repression in that dry run for American fascism, the state of Texas. And to Bernardine or any other critic I would say: show us how to do it better.

The Movement which most of us felt we were joining when we became members of SDS or otherwise affiliated ourselves with the New Left was a movement which ultimately defined itself in terms of certain values. A current stereotype notwithstanding, SDS always accepted an essentially Marxist analysis of American society, even if the "ruling class" was termed the "power elite" and "monopoly capitalism" was termed "corporate liberalism." Yet in addition to this analytical apparatus was a shared commitment to certain ways of behaving toward each other, and toward all human beings. We did not feel this ethical commitment stood in opposition to Marxist analysis. It was one way to begin to "build the new society within the shell of the old."

Is it too much to ask that we try to recover the sense that we face overwhelmingly difficult objective problems, to which no one has ready answers, and that we are all going to need each other in finding a way through them?

Letter to the editor of New Left Notes *written by David Doggett, a member of the Kudzu Commune, Jackson, Miss., who resigned from the Southern Student Organizing Committee (SSOC), which was affiliated with SDS. Published May 20, 1969.*

Parasites of the Youth Revolution

The reason I resigned from SSOC and the reason the rest of the commune is disillusioned with SDS is that SDS (and SSOC in a milder form) is rapidly becoming a new fundamentalist religion. Antiquated classical Marxist-Leninism is the gospel; the works of classical Marxists make up the Old Testament, the Trotskyites have the Apocrypha, and Mao has written the New Testament. The decision-making body of the church (the SDS National Council) interprets the gospel for the people and anyone who opposes the "correct position" utters blasphemy. The world is divided into the saved and the damned. Anyone who does not meekly accept the "correct line" is automatically an "agent" of Satan (the ruling class capitalist pig). There was recently a schism between SDS and SSOC, and SSOC got excommunicated. The neurotic guilt (the sins of the flesh) that creates the motivation for this new fundamentalist puritanism is the belief that somehow one is responsible for the evils perpetuated by the world system of capitalist imperialism.

The guilt that motivates SDS is needless masochism. Only a fundamentalist puritanical sect can develop from such guilt. Intelligent revolutionaries everywhere have constantly reiterated that they are not fighting the American people, they are fighting the capitalist imperialist system. Foreign revolutionaries do not want us to produce a fundamentalist mirror image of their own rhetoric. They know that true revolution can spring only from the felt needs of the people, not from guilt and sympathy.

The only people who feel a need for revolution in this country are young people of all "classes." Therefore, for me "the people" are those young people who feel a need for radical social change (not just political or economic change). The form (centralism) and content (communism) of SDS cannot be integrated. But form and content are integrated in the most advanced segments of the youth revolution and the form/content is tribal communism.

What we are dealing with is the fact that we are creating a new civilization and this new civilization needs a provisional government, a tribal council, to perform the needed political functions. But as we realize the need for political organization SDS and SSOC move into the political vacuum and flood us with inapplicable, abstract, European Marxist theory. SDS and SSOC are the ultimate opportunists. They are parasites capitalizing on our need for political organization and distorting our politics.

I cannot defend the youth revolution against hair-splitting ideologues, however. It is an ideologically imperfect revolution right now. But it is not an abstract rhetorical game of theory; it is real, concrete, human, and dynamic. When one is confronted with the youth revolution, one must choose between the perfect ideas of the scriptures of classical Marxism and the humanly imperfect revolution incarnate in the bodies of thousands of young people of all races and classes and countries.

Fuck the leaders and their "correct line." Power to the people—the tribal youth of the world.

CHAPTER 9

A Cultural Revolution?

Among white radicals there has been a persistent division—evident in the documents in the last chapter—between those who see the movement as primarily involving cultural change and those who see it more as a political and economic struggle. The former are usually oriented toward drop-out cultures and communal values, the latter toward the working class and traditional Marxism. The demarcation between the two tendencies is not sharp, however, and many attempts have been made (e.g., the Revolutionary Youth Movement) to work out positions embracing both. Nevertheless, in some extreme cases, "cultural revolutionaries" have completely rejected politics as a means of change, while their opposite numbers—the Progressive Labor Party, for example—have completely rejected the forms of cultural rebellion (long hair, drugs, rock music, sexual freedom, etc.)

Don Benson, author of the first item in this chapter, advocates cultural change alone, saying, "A person whose mind is dominated by aspirations for power and for the overthrow of the old order can properly be regarded as a victim of the old order." Benson believes that the "directors of empires" should be educated, not attacked, and that radicals should concentrate on developing new life-styles. "The insides are where it's at," he says.

One of the counter-institutions to come out of the cultural movement has been the "free university." Jo Anne Wallace, analyzing a crisis at the Midpeninsula Free University in California, contends that its difficulties are traceable to "middle-class individualism" and concern with self-awareness as a way to resolve problems—Benson's idea that "the insides are where it's at."

During the People's Park campaign, which was itself an attempt to integrate the movement's culture and politics, a group of radicals issued a manifesto called the "Berkeley Liberation Program." In an analysis that appeared in the Communist publication *People's World,* Bob Kaufman attacks the program for not "speaking to" the working class.

Finally, Greg Calvert, former national secretary of SDS, criticizes those like (Wallace and Kaufman) who denigrate individual liberation and who insist that the task of intellectuals is to form a "vanguard party" for the working class. Calvert denies that personal liberation and social revolution are incompatible—or even distinct.

From an article by Don Benson, in Rumors of Change (*U.S. National Students Association*), *Rick Kean, ed., September 15, 1969.*

Restructuring the Universities

A person whose mind is dominated by aspirations for power and for the overthrow of the old order can properly be regarded as a victim of the old order. He too is in need of therapy and education. If we are to create a world without victims and executioners, then we must scrupulously avoid being victims or executioners.

People cling to civilization because they are accustomed to it and out of ignorance and fear. Those in power just don't realize that the exercise of power over people is no longer to their advantage or in their best interests. Certainly the directors have profited from exploiting people, but they are paying a high price in terms of fear, insecurity, and ecological degeneration. They can profit from the new arrangements too—more fully and honorably, without the costs. All the conflict and turmoil and violence which distorts the face of the world today is analogous to the tortured face of someone experiencing a fundamental personality change. You don't further harass and threaten a neurotic person unless you want him to become defensive and retreat to his old, familiar personality structure. If you want a neurotic person to develop a new and healthier personality, it is necessary to provide him with much love and understanding, so that he may feel safe enough to venture. Life, growth and renewal are all essentially acts of love. Out of my experience of love and my feelings of love, I am ready to participate in the development of a viable world culture. Deprived of love and acceptance, I would be dead by now or fighting in the armies of the night.

The Importance of Education. The true revolutionaries are thinking in terms of educating the directors of empires, not attacking them. One function of this educational program is already being carried out rather effectively. The revolutionaries are demonstrating to the establishment that it is futile and absurd to attempt to maintain the old order. This is being accomplished by metaphysical disruption and subversion, guerrilla theater, fun and games, refusal to cooperate, mockery, satirical harassment and courageous honesty in personal encounters. Entire university campuses and cities are being seen as potential living theaters.

In 1968, the old order became sufficiently reduced to absurdity that, even for the establishment's own news commentators, civilization ceased to be a viable reality. The inadequacies of the old order and the potentials of the new order yet to be born have now entered the mainstream of human consciousness.

But let us beware the continuing death throes of civilization. It is very dangerous simply to make it harder for the establishment to carry on. We need also to make it easier for them to act in accord with human purposes. An establishment up against the wall will destroy us, will become paranoid and destroy the world. Therefore, we must think in terms of creating situations in which the directors will realize that it is to their delightful advantage to contribute to the development of [a new culture]. If we can make these changes *attractive* to the establishment (and I think we can) then so much the better. The current mutation involves developing new institutions and technologies for the greater benefit of all, not a mere shift in the power structure to destroy one dominant group in favor of another.

The primary function of our educational program should be to demonstrate thorough-going alternatives. We should invite the directors to participate in developing the new order. Seduce them. Turn them on. Involve them. Use their money and brains. Flatter them by naming communal living centers after them. Women and children will be the most effective change agents vis-à-vis the establishment. We need to conspire with establishment wives and children. . . .

It is tremendously important to develop an effective educational program for the establishment along with all its employees and dependents; we cannot survive without doing so, but let's remember that this is merely public relations. Public relations is not our whole business, merely the interface between our business and the monster. If we concentrate too much on public relations then our program as a whole will be vacuous—a fancy exoskeleton with nothing in it but a chitin factory.

The insides are where it's at. Our real business is learning a better living for ourselves and creating a world culture which will enable us to live on. We shall have to make fantastic structural changes physiologically, psychologically, architecturally and socially. Most of these changes will proceed silently and invisibly. Drop out of civilization. Plug into the cosmos. Turn on. Tune in. Don't worry about your appearance or what kind of noises you make. Let the PR boys play the image game. What counts is the integrity of what is happening inside our heads. Only by respecting, protecting and nurturing the little growing things inside our heads will we be able to invent a sane future. The current revolution is not an external affair to be determined by political, military and economic means. Primarily, it is an internal affair—to be engaged in as a learning experience. The prime purpose of revolutionary action is to restructure the universities.

Article by Jo Anne Wallace in Peninsula Observer, *August 25, 1969.*

Behind the Free University Crisis

The Midpeninsula Free University is in the midst of a severe organizational crisis—a crisis so deep-rooted that it threatens drastic changes and perhaps even the end of the Free U in the near future.

For the past two years, the Free U has tried in principle to have a dual function. It has been, first of all, a counter university sponsoring and advertising hundreds of open courses, most of which deal with members' personal development and personal relationships. On the whole Free U courses are taught by the educated upper middle class for the educated upper middle class, though many Free U members would undoubtedly count themselves as hip and "liberated" rather than "straight" upper middle class.

According to Free U organizers, the Free U is successful as a counter university. Courses are flourishing. The number of course offerings and the enrollment have expanded rapidly—peaking this spring when some 1200 people signed up for almost 300 courses.

But the organizers of the Free U are discouraged. They wanted the Free U to be something more than a counter university. They wanted a vital ongoing community where everyone would be involved in making the Free U go as a way of life, not merely enjoying its recreational benefits. The Free U's coordinator, Bob Cullenbine, said in a recent Free U newsletter interview that most members now are interested in the Free U only as "a course on Tuesday night and a course on Thursday night and certain weekend seminars." Free U classes are remaining "just 'classes,' " he said. "They don't seem to be encouraging people into forming any sort of visible community . . . or a community I can tap into and touch."

So what happens is that eight or nine paid staff members do most of the organizational work and make most of the day-to-day decisions concerning the Free U. They compile a new catalog of courses every three months. They publish an expensive multicolor 50-page newsletter-cum-literary magazine once a month. They stage be-ins and rock concerts. And they handle a steady stream of personal crises that walk through the Free U door. Essentially the staff holds the Free U together—without much interest or support from the rest of the membership.

Since its beginning four years ago, The Free U has been committed in principle to participatory democracy. Theoretically, important decisions have been made by the coordinating committee, a group always open to all interested members. But the coordinating committee is now almost moribund. Two years ago when the organization had 200 members, between 35 and 40 people would attend coordinating committee meetings. Two years and 1000 members later, the meetings have not only about the same number of people, but the same *people.* Recently even those original 35 movers of the Free U have begun to drop out. This is the cause of the present crisis.

Added to these organizational problems are growing financial troubles. The Free U charges all members—both course leaders and participants—$10 per quarter. But this summer membership is down to 900. The Free U has a store in Menlo Park, half boutique, half art gallery, where the wares of local craftsmen and artists are sold on commission. In the last year, however, the store has lost over $1000 because of stolen merchandise. The Free U has a print shop equipped to do commercial job printings, but at present it does not even pay for itself.

Cullenbine said last week that because of these heavy losses he and all but one of the staff members soon may have to resign. Their resignation would strip the Free U down to a minimum operation—only volunteer classes and a catalog to coordinate and advertise them. If this happened, he said, the Free U would have no program, no community function, nothing but Free U courses.

But Cullenbine and his staff are reluctant to let this happen. He said in the newsletter interview that what has kept him going in the Free U is the dream that "we are really doing something that's going to have important ramifications." He believes the Free U can provide important cultural services for the community—be-ins, rock concerts, housing lists for members, job listings for members and so on.

To save the Free U, Cullenbine and his staff are staging a last-ditch benefit rock concert to raise money. It's planned for Sunday, August 17 at Stanford's Frost Amphitheater. If enough money is raised, he says, the Free U show will go on.

The plan may succeed in getting the Free U out of the financial hole. But unfortunately none of the organization's failings as a community will be solved by money.

In fact, it is difficult to know what *could* salvage the Free U and make it into an effective communal organization. As it is now set up, Free U members are encouraged to dabble here and dabble there, "doing their own thing" in as many courses as they may want to take—from bread baking to Zen, from touch encounter groups to Jungian astrology. In theory, anything goes. The Winter 1969 catalog explains:

"One of the cornerstones of Free U philosophy is the principle of an 'open curriculum.' This means that every Free U member is encouraged to offer a course on any subject he wishes and in any manner he wishes to teach it. The Free U exercises no screening, censoring, or directing of any class. We feel that in this way the community can best assess its educational needs."

This is essentially a liberal pluralist position. The Free U is opposed to setting any standards or criteria for distinguishing a good course from a bad one. The members of the Free U are not interested in coming together to decide what they should be learning and doing. Instead, the Free U's liberal position implies that every idea, activity, or concern is equally important. And so to thumb through a Free U catalog is to get a sense that all courses are equally valuable and worth pursuing. It all depends on the individual and his particular tastes, the Free U seems to say.

Another aspect of the Free U educational philosophy—which can be drawn more from the catalog's list of courses than from its statement of purpose—is the idea that the causes of people's problems are personal and psychological. Looking through a course catalog you will find only a few courses which seek political-economic, or even communal, explanations for human problems. Instead, you find, a lot of courses promise to help the individual adjust to society by helping him to understand himself better and to "communicate" more effectively with others. The blurb for a 24-hour marathon called "Encounter" in last winter's catalog stated smugly:

"All kinds of people are interacting for all kinds of reasons: policemen and black militants, criminals and upperclass society matrons, dopers and abstainers, teen-agers and adults, establishment big-shots and restless activists, clergy and laity, libertines and rigid conservatives, gay and straight, you and what-have-you. These people come to this encounter group to learn, to get loose, to acquire self-awareness, to communicate with others, to deal with hangups, to enjoy themselves."

What a beautiful solution for blacks constantly harassed by police in the ghettoes. Just sit a black militant down with a cop, let them shoot the shit awhile, let each see the other as an individual human being, and poof—antagonisms disappear. Why hasn't this technique been used in Vietnam?

But of course my sarcasm is absurd. Confrontation techniques and encounter techniques were created for upper-middle-class individuals to use on each other. Encounter groups and confrontation sessions attempt to convince those participating that they can solve their problems individually if they'll only try harder and better. The essence of such therapy is the way it cures problems: the individual confesses that problems exist, he faces up to them, and then he waits for them to go away while he feels virtuous for having admitted them publicly.

Consider this firsthand account by Peter Smart (an intern working with Husain Chung, a leading influence on Bay Area encounter groups) which tells how a special kind of encounter session called a psychodrama marathon can make a person confront his *real* problems.

"It is a stripping away of psychic layers, a going deeper and deeper into the self. You come in wearing a face, but it is not your real face . . . All the psychodrama, the merciless zapping (why do you lie? why are you so weak, so impotent? why are you such a bitch?), all this is designed to strip away the mask and reveal the real face, the face contorted with hatred and rage, the face with all its marks of weakness and shame. The marathon is a true mirror and for once, you must look at your real face . . . It brings you right up against that monster in you, that dragon, that you've never dared do battle with. It takes you into that secret place in yourself, that ultimate fear of shame, that place you do not want to know, that place you cannot confront, but must confront if you are ever to be whole, to be free. And of course . . . you run shrieking from it. The psychodrama brings on a terrible crisis, an agony of self-knowledge . . . But what you find is that you can always get beyond that place, the dragon can be overcome. That on the other side, there isn't disaster, disintegration, madness, loss of self, but rather self-realization, strength, wholeness, peace. That underneath that ugly face there is yet another face, your true face, and it is a strong, loving face. After the hell, comes this incredible joy, love and peace. Every psychodrama is this kind of trip into the self, a purgation, a cleansing, a trip through your hell to realize your true humanity."

The middle-class, individualistic bullshit is all there. The individual is responsible for his fucked-up life. All he has to do is face up to the demons inside him. Once he acknowledges his hatreds, his fears, he can find peace. Despite the risk of sounding pompous, I can only say that this bit of self-indulgence will work for only a privileged class of people. It is absurd, of course, to think that the Vietnamese peasant whose children have been napalmed is going to make the war go away by stripping off his psychic layers and coming face to face with his hatred for the United States.

Last week, while doing research on the Free U, I asked a leader of one of the more than 100 encounter groups what he thinks the value of such groups is. "I think people become radicalized," he said, "because they are opening up and becoming more aware of their environment. It's impossible to be turned on to more and more things around you without becoming more radicalized." What did he mean by radicalized, I asked. "I mean, aware of the repressive nature of our society," he said. Many of the Free U courses make people see what the society is doing to them, he continued. Once people understand that, they begin to make "cultural demands" on that society—like changing the way they dress and wear their hair, or people drop out of straight jobs, such as jobs with defense contractors. And this radicalization process is necessary for upper-middle-class people, he insisted, because upper-middle-class people can't relate to blacks in the ghetto, for example, if they don't feel their own oppression.

I suspect that not many middle-class people radicalized by the Free U in this way ever *do* move into any collective political activity—either in support of their own interests or any one else's. Whatever radicalism they may acquire is likely to be a privatist kind of radicalism.

A story the same encounter group leader told me confirms this theory. In one of his recent courses, there was some discussion of the housing problems in Palo Alto: the fact that rents are soaring and that it is becoming increasingly hard for people, particularly hippies, to rent houses there. Several months after this discussion, a man from the group phoned the encounter leader and told him that until the group experience, the man and his wife had never realized before what a problem housing was in Palo Alto. And now they wanted to do something about it, he said, so they were going to buy a large old house in Palo Alto and rent it to hippies at reasonable rates.

"This shows that people *can* be radicalized in Free U courses," the leader said. He didn't seem a bit impressed when I pointed out that one couple buying one large old house in Palo Alto will hardly fight the growing crisis in housing, or that Palo Alto financial interests are trying to squeeze all those big, low-rent houses out of the downtown area.

In the last analysis, it seems impossible that the Free U can succeed when it both encourages people's middle-class individualistic tendencies and also hopes to attract them to communal relationships. The two concerns are antithetical. And so, it is completely understandable that members of the Free U are unconcerned and uninvolved in the Free U as a community—most of them are taking courses which encourage them to concentrate on self-awareness, self-fulfillment, and self-gratification.

One final note. Some old Peninsula heads are fond of harking back to the days from 1965 through 1967 when the Free U was first beginning and had a large number of "politicos" as members. These people remember how great the Free U was then and speculate about what the Free U might have become, had the political people only remained.

But according to Barry Greenberg, who was one of the early Free U organizers, it is important to realize that the Free U had the same basic deficiencies then that it has now. "Its politics then were middle-class radicalism," he explained recently. The Free U then was essentially a homogeneous middle-class group—though there were more students then, whereas now there is a preponderance of 25- to 35-year-olds. "The primary view of radical organizing back in the old days was to set the Free U down in the middle of East Palo Alto and educate the blacks and poor whites there to struggle for greater local autonomy within their existing community. We were very naive or very condescending or both," Greenberg continued, "but we thought we had an important message to bring to that community."

Still, the politics of the Free U might have developed and matured had it not been for the liberal anarchistic notion that people should do their own thing. According to Greenberg, this tendency not only made it impossible for the members to debate and collectively decide which courses and political actions were valuable and which should be thrown out; it also made it harder for the political people doing "their own thing" to operate *within* the Free U. "There were very strong pressures by many people in the Free U then to keep others in the organization from taking political action. Membership was used as a stick to keep people in line—the argument was that the large membership of the organization might be jeopardized if the organization or individuals in it took public political stands," Greenberg said.

The political emasculation of the Free U might never have happened if the organization had not suspended its critical judgment.

It is this single characteristic, I think, that is responsible for fragmenting and isolating individual members of the Free U. If the organization's leaders are serious in wanting the Free U to become a real working community, then the luxury of middle-class individualism will, at times, have to be abandoned in order to create an organization with a wider communal perspective. Not until that happens can the Free U serve more than the interests of a thousand separate members. And not until the Free U serves more than just the interests of the upper middle class can it become truly political.

Article by Bob Kaufman in People's World, *San Francisco, June 21, 1969.*

The Berkeley Liberation Program: Whom Does It Speak *for*? Whom Does It Speak *to*?

In the heat of the struggle for People's Park in Berkeley, a full page ad appeared in the *Berkeley Barb* presenting a "Berkeley Liberation Program."

A few days later the program appeared as a wall poster and pamphlet. It also received extensive coverage in the commercial news media.

This program merits serious consideration. First, because it is the collective effort of scores of Berkeley radicals, many of them veterans and some of them leaders, of important struggles the New Left has passed through. Second, because it is an attempt by a cross-section of New Left radicals to produce a program based on the summing up of their experience in struggle.

Finally, it merits consideration because it is a clear-cut statement of the trend to a kind of utopian and subjective escape from the immense difficulties facing socialist revolutionaries in U.S. society.

The program was worked out by a number of "liberation committees" meeting over many weeks. Among those involved in writing it were such New Left figures as Tom Hayden, currently facing federal conspiracy charges for his leadership of the Chicago demonstrations against the Democratic Party convention, and Stew Albert, an influential yippee.

People active in the antiwar movement, Stop the Draft Week, the Peace and Freedom Party, and people of a variety of ideological labels, many considering themselves Marxists, participated in writing this program.

The program begins by declaring, "Berkeley is becoming a revolutionary example throughout the world." but in order to survive the severe attack "by the demons of despair, ugliness and fascism" a movement is needed, "both personally humane and politically radical."

Then the basic idea of the program is stated. "We shall resist our oppressors by establishing a zone of struggle and liberation, and of necessity shall defend it."

This idea is spelled out in 13 points. Here are excerpts from some of them (including the style of the original).

1. *We will make Telegraph Avenue and the South Campus a strategic free territory for revolution.*

2. *We will create our revolutionary culture everywhere.* . . . We will stop the defiling of the earth. . . . The civilization of concrete and plastic will be broken. . . . Many Berkeley streets bear little traffic and can be grassed over. . . . Parking meters will be abolished.

3. *We will turn the schools into training grounds for liberation.* . . . Integration of the (Berkeley) schools is nothing in itself, and only perpetuates many illusions of white liberalism. . . . Students must destroy the senile dictatorship of adult teachers and bureaucrats. Grading, tests, tracking, demotions, detentions and expulsions must be abolished.

4. *We will destroy the University unless it serves the people.* The university is . . . a major brain center for world domination. Students should not recognize the false authority of the regents, administration and faculty. . . . We will build a movement to make the university relevant to the Third World, workers, women. . . . Our battle will be conducted in the classrooms and the streets.

5. *We will struggle for the full liberation of women as a necessary part of the revolutionary process.*

6. *We will take communal responsibility for basic human needs.*

7. *We will protect and expand our drug culture.* Drugs inspire us to new possibilities in life which can only be realized in revolutionary action. . . . Establish drug distribution center and marijuana cooperative . . . All drug busts will be defined as political.

8. *We will break the power of the landlords and provide beautiful*

housing for everyone. . . . Through rent strikes, direct seizures of property. . . . the large landlords, banks will be driven out. We shall force them to transfer housing control to the community . . .

9. *We will tax the corporations, not the working people.* . . . Berkeley cannot be changed without confronting the industries, banks dominating the Bay Area . . . We will demand a direct contribution from business to the community until a nationwide assault on big business is successful.

10. *We will defend ourselves against law and order.* . . . We shall abolish the tyrannical police forces not chosen by the people. . . . All legalistic measures used to crush our movement will be resisted by any means necessary—from courtroom to armed struggle.

11. *We will create a soulful socialism in Berkeley.* . . . We will fight against the dominating Berkeley life style of affluence, selfishness, and social apathy—and also against the self-indulgent individualism which masquerades as "doing your own thing." . . . Within the Berkeley movement we will seek alternatives to the stifling elitism, egoism, and sectarianism which rightly turns people away. . . . We have had enough of supposed vanguards seeking to manipulate mass movements.

12. *We will create a people's government.* . . . We will not recognize the authority of the bureaucratic and unrepresentative local government. We will ignore elections. . . . We propose a referendum to dissolve the present government, replacing it with one based on the tradition of direct participation of the people. People in motion around their own needs will become a decentralized government of neighborhood councils, workers councils, student unions and different subcultures.

13. *We will unite with other movements throughout the world to destroy this motherfucking racist capitalist-imperialist system.* We will make the American revolution with the mass participation of all the oppressed and exploited people. We will actively support the 10 point program of the Black Panther Party.

The program ends with a call to form liberation committees, "small democratic working groups of people able to trust each other."

Striking about this program, at first reading, is how dramatically it turns away from the trend toward Marxism-Leninism and the orientation to the working class so marked in Students for a

Democratic Society, the Black Panther Party, and the many efforts by former student radicals to build the left in shops and working class communities.

There is a perfunctory nod to "oppressed and exploited people," but the "we" spoken of throughout the program is not a social class, or even a strata, like students, but the few thousand radical intellectuals and young people on the periphery of the University of California.

The only orientation toward masses of people implicit in the program is the idea of exemplary action.

When Regis Debray spoke of the guerrilla "foco" mobilizing the mass of peasants in a Latin American country, he was assuming that the masses were already radically hostile to the ruling class, and only had to be shown by the guerrilla's example that the army, the police, the landlords could be effectively resisted.

But the mass of the American people, including workers, black and white, accept capitalism, and the legitimacy of the institutions that run the system. The power of the capitalist system rests at least as much on that as on police.

The "main line" of the Berkeley Liberation Program is the fantasy of the creation of "a zone of struggle and liberation," "a soulful socialism" in Berkeley, or more specifically in the South Campus area. Within this enclave, the power of the capitalist state will be nullified, the police abolished, the landlords driven out.

It is reminiscent of a story about the great 19th-century anarchist Mikhail Bakunin. During the Paris Commune of 1871, Bakunin and a small band of followers seized the city hall in the French city of Lyon. From there was issued a decree, in the name of the revolutionary commune, abolishing the French state. They fled before the police arrived.

Much about this program is similar to classical anarchist doctrine. The preference for direct action by an elite as the central if not the only form of struggle, decentralized government and small group organization, the glorification of action and will as against theory, and above all a purely subjective and rhetorical attitude toward the power of the state.

When the program speaks of abolishing the police, driving out the landlords, or resisting states of emergency and martial law with armed struggle in Berkeley, it is either bombast, or, if it is serious, it presumably reflects an estimate of the comparative strength of the ruling class, and of the Berkeley radical movement.

But does it? Does anyone seriously propose the radical community can hold Berkeley or the south campus area against the armed might of the state? We don't even have the kind of support from masses of people in the society that the French students had, or the students in Argentina. They couldn't hold an enclave either, nor were they interested in holding one.

The whole enclave idea is an escapist diversion, except that it leads to costly and demoralizing adventures. It also has meant the campus radicals have missed real opportunities to link up with the black community and white working people in the whole city of Berkeley to win real victories, like rent control, tenants' rights, control of the police, and people's parks.

The same criticism must be made of the program on the university. As long as this remains a capitalist society, universities, especially universities run by the state, will ultimately, and usually very immediately, serve the interests of the corporate economy and of imperialism. Revolutionary transformation of the university requires revolutionary transformation of the society.

Inroads can be made, however, and concessions won—and a constant struggle to make the university serve truth and the people's needs can and will go on. Even this is seen in the Berkeley program as going on only in the "classroom and the streets," carried on only within the university and its immediate vicinity.

But Chancellor Roger Heyns's power does not rest within the university or its immediate neighborhood. It rests on the power of the state, and that rests on the economic and ideological power of capitalism.

You don't overthrow that kind of power on Telegraph Avenue. More to the point, even to wrest any changes from that power will take the power of masses of people in the state, understanding and supporting the struggle of students and the radical community. The six unarmed Burns guards standing behind the People's Park fence is testimony to that.

With the traditional hostility of the American Left to theory, to the objective examination of just what it will really take to win against the class enemy, a section of the movement is retreating to a life style that really means accommodation to the system, not a revolutionary effort to overthrow it. That is the real meaning of the phrase, "Berkeley will permanently challenge the present system."

It is the idea, popularized in the French student revolt last year, of "contestation," a permanent stance of opposition and confrontation against all the institutions of bourgeois society. Built into it is lack of real confidence that the masses of people can fundamentally transform the society.

The alternative to this is to seriously link up with the constant struggles of the people against all the ways the system oppresses the people, bringing the revolutionary energy and commitment, and the tactical militancy and creativity of the radical movement, to the rest of our people, with a long term commitment to build a mass working class socialist movement in the United States.

From a speech by Greg Calvert, former national secretary of SDS, to a Resistance conference in spring 1969.

A Left Wing Alternative

It is with a certain amount of nervousness that I speak. That's related to a feeling I have had in the last year, a time in which I have wondered, very deeply and with great pain, whether the kind of movement which over the years has made it possible for us to live in America—the kind of movement which, out of the obscenity and sterility of this society, has given us new life—whether in fact that movement was going to survive and grow or whether it was going to die and leave us isolated. . . .

I was asked recently whether I thought there was any possibility that we could avoid the Stalinization of the Left. I said there is only one response: Knowing we are faced with the possibility of the Stalinization of the Left, we must do whatever is necessary to see that it does not happen. . . .

It is very fashionable in SDS these days—an organization to whose national meetings I have not had the emotional energy to return for a year—to denounce something called personal liberation. If you talk about what you feel or what's meaningful to you in a political forum, you're suddenly one of those personal liberation people.

I don't quite understand what that's supposed to mean. I do not believe in a two-story universe; I don't think there's going to be some reward out there somewhere. I don't believe in capitalist ideology, which is the ideology of deferred life, of deferred existence, of accumulation for tomorrow. Unless one does believe in that, then I don't understand what motivation there would be for a biological, physical being to get involved except the liberation of that individual.

In Danny the Red's book, *Obsolete Communism–The Left Wing Alternative,* there's a phrase which I think must be taken seriously. He discusses and puts down people who operate on the politics of guilt—the politics of life deferral, the politics of the acceptance of repressiveness, in the hope that some day there'll be a non-repressive future born suddenly and cataclysmically. He says *the only reason for being a revolutionary in our time is because it's a better way to live.*

I don't think I've ever known anyone in the last five to seven years who was in the movement and in it for good who wasn't there knowing that it was a better way to live. If you think that politics and personality can be split apart and still build a revolution, if you think it's possible to be, in this kind of society, in any sense revolutionary without being engaged to the deepest level of your life, if you think any of those things or do any of those things to your movement, then we will not create that alternative history.

I do not mean that I think it is any longer possible for us to deal with our political responsibilities to ourselves, and to that larger America which we must reach, simply on the basis of existentialist language. But, the alternative is not Stalinist ideology. The alternative to understanding that I'm in this because I want to be free is not economic determinism. Certainly Marx is important; but let us not create a movement based on Marxism as ideology. Let us do more justice to Marx himself. . . .

. . . I think there's been a kind of unrealistic assumption made about where terms like "neo-capitalism" and "new working class" came from, as though we had snatched them from the firmament of Marxist ideology and imposed them on the movement. In January, 1966, we put out the button, "Not With My Life You Don't," to concretize the spirit of, "It's my fight, it's my life." Everyone was talking about strategy for draft resistance, but every time we sat through a three-hour session on strategy for draft resistance, we didn't get anywhere. What we were asking was the impossible: that draft resistance give us the channels for making a total revolution in society.

Then an article was written by Peter Henig in *New Left Notes* called "Manpower Chanelling." That, at least in SDS, was the first time anybody had bothered to read the material that came out of the Selective Service System.* It crystallized a lot of vague notions we'd been playing with in our heads about who students are. What it told us was that this supposed privilege, II-S, was at a deeper level another instrument of oppression. It was part of a larger program, a program of manpower channelling for not only the military but for industry.

It had been written, back in 1947 or whenever, to insure that the military needs of American capitalism and American imperialism would not interfere with the continuing supply of manpower for profit at home. Since the period following the second world war was the period in which the new technology of the coming automation and cybernated production were emerging, it was clear that American capitalism and industry were going to need an enormous number of highly trained, highly skilled workers to plug into those slots in its advanced technological machinery.

It was clear, also, that the university was going to become the training ground for those workers, those scientific, technical and professional workers who were needed by advanced capitalism. The multiversity would become the motor for the transformation of the labor force in the direction of the new technology.

It was out of that set of realizations that we began to see that students are in a tremendously different historical situation than that of Lenin's Russia in 1902, when they *were* the petty bourgeois intelligentsia. There's something different with seven million students in the multiversities of the United States. By 1975, one quarter of the labor force in the country will have had some college training.

We said, then, that the working class was being renewed, expanded; we called these people the "new working class," the university-trained workers.

That was important because it gave us a handle on the long-range question of social change, of revolution in society. It gave us the possibility of a perspective that said students and post-students fighting around the conditions of their own lives are legiti-

* See Vol. I, pp. 195–202, for text of Selective Service memorandum "Channelling."

mately revolutionary strata where they are at, and that that can be their great contribution to a larger movement, which must include other sectors of the population—the blue-collar workers and the poor.

Back to a little history to bring us up to 1968.

After the summer of '67, the Pentagon action and Stop the Draft Week which preceded it, it seemed to some of us that the time was rapidly approaching when the resistance notion of strategy could become the base for a new kind of radical solidarity among a variety of elements within the movement. I mean by "resistance strategy" a notion which included not only draft resistance and non-cooperation, but also resistance to Dow Chemical and other institutions of repression.

Michael Ferber and I talked the other day, trying to dredge out of our unconsciouses the memories of those months from October, 1967 to April 1968. What we came up with was a wealth of memories of political events which affirmed what we believed, events in which representatives of the black militant movement were saying, "Yes, now we have a legitimate basis for an alliance, because in the resistance movement there is a truly radical and potentially revolutionary movement among whites."

I believe that that was true. I do not wish to pretend that events exterior to the movement—such as Johnson's dropping out of the race, and a series of events exterior to the white movement, the series of uprisings that followed King's assassination—did not have an importance in reorienting people's outlooks. The reorientation of SDS in that spring of 1968 was to drop draft resistance and resistance themology almost entirely, and to revert to, "We got to support the black movement, racism is our issue. Anti-racism is the radical position."

What you do to a white man in today's society when you tell him he's got to fight the anti-racism struggle is give him a struggle that doesn't have any outside to it. I do not want to deny that racism is a problem, as male chauvinism is a problem inside of us. But I wish to insist that the only way we can finally fight against racism effectively is to be fighting our battles for our own liberation, in alliance with black people fighting their struggle for their own liberation. . . .

. . . My understanding of the dynamic of the black movement in relation to the other strata in American society is that it has two choices—either it can rely on whites for liberal support, or it can find a radical ally in a radical white movement. When that ally is not there doing his thing, then the black movement, for its own survival, reverts to looking for liberal support. If honky-baiting goes up, it's because we create the dynamic where there's no other response for desperate black militants. I wonder whether once again in that situation we don't have ourselves to blame.

In the ensuing year, having myself left national SDS much disturbed over this question, having opposed the line of racism being our first issue, having opposed the publication of a pamphlet which said liberation will comc from a black thing and having called that pamphlet obscene—in the last year I think we have seen, ... particularly in SDS, a revival of the politics of guilt. There was one major change, however—from 1961 to 1965 the rhetoric was liberal, and in 1968 to 1969, its rhetoric, but only its rhetoric, was revolutionary.

I do not believe that in a society like ours—an advanced capitalist society where mass culture itself is an instrument of oppression, where the repressiveness of all the last 6,000 years of civilization becomes surplus repression, where the authoritarianism of a highly bureaucratized, centralized corporate capitalism requires the inculcation of authoritarian and self-hating values in order to pacify the population—I do not believe we can free ourselves from that society through emotional structures of guilt which were created to keep us from fighting for freedom. No one that I have talked to in this year of isolation has been able to convince me otherwise, either through argument or through political accomplishment.

What's going on in SDS is that, having denied that students have legitimacy as a strata, or that new-working class people have legitimacy as revolutionary strata, we revert to the old Leninist formulations which say that the task of the petit-bourgois intelligentsia is to form a vanguard party which will relate to the proletarian struggle of the factory worker. I do not deny the importance of 20 to 30 million blue-collar workers in long-range revolutionary strategy for the society. To do so would be foolish and absurd on its face. But, coming from a blue-collar working class background, I find it very difficult to believe that the breast beating of white students and white professionals and white technical workers about the fact that they aren't on the production line is going to save my relatives or my high school classmates from the oppressive institutions of capitalism. Nor do I believe that talking that way to them addresses itself to the real concerns of their lives.

I think what addresses itself to the concerns of the lives of young people and others in my home town, where practically everybody works in the lumber mills, is to talk to people about their lives in the way we talk with others about our lives, to organize in the same spirit of openness and commitment and hopefulness and joyousness.

I would go even so far as to argue that to organize otherwise is not to organize for revolution and liberation, but to run the danger of organizing something very different. I know from my personal upbringing what the authoritarian discipline of factories does to the family lives of workers. Not to fight authoritarianism there in the same spirit that we fight it in the university is, I think, to make a grave error, and finally to be of no use to anyone, neither to ourselves nor to those whom we would pretend to reach.

Will it be possible to create that alternative history? Will it be possible to build a movement which talks about the community of free men, about the new selfhood, about new human beings, about new possibilities, about the new man?

Will it be possible for us to have the courage to say, yes, what we want is beauty and freedom, and we think that that could happen and that we become freer and more beautiful on the path to getting there?

It seems to me that such a possibility is not only there in what Marxists call objective conditions, but is also there in the recent history of advanced capitalist civilization itself. It is very much there in the events of France in May and June, 1968.

What were *we* doing in May and June 1968 when revolution almost took place in one of the advanced industrial societies of the world? It was the exemplary action of students fighting first around their own demands that catalyzed the situation. Despite the fact that France has the second-largest Communist party outside the Soviet Union in the industrial world, and despite the enormous reactionary force of that party and its trade union bureaucracy, the students were able to create a language of action which spoke to the other sectors of the population about the control and transformation of our lives, because they fought for control and transformation in a revolutionary sense, of the institution in which they were involved. A left-wing alternative was not only created but its effectiveness in opposition to the reactionary character of existing communist institutions was proven.

What were we doing in those months?

The SDS national office was trying to grind out an elaborate analysis of racism, couched in the most abstruse and dogmatic language so that the line would be right at its national convention in June.

It seems to me that one of our problems, which is a real problem, after 50 years of Stalinism, is the problem of models that give hope. Because of the despair of the new left with the bureaucratic forms of so-called socialism in the Soviet Union, we've always looked and looked for some place where somebody's trying to do it better. It's not so much that we're dumb and unimaginative—although I think we're dumber and less imaginative than need be—but because the question of 20th-century history was: Is human freedom possible? Was there another stage of civilization, or were we headed towards 1984, no matter what the ruling bureaucracies called themselves?

So we are enthusiastic when we think that maybe Cuba is doing something new, maybe there is real popular involvement, or maybe the Vietnamese are in fact embodying a spirit like that which gives us life. I do not want to denigrate our attachment to the heroism of the Vietnamese or of the Cubans; nor do I think we should in any slavish manner suspend judgment when we look at societies which turn us on. What I'm saying is what France should mean, and what I know it does mean for the new left in Europe, is that we now have a concrete set of experiences to look at that can tell us so much more than the Cubans or Vietnamese can tell us, because they are experiences of an advanced industrial society.

Over and over again, as I've read the documents and Cohn-Bendit's book, the experiences tell us we were right. The student movement at Nanterre began really in the spring of 1967, when the university had refused to allow guys and girls to sleep together in the dorms. So a sexual liberation front was created, and they reprinted Wilhelm Reich's sexual liberation manifesto of 1934, and talked about the relationship between authoritarianism, sexual repression and fascism. They began to build a movement which obviously had a most libertarian spirit. That spirit was obviously at the fore when the March 22d movement was crystallized a year later. It was "movement people" doing "movement things" that made France happen.

It may be because most French students had already heard

about Marx, and read through that, put it in perspective, that it was possible for something new to arise, whereas here it seems that every time old Karl's name is mentioned our deep Baptist backgrounds or something out of our repressive pasts come surging to the fore.

One of the things which the French events say to me very deeply and clearly is that most of the traditional conceptions of organization of vanguard parties, of Leninist practice, are not only unpleasant but ineffective. I find myself revising some notions that had been lost as we thought we were getting more radical and more serious. We used to talk in the old days about things like parallel institutions. I don't think that was the right language, but the language pointed to the notion we had, that the revolution was not an event on day "X", but a process that we're into now, and that the structures of revolution and of revolutionary society would begin to be created as we did more work, got involved in more scenes, discovered new things.

What I'm saying is that I think there is an alternative to the question of party, which properly has at least some of its historical antecedents in that tradition which is called by that horrible noun, people's socialist or anarchist or whatever you call it movement. It says also that Marx was serious when he said socialism would grow out of the womb of capitalism. The deadly serious question to ask, if that's true, is how the embryo is conceived: what are the embryonic forms of revolutionary society which must be created, however embryonically, as we work?

Is it not possible to begin to envisage a movement which builds a variety of forms and structures, and uses those instead of a centralized party—structures in which the questions of control and transformation are raised in a way which points toward the historical alternative, in terms of both the form and the content of those embryonic revolutionary institutions?

All of that, I think, is true and possible. All of that requires a great deal of imagination—the imagination which the students at the Sorbonne enthroned in power in those exciting days of May and June. It takes enormous imagination, a willingness to be new, but that is the only way out.

I do not know whether I would or could participate in an organization which did not embody in its immediate present the values and hopes and the fulfillment of need which I have, but I think it no longer, in our society, does any good to say, "I will sacrifice myself to be part of that dehumanizing vanguard for my children in another day." I just don't think there's any evidence that there's anything revolutionary in doing that.

Once again, if the new life which has been created in us in this decade is to be more than a footnote to the last chapter of world civilization, we must take very seriously the lesson of trust in ourselves, of not killing what we feel and need to be true, not blaming objective conditions or using them as a pretext for dehumanizing ourselves, because that's a very silly game. People who argue that game are arguing that the reason I can't be free is because all of that stuff is weighing on me. It's true that the authoritarian forms which are anti-life were not created by us, and we do not need to blame ourselves for them. But we also know in scientific and psychological terms that repression in ourselves does not begin when we touch the outside world. Repression in ourselves begins when we interpret an inner impulse as an exterior threat and call it the world. Since so much of our lives has been learning not only to trust those inner impulses but to rediscover the ones that society, organized as it is, wishes were dead, we should in fact affirm those feelings.

That means hard work, but work with joy. It means trusting ourselves, being willing to be experimental. It means not accepting simplistic either/or formulations of complicated human situations. I think, finally, it means being concerned with effective activity rather than purity of the line. We have to trust other people in the immediate situation who may differ from us in their analyses of things; we must be willing to be wrong and willing to be critical, but clinging to what we knew the movement was all about. Only an ideology of puritanism, religion, capitalism—of deferred existence—can argue otherwise for my life.

I remember one of the most moving and unsettling events in the nine months I spent as national secretary of SDS. I had been out on the road for a couple of weeks, and during that time passed my 30th birthday. When I came back to the office, comrades younger than myself needed to assert their youthfulness in the face of my coming middle age with something resembling guerrilla theater. In rummaging through my desk, they discovered an old passport photo of me from 1961, when I was leaving to go to Europe. I was dressed in a very straight suit, tie, and very short hair. I looked for all the world like what I was at the time, an Ivy League graduate student in history. They put next to it a picture from the *New York Times* of this rather scruffy looking, very tired, but younger looking person—myself.

They wrote underneath it, "The good guerrilla in our society must know how to change his identity in order to fit all new situations."

CHAPTER 10

The Splintering of SDS

The strains that had been building up within SDS finally brought about a series of rifts in the summer of 1969. Two major groupings emerged: the Revolutionary Youth Movement (RYM) and the Worker-Student Alliance (WSA), which was supported by the Progressive Labor Party. In a tumultuous convention at the Chicago Coliseum in July, the two factions split apart, bitterly denouncing each other. Each declared their own organization to be the real SDS. Within a short time, RYM itself divided into new factions: RYM I, better known as "Weatherman," and RYM II; in New York a third short-lived faction formed, RYM I-B, known as the "Mad Dogs." (Another faction, the New York-based SDS Labor Committee, had already been expelled from SDS the previous winter.) Other factions sprouted on the West Coast.

In addition to these groups, which had all belonged to SDS during the "resistance" period, there were a host of other movement tendencies. The "movement press," tried to stand above the conflict, but soon was drawn in. (Within a year the *Guardian,* a weekly paper, split into two rival newspapers.) Old Left organizations, like the Young Socialist Alliance, continued to function. The YSA gained power through the Student Mobilization Committee to End the War in Vietnam (Student Mobe), a national group with chapters on many campuses. Among the cultural revolutionaries, various "collectives" and "communes" formed, each with its own perspective. It was a diversity not unworthy of a pluralist society.

The documents in this section cannot do justice to all the nuances within the left at the end of the sixties. However, they should give some idea of the various tendencies which emerged from the student movement.

One of the most ambitious attempts on the left at a complete analysis of American society was the Weatherman statement written for the SDS National Convention in July of 1969. (The title "You don't need a weatherman to know which way the wind blows" was taken from a song by Bob Dylan.) Though repudiated by nearly every other leftist group, the statement represents the cumulative effort of several years of development and provides some insight into many of the actions taken before the ideas were systematically formulated.

The Weathermen stated their aims, and the ways in which they expected to attain them, with perfect clarity: "The goal is the destruction of US imperialism and the achievement of a classless world: world communism. Winning state power in the US will occur as a result of the military forces of the US overextending themselves around the world and being defeated piecemeal; struggle within the US will be a vital part of this process, but when the revolution triumphs in the US, it will have been made by the people of the whole world."

What distinguished the Weatherman statement from more traditional Marxist writing was the absolute primacy it placed on the Black movement. The Blacks could "win self-determination, abolishing the whole imperialist system and seizing state power to do it" without the help of whites, the Weathermen declared, though they added that white radicals must support the Black struggle. Another distinguishing feature of Weatherman was the tendency to regard American imperialism as being in the "short-term interests" of the working class, an assertion that was to provoke intense criticism from other leftist groups. The Weatherman statement also explained the reasoning behind the revolutionary youth movement strategy and set out a program for high school organizing and attacks on the police. Finally, it recommended the establishment of "revolutionary collectives" throughout the country and the formation of a clandestine Marxist-Leninist party "with discipline under one centralized leadership." *

By the end of August, RYM had split, with the author of the original RYM proposal, Mike Klonsky, forming a separate group (RYM II). Klonsky accused the Weatherman leadership headed by Mark Rudd of failing to communicate with working-class people. According to Klonsky, the Weathermen neglected the issue of the Vietnam War and rejected "struggles for democratic rights" by saying that such struggles only increased the " 'privilege' of the workers." This view was shared by Carl Davidson, who also accused the Weathermen of adventurism and said they had made several essential mistakes in Marxist-Leninist theory.

Unlike Weatherman, the Worker-Student Alliance retained some interest in campus protest during the fall of 1969. Its primary goal was to organize student support for university employees. WSA denounced Weatherman as a "group of police agents and hate-the-people lunatics."

Although the RYM factions and WSA were the most conspicuous remnants of SDS, the majority of students who had formerly belonged to the organization did not join any of the new factions. On many campuses, SDS activity almost disappeared. The sentiments of the disaffected and the discouraged were reflected in an article in *Liberation* by Carl Oglesby, an early president of SDS. Reviewing the development of the radical movement during the sixties, he was clearly unhappy over SDS's reversion to a Marxist-Leninist world view. Oglesby rejected much of the Weatherman position and concluded, "We are not now free to fight the Revolution except in fantasy. This is not a limit we can presently transcend; it is set by the over-all situation, and it will only be lifted by a real breakdown within the system of production."

* In the course of the next year, Weatherman did indeed become a clandestine organization with a centralized leadership (the Weather bureau), but it was no orthodox Marxist-Leninist party. Both drug culture and gay liberation were integrated into its politics, which were accurately reflected in the Weatherman slogan, "Revolutionaries are freaks, freaks are revolutionaries." After a conference and purge at Flint, Michigan, in December 1969, Weatherman divided into underground cells which undertook bombings in major American cities in order to "take a direct toll on the mother country" and to create "political space" for Black revolutionaries. The first casualties were three Weathermen—Ted Gold, Terry Robbins and Diana Oughton—killed in a New York City townhouse allegedly when their explosives accidentally detonated.

Statement prepared for the SDS National Convention, June 1969, submitted by Karin Ashley, Bill Ayers, Bernardine Dohrn, John Jacobs, Jeff Jones, Gerry Long, Howie Machtinger, Jim Mellen, Terry Robbins, Mark Rudd, and Steve Tappis. (Unabridged from text in New Left Notes, *June 18, 1969.)*

You Don't Need a Weatherman to Know Which Way the Wind Blows

1. INTERNATIONAL REVOLUTION

> "The contradiction between the revolutionary peoples of Asia, Africa and Latin America and the imperialists headed by the United States is the principal contradiction in the contemporary world. The development of this contradiction is promoting the struggle of the people of the whole world against US imperialism and its lackeys."
>
> —Lin Piao, *Long Live the Victory of People's War!*

People ask, what is the nature of the revolution that we talk about? Who will it be made by, and for, and what are its goals and strategy?

The overriding consideration in answering these questions is that the main struggle going on in the world today is between US imperialism and the national liberation struggles against it. This is essential in defining political matters in the whole world: because it is by far the most powerful, every other empire and petty dictator is in the long run dependent on US imperialism, which has unified, allied with, and defended all of the reactionary forces of the whole world. Thus, in considering every other force or phenomenon, from Soviet imperialism or Israeli imperialism to "workers struggle" in France or Czechoslovakia, we determine who are our friends and who are our enemies according to whether they help US imperialism or fight to defeat it.

So the very first question people in this country must ask in considering the question of revolution is where they stand in relation to the United States as an oppressor nation, and where they stand in relation to the masses of people throughout the world whom US imperialism is oppressing.

The primary task of revolutionary struggle is to solve this principal contradiction on the side of the people of the world. It is the oppressed peoples of the world who have created the wealth of this empire and it is to them that it belongs; the goal of the revolutionary struggle must be the control and use of this wealth in the interests of the oppressed peoples of the world.

It is in this context that we must examine the revolutionary struggles in the United States. We are within the heartland of a world-wide monster, a country so rich from its world-wide plunder that even the crumbs doled out to the enslaved masses within its borders provide for material existence very much above the conditions of the masses of people of the world. The US empire, as a world-wide system, channels wealth, based upon the labor and resources of the rest of the world, into the United States. The relative affluence existing in the United States is directly dependent upon the labor and natural resources of the Vietnamese, the Angolans, the Bolivians and the rest of the peoples of the Third World. All of the United Airlines Astrojets, all of the Holiday Inns, all of Hertz's automobiles, your television set, car and wardrobe already belong, to a large degree, to the people of the rest of the world.

Therefore, any conception of "socialist revolution" simply in terms of the working people of the United States, failing to recognize the full scope of interests of the most oppressed peoples of the world, is a conception of a fight for a particular privileged interest, and is a very dangerous ideology. While the control and use of the wealth of the Empire for the people of the whole world is also in the interests of the vast majority of the people in this country, if the goal is not clear from the start we will further the preservation of class society, oppression, war, genocide, and the complete emiseration of everyone, including the people of the US.

The goal is the destruction of US imperialism and the achievement of a classless world: world communism. Winning state power in the US will occur as a result of the military forces of the US overextending themselves around the world and being defeated piecemeal; struggle within the US will be a vital part of this process, but when the revolution triumphs in the US it will have been made by the people of the whole world. For socialism to be defined in national terms within so extreme and historical an oppressor nation as this is only imperialist national chauvinism on the part of the "movement."

II. WHAT IS THE BLACK COLONY?

Not every colony of people oppressed by imperialism lies outside the boundaries of the US. Black people within North America, brought here 400 years ago as slaves and whose labor, as slaves, built this country, are an internal colony within the confines of the oppressor nation. What this means is that black people are oppressed as a whole people, in the institutions and social relations of the country, apart from simply the consideration of their class position, income, skill, etc., as individuals. What does this colony look like? What is the basis for its common oppression and why is it important?

One historically important position has been that the black colony only consists of the "black belt nation" in the south, whose fight for national liberation is based on a common land, culture, history and economic life. The corollary of this position is that black people in the rest of the country are a national minority but not actually part of the colony themselves; so the struggle for national liberation is for the black belt, and not all blacks; black people in the north, not actually part of the colony, are part of the working class of the white oppressor nation. In this formulation northern black workers have a "dual role"—one an interest in supporting the struggle in the South, and opposing racism, as members of the national minority, and as northern "white nation" workers whose class interest is in integrated socialism in the north. The consistent version of this line actually calls for integrated organizing of black and white workers in the north along what it calls "class" lines.

This position is wrong; in reality, the black colony does not exist simply as the "black belt nation," but exists in the country as a whole. The common oppression of black people and the common culture growing out of that history are not based historically or currently on their relation to the territory of the black belt, even though that has been a place of population concentration and has some very different characteristics than the north, particularly around the land question.

Rather, the common features of oppression, history and culture which unify black people as a colony (although originating historically in a common territory apart from the colonizers, i.e. Africa, not the South) have been based historically on their common position as slaves, which since the nominal abolition of slavery has taken the form of caste oppression, and oppression of black people as a people everywhere that they exist. A new black nation, different from the nations of Africa from which it came, has been forged by the common historical experience of importation and slavery and caste oppression; to claim that to be a nation it must of necessity now be based on a common national territory apart from the colonizing nation is a mechanical application of criteria which were and are applicable to different situations.

What is specifically meant by the term caste is that all black people, on the basis of their common slave history, common culture and skin color are systematically denied access to particular job categories (or positions within job categories), social position etc., regardless of individual skills, talents, money or education. Within the working class, they are the most oppressed section; in the petite bourgeoisie, they are even more strictly confined to the lowest levels. Token exceptions aside, the specific content of this caste oppression is to maintain black people in the most exploitative and oppressive jobs and conditions. Therefore, since the lowest class is the working class, the black caste is almost entirely a caste of the working class, or positions as oppressed as the lower working-class positions (poor black petite bourgeoisie and farmers); it is a colonial labor caste, a colony whose common national character itself is defined by their common class position.

Thus, northern blacks do not have a "dual interest"—as blacks on the one hand and "US-nation workers" on the other. They have a single class interest, along with all other black people in the US, as members of the Black Proletarian Colony.

III. THE STRUGGLE FOR SOCIALIST SELF-DETERMINATION

The struggle of black people—as a colony—is for self-determination, freedom, and liberation from US imperialism. Because blacks have been oppressed and held in an inferior social position as a people, they have a right to decide, organize and act on their common destiny as a people apart from white interference. Black self-determination does not simply apply to determination of their collective political destiny at some future time. It is directly tied to the fact that because all blacks experience oppression in a form that no whites do, no whites are in a position to fully understand

and test from their own practice the real situation black people face and the necessary response to it. This is why it is necessary for black people to organize separately and determine their actions separately at each stage of the struggle.

It is important to understand the implications of this. It is not legitimate for whites to organizationally intervene in differences among revolutionary black nationalists. It would be arrogant for us to attack any black organization that defends black people and opposes imperialism in practice. But it is necessary to develop a correct understanding of the Black Liberation struggle within our own organization, where an incorrect one will further racist practice in our relations with the black movement.

In the history of some external colonies, such as China and Vietnam, the struggle for self-determination has had two stages: (1) a united front against imperialism and for New Democracy (which is a joint dictatorship of anti-colonial classes led by the proletariat, the content of which is a compromise between the interests of the proletariat and nationalist peasants, petite bourgeoisie and national bourgeoisie); and (2) developing out of the new democratic stage, socialism.

However, the black liberation struggle in this country will have only one "stage"; the struggle for self-determination will embody within it the struggle for socialism.

As Huey P. Newton has said, "In order to be a revolutionary nationalist, you would of necessity have to be a socialist." This is because—given the caste quality of oppression-as-a-people-through-a-common-degree-of-exploitation—self-determination requires being free from white capitalist exploitation in the form of inferior (lower caste) jobs, housing, schools, hospitals, prices. In addition, only what was or became in practice a socialist program for self-determination—one which addressed itself to reversing this exploitation—could win the necessary active mass support in the "proletarian colony."

The program of a united front for new democracy, on the other hand, would not be as thorough, and so would not win as active and determined support from the black masses. The only reason for having such a front would be where the independent petit bourgeois forces which it would bring in would add enough strength to balance the weakening of proletarian backing. This is not the case: first, because much of the black petite bourgeoisie is actually a "comprador" petite bourgeoisie (like so-called black capitalists who are promoted by the power structure to seem independent but are really agents of white monopoly capital), who would never fight as a class for any real self-determination; and secondly, because many black petite bourgeoisie, perhaps most, while not having a class interest in socialist self-determination, are close enough to the black masses in the oppression and limitations on their conditions that they will support many kinds of self-determination issues, and, especially when the movement is winning, can be won to support full (socialist) self-determination. For the black movement to work to maximize this support from the petite bourgeoisie is correct; but it is in no way a united front where it is clear that the Black Liberation Movement should not and does not modify the revolutionary socialist content of its stand to win that support.

IV. BLACK LIBERATION MEANS REVOLUTION

What is the relationship of the struggle for black self-determination to the whole world-wide revolution to defeat US imperialism and internationalize its resources toward the goal of creating a classless world?

No black self-determination could be won which would not result in a victory for the international revolution as a whole. The black proletarian colony, being dispersed as such a large and exploited section of the work force, is essential to the survival of imperialism. Thus, even if the black liberation movement chose to try to attain self-determination in the form of a separate country (a legitimate part of the right to self-determination), existing side by side with the US, imperialism could not survive if they won it —and so would never give up without being defeated. Thus, a revolutionary nationalist movement could not win without destroying the state power of the imperialists; and it is for this reason that the black liberation movement, as a revolutionary nationalist movement for self-determination, is automatically in and of itself an inseparable part of the whole revolutionary struggle against US imperialism and for international socialism.

However, the fact that black liberation depends on winning the whole revolution does not mean that it depends on waiting for and joining with a mass white movement to do it. The genocidal oppression of black people must be ended, and does not allow any leisure time to wait; if necessary, black people could win self-determination, abolishing the whole imperialist system and seizing state power to do it, without this white movement, although the cost among whites and blacks both would be high.

Blacks could do it alone if necessary because of their centralness to the system, economically and geo-militarily, and because of the level of unity, commitment, and initiative which will be developed in waging a people's war for survival and national liberation. However, we do not expect that they will have to do it alone, not only because of the international situation, but also because the real interests of masses of oppressed whites in this country lie with the Black Liberation struggle, and the conditions for understanding and fighting for these interests grows with the deepening of the crises. Already, the black liberation movement has carried with it an upsurge of revolutionary consciousness among white youth; and while there are no guarantees, we can expect that this will extend and deepen among all oppressed whites.

To put aside the possibility of blacks winning alone leads to the racist position that blacks should wait for whites and are dependent on whites acting for them to win. Yet the possibility of blacks winning alone cannot in the least be a justification for whites failing to shoulder the burden of developing a revolutionary movement among whites. If the first error is racism by holding back black liberation, this would be equally racist by leaving blacks isolated to take on the whole fight—and the whole cost—for everyone.

It is necessary to defeat both racist tendencies: (1) that blacks shouldn't go ahead with making the revolution, and (2) that blacks should go ahead alone with making it. The only third path is to build a white movement which will support the blacks in moving as fast as they have to and are able to, and still itself keep up with that black movement enough so that white revolutionaries share the cost and the blacks don't have to do the whole thing alone. Any white who does not follow this third path is objectively following one of the other two (or both) and is objectively racist.

V. ANTI-IMPERIALIST REVOLUTION AND THE UNITED FRONT

Since the strategy for defeating imperialism in semi-feudal colonies has two stages, the new democratic stage of a united front to throw out imperialism and then the socialist stage, some people suggest two stages for the US too—one to stop imperialism, the anti-imperialist stage, and another to achieve the dictatorship of the proletariat, the socialist stage. It is no accident that even the proponents of this idea can't tell you what it means. In reality, imperialism is a predatory international stage of capitalism. Defeating imperialism within the US couldn't possibly have the content, which it could in a semi-feudal country, of replacing imperialism with capitalism or new democracy; when imperialism is defeated in the US, it will be replaced by socialism—nothing else. One revolution, one replacement process, one seizure of state power—the anti-imperialist revolution and the socialist revolution, one and the same stage. To talk of this as two separate stages, the struggle to overthrow imperialism and the struggle for socialist revolution, is as crazy as if Marx had talked about the proletarian socialist revolution as a revolution of two stages, one the overthrow of capitalist state power, and second the establishment of socialist state power.

Along with no two stages, there is no united front with the petite bourgeoisie, because its interests as a class aren't for replacing imperialism with socialism. As far as people within this country are concerned, the international war against imperialism is the same task as the socialist revolution, for one overthrow of power here. There is no "united front" for socialism here.

One reason people have considered the "united front" idea is the fear that if we were talking about a one-stage socialist revolution we would fail to organize maximum possible support among people, like some petite bourgeoisie, who would fight imperialism on a particular issue, but weren't for revolution. When the petite bourgeoisie's interest is for fighting imperialism on a particular issue, but not for overthrowing it and replacing it with socialism, it is still contributing to revolution to that extent—not to some intermediate thing which is not imperialism and not socialism. Someone not for revolution is not for actually defeating imperialism either, but we still can and should unite with them on particular issues. But this is not a united front (and we should not put forth some joint "united front" line with them to the exclusion of our own politics), because their class position isn't against imperialism as a system. In China, or Vietnam, the petite bourgeoisie's class interests could be for actually winning against imperialism; this was because their task was driving it out, not overthrowing its whole existence. For us here, "throwing it out" means not from one colony, but all of them, throwing it out of the world, the same thing as overthrowing it.

VI. INTERNATIONAL STRATEGY AND THE BLACK VANGUARD

What is the strategy of this international revolutionary movement? What are the strategic weaknesses of the imperialists which make it possible for us to win? Revolutionaries around the world are in general agreement on the answer, which Lin Piao describes in the following way:

> "US imperialism is stronger, but also more vulnerable, than any imperialism of the past. It sets itself against the people of the whole world, including the people of the United States. Its human, military, material and financial resources are far from sufficient for the realization of its ambition of domination over the whole world. US imperialism has further weakened itself by occupying so many places in the world, overreaching itself, stretching its fingers out wide and dispersing its strength, with its rear so far away and its supply lines so long."
>
> —Lin Piao, *Long Live the Victory of People's War!* p. 122

The strategy which flows from this is what Che called "creating two, three, many Vietnams"—to mobilize the struggle so sharply in so many places that the imperialists cannot possibly deal with it all. Since it is essential to their interests, they will try to deal with it all, and will be defeated and destroyed in the process.

In defining and implementing this strategy, it is clear that the vanguard (that is, the section of the people who are in the forefront of the struggle and whose class interests and needs define the terms and tasks of the revolution) of the "American Revolution" is the workers and oppressed peoples of the colonies of Asia, Africa and Latin America. Because of the level of special oppression of black people as a colony they reflect the interests of the oppressed people of the world from within the borders of the United States; they are part of the Third World and part of the international revolutionary vanguard.

The vanguard role of the Vietnamese and other Third World countries in defeating US imperialism has been clear to our movement for some time. What has not been so clear is the vanguard role black people have played, and continue to play, in the development of revolutionary consciousness and struggle within the United States. Criticisms of the black liberation struggle as being "reactionary" or of black organizations on campus as being conservative or "racist" very often express this lack of understanding. These ideas are incorrect and must be defeated if a revolutionary movement is going to be built among whites.

The black colony, due to its particular nature as a slave colony, never adopted a chauvinist identification with America as an imperialist power, either politically or culturally. Moreover, the history of black people in America has consistently been one of the greatest overall repudiation of and struggle against the state. From the slave ships from Africa to the slave revolts, the Civil War, etc., black people have been waging a struggle for survival and liberation. In the history of our own movement this has also been the case: the civil rights struggles, initiated and led by blacks in the South; the rebellions beginning with Harlem in 1964 and Watts in 1965 through Detroit and Newark in 1967; the campus struggles at all-black schools in the south and struggles led by blacks on campuses all across the country. As it is the blacks—along with the Vietnamese and other Third World people—who are most oppressed by US imperialism, their class interests are most solidly and resolutely committed to waging revolutionary struggle through to its completion. Therefore it is no surprise that time and again, in both political content and level of consciousness and militancy, it has been the black liberation movement which has upped the ante and defined the terms of the struggle.

What is the relationship of this "black vanguard" to the "many Vietnams" around the world? Obviously it is an example of our strategy that different fronts reinforce each other. The fact that the Vietnamese are winning weakens the enemy, advancing the possibilities for the black struggle, etc. But it is important for us to understand that the interrelationship is more than this. Black people do not simply "choose" to intensify their struggle because they want to help the Vietnamese, or because they see that Vietnam heightens the possibilities for struggle here. The existence of any one Vietnam, especially a winning one, spurs on others not only through consciousness and choice, but through need, because it is a political and economic, as well as military, weakening of capitalism, and this means that to compensate, the imperialists are forced to intensify their oppression of other people.

Thus the loss of China and Cuba and the loss now of Vietnam not only encourages other oppressed peoples (such as the blacks) by showing what the alternative is and that it can be won, but also costs the imperialists billions of dollars which they then have to take out of the oppression of these other peoples. Within this country increased oppression falls heavier on the most oppressed sections of the population, so that the condition of all workers is worsened through rising taxes, inflation and the fall of real wages, and speedup. But this increased oppression falls heaviest on the most oppressed, such as poor white workers and, especially, the blacks, for example through the collapse of state services like schools, hospitals, and welfare, which naturally hits the hardest at those most dependent on them.

This deterioration pushes people to fight harder to even try to maintain their present level. The more the ruling class is hurt in Vietnam, the harder people will be pushed to rebel and to fight for reforms. Because there exist successful models of revolution in Cuba, Vietnam, etc., these reform struggles will provide a continually larger and stronger base for revolutionary ideas. Because it needs to maximize profits by denying the reforms, and is aware that these conditions and reform struggles will therefore lead to revolutionary consciousness, the ruling class will see it more and more necessary to come down on any motion at all, even where it is not yet highly organized or conscious. It will come down faster on black people, because their oppression is increasing fastest, and this makes their rebellion most thorough and most dangerous, and fastest growing. It is because of this that the vanguard character and role of the black liberation struggle will be increased and intensified, rather than being increasingly equal to and merged into the situation and rebellion of oppressed white working people and youth. The crises of imperialism (the existence of Vietnam and especially that it's winning) will therefore create a "black Vietnam" within the US.

Given that black self-determination would mean fully crushing the power of the imperialists, this "Vietnam" has certain different characteristics than the external colonial wars. The imperialists will never "get out of the US" until their total strength and every resource they can bring to bear has been smashed; so the Black Vietnam cannot win without bringing the whole thing down and winning for everyone. This means that this war of liberation will be the most protracted and hardest fought of all.

It is in this context that the question of the South must be dealt with again, not as a question of whether or not the black nation, black colony, exists there, as opposed to in the north as well, but rather as a practical question of strategy and tactics: Can the black liberation struggle—the struggle of all blacks in the country—gain advantage in the actual war of liberation by concentrating on building base areas in the South in territory with a concentration of black population?

This is very clearly a different question than that of "where the colony is," and to this question the "yes" answer is an important possibility. If the best potential for struggle in the South were realized, it is fully conceivable and legitimate that the struggle there could take on the character of a fight for separation; and any victories won in that direction would be important gains for the national liberation of the colony as a whole. However, because the colony is dispersed over the whole country, and not just located in the black belt, winning still means the power and liberation of blacks in the whole country.

Thus, even the winning of separate independence in the South would still be one step toward self-determination, and not equivalent to winning it; which, because of the economic position of the colony as a whole, would still require overthrowing the state power of the imperialists, taking over production and the whole economy and power, etc.

VII: THE REVOLUTIONARY YOUTH MOVEMENT: CLASS ANALYSIS

The revolutionary youth movement program was hailed as a transition strategy, which explained a lot of our past work and pointed to new directions for our movement. But as a transition to what? What was our overall strategy? Was the youth movement strategy just an organizational strategy because SDS is an organization of youth and we can move best with other young people?

We have pointed to the vanguard nature of the black struggle in this country as part of the international struggle against American imperialism, and the impossibility of anything but an internatonal strategy for winning. Any attempt to put forth a strategy which, despite internationalist rhetoric, assumes a purely internal development to the class struggle in this country, is incorrect. The Vietnamese (and the Uruguayans and the Rhodesians) and the blacks and Third World peoples in this country will continue to set the terms for class struggle in America.

In this context, why an emphasis on youth? Why should young people be willing to fight on the side of Third World peoples? Before dealing with this question about youth, however, there follows a brief sketch of the main class categories in the white mother country which we think are important, and indicate our present estimation of their respective class interests (bearing in mind that the potential for various sections to understand and fight for the revolution will vary according to more than just their real class interests).

Most of the population is of the working class, by which we mean not simply industrial or production workers, nor those who are actually working, but the whole section of the population which doesn't own productive property and so lives off of the sale of its labor power. This is not a metaphysical category either in terms of its interests, the role it plays, or even who is in it, which very often is difficult to determine.

As a whole, the long-range interests of the non-colonial sections of the working class lie with overthrowing imperialism, with supporting self-determination for the oppressed nations (including the black colony), with supporting and fighting for international socialism. However, virtually all of the white working class also has short-range privileges from imperialism, which are not false privileges but very real ones which give them an edge of vested interest and tie them to a certain extent to the imperialists, especially when the latter are in a relatively prosperous phase. When the imperialists are losing their empire, on the other hand, these short-ranged privileged interests are seen to be temporary (even though the privileges may be relatively greater over the faster-increasing emiseration of the oppressed peoples). The long-range interests of workers in siding with the oppressed peoples are seen more clearly in the light of imperialism's impending defeat. Within the whole working class, the balance of anti-imperialist class interests with white mother country short-term privilege varies greatly.

First, the most oppressed sections of the mother country working class have interests most clearly and strongly anti-imperialist.

Who are the most oppressed sections of the working class? Millions of whites who have as oppressive material conditions as the blacks, or almost so: especially, poor southern white workers; the unemployed or semi-employed, or those employed at very low wages for long hours and bad conditions, who are non-unionized or have weak unions; and extending up to include much of unionized labor which has it a little better off but still is heavily oppressed and exploited. This category covers a wide range and includes the most oppressed sections not only of production and service workers, but also some secretaries, clerks, etc. Much of this category gets some relative privileges (i.e., benefits) from imperialism, which constitute some material basis for being racist or pro-imperialist; but overall it is itself directly and heavily oppressed, so that in addition to its long-range class interest on the side of the people of the world, its immediate situation also constitutes a strong basis for sharpening the struggle against the state and fighting through to revolution.

Secondly, there is the upper strata of the working class. This is also an extremely broad category, including the upper strata of unionized skilled workers and also most of the "new working class" of proletarianized or semi-proletarianized "intellect workers." There is no clearly marked dividing line between the previous section and this one; our conclusions in dealing with "questionable" strata will in any event have to come from more thorough analysis of particular situations. The long-range class interests of this strata, like the previous section of more oppressed workers, are for the revolution and against imperialism. However, it is characterized by a higher level of privilege relative to the oppressed colonies, including the blacks, and relative to more oppressed workers in the mother country; so that there is a strong material basis for racism and loyalty to the system. In a revolutionary situation, where the people's forces were on the offensive and the ruling class was clearly losing, most of this upper strata of the working class will be winnable to the revolution; while at least some sections of it will probably identify their interests with imperialism till the end and oppose the revolution (which parts do which will have to do with more variables than just the particular level of privilege). The further development of the situation will clarify where this section will go, although it is clear that either way we do not put any emphasis on reaching older employed workers from this strata at this time. The exception is where they are important to the black liberation struggle, the Third World, or the youth movement in particular situations, such as with teachers, hospital technicians, etc., in which cases we must fight particularly hard to organize them around a revolutionary line of full support for black liberation and the international revolution against US imperialism. This is crucial because the privilege of this section of the working class has provided and will provide a strong material basis for national chauvinist and social democratic ideology within the movement, such as anti-internationalist concepts, of "student power" and "workers control." Another consideration in understanding the interests of this segment is that, because of the way it developed and how its skills and its privileges were "earned over time," the differential between the position of youth and older workers is in many ways greater for this section than any other in the population. We should continue to see it as important to build the revolutionary youth movement among the youth of this strata.

Thirdly, there are "middle strata" who are not petite bourgeoisie, who may even technically be upper working class, but who are so privileged and tightly tied to imperialism through their job roles that they are agents of imperialism. This section includes management personnel, corporate lawyers, higher civil servants, and other government agents, army officers, etc. Because their job categories require and promote a close identification with the interests of the ruling class, these strata are enemies of the revolution.

Fourthly, and last among the categories we're going to deal with, is the petite bourgeoisie. This class is different from the middle level described above, in that it has an independent class interest which is opposed to both monopoly power and to socialism. The petite bourgeoisie consists of small capital—both business and farms—and self-employed tradesmen and professionals (many professionals work for monopoly capital, and are either the upper level of the working class or in the agents-of-imperialism category). The content of its independent class interests—anti-monopoly capital but for capitalism rather than socialism—gives it a political character of some opposition to "big government," like its increased spending and taxes and its totalitarian extension of its control into every aspect of life, and to "big labor," which is at this time itself part of the monopoly capitalist power structure. The direction which this opposition takes can be reactionary or reformist. At this time the reformist side of it is very much mitigated by the extent to which the independence of the petite bourgeoisie is being undermined. Increasingly, small businesses are becoming extensions of big ones, while professionals and self-employed tradesmen less and less sell their skills on their own terms and become regular employees of big firms. This tendency does not mean that the reformist aspect is not still present; it is, and there are various issues, like withdrawing from a losing imperialist war, where we could get support from them. On the question of imperialism as a system, however, their class interests are generally more for it than for overthrowing it, and it will be the deserters from their class who stay with us.

VIII. WHY A REVOLUTIONARY YOUTH MOVEMENT?

In terms of the above analysis, most young people in the US are part of the working class. Although not yet employed, young people whose parents sell their labor power for wages, and more important who themselves expect to do the same in the future—or go into the army or be unemployed—are undeniably members of the working class. Most kids are well aware of what class they are in, even though they may not be very scientific about it. So our analysis assumes from the beginning that youth struggles are, by and large, working class struggles. But why the focus now on the struggles of working class youth rather than on the working class as a whole?

The potential for revolutionary consciousness does not always correspond to ultimate class interest, particularly when imperialism is relatively prosperous and the movement is in an early stage. At this stage, we see working class youth as those most open to a revolutionary movement which sides with the struggles of Third World people: the following is an attempt to explain a strategic focus on youth for SDS.

In general, young people have less stake in a society (no family, fewer debts, etc.), are more open to new ideas (they have not been brainwashed for so long or so well), and are therefore more able and willing to move in a revolutionary direction. Specifically in America, young people have grown up experiencing the crises in imperialism. They have grown up along with a developing black liberation movement, with the liberation of Cuba, the fights for independence in Africa, and the war in Vietnam. Older people grew up during the fight against Fascism, during the cold war, the smashing of the trade unions, McCarthy, and a period during which real wages consistently rose—since 1965 disposable real income has decreased slightly, particularly in urban areas where inflation and increased taxation have bitten heavily into wages. This crisis in imperialism affects all parts of the society. America has had to militarize to protect and expand its Empire; hence the high draft calls and the creation of a standing army of three and a half million, an army which still has been unable to win in Vietnam. Further, the huge defense expenditures—required for the defense of the empire and at the same time a way of making increasing profits for the defense industries—have gone hand in hand with the urban crisis around welfare, the hospitals, the schools, housing, air, and water pollution. The State cannot provide the services it has been forced to assume responsibility for, and needs to increase taxes and to pay its growing debts while it cuts services and uses the pigs to repress protest. The private sector of the economy can't provide jobs, particularly unskilled jobs. The expansion of the defense and education industries by the State since World War II is in part an attempt to pick up the slack, though the inability to provide decent wages and working conditions for "public" jobs is more and more a problem.

As imperialism struggles to hold together this decaying social fabric, it inevitably resorts to brute force and authoritarian ideology. People, especially young people, more and more find themselves in the iron grip of authoritarian institutions. Reaction against the pigs or teachers in the schools, welfare pigs or the army is generalizable and extends beyond the particular repressive institution to the society and the State as a whole. The legitimacy of the State is called into question for the first time in at least 30 years, and the anti-authoritarianism which characterizes the youth rebellion turns into rejection of the State, a refusal to be socialized into American society. Kids used to try to beat the system from inside the army or from inside the schools; now they desert from the army and burn down the schools.

The crisis in imperialism has brought about a breakdown in bourgeois social forms, culture and ideology. The family falls apart, kids leave home, women begin to break out of traditional "female" and "mother" roles. There develops a "generation gap" and a "youth problem." Our heroes are no longer struggling businessmen, and we also begin to reject the ideal career of the professional and look to Mao, Che, the Panthers, the Third World, for our models, for motion. We reject the elitist, technocratic bullshit that tells us only experts can rule, and look instead to leadership from the people's war of the Vietnamese. Chuck Berry, Elvis, the Temptations brought us closer to the "people's culture" of Black America. The racist response to the civil rights movement revealed the depth of racism in America, as well as the impossibility of real change through American institutions. And the war against Vietnam is not "the heroic war against the Nazis"; it's the big lie, with napalm burning through everything we had heard this country stood for. Kids begin to ask questions: Where is the Free World? And who do the pigs protect at home?

The breakdown in bourgeois culture and concomitant anti-authoritarianism is fed by the crisis in imperialism, but also in turn feeds that crisis, exacerbates it so that people no longer merely want the plastic '50s restored, but glimpse an alternative (like inside the Columbia buildings) and begin to fight for it. We don't want teachers to be more kindly cops; we want to smash cops, and build a new life.

The contradictions of decaying imperialism fall hardest on youth in four distinct areas—the schools, jobs, the draft and the army, and the pigs and the courts. (A) In jail-like schools, kids are fed a mish-mash of racist, male chauvinist, anti-working class, anti-communist lies while being channeled into job and career paths set up according to the priorities of monopoly capital. At the same time, the State is becoming increasingly incapable of providing enough money to keep the schools going at all. (B) Youth unemployment is three times average unemployment. As more jobs are threatened by automation or the collapse of specific industries, unions act to secure jobs for those already employed. New people in the labor market can't find jobs, job stability is undermined (also because of increasing speed-up and more intolerable safety conditions) and people are less and less going to work in the same shop for 40 years. And, of course, when they do find jobs, young people get the worst ones and have the least seniority. (C) There are now two and a half million soldiers under thirty who are forced to police the world, kill and be killed in wars of imperialist domination. And (D) as a "youth problem" develops out of all this, the pigs and courts enforce curfews, set up pot busts, keep people off the streets, and repress any youth motion whatsoever.

In all of this, it is not that life in America is toughest for youth or that they are the most oppressed. Rather, it is that young people are hurt directly—and severely—by imperialism. And, in being less tightly tied to the system, they are more "pushed" to join the black liberation struggle against US imperialism. Among young people there is less of a material base for racism—they have no seniority, have not spent 20 years securing a skilled job (the white monopoly of which is increasingly challenged by the black liberation movement), and aren't just about to pay off a 25-year mortgage on a house which is valuable because it's located in a white neighborhood.

While these contradictions of imperialism fall hard on all youth, they fall hardest on the youth of the most oppressed (least privileged) sections of the working class. Clearly, these youth have the greatest material base for struggle. They are the ones who most often get drafted, who get the worst jobs if they get any, who are most abused by the various institutions of social control from the army to decaying schools, to the pigs and the courts. And their day-to-day existence indicates a potential for militancy and toughness. They are the people whom we can reach who at this stage are most ready to engage in militant revolutionary struggle.

The point of the revolutionary youth movement strategy is to move from a predominant student elite base to more oppressed (less privileged) working class youth as a way of deepening and expanding the revolutionary youth movement—not of giving up what we have gained, not giving up our old car for a new Dodge. This is part of a strategy to reach the entire working class to engage in struggle against imperialism; moving from more privileged sections of white working class youth to more oppressed sections to the entire working class as a whole, including importantly what has classically been called the industrial proletariat. But this should not be taken to mean that there is a magic moment, after we reach a certain percentage of the working class, when all of a sudden we become a working class movement. We are already that if we put forward internationalist proletarian politics. We also don't have to wait to become a revolutionary force. We must be a self-conscious revolutionary force from the beginning, not be a movement which takes issues to some mystical group—"THE PEOPLE"—who will make the revolution. We must be a revolutionary movement of people understanding the necessity to reach more people, all working people, as we make the revolution.

The above arguments make it clear that it is both important and possible to reach young people wherever they are—not only in the shops, but also in the schools, in the army, and in the streets—so as to recruit them to fight on the side of the oppressed peoples of the world. Young people will be part of the International Liberation Army. The necessity to build this International Liberation Army in America leads to certain priorities in practice for the revolutionary youth movement which we should begin to apply this summer.

IX. IMPERIALISM IS THE ISSUE

> "The Communists are distinguished from the other working class parties by this only: 1. In the national struggles of the proletariat of different countries, they point out and bring to the front the common interests of the entire proletariat, independently of all nationality. 2. In the various stages of development which the struggle of the working class against the bourgeoisie has to pass through, they always and everywhere represent the interests of the movement as a whole." (*Communist Manifesto*)

How do we reach youth; what kinds of struggles do we build; how do we make a revolution? What we have tried to lay out so far is the political content of the consciousness which we want to extend and develop as a mass consciousness: the necessity to build our power as part of the whole international revolution to smash the state power of the imperialists and build socialism. Besides consciousness of this task, we must involve masses of people in accomplishing it. Yet we are faced with a situation in which almost all of the people whose interests are served by these goals, and who should be, or even are, sympathetic to revolution, neither understand the specific tasks involved in making a revolution nor participate in accomplishing them. On the whole, people don't join revolutions just because revolutionaries tell them to. The oppression of the system affects people in particular ways, and the development of political consciousness and participation begins with particular problems, which turn into issues and struggles. We must transform people's everyday problems, and the issues and struggles growing out of them, into revolutionary consciousness, active and conscious opposition to racism and imperialism.

This is directly counterposed to assuming that struggles around immediate issues will lead naturally over time to struggle against imperialism. It has been argued that since people's oppression is due to imperialism and racism, then any struggle against immediate oppression is "objectively anti-imperialist," and the development of the fight against imperialism is a succession of fights for reforms. This error is classical economism.

A variant of this argument admits that this position is often wrong, but suggests that since imperialism is collapsing at this time, fights for reforms become "objectively anti-imperialist." At this stage of imperialism there obviously will be more and more struggles for the improvement of material conditions, but that is no guarantee of increasing internationalist proletarian consciousness.

On the one hand, if we, as revolutionaries, are capable of understanding the necessity to smash imperialism and build socialism, then the masses of people who we want to fight along with us are capable of that understanding. On the other hand, people are brainwashed and at present don't understand it; if revolution is not raised at every opportunity, then how can we expect people to see it in their interests, or to undertake the burdens of revolution? We need to make it clear from the very beginning that we are about revolution. But if we are so careful to avoid the dangers of reformism, how do we relate to particular reform struggles? We have to develop some sense of how to relate each particular issue to the revolution.

In every case, our aim is to raise anti-imperialist and anti-racist consciousness and tie the struggles of working class youth (and all working people) to the struggles of Third World people, rather than merely joining fights to improve material conditions even though these fights are certainly justified. This is not to say that we don't take immediate fights seriously, or fight hard in them, but that we are always up front with our politics, knowing that people in the course of struggle are open to a class line, ready to move beyond narrow self-interest.

It is in this sense that we point out that the particular issue is not the issue, is important insofar as it points to imperialism as an enemy that has to be destroyed. Imperialism is always the issue. Obviously, the issue cannot be a good illustration, or a powerful symbol, if it is not real to people, if it doesn't relate to the concrete oppression that imperialism causes. People have to be (and are being) hurt in some material way to understand the evils of imperialism, but what we must stress is the systematic nature of oppression and the way in which a single manifestation of imperialism makes clear its fundamental nature. At Columbia it was not the gym, in particular, which was important in the struggle, but the way in which the gym represented, to the people of Harlem and Columbia, Columbia's imperialist invasion of the black colony. Or at Berkeley, though people no doubt needed a park (as much, however, as many other things?), what made the struggle so important was that people, at all levels of militancy, consciously saw themselves attacking private property and the power of the state. And the Richmond Oil Strike was exciting because the militant fight for improvement of material conditions was part and parcel of an attack on international monopoly capital. The numbers and militancy of people mobilized for these struggles has consistently surprised the left, and pointed to the potential power of a class-conscious mass movement.

The masses will fight for socialism when they understand that reform fights, fights for improvement of material conditions, cannot be won under imperialism. With this understanding, revolutionaries should never put forth a line which fosters the illusion that imperialism will grant significant reforms. We must engage in struggles forthrightly as revolutionaries, so that it will be clear to anyone we help to win gains that the revolution rather than imperialism is responsible for them. This is one of the strengths of the Black Panther Party Breakfast for Children Program. It is "socialism in practice" by revolutionaries with the "practice" of armed self-defense and a "line" which stresses the necessity of overthrowing imperialism and seizing state power. Probably the American Friends Service Committee serves more children breakfast, but it is the symbolic value of the program in demonstrating what socialism will do for people which makes it worthwhile.

What does it mean to organize around racism and imperialism in specific struggles? In the high schools (and colleges) at this time, it means putting forth a mass line to close down the schools, rather than to reform them so that they can serve the people. The reason for this line is not that under capitalism the schools cannot serve the people, and therefore it is silly or illusory to demand that. Rather it is that kids are ready for the full scope of militant struggle, and already demonstrate a consciousness of imperialism, such that struggles for a people-serving school would not raise the level of their struggle to its highest possible point. Thus, to tell a kid in New York that imperialism tracks him and thereby oppresses him is often small potatoes compared to his consciousness that imperialism oppresses him by jailing him, pigs and all, and the only thing to do is break out and tear up the jail. And even where high school kids are not yet engaged in such sharp struggle, it is crucial not to build consciousness only around specific issues such as tracking or ROTC or racist teachers, but to use these issues to build toward the general consciousness that the schools should be shut down. It may be important to present a conception of what schools should or could be like (this would include the abolition of the distinction between mental and physical work), but not offer this total conception as really possible to fight for in any way but through revolution.

A mass line to close down the schools or colleges does not contradict demands for open admissions to college or any other good reform demand. Agitational demands for impossible, but reasonable, reforms are a good way to make a revolutionary point. The demand for open admissions by asserting the alternative to the present (school) system exposes its fundamental nature—that it is racist, class-based, and closed—pointing to the only possible solution to the present situation: "Shut it down!" The impossibility of real open admissions—all black and brown people admitted, no flunk-out, full scholarship, under present conditions—is the best reason (that the schools show no possibility for real reform) to shut the schools down. We should not throw away the pieces of victories we gain from these struggles, for any kind of more open admissions means that the school is closer to closing down (it costs the schools more, there are more militant blacks and browns making more and more fundamental demands on the schools, and so on). Thus our line in the schools, in terms of pushing any good reforms should be, "open them up and shut them down!"

The spread of black caucuses in the shops and other workplaces throughout the country is an extension of the black liberation struggle. These groups have raised and will continue to raise anti-racist issues to white workers in a sharper fashion than any whites ever have or could raise them. Blacks leading struggles against racism has made the issue unavoidable, as the black student movement leadership did for white students. At the same time these black groups have led fights which traditional trade-union leaders have consistently refused to lead—fights against speed-up and for safety (issues which have become considerably more serious in the last few years), forcing white workers, particularly the more oppressed, to choose in another way between allegiance to the white mother country and black leadership. As white mother country radicals we should try to be in shops, hospitals, and companies where there are black caucuses, perhaps organizing solidarity groups, but at any rate pushing the importance of the black liberation struggle to whites, handing out Free Huey literature, bringing guys out to Panther rallies, and so on. Just one white guy could play a crucial role in countering UAW counter-insurgency.

We also need to relate to workplaces where there is no black motion but where there are still many young white workers. In the shops the crisis in imperialism has come down around speed-up, safety, and wage squeeze—due to higher taxes and increased inflation, with the possibility of wage-price controls being instituted.

We must relate this exploitation back to imperialism. The best way to do this is probably not caucuses in the shops, but to take guys to city-wide demonstrations, Newsreels, even the latest administration building, to make the movement concrete to them and involve them in it. Further, we can effect consciousness and pick up people through agitational work at plants, train stops, etc., selling *Movements,* handing out leaflets about the war, the Panthers, the companies' holdings overseas or relations to defense industry, etc.

After the Richmond strike, people leafleted about demonstrations in support of the Curaçao Oil workers, Free Huey May Day, and People's Park.

SDS has not dealt in any adequate way with the women question; the resolution passed at Ann Arbor did not lead to much practice, nor has the need to fight male supremacy been given any programmatic direction within the RYM. As a result, we have a very limited understanding of the tie-up between imperialism and the women question, although we know that since World War II the differential between men's and women's wages has increased, and guess that the breakdown of the family is crucial to the women question. How do we organize women against racism and imperialism without submerging the principled revolutionary question of women's liberation? We have no real answer, but we recognize the real reactionary danger of women's groups that are not self-consciously revolutionary and anti-imperialist.

To become more relevant to the growing women's movement, SDS women should begin to see as a primary responsibility the self-conscious organizing of women. We will not be able to organize women unless we speak directly to their own oppression. This will become more and more critical as we work with more oppressed women. Women who are working and women who have families face male supremacy continuously in their day-to-day lives; that will have to be the starting point in their politicization. Women will never be able to undertake a full revolutionary role unless they break out of their woman's role. So a crucial task for revolutionaries is the creation of forms of organization in which women will be able to take on new and independent roles. Women's self-defense groups will be a step toward these organizational forms, as an effort to overcome women's isolation and build revolutionary self-reliance.

The cultural revolt of women against their "role" in imperialism (which is just beginning to happen in a mass way) should have the same sort of revolutionary potential that the RYM claimed for "youth culture." The role of the "wife-mother" is reactionary in most modern societies, and the disintegration of that role under imperialism should make women more sympathetic to revolution.

In all of our work we should try to formulate demands that not only reach out to more oppressed women, but ones which tie us to other ongoing struggles, in the way that a day-care center at U of C enabled us to tie the women's liberation struggle to the black liberation struggle.

There must be a strong revolutionary women's movement, for without one it will be impossible for women's liberation to be an important part of the revolution. Revolutionaries must be made to understand the full scope of women's oppression, and the necessity to smash male supremacy.

X. NEIGHBORHOOD-BASED CITY-WIDE YOUTH MOVEMENT

One way to make clear the nature of the system and our tasks working off of separate struggles is to tie them together with each other: to show that we're one "multi-issue" movement, not an alliance of high school and college students, or students and GI's, or youth and workers, or students and the black community. The way to do this is to build organic regional or subregional and city-wide movements, by regularly bringing people in one institution or area to fights going on on other fronts.

This works on two levels. Within a neighborhood, by bringing kids to different fights, and relating these fights to each other—high school stuff, colleges, housing, welfare, shops—we begin to build one neighborhood-based multi-issue movement off of them. Besides actions and demonstrations, we also pull different people together in day-to-day film showings, rallies, for speakers and study groups, etc. On a second level, we combine neighborhood "bases" into a city-wide or region-wide movement by doing the same kind of thing; concentrating our forces at whatever important struggles are going on and building more ongoing interrelationships off of that.

The importance of specifically neighborhood-based organizing is illustrated by our greatest failing in RYM practice so far—high school organizing. In most cities we don't know the kids who have been tearing up and burning down the schools. Our approach has been elitist, relating to often baseless city-wide groups by bringing them our line, or picking up kids with a false understanding of "politics" rather than those whose practice demonstrates their concrete anti-imperialist consciousness that schools are prisons. We've been unwilling to work continuously with high school kids as we did in building up college chapters. We will only reach the high school kids who are in motion by being in the schoolyards, hangouts and on the streets on an everyday basis. From a neighborhood base high school kids could be effectively tied in to struggles around other institutions and issues, and to the anti-imperialist movement as a whole.

We will try to involve neighborhood kids who aren't in high schools too; take them to anti-war or anti-racism fights, stuff in the schools, etc.; and at the same time reach out more broadly through newspapers, films, storefronts. Activists and cadres who are recruited in this work will help expand and deepen the movement in new neighborhoods and high schools. Mostly we will still be tied in to the college-based movement in the same area, be influencing its direction away from campus-oriented provincialism, be recruiting high school kids into it where it is real enough and be recruiting organizers out of it. In its most developed form, this neighborhood-based movement would be a kind of sub-region. In places where the movement wasn't so strong, this would be an important form for being close to kids in a day-to-day way and yet be relating heavily to a lot of issues and political fronts which the same kids are involved with.

The second level is combining these neighborhoods into city-wide and regional movements. This would mean doing the same thing—bringing people to other fights going on—only on a larger scale relating to various blow-ups and regional mobilizations. An example is how a lot of people from different places went to San Francisco State, the Richmond Oil Strike, and now Berkeley. The existence of this kind of cross-motion makes ongoing organizing in other places go faster and stronger, first by creating a pervasive politicization, and second by relating everything to the most militant and advanced struggles going on so that they influence and set the pace for a lot more people. Further, cities are a basic unit of organization of the whole society in a way that neighborhoods aren't. For example, one front where we should be doing stuff is the courts; they are mostly organized city-wide, not by smaller areas. The same for the city government itself. Schools where kids go are in different neighborhoods from where they live, especially colleges; the same for hospitals people go to, and where they work. As a practical question of staying with people we pick up, the need for a city-wide or area-wide kind of orientation is already felt in our movement.

Another failure of this year was making clear what the RYM meant for chapter members and students who weren't organizers about to leave their campus for a community college, high school, GI organizing, shops or neighborhoods. One thing it means for them is relating heavily to off-campus activities and struggles, as part of the city-wide motion. Not leaving the campus movement like people did for ERAP * stuff; rather, people still organized on

* Economic Research and Action Program.

the campus participating in off-campus struggles, the way they have in the past for national actions. Like the national actions, the city-wide ones will build the on-campus movement, not compete with it.

Because the movement will be defining itself in relation to many issues and groups, not just schools (and the war and racism as they hit at the schools), it will create a political context that non-students can relate to better, and be more useful to organizing among high school students, neighborhood kids, the mass of people. In the process, it will change the consciousness of the students too; if the issues are right and the movement fights them, people will develop a commitment to the struggle as a whole, and an understanding of the need to be revolutionaries rather than a "student movement." Building a revolutionary youth movement will depend on organizing in a lot of places where we haven't been, and just tying the student movement to other issues and struggles isn't a substitute for that. But given our limited resources we must also lead the on-campus motion into a RYM direction, and we can make great gains toward city-wide youth movements by doing it.

Three principles underlie this multi-issue, "cross-institutional" movement, on the neighborhood and city-wide levels, as to why it creates greater revolutionary consciousness and active participation in the revolution:

(1) Mixing different issues, struggles and groups demonstrates our analysis to people in a material way. We claim there is one system and so all these different problems have the same solution, revolution. If they are the same struggle in the end, we should make that clear from the beginning. On this basis we must aggressively smash the notion that there can be outside agitators on a question pertaining to the imperialists.

(2) "Relating to Motion": the struggle activity, the action, of the movement demonstrates our existence and strength to people in a material way. Seeing it happen, people give it more weight in their thinking. For the participants, involvement in struggle is the best education about the movement, the enemy and the class struggle. In a neighborhood or whole city the existence of some struggle is a catalyst for other struggles—it pushes people to see the movement as more important and urgent, and as an example and precedent makes it easier for them to follow. If the participants in a struggle are based in different institutions or parts of

the city, these effects are multiplied. Varied participation helps the movement be seen as political (wholly subversive) rather than as separate grievance fights. As people in one section of the movement fight beside and identify closer with other sections, the mutual catalytic effect of their struggles will be greater.

(3) We must build a movement oriented toward power. Revolution is a power struggle, and we must develop that understanding among people from the beginning. Pooling our resources area-wide and city-wide really does increase our power in particular fights, as well as push a mutual-aid-in-struggle consciousness.

XI. THE RYM AND THE PIGS

A major focus in our neighborhood and city-wide work is the pigs, because they tie together the various struggles around the state as the enemy, and thus point to the need for a movement oriented toward power to defeat it.

The pigs are the capitalist state, and as such define the limits of all political struggles; to the extent that a revolutionary struggle shows signs of success, they come in and mark the point it can't go beyond. In the early stages of struggle, the ruling class lets parents come down on high school kids, or jocks attack college chapters. When the struggle escalates the pigs come in; at Columbia, the left was afraid its struggle would be co-opted to anti-police brutality, cops off campus, and said pigs weren't the issue. But pigs really are the issue and people will understand this, one way or another. They can have a liberal understanding that pigs are sweaty working-class barbarians who over-react and commit "police brutality" and so shouldn't be on campus. Or they can understand pigs as the repressive imperialist state doing its job. Our job is not to avoid the issue of the pigs as "diverting" from anti-imperialist struggle, but to emphasize that they are our real enemy if we fight that struggle to win.

Even when there is no organized political struggle, the pigs come down on people in everyday life in enforcing capitalist property relations, bourgeois laws, and bourgeois morality; they guard stores and factories and the rich and enforce credit and rent against the poor. The overwhelming majority of arrests in America are for crimes against property. The pigs will be coming down on the kids we're working with in the schools, on the streets, around dope; we should focus on them, point them out all the time, like the Panthers do. We should relate the daily oppression by the pig to their role in political repression, and develop a class understanding of political power and armed force among the kids we're with.

As we develop a base these two aspects of the pig role increasingly come together. In the schools, pig is part of daily oppression—keeping order in halls and lunch rooms, controlling smoking—while at the same time pigs prevent kids from handing out leaflets, and bust "outside agitators." The presence of youth, or youth with long hair, becomes defined as organized political struggle and the pigs react to it as such. More and more everyday activity is politically threatening, so pigs are suddenly more in evidence; this in turn generates political organization and opposition, and so on. Our task will be to catalyze this development, pushing out the conflict with the pig so as to define every struggle—schools (pigs out, pig institutes out), welfare (invading pig-protected office), the streets (curfew and turf fights)—as a struggle against the needs of capitalism and the force of the state.

Pigs don't represent state power as an abstract principle; they are a power that we will have to overcome in the course of struggle or become irrelevant, revisionist, or dead. We must prepare concretely to meet their power because our job is to defeat the pigs and the army, and organize on that basis. Our beginnings should stress self-defense—building defense groups around karate classes, learning how to move on the street and around the neighborhood, medical training, popularizing and moving toward (according to necessity) armed self-defense, all the time honoring and putting forth the principle that "political power comes out of the barrel of a gun." These self-defense groups would initiate pig surveillance patrols, visits to the pig station and courts when someone is busted, etc.

Obviously the issues around the pig will not come down by neighborhood alone; it will take at least city-wide groups able to coordinate activities against a unified enemy—in the early stages, for legal and bail resources and turning people out for demonstrations, adding the power of the city-wide movement to what may be initially only a tenuous base in a neighborhood. Struggles in one part of the city will not only provide lessons for but materially aid similar motion in the rest of it.

Thus the pigs are ultimately the glue—the necessity—that holds the neighborhood-based and city-wide movement together; all of our concrete needs lead to pushing the pigs to the fore as a political focus:

(1) making institutionally oriented reform struggles deal with state power, by pushing out struggle till either winning or getting pigged.

(2) using the city-wide inter-relation of fights to raise the level of struggle and further large-scale anti-pig movement-power consciousness.

(3) developing spontaneous anti-pig consciousness in our neighborhoods to an understanding of imperialism, class struggle and the state.

(4) and using the city-wide movement as a platform for reinforcing and extending this politicization work, like by talking about getting together a city-wide neighborhood-based mutual aid anti-pig self-defense network.

All of this can be done through city-wide agitation and propaganda and picking certain issues—to have as the central regional focus for the whole movement.

XII. REPRESSION AND REVOLUTION

As institutional fights and anti-pig self-defense off of them intensify, so will the ruling class's repression. Their escalation of repression will inevitably continue according to how threatening the movement is to their power. Our task is not to avoid or end repression; that can always be done by pulling back, so we're not dangerous enough to require crushing. Sometimes it is correct to do that as a tactical retreat, to survive to fight again.

To defeat repression, however, is not to stop it but to go on building the movement to be more dangerous to them; in which case, defeated at one level, repression will escalate even more. To succeed in defending the movement, and not just ourselves at its expense, we will have to successively meet and overcome these greater and greater levels of repression.

To be winning will thus necessarily, as imperialism's lesser efforts fail, bring about a phase of all-out military repression. To survive and grow in the face of that will require more than a larger base of supporters; it will require the invincible strength of a mass base at a high level of active participation and consciousness, and can only come from mobilizing the self-conscious creativity, will and determination of the people.

Each new escalation of the struggle in response to new levels of repression, each protracted struggle around self-defense which becomes a material fighting force, are part of the international strategy of solidarity with Vietnam and the blacks, through opening up other fronts. They are anti-war, anti-imperialist and pro-black liberation. If they involve fighting the enemy, then these struggles are part of the revolution.

Therefore, clearly the organization and active conscious participating mass base needed to survive repression are also the same needed for winning the revolution. The Revolutionary Youth Movement speaks to the need for this kind of active mass-based movement by tying city-wide motion back to community youth bases, because this brings us close enough to kids in their day-to-day lives to organize their "maximum active participation" around enough different kinds of fights to push the "highest level of consciousness" about imperialism, the black vanguard, the state and the need for armed struggle.

XIII. THE NEED FOR A REVOLUTIONARY PARTY

The RYM must also lead to the effective organization needed to survive and to create another battlefield of the revolution. A revolution is a war; when the movement in this country can defend itself militarily against total repression it will be part of the revolutionary war.

This will require a cadre organization, effective secrecy, self-reliance among the cadres, and an integrated relationship with the active mass-based movement. To win a war with an enemy as highly organized and centralized as the imperialists will require a (clandestine) organization of revolutionaries, having also a unified "general staff"; that is, combined at some point with discipline under one centralized leadership. Because war is political, political tasks—the international communist revolution—must guide it. Therefore the centralized organization of revolutionaries must be a political organization as well as military, what is generally called a "Marxist-Leninist" party.

How will we accomplish the building of this kind of organization? It is clear that we couldn't somehow form such a party at this time, because the conditions for it do not exist in this country outside the black nation. What are these conditions?

One is that to have a unified centralized organization it is necessary to have a common revolutionary theory which explains, at least generally, the nature of our revolutionary tasks and how to accomplish them. It must be a set of ideas which have been tested and developed in the practice of resolving the important contradictions in our work.

A second condition is the existence of revolutionary leadership tested in practice. To have a centralized party under illegal and repressive conditions requires a centralized leadership, specific individuals with the understanding and the ability to unify and guide the movement in the face of new problems and be right most of the time.

Thirdly, and most important, there must be the same revolutionary mass base mentioned earlier, or (better) revolutionary mass movement. It is clear that without this there can't be the practical experience to know whether or not a theory, or a leader, is any good at all. Without practical revolutionary activity on a mass scale the party could not test and develop new ideas and draw conclusions with enough surety behind them to consistently base its survival on them. Especially, no revolutionary party could possibly survive without relying on the active support and participation of masses of people.

These conditions for the development of a revolutionary party in this country are the main "conditions" for winning. There are two kinds of tasks for us.

One is the organization of revolutionary collectives within the movement. Our theory must come from practice, but it can't be developed in isolation. Only a collective pooling of our experiences can develop a thorough understanding of the complex conditions in this country. In the same way, only our collective efforts toward a common plan can adequately test the ideas we develop. The development of revolutionary Marxist-Leninist-Maoist collective formations which undertake this concrete evaluation and application of the lessons of our work is not just the task of specialists or leaders, but the responsibility of every revolutionary. Just as a collective is necessary to sum up experiences and apply them locally, equally the collective inter-relationship of groups all over the country is necessary to get an accurate view of the whole movement and to apply that in the whole country. Over time, those collectives which prove themselves in practice to have the correct understanding (by the results they get) will contribute toward the creation of a unified revolutionary party.

The most important task for us toward making the revolution, and the work our collectives should engage in, is the creation of a mass revolutionary movement, without which a clandestine revolutionary party will be impossible. A revolutionary mass movement is different from the traditional revisionist mass base of "sympathizers." Rather it is akin to the Red Guard in China, based on the full participation and involvement of masses of people in the practice of making revolution; a movement with a full willingness to participate in the violent and illegal struggle. It is a movement diametrically opposed to the elitist idea that only leaders are smart enough or interested enough to accept full revolutionary conclusions. It is a movement built on the basis of faith in the masses of people.

The task of collectives is to create this kind of movement. (The party is not a substitute for it, and in fact is totally dependent on it.) This will be done at this stage principally among youth, through implementing the Revolutionary Youth Movement strategy discussed in this paper. It is practice at this, and not political "teachings" in the abstract, which will determine the relevance of the political collectives which are formed.

The strategy of the RYM for developing an active mass base, tying the city-wide fights to community and city-wide anti-pig movement, and for building a party eventually out of this motion, fits with the world strategy for winning the revolution, builds a movement oriented toward power, and will become one division of the International Liberation Army, while its battlefields are added to the many Vietnams which will dismember and dispose of US imperialism. Long Live the Victory of People's War!

From a series of articles by Carl Davidson, in the Guardian, *September–October 1969.*

Adventurism

". . . If it is a world-wide struggle, if Weatherman is correct in that basic thing, that the basic struggle in the world today is the struggle of the oppressed peoples against U.S. imperialism,

then it is the case that nothing we could do in the mother country could be adventurist. Nothing we could do because there is a war going on already, and the terms of that war are set."

—Bill Ayers, SDS Educational Secretary, in "A Strategy to Win," printed in the Sept. 12 issue of *New Left Notes.*

The Weathermen, current leading faction of SDS, have one saving grace: they are usually open about their politics. Because of that, any honest revolutionary reading Ayers' statement above will understand immediately that the SDS national office and a few regional offices are in the hands of a clique of "left" adventurists.

For only a "left" adventurist could say that there is no such thing as adventurism. And the quotation marks are put around "left" because adventurism is only a cover for what is in reality a bourgeois or petit-bourgeois political perspective.

Adventurism is not primarily a matter of militancy. Some people have incorrectly criticized the Weathermen for being "too militant," "too radical," or "too far left." Revolutionaries can't be too far left, since they should be all the way left, diametrically opposed to the bourgeoisie.

Adventurist errors are made when revolutionaries follow a line of action which isolates them from the people, shows their lack of confidence in the people, reveals their contempt for the people, and eventually leads them to substitute themselves for the people. In a tactical sense, adventurism is engaging people in a particular military battle or confrontation leading to certain defeat in the immediate situation.

But the Weathermen's errors go much deeper than any series of tactical mistakes they may have made. In terms of analysis, their most fundamental error can be found in their misunderstanding of the effects of imperialism on the working class of the imperialist countries.

In their basic document, "You Don't Need a Weatherman to Know Which Way the Wind Blows," they state the following: ". . . Virtually all of the white working class also has short-range privileges from imperialism, which are not false privileges but very real ones which give them an edge of vested interest and tie them to a certain extent to the imperialists, especially when the latter are in a relatively prosperous phase."

In other words, the mass of white workers and the monopoly capitalists have a real, common "national interest" in exploiting the oppressed nations. This has been the political line of the ruling class ever since the imperialist epoch began.

In arriving at this conclusion, the Weathermen revise several basic tenets of Marxist-Leninist theory.

First, they fail to make a distinction between the "labor aristocracy" or upper strata of highly skilled, privileged workers and labor officials and the mass of ordinary workers in the imperialist countries. Lenin put it this way: ". . . While trusts, the financial oligarchy, high prices, etc., *permit* [Lenin's italics] the bribing of small upper strata, they at the same time oppress, crush, ruin and torture the masses of the proletariat and semi-proletariat more than ever." ("Imperialism and the Split in the Socialist Movement.")

The second mistake is the view that the white-skin privilege, the relative advantages given white workers over blacks, is in the real class interests of white workers. Weathermen say these false privileges are in the real interest of whites because there are material benefits—such as better housing, higher pay, or more services than those received by blacks.

But this is only one side of a relative situation. The other side is this: it is in precisely those situations where the relative advantages of whites over blacks is the greatest that the over-all material conditions of all workers, including whites, are the worse—such as exist in the South.

Some, but not all, of these relative advantages are at the immediate expense of blacks. But none of them are in the real class interests of white workers, any more than the bait on a hook is in the interests of a fish—no matter how fat, juicy and "material" the worm might be.

The Weathermen try to get around this differentiating between the "short-range" and "long-range" interests of the white workers, with the "short-range" interests being held in common with the imperialists. This is a third mistake.

Actually, if a distinction is to be made, it should be between the class interests and solidarity of the workers as a whole and the fancied selfish "interests" of each worker as an individual. Naturally, any worker who looks out only for himself, or his or her own small group of friends and say to hell with the rest of the class will ultimately end up taking sides with the boss.

* * * * *

. . . Weathermen see almost all struggles for immediate reforms, whether for material needs or for equality and democratic rights, as struggles for "more privileges." While white workers and students in this country have fought to maintain and extend certain white privileges, no one, except the Weathermen and the ruling class, has maintained that these struggles served or met the needs of the people.

In fact, in relation to the student movement, Weathermen in the past have opposed the slogan, "the schools must serve the people" with the line "destroy the university." With that in mind, when black and brown students raise the demand for open admissions this year, it might be interesting to see which way the wind blows the Weathermen. . . .

From an article by Fred Gordon, SDS leader (Worker-Student Alliance), in New Left Notes *(WSA), September 20, 1969. Rights were granted by Students for A Democratic Society, 173-A Massachusetts Avenue, Boston, Massachusetts.*

Build the Campus Worker-Student Alliance

During the past few years, many SDSers have seen that a mass-based student movement that can fight imperialism and racism must ally with working people. Thus we developed the idea of worker-student alliance. Students (and the mental workers most become) *need* in fact to ally with working people. Both groups are oppressed by the same class, which owns the industries in which workers are fiercely exploited, and which controls the schools as well. In order to make a worker-student alliance possible, we've tried to develop a pro-working class student movement. Thus we've backed strikes, from telephone to transit to United Parcel, trying to involve many other students, raising our politics with the workers. We've supported welfare and other community struggles, fought the racist attitudes dividing white and Black workers. On campus, we've fought anti-working class ideas among our fellow students, tried to organize struggles in an explicitly pro-working class way. For example, we've come to see that students should fight ROTC because it trains officers for wars like Vietnam and for putting down Black rebellions and strikes in the US—that is, ROTC attacks working people. Other ways of fighting ROTC, aimed at "purifying the university," really build the students' anti-worker attitudes, and must be rejected.

The idea of a pro-working class student movement has been key in drastically changing SDS. Last fall, the old national leadership was able openly to write off workers as "reactionary, bought off," etc. These ideas are still around, but many SDSers have rejected them. We have seen that just building a student movement —*any* student movement—is not enough, that we need a mass student movement *that serves the people,* that serves working people here and all over the world. This understanding is no small gain.

But it's not enough. The purpose of a pro-working class student movement is to win students and mental workers to ally with other workers. But this strategy can't succeed unless, in practice, that alliance gets built. After a certain point, either you reach your goal or you stop running. It is impossible to build a pro-working class student movement indefinitely without more and more building actual alliances with workers.

This has been discussed a good deal over the summer, especially by roughly a thousand people involved in the SDS Work-In . . . How should we develop the alliance—what steps do we have to take?

A Real Alliance

The conclusion of many is that the best way to begin the transformation of SDS from an increasingly *pro-working class* movement to one in fact *allied with workers,* is to begin on campus. In a sense, the fact that we didn't realize this earlier is a serious criticism. In some places where this strategy was discussed, people thought there weren't any campus workers at their schools . . . it turned out there were "only" a few thousand. Supposedly trying to build a pro-working class movement, nevertheless our anti-working class attitudes led us to miss the exploitation going on on "our" own campuses!

The University as Boss

The universities are bosses, plain and simple, employing hundreds of thousands of workers. These people are terribly exploited—lousy pay and working conditions, no job security, student part-timers used to cut down the full-timers' pay, racist pay differentials and employment practices. Many have been fighting school administrations harder—and a lot longer—than SDS. Allying with these workers is very possible—and absolutely necessary, if we are serious about serving the people. . . .

Tactics

. . . Here are some tactical ideas on how we can proceed:

1. We should get jobs, now, in school cafeterias, libraries, hospitals, offices, print shops, as janitors, gardeners—everywhere. Find out the real situation from the workers. (Our limited experience shows that it's usually pretty horrendous and getting worse.) A related step is for those of us who've moved off campus to go back to the dorms. Being "radical" doesn't mean keeping away from the people. This means taking other students' problems more seriously and linking the struggles of campus workers to our fight against anti-working class and racist ideas among students. This will help us get to know dorm workers also.

2. As soon as possible, issue a pamphlet and/or leaflets exposing your particular school as a boss. Find out the history of your school as a boss and let people know that, as well as exposing the current situation.

3. Where workers are already engaged in organized struggle against the administration, we should organize mass support. Where they're not, chapters should study the situation and launch struggles against particular abuses.

4. Get to know the workers, discuss politics with them. Bringing the issue to students in a mass way (as discussed in point 3) will help show the full time workers we're serious. Our attitude should be humble, but not opportunist. That is, racist ideas, mistaken notions about the war, etc., should *always* be argued against. At the same time, we should remember that campus workers have been hurt a lot more by these things than we have. They understand the situation, in many ways, far better than we do. If you want to serve the people you have to learn from them.

Two things should be kept in mind in general. One is that fighting around campus worker-student alliance is often an excellent way to fight racism. Many campus workers are Black—often they have the most difficult jobs. Racist hiring, pay, and employment practices are used to squeeze more out of non-white workers as well as to build racism among whites. . . . Fighting the super-exploitation of non-white campus workers hits at the very roots of racism and helps expose the racist nature of the university as well as challenging the racist attitudes of white students and workers. (Our previous failure to organize such struggles in most places reflects our own racism!) Some of the biggest campus struggles of the last year grew out of campus worker-student alliances—for instance, at Duke and the University of North Carolina.

Second is that we can start *right now.* While many fights—for union recognition, overall changes in conditions, and wage raises—usually require the mass participation of campus workers, we can raise certains demands immediately, even if the workers aren't themselves already fighting openly around these questions. . . . Doing this is only possible if, by working side by side with full-timers, we learn examples of flagrant abuses. Initiating struggles around these grievances will help us develop really close ties with campus workers and begin to raise the issue of campus worker-student alliance in a mass way on campus.

Excerpts from a national press release of SDS (WSA), October 1969.

Provocateurs

On Wednesday, October 1, a group of provocateurs claiming to be from SDS attacked students and teachers at Boston English High School. The week before, this same gang had attacked campus workers at Harvard's Center for International Affairs. Similar incidents have occurred in other parts of the country. These actions were all the work of a group of police agents and hate-the-people lunatics who walked out of SDS at the June convention because their ideas had been rejected. No SDS chapter supports them!

The bankers and big businessmen who run the country are using this clique (led by Mark Rudd) for two purposes. First, to divert people so that they won't fight back anymore. Second, to discredit SDS and radical ideas in general.

This group's "Days of Rage" planned for Chicago, Oct. 8–11, is a police trap—no one should go to it. Their newspaper says "We're going to Chicago to fight anyone who plays pig." What they've done previously makes it clear that they plan on fighting anyone in sight! And they're building for this action saying that it won't be a success unless some are killed.

People will see through this trick. The big businessmen who run this country and who benefit from the war in Vietnam are responsible for the rotten conditions in the schools, in the cities, and on the job. SDS supports students', parents', and teachers' fights for better conditions in the schools; and SDS supports working people's struggles against their bosses. In general, we are trying to fight on the side of working people, not against them like Rudd's gang.

From an article by Carl Oglesby, former president of SDS, in Liberation, *August–September 1969.*

Notes on a Decade Ready for the Dustbin

The idea of trying to visualize ourselves five or ten years from now seems to me hopeless but necessary, so I'm writing a letter instead of a paper just because it seems easier in the former to float, stammer, and skip.

Hopeless—to put it most abstractly—because I don't think we have anything like a predictive science of political economy. We *approach* having an explanatory art of history, I think, and sometimes we can build up a head of steam-bound analogies and go crashing an inch or so through the future barrier, but it always turns out we land sideways or even upside down. And more practically, hopeless because in a situation as sensitive as what the world's in now, mankind as a whole lives under the permanent Terror of the Accidental.

But necessary, too, this idea, because even if we're never going to surpass improvisatory politics, we could still improvise better if we were clearer about ourselves and the country, and the effort to think about the future always turns out to be an effort to think about the present. Which is all to the good. So I'll start with the past—to get a sense of trajectory, if any, or the rhythm of our experience, to see if there's a line of flight:

1960–64

. . . . Whenever it began, this was the Heroic Period, the movement's Bronze Age. In transition ever since, the movement has yet to prove it will have a Classical Period, but maybe we're on the verge. Essentially, a single-issue reform politics; integration the leading public demand, although underneath that demand, there's a sharply rising sense that a structural maldistribution of wealth won't be corrected by the abolition of Jim Crow. An implicitly radical democratic communitarianism, projected correctly as both a means *and an end* of the movement, can still co-exist with a formless and rather annoyed liberalism because (a) the Peace People are obfuscating the Cold War without yet having become suspicious characters, and (b) the reform tide seems to be running, picking up velocity and mass, and has still to hit the breakwater. But there's a richness in the decentralist idioms of this period that has only been neglected, certainly not exhausted, or even barely tapped, in the intervening half decade of transition.

1965

Very quick, sharp changes, engineered in part by Johnson, in part by self-conscious growth within the movement.

• The war abruptly becomes the leading issue for most white radicals. But not for community organizers, some of whom in fact are bitter about the new preoccupation. This is neither the first nor the last time that this sort of friction develops. What is its general form? A nationalist vs. an internationalist consciousness? It appears that some activists will always tend to visualize the American people mainly as victims, and others will tend to see them as criminal accomplices (passive or not) of the ruling class. . . .

• The teach-ins and the SDS April March on Washington repeat in a compressed time scale the civil-rights movement's growth from Greensboro to Selma. It's in this very brief, very intense period that SDS projects an unabashedly reformist critique of the war, our naive attack on the domino theory being the best illustration of this: "But the other dominos *won't* fall," we insisted, happy to give such reassurance to the Empire.

• SNCC formalizes its transformation from reform to revolution, first, by explicating the connection between racism and the war; and second, by focusing the metaphor of Black Power, which clearly (at least to hindsight) implied the forthcoming ghetto-equals-colony analysis and the shift from an integrationist to a separatist-nationalist politics, which of course was to bring two problems for every one it solved. This shift seems to have been necessitated by the impasse which integrationism confronted at Atlantic City the previous year.

• What was the Atlantic City of the white student movement that was to go from pro-peace to anti-war, anti-war to pro-NLF, pro-NLF to anti-imperialist to pro-Third World revolution to anti-capitalism to pro-socialism—and thence, with much more confusion and uncertainty than this schedule implies, to anti-peace (i.e., no co-existence) and anti-democracy ("bourgeois jive"), and which finds itself at the present moment broken into two, three, many factions, each of which claims to have the *real* Lenin (or Mao or Che) in its pocket? Riddled with vanguarditis and galloping sectarianism, and possessed of a twisty hallucination called the "mass line" like an ancient virgin her incubus (or is it just a hot water bottle?) the Rudd-Jones-Ayers SDS is at least an SDS with a past. I'll say later what I think is wrong with the mass-line stance, but the point here is to understand that it didn't just come upon SDS out of nowhere, not even the nowhere of the PLP, and that in the end, whatever you think of it, it has to happen: (a) because there was no way to resist the truth of the war, no way, that is, to avoid imperialism; (b) because once the policy critique of the war had been supplanted by the structural critique of the empire, all political therapies short of socialist revolution appeared to become senseless; and (c) because the necessity of a revolutionary strategy was, in effect, the same thing as the necessity of Marxism-Leninism. *There was—and is—no other coherent, integrative, and explicit philosophy of revolution.*

I do not want to be misunderstood about this. The practical identity of Marxism-Leninism with revolutionary theory, in my estimate, does not mean that Marxism-Leninism is *also* identical with a genuinely revolutionary practice in the advanced countries. That identity, rather, constitutes nothing more than a tradition, a legacy, and a problem which I think the Left will have to overcome. But at the same time, I don't think the American Left's first stab at producing for itself a *fulfilled* revolutionary consciousness could have produced anything better, could have gone beyond this ancestor-worship politics. It was necessary to discover—or maybe the word is confess—that we had ancestors in the first place; and if for no brighter motive than gratitude at not being so alone and rootless, the discovery of the ancestors would naturally beget a religious mood. That of the revival tent, no doubt, but religious all the same. . . .

The main point here is that 1965 was the year in which both the black and white sectors of the movement explicitly abandoned reformism and took up that long march whose destination, not even in sight yet, is a theory and practice of revolution for the United States. For the West.

1966–67

The rise of the resistance (in all its variety) and experiments with a "new-working-class" analysis, both motions strongly influenced by Greg Calvert and Carl Davidson. Superficially, these developments seemed to be congruent and intersupportive. But it looks to me now as if they were in fact opposite responses to the general problem of conceiving and realizing a revolutionary strategy, each one being a kind of political bet which the other one hedged. There was, I know, a lot of heavy theorizing about the politics of resistance, and I don't want to turn a complex experience into a simple memory. Still, I think it's fair to take the slogans as being indicative of its political atmosphere—"Not with my life, you don't!" for example, or "A call to resist illegitimate authority." Even if only in embryo, I think "resistance" was at bottom a youth-based anti-fascist front whose most central demand must have appeared to any outsider's eye to be for a return to the *status quo ante.* That's not to say that its organizers were not radicals or that its inner content was anti-socialist or non-socialist. But in basing itself on the individual's rights of self-determination (mythical, of course: we were all hip to the con), and in trying to depict Johnson's as an impostor ("illegitimate") regime, the Resistance was easily as unassuming in its politics as it was extravagant in its imagination.

At the same time, Carl ("I Blush to Remember") Davidson, among others, was trying to work out a new-working-class concept of the student rebellion, the main purpose being to discover in this rebellion that revolutionary power which one feared it might not have. Wanting revolution (with all that implies about the power to make one) but only having spasms of campus rebellion, the student syndicalists needed to show that at least the seed of the first found fertile ground in the latter. . . .

1968

Confidence reappeared with Columbia and France, and then took an important turn with Chicago.

Columbia: (1) Conclusively, students have severely limited but formidable power to intervene in certain processes of oppression and to compel certain institutional reforms. (2) A practical alliance between blacks and whites became a concrete fact for the first time since Selma. The campus continues to be the main current locus of this alliance. (I say this, obviously, in view of Columbia's subsequence: Columbia's innovations proved repeatable elsewhere.) (3) Production relations constitute the life of class economy; distribution relations constitute the life of class society; consumption relations constitute the life of class politics. The stormed or barricaded factory gate of classical revolutionary vision is not the definitive image of any "final" or "pure" proletarian consciousness. The struggle at the point of production, when it occurs, is merely one expression of a more general struggle which, much more often than not, is ignited and fed by consciousness of inequities of consumption. . . . In fact, it's much more often a failure in the distributive or consumptive functions that creates political trouble for capitalism. How to finance further expansion? How to empty these bursting warehouses? And it could even be argued that as between the ghetto rising and the militant strike in heavy industry, the former is closer to that famous "seizure of State power" than the latter is. But why try to choose at all? We are dealing here only with aspects of a unitary complex, not with elements of a compound, and the tendencies of a method of analysis to reproduce reality as a set of correlative abstractions should never be permitted to reduce aspects of a continuous social process to the elements of its model. What happened at Columbia/Harlem in the spring of '68 is just as important, just as pregnant and portentous, as what happened in Haymarket Square—but at the same time, *no more important either*. . . .

A few other points about Columbia: (4) "Co-optation" is obviously a useful concept. It warns you against being hoodwinked by those who've learned to smile and smile and still be villains. Unfortunately, just beyond that point at which it remains useful, it flops over completely and becomes disastrous: it can become a no-win concept masquerading either as tactical cunning or strategic wisdom. It instructs people to reject what their fight has made possible on the grounds that it falls short of what they wanted. If the Left allows its provisional victories to be reaped by the Center-Left, trust that those victories will very promptly be turned into most unprovisional setbacks. Am I saying that we should sometimes have people "working within the system's institutions?" Precisely, emphatically, and without the slightest hesitation! You are co-opted when the adversary puts his goals on your power; you are *not* co-opted when your power allows you to exploit his means (or contradictions) in behalf of your goals.

(5) The SF State strike retrospectively clarified one difficulty, maybe a shortcoming, of the Columbia strike. Other BSU-SDS-type eruptions suffered from the same lapse. Namely: *We very badly need a clear, sharp formulation of the white interest in overcoming racism.* All of us feel that this "white-skin-privilege"—if it is even a privilege at all—costs us something, and that the cost exceeds the gain. Yet we've had difficulty making it clear why we feel this way, and for the most part in the hurry of the moment have simply had to abandon the attempt, opting either for a purely moralistic explanation (which has meant that the white base of the strike is not represented in the strike leadership committee) or for the adding on of "white demands" (which tended to obscure the specifically anti-racist character of the action). Neither approach is any good. It is wrong for the base of the movement, any action, not to have a voice in tactical and strategic policy—witness, for one thing, the general bewilderment of the white SF State students who, when the strike was over, had little to do but return to business-as-usual classrooms. It is also wrong, or at least not quite right, for whites to demand "open admissions for all working-class youth" at the same time that the same whites are (a) trying to help make a point about the *racist* nature of colleges, and (b) attacking the *content* of the basic college education on the grounds that it's a brainwash. The German SDS idea of the critical university, somehow adapted to our particular political objectives, might break through the current dilemma at the level of program. But especially since the dilemma may shortly materialize in noncampus settings, it's first necessary to break it at a theoretical or general level. Why does racism hurt whites? Or *which* whites does it hurt, and why and how?

France, the May Days: "The revolt of the students is the revolt of the forces of modern production as a whole," writes Andre

Glucksmann, a leading theoretician of the March 22 Movement. This intriguing formulation, like all new-working-class theorizing, is at bottom nothing but an attempt to find a new face for the old Leninist mask: Only "workers" can make 20th Century revolutions, so those who are creating a big revolution-sized fuss, even if they come outfitted with a few electrifying Sartrean neologisms, must therefore be some new kind of workers. I think this souped-up "New Left" scholasticism is worse than the Old Orthodoxy. Any common-sensical reading of the Glucksmann map would lead the revolution-watcher straight to the faculties of administration, technology and applied sciences, since it's within the meanings of the New Technology that these "forces of modern production as a whole" are being visualized. Maybe at Nanterre, where the fuse was lit. But certainly not at the Sorbonne or anywhere else in Paris, where the student base of the revolt, just as in the United States, came out of the faculties of liberal arts and the social sciences. Quite contrary to Glucksmann, the revolt of the students is the revolt *against* the forces of modern production as a whole—a fact which would doubtless be apparent to everyone if it weren't for the intellectual tyranny of Marxism-Leninism. . . .

The main fact about the Almost-Revolution is that it was *almost* a revolution, not that it was almost a *revolution.* As parched for victories as the Western Left has been in the post-war period, it may be forgiven its ecstasy at scoring a few runs. But what are we left with? No questions, Pompidou is not the only or the main or even a very important result of the May Days; as a minimum, the feudalism of the French academy has been jolted, and maybe it's still a big deal in the 7th decade of the 20th century to give academic feudalism a jolt. But it seems to me that all the lessons people are claiming to have learned are not lessons at all, only so many brute-force misreadings of the event. To claim that the student *foco* was a worker "detonator" is to dodge the awful question of the vanguard, not to face it and overcome it, and besides that, it tortures a meaning into "student" that has nothing to do with the students' evident meanings. On the other hand, the claim that the old problem of the "worker-student alliance" has found here the possibility of its solution seems to me the very opposite of what the facts indicate: Under propitious, even ideal circumstances, with the State isolated and virtually dumb before the crisis, with DeGaulle offering nothing more spiritual than an old man's resentment or more concrete than a diluted form of the students' program, with the army out-flanked politically and the police widely disgraced, with production mired in fiscal doldrums, the industrial workforce caught with a deep unease and its bureaucratized leadership dozing, it still proved hard for students and young workers to make contact, and (so it now seems) all but impossible for them to forge a lasting and organic revolutionary union. . . .

Chicago: (1) Liberalism has no power in this country. It is not politically organized. The few secondary institutions in which it lives its hand-to-mouth existence are, at best, nothing more than insecure and defenseless sanctuaries. In none of the estates—not the church, not the media, not the schools—does it exhibit the least aggressiveness, the least staying power, the least confidence. *This country, in the current situation, is absolutely impotent before the threat of what Fulbright has lately called "elective fascism".* . . .

(2) If only because it sharpens the melodrama, we may as well pinpoint Chicago, August, as the place and time of the "mass line's" formal debut: an unforgettable lit-up nighttime scene, Mike Klonsky taking the bullhorn at Grant Park to harangue the assembly about its "reformist" politics.

I've already indicated that I see nothing promising in *any* version of Marxism-Leninism—not PL's, not that of the now-defunct "national collective" of the Klonsky-Coleman period or of its apparent successor, the Revolutionary Union, and not that of the more diffuse and momentarily hazier grouping, the Revolutionary Youth Movement. But of course I don't claim that a mere statement of this view constitutes either an explanation of it or an argument for it. The argument will have to be made, very carefully, in another place, and I have to confine myself here to the observation that any revolutionary movement will all but inevitably adapt itself to Marxism-Leninism—or the other way around—because there is just no other totalizing philosophy of revolution. This philosophy then enables a representation of reality in something like the following general terms: "A desire in pursuit of its means, a means in flight from its destiny—these conditions constitute The Problem. Solution: tomorrow, when history's preplanted timebomb at last goes off, blasting false consciousness away, the words of the prophets will be fulfilled."

Chicago, in any case, occasioned these two terminal moments: the humiliation of liberalism, and the "official" reversion of SDS to a Marxist-Leninist worldview.

1969

The leading events so far: The SF State strike and the structurally similar conflicts that erupted across the country, the People's Park showdown in June, the SDS convention, and the Black Panther call for the Oakland conference.

San Francisco State: I want to make just two observations on this much-studied event.

First, the movement's characteristic attitude toward partial victories—more particularly, toward what is disparaged as "student power"—is mechanistic. It appears that every change which is not yet The Revolution is either to be airily written off as no change at all, or further than that, to be denounced as co-optation into the counter-revolution. People should only try to remember that the SF State strike did not materialize out of thin air, that it had a background, that it was that particular moment's culmination of a long conflictual process, and that just as with Columbia, where political work had been sustained at a generally intense level at least since May 1965, the explosive strike at State was made possible, maybe even necessary, by a long series of small moves forward, any one of which could have been attacked as "bourgeois liberal reform." More precisely, it was in large part those incremental "reforms" of curriculum and student-teacher and teacher-administration relationships carried out under the unseeing eyes of President Summerskill that created the general conditions in which the strike could take place. As with Columbia, the atmosphere had long been thoroughly politicized—that is to say, charged with consciousness of national issues. And a long reign of liberalism had, in effect, already *legitimated* the demands around which the strike was fought through, just as a long reign of reformism had created the institutional means of the strike. In the same way, the fact that the Third World Liberation Front leadership did after all negotiate the "nonnegotiable" demands, the further fact that this leadership then moved *to consolidate these bargaining-table victories within the changing structure of the institution itself*—this meant not that the fight was over, not at all that "capitalism" had suffered a tactical defeat only to secure a strategic victory, but rather that the stage was—and is—being set for another round of conflict at a still higher level of consciousness within a still wider circle of social involvement. For the net result of the strike's victories is still further to break down the psychological, social, and political walls that had formerly sealed off the academy from the community. This is a big part of what we are about—the levelling of all these towers, the redistribution of all this ivory, the extroversion of these sublimely introverted corporate monstrosities: and not just because we have willed it, whether out of malice or chagrin or a blazing sense of justice, but rather because capital itself, in all its imperial majesty, has invested these schools with its own trembling contradictions. . . .

. . . Thc winning of a "reform" isn't always a bad business, and Leftists should stop being scared of being reformed out of things to do. The only real strategic necessity is to make sure the reform in question reforms the power configuration so that it becomes the basis for further and still more fundamental challenges to class rule.

. . . The formula attack on the making of demands for such things as curriculum reform and greater student participation in campus government goes like this: "The young bourgeois, privileged already, exhibits here only his desire to extend his privileges still further. This desire must be fought by radicals. If not exactly in the *name* of the working class, we must see ourselves as fighting at least in its *behalf*, and since its interests are hardly served by the abolition of grades or the reduction of required credits, we must oppose such demands."

First, the outlines of a speculation. What if the multiversity is in some substantial part the creation of the advanced-world proletariat—not merely the plaything and mistress of the imperialists? What if it is partly in the multiversity that the proletariat has banked and stored up its enormous achievements in technology? What if the multiversity—the highest realization yet of the idea of mass education and the rationalization of productive labor—is in one of its leading aspects the institutional form through which the proletariat continues its struggle for emancipation? Behind how many of these so-called "bourgeois" children, one or two generations back, stands a father in a blue collar, a mother in an apron? The proletariat, says Marx, will have to prepare itself for self-government through protracted struggle. What if this struggle is so protracted that it actually must be seen as taking place, in one of its aspects at least, across *generations?* The revolutionary aspiration of whites in the 1930's manifested itself most sharply in factory struggles. In the 1960's, that aspiration has materialized most sharply on the campuses. What have we made of this fact? The function of a method of social analysis is not to reprimand reality for diverging from its model, but on the contrary to discover in reality the links and conjunctures that make history intelligible and life accessible to effective action. An abstraction is not something to stand behind like a pulpit but a lens to see through more discerningly. Obvious? Then it is high time to confess: At the same time that it has been trying so desperately to live forwards, the New Left everywhere, in West Europe as well as here, has been just as desperately trying to think backwards. If Marxism is any good, and if we can prove it worthy of the moment, then we ought to be able to say what it is about contemporary relations of production that makes the campuses a primary site of contemporary revolutionary motion. Only when that question is answered will we have any right to pontificate about "correct" and "incorrect" lines, and it has not yet been answered. Meanwhile, even if it is good and sufficient, as I am almost sure it is not, to characterize "student power" as a fight for "bourgeois privilege," we would still have to ask: What *kind* of privilege? Assuming that there is nothing here at all but an intra-class struggle against the contemptuous indifference of institutions, against the mindless blather of the dons, the deans, the sycophants and the liars, against authority in particular and authoritarianism on principle, we would still have to say that the political balance of this struggle is *progressive and portentous.* To those who tell me that this fight neither equals, approximates, initiates, nor reveals the form of The Revolution Itself, I answer first, Neither did Nanterre, neither did Watts, neither did anything else in man's social history but a bare handful of uniquely definitive and epochal convulsions, each one of which moreover appeared only at the end of a painfully long train of indeterminate events which escaped their ambiguity only thanks to the denouement; and I answer second, If you are trying to tell me you know already what The Revolution Itself will look like, you are either a charlatan or a fool. *We have no scenario.*

Second, for what it's worth to a movement suddenly infatuated with the words of the prophets, Lenin faced a somewhat similar question in 1908 when certain radicals refused to support an all-Russia student strike on the grounds that "the platform of the strike is an academic one" which "cannot unite the students for an active struggle on a broad front." Lenin objected: "Such an argument is radically wrong. The revolutionary slogan—to work towards coordinated political action of the students and the proletariat—here ceases to be a live guidance for many-sided militant agitation on a broadening base and becomes a lifeless dogma, mechanically applied to different stages of different forms of the movement." Further: "For this youth, a strike on a large scale . . . is the beginning of a political conflict, whether those engaged in the fight realize it or not. Our job is to explain to the mass of 'academic' protesters the objective meaning of the conflict, to try and make it *consciously* political."

The People's Park: Those few SDSers, unfortunately conspicuous this past year, who think Stalinism is more or less right on, ought at least to have admitted that "socialism in one country" is not exactly the logical antithesis of "socialism in one park." But it was the Stalinists, both pure and off-breed, who among all the Bay Area radicals found it hardest to relate to the park before the attacks, were most puzzled by the attack itself, and produced the most opportunistic "support" in the aftermath. Mainly because these curious rumbles of the hip are so hard to focus politically in terms of a mass-and-vanguard model, it's hard for people with old minds to figure out how to relate to them. That fact may be the basis of a touching epitaph; but a living politics for our period will have to understand that "decadence" is as "decadence" does, that the "cultural revolution" is not merely a craven and self-serving substitute for the "political" one, and that if the West has, indeed, a leftwards destiny, then neither its particular ends nor its modes of organization and action will be discovered through archeology. My guess: People's Park was one among many episodes of a religious revival movement—exactly the kind of movement that has heralded every major social convulsion in the United States—and as with all such movements, its ulterior target, its enemy, is the forces of the industrialization of culture. The difference now is that the virtual consummation of the Industrial Revolution, *within the West,* lends a credibility and relevance to such a program that it formerly has not had. That is: The anti-industrialism of early radicals like Blake and Cobbett, though it was fully anti-capitalist, could confront rampant capitalist industrial progress with nothing more powerful than a retiring, improbably, defenseless nostalgia; could argue against the system of "masters and slaves" only in behalf of the older and no doubt mythical system, allegedly medieval, of "masters and men." Every time it became a *practical* movement—whether revolutionary or reformist

—socialism had to put forward simply a more rational version of the program of industrialization itself. This is not an irony or tragedy of history, it's just the dialectics of historical process. That it has so far been unsurpassable is in fact the essence of revolutionary socialism's general isolation to the backwards countries, or put differently, this limit merely expresses the wedding of revolutionary socialism to anti-colonialism, and on the other hand, its impotence in countries in which the industrialization process has been carried forward effectively (however ruthlessly) by the bourgeoisie. The thesis of People's Park, rough as it may be to deal with both in terms of our tradition and our current practical needs, is that the essentially *post-industrial* revolution, embodied most fully but still (we must suppose) very incompletely in the hip communities, portends the historically most advanced development for socialist consciousness.

"Most fully" because it goes beyond industrialization, and in doing so, implies (much more than it has so far realized) a genuinely New Man—just as new compared to Industrial Man as Industrial Man was new in comparison to the artisans and small farmers who foreran him.

But it would be useless just to approve of this cultural revolution without being very clear about its terrible limits. I see two limits. First: The "new values" (they are, of course, very old) can claim to be subversive only of the standing values of work, but not really of consumption, there being nothing in the structure and precious little in the texture of "hip leisure" that keeps it from being commercially copied (deflated) and packaged. Thus, in effect, the target of the attack detaches itself, refuses to defend itself, and in offering itself as the apparent *medium* of the attack is able (persuasively to all but the sharpest consciousness) to pose as the "revolution's" friend. There are a thousand examples of this process, whose minimum result is vastly to complicate the cultural critique, and which at the other limit succeeds wholly in disarming it. The quietism of which the hip community is often accused may thus be much less the result of a principled retreat to cosmology than of its flat inability to confront commercialism with a deeply nonnegotiable demand.

Second, even though the new anarchism is morally cosmopolitan—affirming in a rudimentary political way the essential oneness of the human community—its values are *practical* only within the Western (imperalist) cities, and are far from being universally practical even there. So the second and bigger problem the cultural revolution needs to overcome is its lack of a concrete means of realizing its ideal sympathy with those globally rural revolutionary movements whose social program necessarily centers around the need for industrialization, not the surpassing of it. A solution of this problem would no doubt also solve the first. This is why it's so important to subject the cultural revolution to a much more profound and critical analysis than what has been produced so far. For the point at the moment is not to be for or against the current reappearance of anarchism. It will be necessary rather to explicate its tradition (too many hippies think they are saying brand new things) and then to try to see if the balance of forces has changed sufficiently that this old movement for a cultural revolution against industrial society has begun to acquire a power which it formerly has not had. . . .

Yesterday's *New York Times* carries a full-page political ad—the American Institute of Architects, it seems, has come out against the war. What will the Panther or the SDS national office do? Send a wire? Make a phone call? Investigate the possibility of a combined action? Try to make two or three new friends in order to make a hundred or a thousand later. I guess not. For the AIA is as *bourgeois* as they come, awfully *liberal,* too. When even the Oakland 7 and the Chicago 8 are suspect, what chance does a lot of architects have? So the architects will never hear what we have to say about the empire, about the houses that are being built in Cuba, about what we take to be the extent and causes of the present world crisis.

But this loss is presumably compensated by our clarity about the "vanguard." Clarity! Any close reading of the RYM's Weatherman statement will drive you blind. Sometimes the vanguard is the black ghetto community, sometimes only the Panthers, sometimes the Third World as a whole, sometimes only the Vietnamese, and sometimes apparently only the Lao Dong Party. Sometimes it is a curiously Hegelian concept, referring vaguely to all earthly manifestations of the spirit of revolution. At still other times, it seems to be the fateful organ of that radicalized industrial proletariat (USA) which has yet to make its Cold War-era debut. Mostly, though, it's the poor Panthers, whose want of politics was never challenged by the few SDSers who had access to their leaders; this appointment—Vanguard to the People's Revolution—being, presumably, SDS's to make—and one which is defended, moreover, in terms of a so-called revolutionary strategy (see the Weatherman statement) in which the United States is to experience not a social revolution at the hands of its own people, but a military defeat at the hands of twenty, thirty, many Vietnams—plus a few Detroits.

But perhaps the ghetto-colony analysis means that the Detroits are already included in the category of Vietnams? In that case, for all real political purposes, (North) American-white; and the historic role of these whites, their "mission" in the many-sided fight for socialism, is most basically just to be overcome. The authors of the Weatherman statement are of course perfectly right in trying to integrate what may appear to be *decisive* international factors into a model scenario of domestic change. From no viewpoint can an empire be treated as if it were a nation state. But although they face this problem, they do not overcome it. They might have said that the leading aspect of the US industrial proletariat remains, classically, its exploitation at the hands of US capital, and that it therefore still embodies a momentarily stifled revolutionary potential. Contrarily, they might have said that what we have here is a giganticized "labor aristocracy who are quite philistine in their mode of life, in the size of their earnings and in their outlook . . . [and who are] real channels of reformism and chauvinism" (Lenin, *Imperialism: The Highest Stage of Capitalism*). On its face, neither view is silly, but neither is one more satisfactory than the other. Weatherman's refusal to settle for one or the other seems to me to express a realistic *intuition;* but the problem is not solved simply by asserting one theory here and the other theory there. They cannot both be equally valid. I think the difficulty is embedded in the method of analysis: Weatherman takes class to be a thing rather than a process, and consequently tries to treat class as if it were, in and of itself, *a definite political category.* (That is, labor is fated to be Left.) But Weatherman also has a certain level of historical realism, and this realism always intervenes (happily) to obstruct the mostly theoretical impulse—a kind of social Freudianism—to idealize labor, to strip it of its historical "neurosis" by the simple and fraudulent expedient of viewing its neurosis as *merely* superstructural. In other words, Weatherman's confusions and ambiguities stem from a conflict between its model and its data, and it comes close to escaping this dilemma only when it forgets its static model of class for a moment, and gives freer rein to its sense of history and process. At such moments, it comes close to saying something really important, which I would paraphrase, over-optimistically no doubt thus: "The labor force we are looking at today is not the one we'll see tomorrow, and the changes it will undergo have everything to do with the totality of its current and forthcoming experiences, which range all the way from the increasingly sensed contradiction between the rhetoric of affluence and the fact of hardship to the blood and money sacrifices it will be asked to offer in the empire's behalf." But this ought to be said up front, and it then ought to lead to the most exhaustive analysis of the real, living forces that impinge upon not just labor but the population as a whole. Everytime something like this starts to happen, Weatherman breaks off and reverts to its concealed paradox: the vanguard of the US (Western would be better) revolution will be those forces which most aggressively array themselves *against* the US, those forces, in other words, which are most *distant* from white culture. Thus, *cause becomes agency:* the living proof of a *need* for change—the Panthers, the NLF, etc.—is defined as the political *means* of change; an almost absent-minded abstraction converts white America's sickness into the remedy itself.

The most succinct case of this kind of bad reasoning I've heard came at the end of a speech Bob Avakian made at the Austin NC. The racism of white workers would have to be broken, he said, because, when the revolution comes, it will be led by blacks, whose leadership whites must therefore be prepared to accept. If this were only an unconsidered trifle, it would be pointless to snap it up, but it appears to represent a serious, persistent, and growing school of thought in the New Left. The problem with it is just that it implies that there could be a revolution in the absence of a profound radicalization of the white working class, in the absence of profound changes in the political character of that class. What would make it possible for white workers to revolt would also make it possible—and necessary—for white workers to help *lead* that revolt. The very idea of a white working class revolution against capitalism, that is, necessarily *presupposes* either that racism will have been overcome or at least that the conditions for that triumph will have been firmly established. The problem with this dreamed-of revolution will not be anti-blackism within its ranks, but the anti-communism of its adversary. "In revolution, there are no whites or blacks, only reds."

But beyond this, Avakian (as with the Weathermen) wants it

both ways: blacks are a colony, on the one hand, outside the colonizing political economy and set over against it; and on the other hand, they are in and of the empire's proletariat. In the first mode, they press against the empire from a position which is outside it in every sense but the geographical. In the second mode, they press upwards against the bourgeoisie from within capital's system of social classes. It is of course not impossible that these modes really do coexist and interpenetrate one another. In fact, it is likely that they do. But both modes cannot be represented as simultaneously co-leading aspects of the black situation *vis-à-vis* white society. A white revolutionary strategy requires a decision as to which aspect is dominant and which secondary, *as well as an understanding that what is dominant now may become secondary later, may even disappear.*

So—an attempt at a clarification (which, as with certain other points I've tried to make in this letter, I'll have to elaborate and defend in some other, more ample space):

1. The persistence of integrationism, in a dozen disguises, and nationalism's struggle against it, make a strong circumstantial case for the view that blacks are above all blacks. They are not just another part of the workforce, not even just the main body of the lumpenproletariat. Nor do they make up a *caste.* Industrial societies do not have, cannot afford, castes; castes belong to precapitalist formations (or, at latest, to agrarian capitalism) and are in fact destroyed by the imperatives of industrial organization.

Obviously, blacks are assigned an important role in the US production-consumption process. So were pre-revolutionary Cubans. So are contemporary Venezuelans. The low-skill aspect of black production and the importance of the credit and welfare systems in black consumption constitute, in themselves, the leading features of a *colonial* relation to a colonizing political economy. It is therefore appropriate to see the black ghetto as a colony. Thus, *true* black nationalism (much "nationalist" rhetoric is merely a Hallowe'en mask for integrationist or even *comprador* demands) is necessarily anti-imperalist, and could consummate whatever military or political victories it might achieve in the independence struggle only through a socialist development of the means of production.

2. No more than the struggle of the Vietnamese can the struggle of the blacks play a "vanguard" role in the problematic revolution of white America. *Vietnam and Detroit, the NLF and the Pan-*

thers, do not constitute the means of white America's liberation from imperalist capital. They constitute, rather, the necessity of that liberation. They exist for white America as the living embodiment of problems which white America must solve. There are, obviously, many other such problems: the draft, high taxes, inflation, the whole array of ecological and environmental maladies, Big Brotherism at all levels of government, the general and advanced hypertrophy of the State, the fractionalizing of the civil society. Most of these problems are relatively diffuse; they are not experienced so acutely as the war or the ghetto risings. But they are still real to people, and they all have the same general source in the hegemony of capitalism: What sets Vietnam aflame is the same force that brutalizes the black population and poisons everybody's air.

3. The function of the white Western socialist is therefore, at this moment, to confront white America (white France, etc.) with the truth about the problems that harass it, to explain that these problems cannot be solved merely by repressing those people in whose lives the problems are embodied, cannot be solved by prayer or petition, and above all that they cannot be solved so long as the means of production, the wealth of that production, and the monopoly of political power that goes with those means and that wealth are locked up in the hands of the big bourgeoisie. You would as wisely ask the bullet to sew up the wound it made as ask the monopoly capitalist to solve these problems. The capitalist cannot do it. But the socialist can. That is the point we have to make.

4. The rebellion of white students is provoked most fundamentally by the general *extrinsic* failure of capitalist production—by the fact, that is, that production has become so conspicuously anti-social. This is what gives the student rebellion both its power and its very real limits. But this extrinsic collapse has not yet been followed by an *intrinsic* collapse: the system of capitalist production is at the moment *both insane and rational.* If a failure of its administration should produce also an *intrinsic* collapse—if suddenly no one could buy and no one could sell—then the people of the West would come again to the crossroads of the 1930s, and would have to decide again whether they would solve their problems by means of war or revolution. It is at that point that the fight for the loyalty of the proletariat will become truly historical instead of merely theoretical, necessary instead of merely right,

possible instead of merely desirable. *But no will, no courage, no ingenuity can force this eventuality.* If it develops, and if the crisis is prolonged enough for white American workers to grasp the need for revolution, then with the same motion in which they change their rifles from one shoulder to the other, they will simultaneously *de-colonize* the blacks, the Vietnamese, the Cubans, *the French*—for at such a moment, all the old paralyzing definitions will die and new definitions, revolutionary ones, will take their place. The world proletariat will have achieved, at last, its dreamed-of world unity. This possibility, this towering historical power, is merely the other side of what it means to be a white American. But again: no matter how well it is organized or how combative and brilliant its performance is, no Western socialism has it in its power to force or even to hasten the intrinsic collapse of capitalist production. If you are an unreconstructed Marxist, you believe that it will come about sooner or later; if, like myself, you are not, then you don't know. It could happen: the market seems pale, inventories are large, the need to fight inflation in behalf of the international position of the dollar may lead to harder money, more unemployment, and still further slippage in demand; and if Nixon does not get the ABM, the whole system of the US Cold War economy will have received an ominous if mainly symbolic jolt. My view is that if this process starts unfolding, labor will have scant need of student organizers, and in the second place, that it will actively seek the support of student radicals. The "worker-student alliance" will happen when workers want it to happen, they will want it when they need it, and they will need it when and if the system starts coming apart. At such a conjuncture, students will have a critical contribution to make no matter what happens between now and then; but their contribution will be all the greater if they will have employed this uncertain threshold period to secure some kind of power base in the universities and such other institutions as they can reach, and if they will have used the opportunities of their situation to take the case for socialism to the country as a whole, aware certainly that class implies a political signature, but just as aware that it does not *necessitate* one. It is mainly to the extent that the white movement has done just this, in fact, that it has been of some occasional concrete service to the black movement, and the same will be true of any forthcoming relationship with a self-radicalized labor force.

Let me put this more bluntly. We are not now free to fight The Revolution except in fantasy. This is not a limit we can presently transcend; it is set by the over-all situation, and it will only be lifted by a real breakdown within the system of production. Nor will the lifting of the limit be the end of our fight; it will be just the possibility of its beginning. Meanwhile, there is no point in posing ourselves problems which we cannot solve, especially when the agony of doing so means, in effect, the abandoning of humbler projects—"humbler"! . . . as for example, the capture of real power in the university system—which might otherwise have been brought to a successful head. Just look: Very little, even insignificant effort was invested in the idea of "student power," and the SDS leadership even debunked the concept as, of all things, "counter-revolutionary." Yet we have just witnessed a moment in which a few key universities very nearly chose to collide head-on with the State over the question of repression of the Left. That would have been a momentous fight, especially coming on the heels of the black campus insurgencies. It's our fault that it didn't happen. The fault may be immense.

This was supposed to be about the future. Thousands of words later, I have still said very little about the future. I'm not really surprised at myself, and I won't apologize, but simply sum it up by saying that if SDS continues the past year's vanguarditis, then it, at least, will have precious little future at all. For what this movement needs is a swelling base, not a vanguard.

Or if a vanguard, then one which would rather *ride* a horse than look it in the mouth. One which wants students to get power and open up the campuses, blacks to win the franchise and elect some mayors, architects to be against the war and advertise that fact in the *Times,* clergy to be concerned and preach heretical sermons, inductees to dodge the draft and soldiers to organize a serviceman's union, workers to have more pay and shorter hours, hippies to make parks on private property, liberals to defeat the ABM, West Europe to escape NATO, East Europe the Warsaw Pact, and the global south the Western empires—and the American people as a whole (by any means necessary!) to be free enough to face their genocidal past for what it was, their bloody present for what it portends, and their future for that time of general human prosperity and gladness which they have the unique power to turn it into. And for being still more "revolutionary" than this implies, let us confess that time alone will tell us what that might mean.

PART III

THE ROLE OF THE FACULTY

Two major issues arose concerning the role of the faculty in student rebellions. The first issue involved the faculty's role as a "third force": Should the faculty as a group support the administration or establish itself as an independent mediator?

The second issue involved the role of individual professors sympathetic to student demonstrators. To whom did such persons owe responsibility? What constituted proper and improper conduct on their part?

CHAPTER 11

Faculty as Mediators

For the arch-opponents of appeasement in university crises, the faculty became the incarnation of spinelessness. This disdain for the faculty is evident in the first document in this section, "Harvard: The Voice of a Non-Striker." The author, J. C. Helms, a graduate student in classics, singles out the Harvard faculty—"its leniency, its blindness, and its cowardice"—as the source of the university's problems. (Helms later became a speechwriter for Vice-President Spiro T. Agnew.)

Two statements from Columbia defend faculty intervention. A brief declaration by the left-liberal Independent Faculty Group, written in late May 1968, maintains that students and the administration at Columbia were linked in "antagonistic cooperation" and that if the university was to survive, the "confrontation system" had to be broken.

Walter Metzger, a professor of history at Columbia, presents a more extended defense of the faculty's actions during the university's 1968 crisis. Metzger stated that although SDS leaders had no intention of negotiating a settlement, faculty efforts at mediation and arbitration might have succeeded because many students in the building were interested in a negotiated settlement. He concluded, however, that the Columbia faculty effort at mediation was almost doomed to fail, essentially because it was *ad hoc*: "To salvage authority, one needs authority—or at least some authorization."

Column in The Wall Street Journal, *May 6, 1969, by J. C. Helms, a graduate student at Harvard University.*

Harvard: The Voice of a Non-Striker

The problem at Harvard is not SDS. The problem is not the use of police, nor is it the student strike. The problem is the Harvard faculty: Its leniency, its blindness and its cowardice.

On April 9, several hundred students seized University Hall by force. They came armed with crowbars for smashing windows and chains to secure the doors once they were inside. They evicted nine deans, dragging some of them through the halls: one was even carried out, slung over a student's shoulder. They physically beat an undergraduate in University Hall, who was not in sympathy with their action: he was alone, and five of them held his arms and his hands while two others beat him. They rifled the faculty files and published the private letters of the dean. And the next morning one of their leaders urged a mob of many hundreds to pelt President Pusey's house with rocks.

The community was startled.

But how can it surprise us that such an incident occurs, when two years ago Robert McNamara was humiliated and subjected to mob coercion, and the university did next to nothing? How can it surprise us that such an incident occurs, when last year a mob of students held an interviewer from Dow Chemical Co. prisoner for seven hours, and the university did next to nothing? Will the faculty never see that it is only reaping the reward of leniency and indecision in the past?

Yet this time, too, our faculty has failed to take swift action. Instead of bringing the matter before the administrative board, a body established to deal with problems of discipline, the faculty has thought it wise to abandon, in the middle of a crisis, proven and equitable procedures and to grasp at the untried compromise of an elected punishing committee of ten professors and five students.

And so they add confusion to confusion. Or do they suppose that elections held on one day's notice at a time of high emotion are going to select the best jury to pass judgment on the offenders? It is a travesty of justice, whatever the decision of the jury. But, in any case, that decision will most probably be lenient, for the watchwords of today are popularity and license, not rightness and order.

Can our faculty not see the damage that will surely come to this university if it is not made crystal clear that lawless forces can never be permitted here? Or is the faculty always blinded by the argument that these militant moralists are fighting in a good cause?

I think it's time somebody called nonsense nonsense. I think it's time somebody calls nuts nuts. Isn't this the generation that wants to tell it like it is? Why, then, is everyone mincing words? The students who occupied University Hall are violent people, they do not belong here. Their wrongdoing is not just youthful restlessness, it is not just misdirected idealism: It is a crime, and those who committed this crime should be expelled immediately and never allowed to return.

Why, then, does our faculty hesitate? Is it because it recognizes a certain validity in the demands of SDS? So what? All thinking men at Harvard grant that these demands are not without some merit, but there is still no justifying SDS' use of force and violence. Not even a comparison with the civil rights movement can justify these tactics. It is true that in the civil rights movement just ends were attained by illegal means, but this achievement sets a dangerous, very dangerous, precedent, because such action opens wide the door to all sorts of selfish people who are only too willing to circumvent the law in order to attain their ends—ends that they invariably call good, but which are all too often bad.

Just several days ago one of SDS' members told me in The Yard that if by killing one, specific person, he could end the war in Vietnam, he would kill that person. How about two persons? How about 10? How about Robert Kennedy or Martin Luther King? Nobody likes the war in Vietnam, but how far will they go to achieve a goal that they're convinced is good?

But let there be no doubt about it: what has happened here has not been good. Or do you think we should be thankful to the students who have caused this mess? Do you think the mass-meetings and the television cameras and the bull-horns have made us better? It is loathsome to men of good sense to listen and listen and listen to people who talk about peace in Vietnam and make war here. It is loathsome to men of good sense to see these faceless mobs and committees and organizations all marching behind one banner, all wearing one ribbon, all chanting one song, all shouting one word: Strike, Strike, Strike. Where are the individuals I hoped to find at Harvard? Where are their individual thoughts? Where are the careful distinctions, where are the subtle refinements?

They have been swept away by passions, by crude and simple passions, that are usually covered for our common welfare by the merciful veneer of civilization. But this veneer is very thin, and those who expose themselves to the abrasive activity of revolution will see it quickly stripped away. It is an unfortunate inequity that thousands of years are required to make men civilized, while only one generation can reduce us to beasts. We swim against a current of barbarity: it takes great effort to hold our own, and superhuman effort to advance, but if we give up for a single moment, we are swept back into darkness.

The noise and the chaos and the violence have not been good, yet there are some who feel that we have gained in recompense a new sense of community. That is not surprising: for 10 days there was a carnival on campus and we saw our friends and watched the light show in The Yard and listened to the rock bands and let the orators entertain us in the stadium, and we had bull-sessions all night long. If this is "community" and this is what we want, then let's go on with it all year. But let's not fool ourselves by calling it a university.

A bull-session can be a good thing, but it is not a substitute for thought, and a party is certainly pleasant, but it is not a substitute for learning. Learning is difficult. It can also give great pleasure, but it is not the pleasure of a carnival: It is a pleasure that is hard-won, it demands sacrifice and discipline and is attained by few.

The sit-ins and the be-ins and the mill-ins are communal, they are cozy, they are fun. But their coziness does not develop leaders, for leadership is lonely. And that is why this campus has always been a lonely place. Perhaps some day Harvard will be one big happy tribe, but on that day Harvard will no longer be significant, for she will have lost the courage to accept the loneliness of leadership.

But the issue is not only Harvard. At stake is more. At stake is

American education. At stake is the survival of a vision in our young that there is goodness which transcends the many and obvious evils of the "real world." It is a vision of gentleness and decency and order, of nobleness and generosity and justice. A naive vision, but a good one.

And it is a vision that can be strengthened by the teachers in our universities, for teachers are not mere conveyors of facts or masters of scholarly method. They are spiritual leaders. They stand before the young, whose minds are plastic and receptive, and they have a power greater than kings, for they have the power to shape the character of men who will live and think and act for another 50 years. This shaping is done by example and by lesson. But what lesson do we want our young to learn? That might is right?

Yet this is what we have learned at Harvard recently, for our faculty has yielded to force. Out of fear of student anger it has instituted student participation in the punishment of colleagues, out of fear of violence it has reconsidered an earlier decision on the ROTC. These new decisions may be sound in substance, but they were not made on the merits of the issues, and the students know it. Need we ask then, why our faculty is hesitating to expel the radicals who seized University Hall and threw our campus into chaos? It hesitates because it is afraid, afraid that if the punishment is severe, there would be a serious student reaction. And perhaps there would be.

So what?

It is time to call an end to playing politics with students. It is time to call an end to appeasement. It is time to call an end to making all decisions out of expediency. If there is one, large group in our society apart from organized religion that can and must still show the world that principles are preferable to politics, it is the teachers. For if they do not show us, who will?

We need change at Harvard, much change. We must free ourselves from outside control; the students should play a more active role in university affairs; Harvard must show greater concern for the community around her. All this is true. Moral sensitivity and an eagerness to make reforms are admirable, necessary and rare, and must not be discouraged.

But there are dangers in untempered zeal, and we need courage as well as change, perception as well as compassion. If the faculty fails to perceive the long-term effects of its decisions, if the faculty loses its courage in the face of student disorder, if Harvard does not deal swiftly and severely with people who are bent on destroying American universities as a prelude to destroying all of American society, then Harvard is through.

From a statement by a Columbia faculty organization, The Independent Faculty Group, issued on May 24, 1968.

The Confrontation Crisis

Columbia University is being torn apart by the remorseless operation of a confrontation system. Two parties are required for such a system. On the one side, an Administration, stubbornly reluctant to manifest the spirit of reform demanded by the situation, defends its compromised authority by confusing, ungenerous, and provocative actions. On the other side, a group of students, some of whom are far less interested in reforming this University than in using it as a political staging area, have concertedly violated basic rules and refused to engage seriously in mediation or negotiation.

Such postures predictably produce repeated interventions by police. Both parties, claiming an impeccable moral position, call upon all others to join them. Both parties, linked in antagonistic cooperation, are reluctant to save and support the first steps, admittedly imperfect and improvised, towards a reformed University. Both cooperate in creating a polarized moral world. Those committed to the preservation of the University—and not to its use as a political background, or to the maintenance of distant, unresponsive, and rigid Administrative powers—are faced by a series of searing crises that further shatter the trust indispensable for the relationship of student to teacher, and of scholar to scholar.

Intransigent student leaders and inflexible administrative officers are thus locked into a series of acts, each of which amounts to a self-fulfilling prophecy. The student leadership claims that this University can function at present only by the Administration's use of force; they proceed to behave in a manner that makes this use of force inevitable. The Administration claims that one group of students bent on destroying the University will refuse, under any conditions, to abide by University procedures. It then behaves in a confusing, inconsistent, and small-minded manner that leads students to distrust the possibility of reform.

Neither party accepts responsibility for the consequences of its acts. The student leadership will not share any part of the moral burden for the police presence; the Administration will not admit that it is at all responsible for the behavior of the police, once called in, or for the predictable consequences of disciplinary actions undertaken hastily and in confused ways in so inflamed a situation.

This confrontation system must be broken if this University is to survive and be recreated.

Statement by Professor Walter Metzger, Department of History, Columbia University, in Daedalus, *Fall 1969, as part of a "Dialogue on Governance of the Universities."*

Authority at Columbia

Let me address myself to the problem of authority—a theme which any storyteller from Columbia is likely to think of first. Last spring, a large number of Columbia students not only violated the rules of the institution, but challenged the legitimacy of the rule-makers. A self-constituted body of the faculty interposed itself between the students and thc administration and attempted to mediate their differences. This *ad hoc* intervention failed, for reasons that shed a certain light on why *ad hoc* interventions of this sort often fail. The administration called in the police (not once but twice within a fortnight and each time with bloody results). Failing to anticipate, constrain, or condemn police misconduct, the "authorities" of the institution lost most of the moral credit they had left. For a time, there was no authority at Columbia, but two competing and incompetent seats of power—an officialdom that could summon force, but could not gain the consent of the governed; a student strike committee that could shut things down, but could not gain and keep allegiances, even within its ranks. Gradually, a committee of the faculty, set up by professors assembled in full strength, acquired sufficient moral standing to become, if not a new authority, then at least the instrument through which authority might be restored. It prevailed upon the trustees of the university not to press charges of criminal trespass against students accused of one offense; it supported the efforts of another body to judicialize the discipline of the university; it appointed a commission of outsiders to investigate the causes of student anger; it began the framing of a constitution that would give students and professors a more important role in the running of the institution. Whether these techniques will work—whether a calculated policy of forgiveness, a more thorough commitment to due process, a willingness to submit to outside judgment, and a more democratic form of governance will reknit our shattered community—it is still too soon to tell. The way the spring term ended admonishes against facile optimism: The official graduation ceremony had to retreat to a nearby church in order to protect itself against disruption; a radical student counter-ceremony took over the embattled campus grounds.

I think it can be said that at no other university up to that moment was the attack on authority so jugular, the crisis of legitimacy so complete. Yet, when one looks back, one finds little evidence that this attack and this crisis were anticipated. Those in charge of the university knew that students were restive, but they felt that student restiveness was a chronic illness, not one that reached climatic peaks. A minority of radical students was attacking the alleged seduction of the academy by the social institutions of war and profit, but it was believed that numbers were decisive, and that those who were complaining about the CIA, ROTC, and grades for selective service could command the soap boxes, but not win the troops. I would attribute this false sense of security in part to conceptual failings. What produces and sustains authority? President Kirk seemed to employ a "rational-legal" model: Authority, he appeared to believe, is the gift of the charter and the statutes conferred on the holder of a specific office. Vice-President Truman seemed to use a pluralistic-pragmatic model: Authority, he appeared to believe, is the product of the capacity of a system to recognize and satisfy divergent interests. The senior professors seemed to favor yet another concept: Authority, many of them seemed to believe, is an attribute of personal competence, as attested by institutional credentials and by disciplinary repute. A sanguine corollary could be drawn from each of these conceptual models. President Kirk made the Weberian assumption that as long as he stayed within his sphere of competence and obeyed the general rules, his orders would be obeyed. Vice-President Truman seemed to infer from his political science that as long as students had access to the administration and could negotiate with it for concrete rewards, they would be socialized into the going order, even as the Populists and the CIO had been in another day. The senior professors seemed to think that of all authorities, their own, a product of mandarinism and charisma, was the most natural, the most winning, and the most secure.

What these models failed to take into account was the thrust of black student militancy and the animus of white student revolutionism—two very different forces which joined at Columbia for one frightful week. To the black students on campus, who had gathered in numbers large enough to make the assertion of race consciousness a collective rather than a lonely task, academic authority was white authority and thus congenitally suspect. They did not test the moral quality of an official action by asking whether it was authorized or *ultra vires:* In their eyes, the rules, though general, were not neutral with respect to race. Nor would they automatically accord to a white professor the respect due knowledge and renown, for knowledge could be tainted by prejudice and fame could be accorded evil men. This did not mean that they would never treat with white officials. To the extent that they regarded the university as a dispenser of occupational advantages and the arbiter of racial rewards, they did conform to the Truman doctrine and bargain for specific gains. But black confrontation with white authority was no longer just an ask-and-get affair. It served an expressive function: It was a way of acting out resentments, a way of exorcising inner doubts; it involved a purging of the servile images incorporated into the black man's psyche through centuries of social subordination. To use a convenient shorthand, the black students were concerned not only with de-exploitation, but also with de-victimization. The goal of de-exploitation is a fairer allocation of resources, a more even division of the pie. In the context of the campus, it took the form of demands for greater black enrollments and for larger scholarship funds for the poor. The goal of de-victimization is to repair the psychic consequences of prolonged subjection. Whatever forms it takes, it cannot have so finite an agenda. Historically, the prime vehicle of de-victimization has been de-colonization—the replacement of the foreign superordinate by the indigenous subordinate in every position of power and prestige. The demography of this country may not permit so drastic a solution. Still there is room for colonial analogies: Population movements have concentrated blacks in ghetto pockets; administrators, social workers, and policemen, entering the "native quarters" by day and leaving them by night, do bear a certain resemblance to foreign officers, religious missionaries, and expeditionary armies. The fight for community control of schools is somewhat akin to a bid for sovereignty, although it is more partial and oblique. When Columbia decided to build a gymnasium in the park that separated Harlem from the Heights, it failed to consider these analogic possibilities. On its face, the move was not exploitative. The facility would be used by both the community and the college; located in a city park, it would not force any tenants to be relocated and reduce the limited housing stock. Ten years ago, these considerations had weighed heavily with Harlem's leaders, who had helped pass the enabling laws. But now a new set of leaders, reflecting a new black power mood, was inclined to see things very differently. To them, Columbia was a white settler's city on the hill—a Salisbury, a Johannesburg, a Nairobi—rising high and mighty over the native flats. Like them, it had seized the land around it through a policy of purchase and chicane and had expelled the native population so as to protect its safety and hygiene. Now, its appetite unappeased, it was about to appropriate more tribal territory that had struck it as desirable and green. No matter that it was willing to share the building's floor-space, the control of the building would not be shared; moreover, the very plan for sharing betrayed an *apartheid* prejudice—one entrance on the high ground for students, another for the lesser breeds below. I am not certain that every student at Columbia who was black saw the gym as a colonial intrusion. But almost every student who was black took sides with the black community, rather than with the white-led institution, once these Mau Mau symbols had been raised. To put race above status was to prove that one had not been suborned by white preferment; this was essential to self-esteem, and self-esteem was now of the very essence. (I recognize, as I say this, that Columbia had been harsh toward its neighbors, and that this imagery, though exaggerated, had a germ of truth.)

At the start of the week that shook the ivy, Hamilton Hall was seized and occupied by black militants and white revolutionaries joined together. Soon, however, this alliance fell apart. After a night of squabbling, the whites were sent out into the early morning cold to colonize another building, and the blacks had Hamilton to themselves. Why this separation? In part, because the blacks demanded autonomy. (In a crude way, the building was for them a kind of country; the negotiations for its release, a kind of foreign policy; the removal of the white contingent, an assertion of their own self-determination.) In part, because the blacks did not trust their allies. (At first, the whites opposed the barricading of the building and proposed to block administrative rooms instead, seeking thereby to avoid embroilment with the student body. The blacks interpreted this to mean that these white rich men's sons in their Skid Row clothes were willing to take the risk of words, not deeds. To prove they had the courage of their convictions, the whites jettisoned selective tactics when they struck out on their own, and the idea that confrontation should be discriminating in its choice of target fell a casualty to this contest of zeal.) But as much as anything else, the blacks parted company with the whites because of differences over ideology. Where the whites spurned the materialism of society and regarded social mobility as an anaesthetic, the blacks maintained a strong commitment to the stratification system and to conventional notions of success. Where the whites saw the enemy as "capitalism," the blacks saw the enemy as "racism," and these symbols, while they touched, were not the same. Most of all, they had different attitudes toward academic authority. The black militants wanted to face the "Man," both in order to redress their grievances and to address their wrath. They sought, therefore, a responsible and responsive adversary. (It is interesting that, of all the student groups in the buildings, only the blacks failed to call for the resignation of Mr. Kirk.) The whites would not render the administration the tribute of being needed. In the revolutionary credo, the social system was congenitally corrupt and those who served to sustain it had to be attacked and overthrown. The weakness of university authority, a sometime source of despair to the black students, was for the whites an opening to be exploited, a point in the social organism where one could inject the redeeming plague. The blacks used ingestive and obstructive images ("let more of us in," "stop the juggernaut"), but they did not use toxic or gangrenous metaphors.

At Columbia, there existed no faculty body that could debate important academic issues, generate a consensus about them, and make sure that that consensus took effect. (There was a University Council, but it was dominated by administrators and traditionally had concerned itself with bagatelles.) Consequently, the brunt of this assault upon authority was borne by the emplaced authorities, which is to say, by two individuals—the president and vice-president of the university. To say that it was not borne well is not to ignore the difficulties under which they worked. They were—to start with—only two, hardly an optimum number for gaining the sort of intelligence and instigating the sort of argument that were needed to correct mistaken views. Men younger than they would have been overtaxed; men less able than they would have been overwhelmed. Then, too, they had inherited from the last great president of the institution, Columbia's own demonic St. Nick, the worst of all possible executive worlds—too much uncommunicativeness on high policy to receive the benefits of feedback, too little control over subdivisions to implement any central plan. In a time of crisis, this combination of an overabundance of prerogative with an insufficiency of power turned out to be particularly perverse. Added to all this were the pressures that outsiders exerted on them. Alumni who had been students in a more tranquil day saw their successors as engaging in a temper tantrum that would grow if it were in any way placated; men of property saw property rights invaded and demanded instant recourse to the law's defense; other administrators begged ours to hold the levee, lest the radical torrent engulf them too (this was a liquefied version of the domino theory and doubtless just as hyperbolic). For a while, these pressures were resisted. The separation of the black students from the white students had created an all-black citadel in a predominately white institution that stood cheek-by-jowl with Harlem. To allow them to stay ran one sort of danger, but to dislodge them by force ran another—the danger of arson and riot—and the balance of risks had to be gravely weighed. The hostaging of a dean also bought the sit-ins time and allowed them to spread to other buildings. But procrastination was not adopted by the administration as a policy; to the external publics of the university, this would have been taken as a sign of weakness, and the regard of these external publics counted much at Low. This is not to say that a Fabian approach would have been adopted had there not been so much prompting from outside. I do not know exactly at what point the president and vice-president concluded that negotiations with the SDS-dominated strike committee were useless, that the issues of the gym and of IDA (an institute of weapons analysis with which Columbia had nominal connection) had been raised to embarrass not reform the university, that the longer the sit-ins lasted the more they became a counter-government competing with the legal one for mass support, that so ultimate a challenge to authority had to be met by something no less ultimate—the arbitrament of force. Perhaps they reached this point when the SDS took over the president's suite and began to affirm the revolutionary counter-ethic that establishment property, being theft, is therefore eminently seizable and that privacy is never a right that can be said to adhere in official persons. With the blacks, who were less wounding in words and conduct, the administration did make an effort to come to terms; it would not, however, pay the ransom asked for—the abandonment of the gym; and so these negotiations did not prosper. On the third day, the vice-president told the faculty that he had reached the end of his political string. He was about to submit to the harsh protectorship of the police.

But a group within the faculty would not accept this, and their intervention was to produce another chapter in the crisis of authority at Columbia. I shall not burden you with the details of how the Ad Hoc Faculty Group took form. Let it suffice to say that it arose spontaneously, rather than by any plotter's will. Nor shall I try to examine all the motives of those who joined it. Assuredly these were varied and in certain persons quite complex. It may be enough to say that, as far as its steering committee was concerned (as a former member of it I can describe its mind with modest confidence), there was little sympathy for the insurrection. One fear brought us into action—the fear of violence on the campus—and one hope sustained us through four sleepless nights—the hope that third-party intervention, free from the intransigencies of either side, could find a placable and equitable way out. Subsequent commentators have charged that this was a partial fear and a naïve hope—the Ad Hoc Faculty Group has not received what one would call a glowing press. I do not doubt that there is some substance to these charges. We *were* more concerned about imported violence than about the violence boiling up in our midst (though we did constitute ourselves a constabulary to try to keep the left- and right-wing students from each other's throats). And we *did* misjudge the temper of the revolutionaries, which was far more Sorelian than we anticipated. Between our desire to pacify the campus and their desire to traumatize and radicalize it, between our sense of politics as accommodation and their sense of politics as war, stretched a gap that was probably unbridgeable. Yet, it seems to me, there was more wisdom in our course than has been noticed or than even we at the time realized. When the police came with their covered badges and flailing nightsticks, when they not only made arrests but inflicted punishments—and on the innocent and the lawbreaker alike—when they disobeyed the instruction of their own officials in venting their fear and spite, they did more to jeopardize authority than ever did the students at their barricades. To have tried to sustain the life of the university around the confiscated buildings would probably better have preserved the social compact than to have invoked what turned out to be an indiscriminate and ungoverned force. Moreover, it is possible that, in time, the area of disaffection might have shrunk. By dealing substantively with the issues, the Ad Hoc Faculty Group took cognizance of an important fact—that most of the students in the white communes were not revolutionary and had not written their manifestoes tongue-in-cheek. If most shared with the revolutionaries a radical critique of society, they did not draw the same nihilistic inferences; if they agreed that the university had been corrupted, they did not agree that its improvement was beyond all hope. The very innocence of our rationalism allowed us to discern complexities—to see that the buildings had not been occupied by eight hundred anarchistic Rudds, that there were many communards who were not *enragés* and who were tense under the latter's leadership, and that time and a concessionary stance might result in their defection.

And yet I now see that our intervention was doomed to fail—not because it was inept, but because it was *ad hoc.* To salvage authority, one needs authority—or at least some authorization; to exercise power without anointment, to mediate at no one's behest, is almost to guarantee defeat. We were made aware of this in many ways. In our first phase of mediation, when we simply tried to repair communications between the students and the administration, we were seen as abdicating our role as teachers and turning ourselves into colorless connecting links; in the second phase, when we tried to impose a settlement and speak with our own authentic voice, we were seen as making promises we lacked the mandate to put forward and the power and stature to enforce. By going our self-made way, we became an object of suspicion to colleagues who valued due procedures. Some seemed to think of us as intruders, well-intentioned perhaps but too presumptuous;

while others seemed to think of us as adventurers capitalizing on crisis to advance our own careers. Perhaps the worst of the liabilities of our *ad-hoc*ism lay in the indefiniteness of its contours. Who belonged to the Ad Hoc Faculty Group? To what extent did the Faculty Group speak for the faculty as a whole? The debate over the issue of amnesty made it clear that these questions were critical and that the answers would be indistinct. "We will not accept judgment of punishment from an illegitimate authority," said Mark Rudd, referring to the corporate authority that emanated from the legal fount. The *ad hoc* steering committee, which was largely made up of senior faculty, proposed that the disciplinary punishment be light (for those who voluntarily left the buildings), but that some sort of disciplinary judgment be made—in short that the students be granted amnesty *de facto,* not *de jure.* Critical as they were of the administration, they did not regard its authority as illegitimate; much as they sought a settlement, they would not agree that the revolutionaries were in the right. Doubtless, for professors who were not so critical of the administration or were not so eager to arrange a pact (and these included some of the most distinguished members of the faculty), even amnesty *de facto* went too far toward immunizing lawlessness and acknowledging its moral claims. But in the group that called itself the *ad hoc* membership, there was a surprising amount of "faculty" sentiment in favor of a prescriptive amnesty. A certain part of this variance in sentiment was clearly an artifact of composition. Existing outside the rules, the Ad Hoc Faculty Group had no standard by which it might define itself except that of an incontinent egalitarianism. Some who came to vote and argue had fewer ligatures to the faculty than to the students (some indeed *were* students, with relatively minor teaching responsibilities). Some were of a rank and office that would have barred them from a seat on the established faculties or would have admitted them without a vote. In regular academic governance, there may be something to be said for open doors and an elastic franchise; in irregular modes of operation, there is not. Because we did not know what we were, we could not maintain confidentiality; whatever happened in our sessions was instantly reported by double agents to the SDS. As the votes on the issue of amnesty teetered back and forth, depending on the vagaries of attendance, the student rebels came more and more to believe that "the faculty" might declare itself their moral ally. Clear-minded observers would have known that, whatever happened in these frenzied meetings, the bulk of the tenured faculty would not dissolve the thousand ties—personal, contractual, and customary—that bound them to the given order, and the idea that they would have preferred to live in anarchic confraternity with the students rather than in orderly relations with the legal powers should have strained credulity from the start. But crisis is not a time for clear-minded observation, and the rebelling students did believe that they would get large pickings if they stood pat.

The Ad Hoc Faculty Group failed. The lessons of its failure have not always been correctly drawn. Its failure does not prove that whenever authority shows cracks it crumbles. "United we stand and divided we fall" is a precept for preserving power, not legitimacy; a flawless alliance between Columbia's professors and administration might have brought the police in sooner, but would have made for greater difficulties when they left. Nor does it prove that mediation in a polar world is fruitless. True, our even-handed formulas were rejected—politely by the administration, contemptuously by the students; we did seem, from each perspective, to be disingenuously partial to the other side. But one rejection after five days' trying can hardly be generalized into a law of nature, and it remains to be seen what mediation can accomplish when time is less at a premium, and there is less need for a climactic "yes" or "no." For me, the primary lesson of that failure is that structures should anticipate, not trail, events. For what we were trying to do, we needed an established mechanism that could draw on the legitimacies of tradition, that could enjoy collegial proxies, that could define itself. We needed a faculty organ; all that we could manufacture, on the spur of the moment, was a crowd.

The coda to the story I am telling involved the effort to create just such an instrument in the dark period following the "bust." On the day after the police retook the buildings, all the professors from the varied divisions of the university met together in the chapel, one of the few places free of the stains and debris of war. Only once before had they met as a collectivity; this had been on the eve of battle, when the administration had convoked them for the purpose of gaining their general support. On this occasion, the members of the Ad Hoc Faculty Group had been able for the first time to address their peers on the dangers of a stiff-backed policy and the virtues of mediation; they had not, however, submitted their proposals to a vote, fearing that a negative or closely-won result would hamper their negotiations with the students. (Whether they had thus let slip an opportunity to gain majority support for their own position, it is difficult to tell. Clearly, they had made a greater impact on their audience than their pariah instincts had supposed they would. Nevertheless, the only formal outcome of that meeting was a bland vote of confidence in the administration.) Now, in its second convocation, the assembly had to face the consequences of decisive action: almost two hundred students bloodied, four or five thousand students on strike, an armed patrol at every gateway, every civility effaced. The inclination of this body was now to find some way to go back—to retrieve a community based on shared assumptions that had so suddenly developed into a regime of force. It sensed it could not do this by rallying again to the administration; it needed its own instrumentality and one that would not be factional or outcast. Out of this sense was born the Executive Committee of the Faculty, something new under the academic sun. It was given a nostalgic mandate—"to return the university to its educational tasks." But the past could not be recreated; the very existence of this body was a rebuke to the old regime; the disaffection of the mass of students had to be coped with, not wished away. In a short time, the Committee became an advocate of reform as a key to recovery, and "restructuring" became its motto and major aim.

For all its advantages of birth, the Executive Committee of the Faculty had to struggle for legitimation. At the beginning, it did not transcend the deep divisions of the faculty. Its parliamentary sponsors, hoping to have it do so, had fixed its membership in a slate composed of old *ad-hoc*ers, staunch supporters of the administration and a few members heretofore disengaged. This *politique* approach, instead of creating a committee of the whole, created a committee of warring parts, and it took time before the conciliations of an able chairman and the unifying effects of the committee process could work to solidify the group. At the beginning, it was distrusted by the students. In an effort to restore the peace, which it saw as a precondition to reform, it became deeply involved in crisis management and lost credibility as a force for change. Moreover, its notion of the changes called for—a greater voice for faculty and students in a government that would leave old forms intact—aroused a great deal of student skepticism in quarters where "co-option" was a fighting word. It was not until the summer brought composure that a *rapprochement* of sorts could take effect. A radical, but not revolutionary student group, which had broken away from the diehard leadership, turned its energies to "restructuring" and became the critic and the partner of a faculty similarly engaged. With the Kirk administration, the Executive Committee of the Faculty had very strained relations. This was a third block to legitimacy. But for the recognition accorded it by the trustees, the Committee might have found itself in the role of its *ad hoc* predecessor. As it happened, the exigencies of the moment impelled the board to turn, not to their deputies, but to an agency of the faculty for advice. It was a marriage of convenience, not without its points of discord. The board thought the way to restore authority was to invoke full disciplinary sanctions; the faculty argued—in part, successfully—that a punitive university would be a university beset by enemies, that retribution without mercy would lead to confrontation without end. The board wanted to continue to allow the president to raise intramural punishments at his own discretion; the faculty argued—more successfully—that this was as judicially untenable as it was politically unwise. Not all the arguments were won by the faculty and not all the arguments of the faculty were sound. What mattered as much as the score on issues were the utilities gained by the debate. The trustees came to know their campus; the Executive Committee of the Faculty received the accolade of their regard. I think I have located one of the latent functions of trustees—they can validate new agents of authority when the old no longer work.

The returns are not yet in. The relegitimation of authority has not yet been accomplished at Columbia. We are only at the point where we may think that we have learned something from our distress.

CHAPTER 12

Professional Responsibility

A young professor leads a student demonstration into the administration building. The next day the chairman of his department recommends his dismissal. More demonstrations ensue.

The young professor was John Gerassi, expert on radical movements in Latin America and a leader of the New Left. The departmental chairman was Marshall Windmiller, an outspoken opponent of the Vietnam War. Close on certain political questions, they were poles apart on the proper role of the faculty. The debate that follows speaks for itself.

Exchange between Marshall Windmiller and John Gerassi of San Francisco State College, in New York Review of Books, *April 11, 1968.*

Trouble at San Francisco State: An Exchange

Marshall Windmiller:
On January 11, 1968, John Gerassi, well-known as a militant opponent of the war in Vietnam, was dismissed from the faculty of

San Francisco State College where he held the post of Visiting Lecturer in International Relations. As Acting Chairman of the Department of International Relations, I had joined with the other tenured members of the department in recommending his dismissal.

The firing of a professor is a serious matter which always sends shock-waves through the academic community. This case was especially upsetting, not only because it raised important questions about academic freedom, but because it was falsely linked with the issue of racism and with campus protest against the war in Vietnam. The events which led to the dismissal caused the college to be temporarily closed down, seriously damaged faculty and student morale, and increased right-wing political pressures on the college administration.

Interest in the Gerassi case is found not only among those who want to know why he was fired, but from many who wonder why he was hired in the first place. He was hired because the Department of International Relations wanted a Latin American specialist who would contribute to its efforts to build courses that are relevant to current international events, and who would not shrink from confronting the difficult intellectual and moral problems raised by American policy in Latin America.

Gerassi had wide experience in Latin America, had been an editor of *Newsweek* magazine, and had written a book called *The Great Fear in Latin America* which had been used in the department and found valuable. Gerassi has an M.A. in philosophy from Columbia, speaks fluent French and Spanish, taught at the New School, at Windham College, and was an Assistant Professor of Journalism at NYU when we invited him to come to San Francisco. He had published articles in *The New York Review, Book Week, Commonweal,* and *Esquire,* and he was Latin American Editor of *Ramparts* magazine. We checked with academic colleagues who knew him and they responded favorably, so we offered him a one-year appointment, which he accepted.

The members of the department were in general aware of Gerassi's political views as they had been expressed in his articles and in *The Great Fear.* The latter was a critique of American policy in Latin America and a plea for "a policy of reconquest" of the area "with the arms of a new and lasting friendship." It was critical of American economic exploitation and military intervention. It advised the United States to support Latin American nationalism or face the growth of Communism. We knew that Gerassi opposed the war in Vietnam, was sympathetic to the Cuban revolution, and believed that armed struggle was the only way that Latin America could free itself from United States domination. While these views were not shared by all of us, and were vigorously opposed by at least one, we thought they would enliven the dialogue among faculty and students and precipitate controversy of educational value. We had had similar aims when we sought and hired an extremely conservative colleague the previous year. In making our decision, we looked upon Gerassi as a "high-risk, high-gain" person, a term used by the Peace Corps to describe the livelier volunteers. Six members of the department, including myself, voted for the appointment; only one thought it was a bad risk.

By the time Gerassi arrived in San Francisco, his views had moved considerably beyond those expressed in *The Great Fear.* Between May, when we hired him, and September, when he began work, he had visited Cuba and had attended the OLAS conference. That meeting was also attended by Stokely Carmichael, who was lionized by the Cubans as an authentic American revolutionary. Gerassi returned fired up with revolutionary fervor and entranced by the romanticism surrounding Fidel, Che Guevara, and Régis Debray. In a formal lecture, sponsored by the International Relations Department, he told an enthusiastic student audience:

> What it means . . . for the individual that goes to Cuba—what it means for an individual American that goes to Cuba—and sees the committedness, and sees the strength, and sees, therefore, because of that committedness, the incredible freedom, as I said, the complete and total relaxation of any kind of repressive measures, the lack of police, the lack of check-ups, the lack of all these things, because the youth is committed, and when you have the youth committed you don't need it anyway; even from a practical point of view, there's no need for any of it. When you see all that, and you consider yourself radical, or you consider yourself revolutionary, and you realize that it's true that the example sets the tone; the example is what influences people—not the talk; not the theory; not even the writing of the books—ulti-

mately it's the example. You go to Cuba. Cuba, without trying to be nasty to you, puts you right on the spot. It makes you at all times while you are visiting there say "and what are you? Because if you're a revolutionary, then put up or shut up!"

Gerassi's revolutionary romanticism came to the campus at a time when it could have maximum impact. The Students for a Democratic Society were circulating nationwide an article by its Inter-Organizational Secretary, Carl Davidson, entitled "Toward Institutional Resistance." * Davidson described the American university as a " 'knowledge factory' adjunct to the multinational corporations of American capitalism." He said that "the social order we are rebelling against is totalitarian, manipulative, repressive, and anti-democratic. Furthermore, within this order of domination, to respect and operate within the realm of bourgeois civil liberties is to remain enslaved, since the legal apparatus is designed to sustain the dominant order, containing potential forces for change within its pre-established and ultimately castrating confines. As a result, it is the duty of a revolutionary not only to be intolerant of, but to actually suppress the anti-democratic activities of the dominant order."

John Gerassi had returned from Cuba with its "incredible freedom" and "complete and total relaxation of any kind of repressive measures," ready to do battle with the American Establishment. He gave an interview to the campus newspaper, *Open Process,* which was published on October 27: "The whole educational system in this country," he said, "is really part of the Establishment, and it has to be challenged and confronted just as much as the military. . . . Of course, the risk involved is great. If you really accept this—if you're going to have that kind of confrontation on campus—it means you're risking bringing the whole thing to a standstill. But is that so bad?"

In the same interview, Gerassi discussed the free speech issue that had arisen in connection with war recruiters. "You don't have freedom of speech in this country with regard to whether you go fight or whether you don't want to go fight. . . . You don't have freedom of speech about the system under which you live. It

* For text, see pp. 129–38.

can't even be considered whether General Motors should be nationalized. . . . There is no free speech objectively. They have the loudspeakers. Let's face it—we don't."

If Gerassi meant by this that minority opinion in the United States has less access to the mass media than majority opinion, then it would be hard to disagree with him. But the language he used is difficult to square with a statement he made elsewhere in the interview. "Any individual," he said, "can get up and say what he wants to in this country and openly advocate sedition and have nothing happen to him, or at worse have to settle for a $50 honorarium instead of a $500 one." He implied that a little repression would be a good thing because it would unite the Left. Unfortunately, as his post-suspension interview with Elsa Thompson of Pacifica Radio revealed, San Francisco State College had not produced that oppression:

> THOMPSON: When you were invited to come to San Francisco State, both Marshall Windmiller and the other people involved in okaying your appointment were in fact thoroughly familiar with your background?
>
> GERASSI: Oh, yes, they used my book, *The Great Fear in Latin America,* and have used it for a couple years right in the Center.
>
> THOMPSON: And since you have been at San Francisco State, until this difficulty which has arisen within the last few days, has there in fact been any interference in anything you wanted to do with your students or with what you had to say in the classroom?
>
> GERASSI: Well, I've been suspended.
>
> THOMPSON: Yes, I understand that now . . .
>
> GERASSI: Oh, prior . . .
>
> THOMPSON: Yes . . . prior to . . .
>
> GERASSI: No, none at all . . .
>
> THOMPSON: . . . you were allowed—you were in fact doing what you wanted to do at San Francisco . . .
>
> GERASSI: Exactly.
>
> THOMPSON: Then really, insofar as one can tell, this suspension is in fact hinged around the events of the past few days.
>
> GERASSI: That's right, and in a way, if I may say so, I consider it really very unfair, not to me, but to my students.

The reason given by Gerassi for the suspension was correct. It, and the dismissal which it preceded, were both based on his actions on December 6, not on his teaching or other activities.

December 6 was the day when long-simmering campus tensions exploded. The tensions had many causes, but they were focused on the action of College President John Summerskill in suspending two groups of students. The first were nine black students who had allegedly beaten up the editor of the student newspaper, *The Gater.* (The paper had a history of insensitivity to the concerns of black students, and had published a column on world heavyweight champion Mohammed Ali which had racist overtones.) A subsequent hearing resulted in the lifting of five suspensions, but four remained in effect.

The other suspensions were directed against the white editor and a columnist for another campus paper, *Open Process,* for publishing a poem which described a bizarre act of masturbation in four-letter words and which the poet dedicated to a member of the faculty. When the ACLU threatened Summerskill with a lawsuit over the *Open Process* suspensions, he consulted attorneys, discovered he was on weak ground, and lifted the suspensions. The black students, who claimed that their due process had been impaired by the prehearing suspensions, then demanded that the four suspended black students also be reinstated. The two cases were not parallel, however, for violence had occurred in the black student affair and the student editor had been hospitalized. According to the *ACLU News,* the ACLU Staff Counsel told Summerskill that "considerations of immediate personal violence to members of the academic community might allow suspensions and expulsions before a hearing, but that the *Open Process* matter was not such an emergency."

Summerskill refused to lift the suspension of the black students. Whether his decision was wise or not is debatable, but it was certainly legal and within the requirements of due process. The black students, however, attributed it to racism, and began to organize a confrontation. They were supported by the Progressive Labor Party, Students for a Democratic Society, and members of the *Open Process* staff. The white radicals organized the Movement Against Political Suspensions (MAPS) to join the Black Students Union in confronting Summerskill. Leaflets were issued that called him a "liberal racist" and compared San Francisco State with Mississippi.

It was on this basis that the BSU and MAPS planned for a demonstration on December 6. Jimmy Garrett, a BSU leader, said he would bring in 5,000 off-campus blacks. While some MAPS people said there would be no violence, the rhetoric of many suggested otherwise.

George Murray, a BSU member and part-time English instructor, was quoted by the *Gater* as telling a rally: "We must defend our rights by any means necessary, which means closing the school." * Jimmy Garrett said: "If you are serious, then you had better act in a serious manner. That act should be in the fullest extent—close down the Ad building if you are serious. You should have no hassle about tearing it up."

This was the kind of rhetoric that preceded December 6. It had been accompanied by rumors and fairly reliable information that some of the black students were armed with handguns. At the same time, some of the white athletes were spoiling for a fight. The administration and the faculty were greatly alarmed, for the situation had considerable potential for violence.

The events of December 6 began with a rally on the free speech platform 100 yards from the administration building. Gerassi was one of the speakers, as he had been on several previous occasions. Word reached the rally that Summerskill, fearing violence, had locked up the administration building. Some of the student speakers called it a victory. "It is a victory," Gerassi told the rally, "no doubt about it. But I say it is not enough. Either we have to keep it closed down permanently or we have to go in."

The rally subsequently moved across the lawn and approached the locked administration building. "The first act of violence," Gerassi later told the *San Francisco Chronicle,* "was in locking the door against us. What we did was an act of self-defense and self-expression." Gerassi expressed himself by boosting a student through an open window and then climbing in himself. As he described it in the December 23 *National Guardian:*

> Someone spotted an open window. A student and I pulled ourselves up and we went in. My objective was to reach the

* Murray was quoted by the *San Francisco Examiner,* December 13, 1967, as saying: "Black people cannot commit any crimes against white people. . . . Anything we do to the 'dog' cannot be wrong. . . . The only crimes we can commit are crimes against humanity. And white people aren't part of humanity."

> door and unlock it but I was stopped by security guards. By the time I freed myself from them, students had smashed the main glass doors and had started streaming in. As we embraced on the inside, I realized they were all shaking. They were scared. They knew there were hundreds of cops nearby. . . . They came in anyway, willing to risk their way of life. They had become radical.

The *Examiner* next day carried a poignant photo of Gerassi standing at the shattered doorway extending a warm *abrazo* to a girl who was wearing an old army shirt complete with First Cavalry shoulder patch. It was the Moncada Barracks, the Sierra Maestra, and the battle of Santa Clara all together, with the liberal Summerskill presumably playing Batista.

If the students were "willing to risk their way of life," as Gerassi asserts, what did he think that *he* was risking? Elsa Thompson raised this question in the Pacifica Radio interview:

> THOMPSON: . . . I assume that you are not sufficiently naive so that you thought that this was going to be with impunity.
> GERASSI: No, I realized of course that immediately a hearing would be set up, and as far as I am concerned personally, now, as a result of that hearing we could really begin to talk about the *real* causes for the unrest in general. They can get rid of me, they can rid themselves of other student leaders, they can get rid of Black Student Union leaders, the unrest will continue unless the causes are coped with in some way, tackled. I hoped, number one, that to a certain extent attention would be focused on me, and therefore there would be no reprisals against the students. That's why I felt that as soon as I noticed that the students were going to go in no matter what, that I should immediately go in myself. . . .

Whether Gerassi went into the building to help carry out his own instructions at the rally—that is, go in or close it down permanently—or whether he went in to sacrifice himself for the sake of the students as he told Elsa Thompson, is of psychological interest only. The fact is that he did go in and he expected to get in trouble for it. In so doing, he contributed to a dangerous situation which could have resulted in tragedy. By the end of the day several people had been roughed up, the bookstore had been entered, merchandise stolen and a small fire started, some classes had been invaded and dispersed by black students threatening violence, and the second floor of the administration building was ransacked. Summerskill remained cool, cancelled all classes, but didn't call the uniformed police. It was an act of courage which may have saved lives.

Gerassi saw his own actions on December 6 as a great contribution to education, "much more beneficial than a year's worth of classes," he told Elsa Thompson. In the sense that a man who contracts cholera learns something profound about tropical disease, Gerassi may be right. But there are other questions.

Not long ago the college learned that one of its professors had passed around a marijuana cigarette to the students in his classroom. Like Gerassi, he believed that he was educating them, but his method made them technically liable to prosecution for a felony. Both men had used their professorial authority to encourage students to do things which might result in injury or jail sentences. Are such "pedagogical techniques" protected by academic freedom? Can a publicly financed college which wants to continue in operation retain such professors on its staff? It seems to me as a professional educator that the answer to both these questions is obviously no.

The Hiring, Retention, and Tenure (HRT) Committee of the Department of International Relations met on December 7 to consider what to do about Gerassi. They heard his side of the story, and then recommended to the President that he be suspended for thirty days with pay and charged with "unprofessional conduct," an offense listed in the state education code as grounds for dismissal. An ad hoc committee of faculty members was appointed by the Academic Senate to make a recommendation. Its four members concluded unanimously that Gerassi's conduct was unprofessional, but, in the words of the official announcement, the committee "was evenly divided in its recommendations to the President concerning disciplinary action." All four tenured members of the International Relations Department, including myself, wrote the President recommending dismissal. Gerassi was fired, but before it was over faculty members and administration were forced to endure numerous meetings, conferences, and phone calls, as well as malicious propaganda attacks and threats to personal safety. It was not a pleasant experience, but there are certain issues that are illuminated by it.

A writer in the January issue of the *Movement,* an SDS and SNCC affiliated paper in San Francisco, described San Francisco State College as "generally more liberal than others." "For a public supported school," he said, "the college has been amazingly creative in its attitudes toward education and the role of the college in relation to the rest of society. Educational and political experimentation has been the rule rather than the exception over the past few years."

If this is true, as I believe it is, then what measures should responsible professors take to protect such an institution from student militants and men like Gerassi who, wrapping themselves in the banners of racial justice and opposition to the Vietnam war, attempt to tear it apart? It seems to me clear that so long as there is war against Vietnam but no real war on poverty and racial injustice, educators will increasingly encounter the dilemma of choosing between calling the cops and seeing their institutions destroyed.

Some portent is contained in the article which the anti-war leader and former student, Jerry Rubin, wrote for the February 2-8, 1968, *Berkeley Barb:*

> . . . I think the thing to do is to get a traveling yippee guerrilla theater band roaring through college campuses burning books, burning degrees and exams, burning school records, busting up classrooms, and freeing our brothers from the prison of the university. We'll probably get beat up or arrested, because physical force is the final protector of law and authority in the classroom. The universities cannot be reformed. They must be abandoned or closed down. They should be used as bases for actions against society, but never taken seriously. The professors have nothing to teach; we learn in action confronting America. We can learn more from any jail than we can from any university.

The complicity of some universities with the military-industrial complex is a scandal that cries out for reform of the academy, but not its liquidation. If the colleges, with all their faults, keep alive some respect for reasoned discourse, afford some opportunity for the development of new political leadership, provide a base from which constructive work can be undertaken, as many of them do, then I believe they should be protected. Protecting them will not be painless, and it will expose the defenders to attacks as fascists, finks, racists, and warmongers. It will also cause those who believe in student protest and who oppose the war and racial injustice many agonizing hours of self-doubt as they wonder whether they have somehow gotten themselves aligned with the forces of the *status quo.* But there is no escape from this unless they are willing to allow the most insane and suicidal students to set the style of political deportment.

Another factor illuminated by the travail of San Francisco State College is the extent to which the ethical and semantic environment fomented by Lyndon Johnson has corrupted even those who oppose his policies. Johnson's misuse of the authority of his high office has rendered all authority illegitimate in the eyes of many young people, and his misuse of words ("unconditional discussions," etc.) for purposes of deception has made it seem less outrageous for a college professor to refer to the locking of a door as an "act of violence," or a black student leader to say that white people "are not part of humanity."

The issue of *Open Process* for which the two students were suspended bore a cover which carried the thrice-repeated headline, "Beauty Is a Defiance of Authority," and the poem which caused all the trouble was introduced by the author with these words: "Just to be inconsistent, I guess I'll break my pledge against writing about sex." If the President of the United States cares nothing about his pledges to the American electorate concerning Vietnam, does he set an example that influences the attitude of a student toward pledges *he* has made? And who is to say that the Johnsonian example is not also in some measure responsible for the ethical posture of John Gerassi, who on the one hand says that the Peace Corps is an instrument of American imperialism but on the other hires himself out to it as a consultant during the period of his suspension? If it is true, as Gerassi says, that "the example sets the tone; the example is what influences people," then professors must be especially careful if they are to teach the young not to emulate the unethical example of Lyndon Johnson.

One of the components of the troubles at San Francisco State was the issue of "student power." It is an issue which has legitimate origins in student rebellion against unfair and authoritarian controls existing on some campuses, and resentment against the depersonalized, assembly-line character of much higher education. While this feeling tends to be concentrated among New Left groups, it is shared by enough other students to cause a polarization of students and faculty on some campuses into two hostile camps. This did not appear to be happening at San Francisco State until the fall of 1967, when it seemed to be related to the issue of authority.

The faculty member is inevitably an authority figure. I mean this not in the psychological sense, but in the educational and legal sense. He derives his authority from his superior knowledge of the subject matter he teaches and from the institution which requires him to allocate grades and serve on committees that decide on scholarships, curriculum, and many other matters affecting the students' academic careers. The inseparable companion of authority is responsibility. The faculty member has the authority to reward the student with good grades and letters of recommendation. He also has the responsibility to preserve the integrity of the institution by identifying and giving poor grades to those students who lack the ability or the initiative to do competent work.

Although there is a great deal of controversy about grades, in most institutions the professor is required to evaluate the performance of each of his students. It is always a painful process, for it invariably involves telling some students that they did less well than others. Many a professor has perceived a marked change in his rapport with a class immediately after the announcement of the midterm grades. The experience can be painful for student and professor alike. It is not surprising that there are many who would like to abolish the entire grading system.

One explanation of Gerassi's popularity with his students was his understanding of their attitudes on this question. "My feeling," he told Pacifica Radio, "has always been that a teacher must not separate himself from his students. There must be a relationship that's direct. I must learn from them, and they must learn from me. And, as far as experience is concerned, they are perfectly my equal. Their experiences are just as meaningful for them as my experiences are meaningful for me. And if I've lived maybe five years more than they have [Gerassi is thirty-six], that doesn't make me superior in any way."

While there can be no quarrel with the assertion that the experiences of students are just as meaningful for them as those of faculty members are for them, the notion that a student is "perfectly my equal" and that the professor is not "superior in any way" requires more careful consideration. It received such consideration by the Study Commission on University Governance composed of students and faculty of the University of California, Berkeley. Their scholarly report, published in January, makes a persuasive case for increased student participation in all aspects of the governance of the university, and I am in general agreement with it. On educational policy matters, where the Commission felt that professional judgment is critical, the report pointed out that "by comparison with faculty and administrators, students are substantially disadvantaged in experience, professional judgment, and long-term responsibility to the institution." But while granting authority to faculty and administrators in matters of educational policy, the report correctly cautioned against using this authority in other areas. "We think students today distinguish," the report said, "intuitively at least, between the natural authority which stems from scholarship and the misuse of authority which stems from status. One cannot expect academic status of administrators or the claims of academic or administrative expertise to provide legitimacy for decisions in such areas as lock-out hours for a dormitory, the penalty for stealing a book from the library, or the size of a political poster allowed to be displayed on a plaza or bulletin board."

But the question arises: if it is improper to use the authority which stems from scholarship to give legitimacy to decisions on lock-out hours, etc., is it not also improper to use that authority to give legitimacy to violent methods of protest on the campus? And when a professor who is a specialist on revolution tells an audience of students that they should close down the administration building, do all the students, intuitively or otherwise, dissociate the professor from the status he possesses? The Gerassi case provides little hard evidence on these difficult questions, for he declined to exercise the normal responsibility of academic authority. For example, he gave all his students "A's." In style, dress, associations, and deportment he made it clear that he regarded the students, and not the faculty, as his peer group. This may explain why his dismissal has caused concern primarily among students, and why no faculty defense committee was formed in his behalf.

While authoritarianism is as inimical to the academy as it is to democracy and must certainly be resisted, there can be no lasting social or political organization without some form of authority. It is one of the aspects of the unhealthy state of the American society that all authority is losing its legitimacy in the eyes of many young people. The way to restore society to health, however, is not simply to assert the importance of authority or merely to back it up with overwhelming force, although force at times may be necessary. The re-establishment of respected authority on college campuses requires something more. It requires the restoration of legitimacy, and that may not be possible as long as there is so little confidence in the integrity and legitimacy of the national government. So long as the Vietnam war continues, so long as young students must confront the terrible dilemmas caused by the draft, so long as some universities and many professors support the war or remain indifferent to it, it will be hard to arrest the disintegration of morale and the feeling of despair that gives rise to phenomena like John Gerassi.

One of the great ironies involved in the spread of the mindless notion that "Beauty Is a Defiance of Authority" is that it will hurt the student antiwar movement as much as it hurts the universities, for it breeds a mood in which the movement itself can have no authority—neither the authority of leadership nor the authority of ideology. Without authority the movement will have no structure or discipline, and without discipline its effectiveness will be ephemeral.

John Gerassi replies:

Professor Marshall Windmiller is a liberal, and like all liberals, he has problems reconciling his basic faith in the American system and his undoubtedly genuine revulsion at the crimes perpetrated by that system. As long as the battleground is outside academia, he can remain on the moral offensive—verbally—and condemn the war in Vietnam, the invasion of Santo Domingo, the Congo massacres, even racism in Oakland, Detroit, and Mississippi.

When, however, the battleground narrows onto the soft green commons below his academic window, the contradictions inevitably must reveal themselves. To soften them to his own conscience and to try to conceal them from his academic peers, he must wage an attack laden with "academic objectivity"—quotes out of context, innuendoes by association, even personal diatribes and attempts at character assassination. Thus, the real issue of the responsibility of the academic intellectual who profits from a system he would like to condemn becomes blurred by irrelevant arguments and statements. And, in this case, it forces me to counter these statements. But I shall broaden my case so as to draw more universal lessons from it.

Windmiller's contention is that the academic dissenter should play a passive role on campus, limiting his dissent to legal opposition off campus. As a corollary he must defend the proposition that on campus the teacher should stick to teaching, and counseling students according to their individual scholarly (and, it turns out, career, i.e., employment) needs. To maintain this position, he must then differentiate between education and propaganda, and insist that anyone who propagandizes, who plays an active role in dissent on the campus, must be fired. Since this would lead him, were he to be consistent, to advocating the end of academic freedom (with officials having to check up on teachers in their classrooms and the ensuing witch-hunts), and since he personally played the principal role in my being fired, he must justify his position by contending that taking an active part in dissent on campus, as I did, necessarily leads to violence. The outside world is violent, he says, but the university must not be. The only way to accomplish this separation is to turn the academy into a sanctuary. And that can only be achieved by keeping all dissent passive.

My argument is that students are not bracketed off from the world when they are on campus, and neither should be teachers; that the academy produces the cogs which will keep our society violent precisely because the academy is a crucial institution in the fostering and strengthening of our system; and that this system is violent by its very nature. I further insist that the responsibility of teachers should be to the students and not to the administration or to some abstract concept of what the academy ought to be. That such responsibility entails the awareness that unless the system-academy is constantly challenged the average student graduated by it will inevitably end up fortifying the system and hence help increase violence. That, therefore, the politically aware teacher must play an active role in dissent, must confront the system at all levels and most specifically on campus—in the classroom, at the war recruiters' booths, in the academic senates, in faculty meetings and so on. He must fight grade regulations, curriculum standards, administration edicts, entrance discriminations, as well as the arbitrary power of the trustees. Wherever and whenever the student demands involve not only campus restrictions but also their opposition to the system "outside," it is the duty of that teacher to join the students in militant action—even at the risk of losing his job. What should guide that teacher in evaluating the risk is not abstract concepts but his own effectiveness (and that, inevitably, will sometimes lead to miscalculations) in contributing to the destruction of the violent system as a whole.

I further believe that those "dissenting" academicians who do not take such risks do so only because they do not want to lose their jobs, no matter how they rationalize it. For example, it is absolutely clear to me that Professor Windmiller saw a direct threat to his leadership status in the events at State. And so did all "faculty-ized" liberal faculty members. For so long as dissent is restricted to a passive verbal level, such "dissenters" as Windmiller can remain in the forefront. The events destroyed that. Hence in his article, Windmiller must try to discredit me personally.

Let me point out, first, that Windmiller was fully aware of my political position long before I was "fired up," as he says, by my trip to Cuba. In April, 1967, shortly after my return from North Vietnam, I spoke at San Francisco State College. Windmiller was in attendance when I described that trip and when I concluded by saying that genuine American patriots must not just be opposed to the War in Vietnam, but must work for the downfall of American imperialism even if this means joining international brigades should the Vietnamese request them. It was after that speaking tour that I was offered the job at San Francisco State, and I shall explain why in a moment.

(Incidentally, why does Windmiller stress the fact that also in attendance at the OLAS meeting was Stokely Carmichael, "who was lionized by the Cubans as an authentic American revolutionary," and not the fact that correspondents from *The Washington Post, Look, Life, The New York Review of Books,* etc., were also present? Is he trying to associate me with Stokely and thus discredit me to *New York Review* readers who, by and large, tend to consider Stokely irresponsible? If so, fine, since there are very few men in America whom I respect more than him. But what relevance does this have to the issue at hand?)

Next, Windmiller quotes a long passage from an extemporaneous speech that I delivered on Cuba, in which I insisted that there was "incredible freedom" there. Of course, he does not mention the fact that I was talking about *meaningful* freedom, by which I clearly meant that in Cuba today criticism is seriously considered at the highest official levels, which is not the case in America. And that is so: there is nothing that Fidel and the other Cuban leaders take more seriously, debate more profoundly than the constructive criticism of the young. But again, what relevance does this have to the issue of protest on the campus?

Be that as it may, I did say and I do say that the power structure in America does profit from the kind of dissent that liberals like to voice; it reinforces the myth that America is an open society. That is why the Establishment (if not Johnson) encourages people like Windmiller to condemn the War in Vietnam on Pacifica radio stations. And that is why people like me are paid honorariums to address Establishment academic gatherings. So long as all we do is talk, we reinforce the myth. We thus function as cogs in the over-all structure, which, as everybody knows, defends freedom "at home and abroad."

Windmiller then uses an exchange between radio interviewer Elsa Knight Thompson and me to claim that I admit that I was fired *only* for my activity in the demonstration of December 6. Please read that passage again. I made no such admission. I did say, correctly, that I was *not* suspended (now fired) for my teaching, but where "other activities" creeps in is puzzling. On the contrary, it is my conviction that I was fired for *all* my non-teaching activities. In fact, prior to December 6, Windmiller himself warned me that if I wanted to be rehired next year I should keep my political activities off-campus and should be "around" more often with my "peers," i.e., fellow faculty members, not students. I point out these details because they are not characteristic only of Windmiller, but are typical of the academic mind.

In this respect, I must relate the following. During the October 16-21 Stop-the-Draft-Week confrontation at Oakland, two San Francisco State professors were arrested. Their names were listed in the local newspapers. At State, their pay was docked for their absences. I was also at Oakland, but was not arrested (nor were twenty-odd other San Francisco State teachers from other departments). My pay, however, was also docked. Why? Because Windmiller, who knew that I was at Oakland, reported it to the appropriate authorities "in the name of fairness." Windmiller then explained that "members of the Department, including myself, who support the Anti-War Movement, then contributed to a fund designed to make up the financial loss to the faculty members involved."

This, to me, is very revealing of the Liberal's purism—and that is why I mention it. The Liberal believes in following the letter of the laws and regulations of a system he criticizes as unjust (which, hence, presumably enacts unjust laws and regulations), even to the extent of becoming its policeman or informer, and then tries to buy back justification to soothe his conscience. I know that most academics will approve of this highly—and that position, to me, is symptomatic of academic liberals' inability to participate in the destruction of that injustice we all recognize.

The list of logical fallacies, motivated by the Liberal's obsession with keeping his cause pure and his hands clean, is endless. Take, for example, this Windmiller statement: "When the ACLU threatened Summerskill with a lawsuit over the *Open Process* suspension, he consulted attorneys, discovered he was on weak ground, and lifted the suspension." The implications of this apparently do not shock him. That Summerskill should have such arbitrary power in the first place is not even questioned.

And so on! There's Windmiller's attempt to discredit the Black Student Union leaders, Jimmy Garrett and George Murray, by quoting passages appearing in the *Gater* (which is a Hearst scandal sheet) when both Garrett and Murray deny those statements (and Windmiller himself has often been outraged by the *Gater*'s inaccuracy in reporting *his own* statements); there's that absurd reference to the army clothes worn by one demonstrator when Windmiller knows full well that many poor students wear such second-hand garb because it is cheap and lasting; there's that outright distortion that the four-man committee of my peers hearing my case "was evenly divided in its recommendations . . ." when their official report said that three members "recommended that the suspension of Mr. Gerassi be lifted immediately," while *one* recommended that I be dismissed.

Windmiller's concern over my "ethical posture," which is put into question because I spoke to Peace Corpsmen, is central to his case. Though meant to discredit me, it is an important issue since it reveals again the Liberals' purism. Windmiller, who used to think the Peace Corps was "one of the most hopeful creations of the twentieth century" and a possible "instrument of change and enlightenment," now has second thoughts. Under Johnson and Peace Corps Director Jack Vaughn, Windmiller says, it has become "not a revolutionary organization, but a counter-revolution organization. It is the advanced guard of the Marines—counter-insurgency in a velvet glove. Young people who sincerely want to see progressive change in the world would be best advised to stay out of it. The places where their efforts are really needed are right here at home."

But how do you get those young people to stay "here at home?" You talk to them. Before they join? Yes, says Windmiller. After they join? No, says Windmiller. Why? Because to talk to them at their training camps means to become a paid consultant, accepting their dirty money. No matter how many crimes he could prevent by accepting such money, a good Liberal (one who never did accept CIA funds) must never do so. And yet the Movement is full of Peace Corps drop-outs. Why did they quit? Because radicals, people who are more concerned about stopping the crimes than accepting "dirty money," people like Saul Landau, James O'Connor, Timothy Harding, and so forth, went to the Corps camps, sought out those volunteers who wanted to see progressive changes, and explained to them why there can never be meaningful changes in the underdeveloped world until the country that exploits that world is itself changed—the USA. To Liberals, neither the people of the underdeveloped world nor the flesh-and-blood idealistic youths who join the Peace Corps really matter. What does matter, as Windmiller honestly says, is their own ethical posture.

This concern with abstract morality has peculiar consequences. Before December 6, for example, the students and faculty members of the International Relations Department met to discuss "important issues." Some students presented this petition:

> We, the undersigned, believe that the present administration by engaging in an unjust and illegal war has lost the right to represent us.
>
> We feel that a condition of crisis exists and that the present policy of aggression in Vietnam constitutes a threat to national security by undermining our democratic values.
>
> We believe that officials of the Department of Defense, Department of State, the Central Intelligence Agency, and the United States Information Agency are subversive who are acting against the interest of the American people by supporting the war.
>
> Therefore, we ask that the Department of International Relations inform any officials of the above agencies who wish to speak in this department that they are not welcome until American involvement in the War in Vietnam is ended.

A vast majority of International Relations students present approved this petition. So did all department teachers, save two. One opposed it. The other, Windmiller, abstained, explaining in a long monologue that he could not vote in favor of the petition so long as any student sought his help in obtaining a job from these Federal agencies; he could not take the responsibility of stopping him from doing so, he said. He had to be open to all students. In other words, his argument was that if some student asks him how best can he go about killing Vietnamese, he considers it his duty, so long as he teaches International Relations, to give him such advice, even if he thinks the war is immoral.

Well, what did happen at San Francisco State on December 6 and why? In the first place it is not true that the college is radical. In a lengthy and highly documented article, published both in *Open Process* (January 10, 1968) and in the *Mid-Peninsula Observer* (January 22-February 5, 1968), Professors Anatole Anton (Philosophy) and Richard Fitzgerald (History) insist that San Francisco State, "far from being a citadel of freedom, sorely reflects the complete capitulation of the academy in the United States to industry and government. In addition, its internal structure reflects the undemocratic paternal nature of outside American society, displaying no more than a shred of commitment to liberal values."

And even if it once was radical (due to its student body, not its staff), it no longer is. As Professor Rudolf H. Weingartner, in his January 15, 1968 letter of resignation as Chairman of the Philosophy Department (he subsequently quit altogether), complained:

> . . . the San Francisco State administration is rapidly becoming a "team" with an interest of its own. It is shaping itself into a technocracy that is rapidly losing touch with the best creative impulses in the faculty and the student body. The administration now is coming to serve the "silent majority" of the faculty for the sake of quiet and order. . . . Instead of being a bulwark against the desires of politicians, outside pressures have made out of our own administration a funnel as well. . . . Throughout this, the faculty has remained supine. It has been unable to deal with the pressures from the outside, nor does it seem able to face the demands of student groups on campus. The power has shifted from the

> faculty (whose grasp was never firm) to an administration intent upon keeping the wheels turning smoothly. I have no doubt that law and order will soon be restored; I only doubt that there will be a College in San Francisco, rather than merely a branch of the System.

It was precisely to offset this new image of reality that campus Liberals, including President Summerskill and Marshall Windmiller, had been shopping around for visible moves to offer as proof of their continuing liberalism. Thus did Windmiller hire me. Perhaps unconsciously, he saw in the act of bringing "a revolutionary" into his department a way of exhibiting, mostly to himself, the sincerity of his "ethical posture." The expectation, of course, was that I would keep my "revolutionary" activity off campus.

But America's youth can no longer be fooled by gestures. They judge institutions by their actions, and San Francisco State—by its racist daily newspaper (the *Gater* was controlled by the Journalism Department), by its policy of allowing war recruiters, Dow Chemical, ROTC, the CIA and so forth, on campus, by the simple statistical fact that fewer blacks were registered this year than last—was constantly proving itself to be a typical American institution. Liberals at State could well talk about their relatively free Experimental College, just as Washington Liberals talk about their War on Poverty; the fact is that life on campus was and is a microcosm of life in America.

Like any other college, State has a Business Administration School, but no Union Administration School, no Community Organizing School, no student court of appeals, no student board of supervisors on curricula, teachers or administrators, no student policy board, etc. In other words, students at San Francisco State, as on any other campus, are forced either to leave or adapt to the standards and policies of their elders, whose values they no longer respect. And when teachers take their side, teachers such as Dr. Juan Martinez, a Mexican-American who sided with the Black Students Union, or Richard Fitzgerald, who offered to sponsor BSU courses in the Experimental College, they are fired (in the case of Fitzgerald, the day after he had been rehired and taken his BSU stand; "a clerical mistake," said the History Department).

The Administration at State, as in Washington, is authoritative and arbitrary. First it acts, against students or in the Gulf of Tonkin, then it offers vague explanations. And the System, with its elections every four years or a Free Speech area where any student can say what he feels, remains unaffected. For both the elections and the speeches are used to reinforce the System itself.

Against such domination, people inevitably, sooner or later, rebel. First the Vietnamese, then the Dominicans, then the blacks and finally the students. In the San Francisco area, this year, it began in earnest at Oakland during the October 16-21 Stop-the-Draft Week. On the first day the students were pacifists. On the second they were civil disobedients—and were beaten. On the third and fourth, they trained, planned, and learned. On the fifth they fought—and held their own. They were jubilant and they were proud.

To campus liberals, this newly visible militancy became a threat. Brought back to campus, it could shatter their sinecures. Suppose the students understood that, as Professors Anton and Fitzgerald put it, "We simply do not have today (since the beginning, at least, of the cold war in 1945) the kinds of free choices to make that Windmiller assumes"? Suppose the students realize that American academia, for all its fostering of verbal dissent, is not a marketplace of ideas, but an essential institution in producing the cogs and technocrats and ideologues needed to run, justify and rationalize American imperialism? The Vietnamese know that their enemy is the American System, but to fight it they must stop ordinary soldiers. The blacks know that their enemy is the American System, but to fight it they must stop ordinary cops. Suppose the white students, who also realize that their enemy is the American System, concluded that to fight it they must confront their ordinary teachers, who, through liberal rhetoric about choices, pervert their goals and corrupt their ideals? It must not happen. Thus, to channel, sublimate, and co-opt their militancy, San Francisco State's astute Liberals invented the Convocation.

A week-long affair in November, the Convocation was simply one mammoth bull session, run in academic orderliness. All teachers were requested to cancel their classes (with no dock in pay, naturally) so that students could all come to discuss the issues, in a neatly separated agenda. From the Convocation's topics, resolutions were drawn and then put to a campus-wide vote. As expected, the keep-the-campus-open resolutions won. Thus Summerskill could now say—and he and campus liberals did say—that though the War was immoral, he was bound by the consensus: war recruiters would be invited on campus. It was like a

German intellectual saying that though killing the Jews was immoral, the majority of Germans want to do so, hence my individual duty is to help. Strangely, the Liberals did not push their theory consistently: they did not say that since most white Americans are racists, it is their duty to encourage racism.

But to the black students at SF State, it was as if they had said it. Previously, on November 6, a group of them, fed up at the racist columns in the *Gater,* went to their immediate source, the *Gater* editor and staff (the ordinary soldier to the Vietnamese, the ordinary cop to the ghetto black) and a confrontation ensued. The editor was allegedly knocked out. Immediately, the campus liberals condemned the "violence," and approved Summerskill's suspensions of four black students involved in the incident. Windmiller agreed. The case of the *Open Process* suspensions and that of the blacks "were not parallel," he says, "for violence had occurred in the black student affair." This simply shows his inability to understand America. To whites, who do not suffer as directly as blacks, a put-down can be nothing more than censorship. But to the blacks, who suffer physically, psychologically, constantly and consistently from racism and its *direct* consequences—police repression and terror, unwarranted arrests and harassment, poverty and indignity—racist columns do constitute violence, for they reinforce, encourage, and broaden the physical and psychological oppressions. Thus, Windmiller and other liberals may call the BSU's confrontation with the *Gater* editor "violence" if they wish; to the campus radicals, to the blacks and to me, their act was self-defense, perhaps a tactical mistake but as justifiable as a Vietnamese counter-attack or as Black Panther leader Huey Newton's alleged gun-down of Oakland cops (which is probably a frame-up anyway).

To student radicals at State, the Convocation co-optation, the *Gater* incident, the reinstatement of the white staffers on *Open Process,* the firing of popular anti-war teachers, Oakland, the war recruiters, the War itself, the university's role in that war, the lack of student voice in their own and in the college's affairs were all interwoven. And the series of protest rallies which preceded December 6 directly related to all of them. But the students' demands were specific: "(1) Drop the suspension of the six students [the four blacks and the two whites who had not yet been reinstated]; all trials in the future shall be conducted by a board of elected peers; (2) reinstate *Open Process;* (3) end political harassment of faculty, students, and administrators; (4) no outside police on campus; (5) student control of student affairs, specifically of student publications."

These were reasonable demands. These were demands that liberals should have supported (and the American Federation of Teachers local did support them). These were demands continuously ignored by the administration (which publicly promised to enforce its rejection by threatening to call outside police if necessary). The demands amounted, perhaps, to a weak call for student power, and that was enough to be considered a threat to those on the faculty who view the academy as a sanctuary; for with even such a mild dose of power, the students, who do not live outside the nasty everyday world, would obviously bring it back onto the campus, from which it is now excluded.

Conversely, my support of these demands was also deemed a threat. Windmiller means just that when he says: "in style, dress, associations and deportment, he made it clear that he regarded the students and not the faculty as his peer group." True enough, for I respect students, as a group, far more than the faculty-ized faculty (as opposed to the Antons, Fitzgeralds, Martinezes and other committed teachers). The reason is simple enough. The students genuinely try to understand the society in which they live. The teachers, however, try to justify it. The students have no awesome admiration for America's institutions, nor do they profit from them. They are aware that those institutions lead to the criminal American foreign and internal repressive policies.

In any case, the students' demands were not met. In fact, they were not even considered. Finally, a deadline was fixed: noon on December 6, or else the students would mill-in at the Administration Building. MAPS and BSU issued leaflet after leaflet calling for support, explaining their aims, promising a non-violent demonstration. On December 6, as the noon hour approached, word came that the administration had sent most of its employees home—to avoid violence, it said—and had closed down the building. It was a lock-out.

I called it an act of violence. A factory lock-out is considered an act of violence against workers. Why shouldn't an Administration Building lock-out be considered an act of violence against students? Because liberal academics, who consider all university intellectual adults their peer group, look upon academia as belonging to them, not to students. Notice, for example, how

Windmiller says that "educators will increasingly encounter the dilemma of choosing between calling the cops and seeing *their* institutions destroyed [italics mine]." Because of their financial, psychological, and political identification with the administration (and, therefore, the power structure), such academics necessarily end up viewing students as "the enemy." Windmiller is intelligent enough to realize that this could lead to class distinctions, so instead he must create a weird relationship model of authority-respect-responsibility. But the result is a caste system.

Anyway, the students went in. So did I—through an open window. It did not take great courage for Summerskill not to call the uniformed police, waiting off campus—just shrewdness and an awareness of the dialectics of over-reaction. Meanwhile, as some students broke the glass doors to go in, others abandoned the cause. Respect for private property is hard to shake, even when that property is yours but is being used as a bastion against you. At stake, after all, is our whole American way of life, based on the greed of competition, evaluated in material possessions, justified by the concept of free enterprise, propagandized by the cult of the rich, ending in imperial domination.

Summerskill cooled it. With plainclothes police, photographers, reporters, TV cameramen, and a battery of administrators and "acceptable" faculty members on the inside, he simply waited. Of the 2,000 students who surrounded the Administration Building, only 300 went in. Not enough political work had been done, not enough of a base had been established. In that light, the student action was probably a mistake. I let the justness of the students' cause carry me into losing my forum. I was suspended—not because I went in (other professors who felt strongly about the students' demands had also gone in), not because a reactionary administration chose me as a scapegoat, but because Windmiller and other liberals in my department recommended that I be suspended. They did so as a warning to all other non-faculty-ized teachers not to dissent actively. Later, Liberal Summerskill signed criminal complaints against eleven students and against me. Were these eleven leaders in the demonstration? Had they perhaps been the ones who broke the door? No. They were radical student leaders: four members of Progressive Labor, the two co-chairmen of Students for a Democratic Society, members of the powerless student legislature, and Jimmy Garrett, the head of the BSU, who arrived at the Administration Building half an hour after it had been entered.

On January 2, 1968, I had my hearing at San Francisco State. Windmiller testified, insisted that I be fired because I was a propagandist, not an educator. He was asked to define the difference. Propaganda leads to action, he said; education does not. And there is the crux of the liberals' creed. Action must be avoided at all costs and the ethical posture of purity always maintained. (Although that too can be twisted, as when Windmiller made a formal request that my hearing be set aside on the grounds that it was open to students who, presumably, intimidated my hearers; but Summerskill, basing himself on the hearing chairman's statement to him that "The Committee further recognizes that the ultimate decision must be yours, . . ." ignored the hearers' 3 to 1 split in my favor and fired me anyway. Why the farce then? I was even billed for the transcript cost.)

What lessons are to be derived from all this? There are many. Radical students learned that a just cause cannot be explained and propagated just by rallies and leaflets; hard grass-roots work must precede action. Though talk of a base is often used in the Left, especially the old Left, as an excuse for inaction, and though it is often true that action itself can be an organizing tool, it is equally true that militant action without a strong base of support often results in failure.

Personally, I learned how easy it is to derive faulty consequences from accurate analysis; the only check against confusing objective and subjective conditions is to work within a collective. Such a collective might have reminded me that so long as the young continue to go to colleges, the role of the radical teacher is to work with them. Just as a radical must jump at the opportunity of politicizing Peace Corpsmen, so must he not sacrifice his possibility of politicizing students—unless the sacrifice itself leads to a major political breakthrough. Also, by its criticism, such a collective might have given me the distance necessary to deal with my own actions more objectively in print, in my *National Guardian* article which, though badly edited, repeated my mistake by stressing the faulty consequences rather than the accurate analysis.

Most important of all, however, was the students' realization that they must never trust anyone who profits from the structure, even if he is objectively only a pawn. By analogy, therefore, many white radical students at State have now understood why black liberation leaders cannot and must not trust white radicals, for the white, by the simple fact of color, can survive and flourish materially within the white racist structure—unless, by his life-commitment, he is no longer reconcilable. That is why all talk of black-white alliances is just that—talk. Such alliances can exist only in practice, on the battlefield so to speak, and on the blacks' terms. For, as blacks point out, they *need* a change, the whites only *want* one. That difference is crucial.

In academia, the analogy is between the liberal faculty-ized member and the radical student. The student needs a change to survive, not physically (though he faces death in Vietnam), but mentally, as he is. The teacher may like to see a change, but does not need it. On the contrary, he is really wary of changes lest they destroy his career, his sinecure, his rationale, his whole life-style. His objection to the system is that it is eating away at his authority, at his "legitimacy," as Windmiller says. His concern is "to restore society to health." What health? What garden of Eden? It is not just the restoration of the "legitimacy of the national government," that liberals seek, but their own. Their world is meaningless without authority and they correctly understand that their authority is destroyed in a world based on collective humanism rather than on competition. This is implicit in Windmiller's statement that giving of grades "is always a painful process, for it invariably involves telling some students that *they did less well than others.*" Only if that's the way you think.

To others, who would not reject the system, a grade could mean telling the student how well he is doing, *not* in relation to *others,* but in relation to himself and his own potential. I tried an experiment this year: I told students they would all receive A's and then asked them to do what they wanted—for themselves—whatever the course inspired them to really want to say. The result was revealing. Some didn't do anything, true. But never before have I received such solid, thoughtful, meaningful work from not only registered students, but also auditors. Most illuminating, however, was the amount of work I received that was the product of a collective—including a twenty-page poem about Nicaraguan rebel "General of the People" Sandino, written by six students working together. Does it matter whether or not it was good? To Windmiller that's all that would matter. To the future of mankind, what will matter will be the attitude of such students who can relate and correlate their egos *to try to create together*—that is if they are allowed to continue.

The American System cannot let them. For what would happen if such an attitude spread? Sooner or later workers would manage General Motors together, the distinction between foreman and lineman—a distinction imposed not by respect but by authority—would disappear, and then before you know it, there would be no academic department chairmen, no associate professors with tenure, holding literally life-power over instructors. No grades, no authority—except the authority willingly delegated because of respect earned not through knowledge and "objective" competitive accomplishments, but through the use of that knowledge in warmth and human consideration.

That is why the liberal, ingrained, faculty-ized academician has no choice but to defend the System as it is. He is no different than the conservative ingrained academician. He belongs to the same class, the sub-power-class.

Thus did liberals and social democrats, who have always talked of individual human values, inevitably betray these values when their own authority and that of their class were at stake. German social democrats voted for rearmament. Léon Blum stopped arms shipment to Spain. Guy Mollet shouted (February 9, 1956): "France will fight in Algeria and she will stay." Two years later François Mitterand, now revered by American intellectuals as the greatest leader of France's non-communist Left, added: "Algeria is France. From Flanders to the Congo, only one law, only one nation, only one parliament. That is the constitution and that is our will. The only negotiation is war." A true inspiration to LBJ.

And here at home, American liberal intellectuals objected (usually privately) to Joe McCarthy's tactics, not his goals. (Today they tell activists, as Henry Steele Commager points out in his eloquent *New Republic* article of February 24, 1968: "I may agree with you, but I disagree profoundly with the manner in which you say it.") They heralded Diem. They praised the Alliance for Progress. Until Johnson took away its liberal rhetoric, they considered the Peace Corps "one of the most hopeful creations of the twentieth century." They let America execute the Rosenbergs. They, the Liberals, the Harrimans, the Kennans, then the Schlesingers and Hilsmans, invented and propagated the whole Cold War. And now they will vote for Robert Kennedy—and make impotent speeches when the police of Oakland, Detroit, Carolina, and

Newark unleash their systematic "final solution" to the black problem. Why? Because to do anything more than march, sit-in, and talk might challenge the whole "legitimacy"—and their own hard-earned authority.

And when their consciences cannot stand it anymore, when they can no longer claim that Vietnam, Detroit, Santo Domingo, Guatemala, the Congo, Brazil, etc., were inevitable but understandable mistakes of American "pluralism," then, like Camus, their hero, perhaps a great writer but surely not a great man, they will withdraw even more into their search for the pure cause, putting down the activists' mistakes (for all men who act *do* make mistakes) by concentrating their efforts on discrediting them—to placate their own frustrated consciences.

Finally, when the New Left will condemn them for supporting the whole System, with its legal machinery, its "free" press, its "right to dissent," and, yes its educational apparatus, all designed, as Carl Davidson said, "to sustain the dominant order, containing potential forces for change within its pre-established, ultimately castrating, confines," they will shout "romanticism" (heresy)—and resort to smears.

Academic liberals are the scholastics of the modern era, and like their medieval colleagues, the consequence of their actions in life is to keep God omnipotent. The only difference is that today God is Imperial America.

Ed. note: A further exchange of correspondence took place, and can be found in the New York Review of Books, *July 11 and August 1, 1968.*

PART IV

THE ESTABLISHMENT: HOW TO RESPOND TO TURMOIL

Student rebellions on college campuses confronted the faculty, administration, and local and Federal government with a series of dilemmas. Strategy was as much a problem for the establishment as it was for the radical movement. Some maintained that the student revolt should be condemned categorically as a threat to law, order, reason, and progress; others said it should be excused in part because there were legitimate grievances. Some insisted that authorities take a hard line on every transgression; others advised that they overlook minor infractions on campus rules and propriety. Some suggested concessions to win over moderate students and cut into the radicals' base of support; others insisted that any concession made to force would only encourage the further use of force. Some called for stiffer legislation against campus disruption; others cautioned that it was not necessary and would only help the radicals.

At stake in this dispute was the maintenance of authority. Would authority be strengthened or weakened by granting concessions? calling in police? overlooking minor disruptions? enforcing rules even for trivial actions?

These were the tactical considerations on the establishment side. To one wing of the establishment, the authorities faced a choice between firmness and appeasement. To another wing, the choice was between inflexibility and strategic compromise. To the radicals, however, watching from the outside, the establishment was merely debating whether to use repression or co-optation against them.

CHAPTER 13

Official Responses

In June 1969, following a spring of disturbances at Harvard, Cornell, and San Francisco State, the National Commission on the Causes and Prevention of Violence issued a statement on campus unrest.* The commission, which had been created in the wake of the assassinations of Martin Luther King, Jr. and Robert F. Kennedy, made a series of recommendations, both to universities and to the public. The statement advised university communities to develop a "broad consensus" on rules for protest. Administrators were urged to prepare contingency plans for campus disruptions and to institute reforms in governance to "permit more rapid and effective decision-making."

While the commission's statement decried the use of force and violence, it did recognize that many students were genuinely and legitimately concerned about national problems. In a dissent from the statement, one committee member insisted that campus violence be condemned "without extenuation."

A third view of student unrest came from the Cox Commission, a panel established by the Columbia University faculty with the concurrence of the trustees to investigate the 1968 upheaval at that campus. The commission, chaired by Archibald Cox, Profes-

* For the report of a second Presidential commission made a year later, see below, Appendix B.

sor of Law at Harvard University and former Solicitor General of the United States, rejected the view that the uprising was the result merely of a "conspiracy of student radicals." Rather, Columbia was buffeted by storms that had their origin outside the university. Internal difficulties—"an administration that too often conveyed an attitude of authoritarianism and invited distrust"—aggravated the situation. The commission denied violence was a legitimate tactic for change, but insisted change was necessary. It called on the university and especially "the liberal and reform-minded students" to convert the crisis into a "creative source of renewal."

Statement of the National Commission on the Causes and Prevention of Violence, June 9, 1969.

Interim Statement on Campus Disorder

MEMBERS OF THE COMMISSION
DR. MILTON S. EISENHOWER
CHAIRMAN
JUDGE A. LEON HIGGINBOTHAM
VICE CHAIRMAN
CONGRESSMAN HALE BOGGS
TERENCE CARDINAL COOKE
AMBASSADOR PATRICIA ROBERTS HARRIS
SENATOR PHILIP A. HART
ERIC HOFFER
SENATOR ROMAN HRUSKA
LEON JAWORSKI
ALBERT E. JENNER, JR.
CONGRESSMAN WILLIAM M. MCCULLOCH
JUDGE ERNEST W. MCFARLAND
DR. W. WALTER MENNINGER

The members of this Commission, along with most Americans, are deeply disturbed by the violence and disorder that have swept the nation's campuses. Our colleges and universities cannot perform their vital functions in an atmosphere that exalts the struggle for power over the search for truth, the rule of passion over the rule of reason, physical confrontation over rational discourse.

We are equally disturbed, however, by the direction of much public *reaction* to campus unrest. Those who would punish colleges and universities by reducing financial support, by passing restrictive legislation, or by political intervention in the affairs of educational institutions, may unwittingly be helping the very radical minority of students whose objective is to destroy our present institutions of higher education.

So threatening is the situation, so essential is the need for understanding and calm appraisal, that this Commission feels compelled to speak now rather than to remain silent until publication of its final report next fall. We offer our comments during the summer pause in the hope that they will contribute to constructive thought and action before the beginning of the new academic year in September.

The problem of campus unrest is more than a campus problem. Its roots lie deep in the larger society. There is no single cause, no single solution. We urge all Americans to reject hasty and simplistic answers. We urge them to distinguish between peaceful protest and violent disruption, between the non-conformity of youth and the terror tactics of the extremists. We counsel patience, understanding and support for those in the university community who are trying to preserve freedom and order on the campus. We do so in the conviction that our universities and colleges are beginning to learn how to achieve change without disorder or coercion.

I.

During the past year, many of America's universities and colleges have been seriously wounded. These wounds arise from multiple causes. One is the increasingly violent expression of widespread student discontent. Although much of this discontent often focuses on grievances within the campus environment, it is rooted in dissatisfactions with the larger society that the campus can do little about.

Students are unwilling to accept the gaps between professed ideals and actual performance. They see afresh the injustices that remain unremedied. They are not impressed by the dangers that previous generations have overcome and the problems they have solved. It means little to them that the present adult generation found the way out of a major depression to unparalleled heights of economic abundance, or that it defeated a massive wave of vicious totalitarianism and preserved the essential elements of freedom for the youth of today. To students, these triumphs over serious dangers serve primarily to emphasize other problems we are just beginning to solve.

Today's intelligent, idealistic students see a nation which has achieved the physical ability to provide food, shelter and education for all, but has not yet devised social institutions that do so. They see a society, built on the principle that all men are created equal, that has not yet assured equal opportunity in life. They see a world of nation-states with the technical brilliance to harness the ultimate energy but without the common sense to agree on methods of preventing mutual destruction. With the fresh energy and idealism of the young, they are impatient with the progress that has been made but seems to them to be indefensibly slow.

At a time when students are eager to attack these and other key problems, they face the prospect of being compelled to fight in a war most of them believe is unjustified. This traumatic experience has precipitated an unprecedented mass tension and frustration.

In assessing the causes of student unrest, it would be a mistake to assume that all causes are external. There are undoubtedly internal emotional pressures and internal value conflicts in many students which contribute to their own dissatisfaction and thus to the tension and turmoil of campus life.

Students attribute the shortcomings they see to the smugness of their elders and the weaknesses of social institutions. They see the university, guardian of man's knowledge and source of his new ideas, as an engine for powering the reform of the larger society, and as the first institution they are in a position to reform.

We emphasize that most students, despite their view of society's failures, accept as valid the basic structure of our democratic system; their main desire is to improve its ability to live up to its stated values. Their efforts to do so are welcome when they take the form of petitions, demonstrations and protests that are peaceful and non-violent. Although many persons are unsettled by these activities (which are often of a bizarre nature), we must all remember that peaceful expression of disturbing ideas and petitions for the redress of grievances are fundamental rights safeguarded by the First Amendment of our Constitution. Methods of dealing with "campus unrest" must not confuse peaceful protest and petition with violent disruption. To do so will aggravate rather than solve the problem.

A small but determined minority, however, aims not at reform but at the destruction of existing institutions. These are the nihilists. They resort to violent disruption as the means best suited to achieve their ends. By dramatic tactics of terror, they have focused widespread public attention upon themselves and have often induced university authorities either to surrender or to meet force with force. When they have managed on occasion to provoke counter-force to an excessive degree, they have succeeded in enlisting the sympathies of the more moderate campus majority.

They are the agent that converts constructive student concern into mindless mob hysteria. They are the chief danger to the university and its basic values.

There is also a minority of students who are not nihilists, but who feel that violence and disruption may be the only effective way of achieving societal and university reform.

II.

Forcible obstruction and violence are incompatible with the intellectual and personal freedom that lies at the core of campus values. In its recent *Declaration on Campus Unrest,* the American Council on Education noted that "there has developed among some of the young a cult of irrationality and incivility which severely strains attempts to maintain sensible and decent human communications. Within this cult is a minute group of destroyers who have abandoned hope in today's society, in today's university, and in the processes of orderly discussion to secure significant change." These "destroyers" seek to persuade more moderate students that verbal expressions of grievance go unheeded, while forcible tactics bring affirmative results.

Despite some eloquent and subtle rationalizations for violent methods of protest, the record of experience is incontrovertible. While violent protest is sometimes followed by the concessions sought, it more often produces a degree of counter-violence and public dismay that may gravely damage the cause for which violence is invoked.

Even when violence succeeds in achieving immediate social gains, it tends frequently to feed on itself, with one power group imposing its will on another until repressive elements succeed in reestablishing order. The violent cycles of the French and Russian revolutions and of the decade resulting in the Third Reich are stark summits of history to ponder. All history teaches that as a conscious method of seeking social reform, violence is a very dangerous weapon to employ.

That is why our nation has sought to avoid violent methods of effecting social change, and to foster instead the principles of peaceful advocacy proclaimed in the Bill of Rights and the rule of law. As the President has just reminded us:

> "The purpose of these restraints is not to protect an 'establishment,' but to establish the protection of liberty; not to prevent change, but to insure that change reflects the public will and respects the rights of all."

The university is the citadel of man's learning and of his hope for further self-improvement, and is the special guardian of this heritage. Those who work and study on the campus should think long before they risk its destruction by resorting to force as the quick way of reaching some immediate goal.

Father Theodore Hesburgh of Notre Dame has observed that the university, precisely because it is an open community that lives by the power of reason, stands naked before those who would employ the power of force. It can survive only when the great majority of its members share its commitment to rational discourse, listen closely to those with conflicting views, and stand together against the few who would impose their will on everyone else.

Kingman Brewster of Yale has persuasively articulated this policy:

> "Proposition one is the encouragement of controversy, no matter how fundamental; and the protection of dissent, no matter how extreme. This is not just to permit the 'letting off of steam' but because it will improve [the university] as a place to be educated. Proposition number two is a convincing intention to deal speedily and firmly with any forcible interference with student and faculty activities or the normal use of any [university] facilities. . . . I see no basis for compromise on the basic proposition that forcible coercion and violent intimidation are unacceptable means of persuasion and unacceptable techniques of change in a university community, as long as channels of communication and the chance for reasoned argument are available."

Several attitudes held by members of the university community have often interfered with the application of these sensible standards. One is the belief of many that the civil law should not apply to internal campus affairs. They feel that the academy is an enclave, sheltered from the law, that the forces of civil authority may not enter the campus, save by invitation. This is a serious misconception—a residue of the time when the academy served *in loco parentis,* making and enforcing its own rules for students' behavior and protecting them from the law outside, save for such extreme crimes as murder and arson. Now that students themselves have firmly discarded school authority over their personal lives, they must logically accept the jurisdiction of civil authority. They cannot argue that of all Americans they are uniquely beyond the reach of the law.

At the same time, the university is ill equipped to control violent and obstructive conduct on its own. Most institutions have few campus police; most of these are not deputized and thus do not possess true police power. Few schools have explicit rules either defining the boundaries of permissible protest or stating the consequences if the boundaries are crossed. Some have very loose rules for disciplinary proceedings; others have diffused disciplinary power so widely among students, faculty and administration that effective discipline is difficult to impose, and is seldom imposed quickly enough to meet an emergency. And in most institutions the ultimate internal disciplinary sanction of suspension or expulsion lies unused because the campus community shrinks from its probable consequence—exposure of dismissed students to the draft and what students call the "death sentence" of Vietnam.

III.

Out of many discussions with faculty members, students and administrators, and with full appreciation that no two institutions are the same, we offer the campus community the following specific suggestions:

(1) A broad consensus should be achieved among students, faculty and administration concerning the permissible methods of presenting ideas, proposals and grievances and the consequences of going beyond them. Excellent guidelines have been provided by the American Council on Education's recent Declaration on

Campus Protest. These could usefully be supplemented by more detailed statements developed by representatives of the American Association of University Professors, the American Association of Universities, the American Council on Education, the Association of Land Grant Colleges and State Universities, the National Student Association, and possibly others. Where agreed upon and explicit codes of student conduct and procedures for student discipline are lacking, they should be adopted; where they already exist they should be reviewed and, if necessary, improved.

Students have the right to due process and to participate in the making of decisions that directly affect them, but their right of participation should not be so extensive as to paralyze the disciplinary process itself. Codes for campus conduct should place primary reliance on the power of the institution to maintain order in its own house, and on its courage to apply its own punishment when deserved. These codes should also recognize the universal duty to obey the civil and criminal laws of the larger society, and the right of the civil authorities to act when laws are violated.

(2) Universities should prepare and currently review contingency plans for dealing with campus disorders. Advance plans should be made to determine, insofar as possible, the circumstances under which the university will use (i) campus disciplinary procedures, (ii) campus police, (iii) court injunctions, (iv) other court sanctions and (v) the civil police. A definite plan, flexibly employed at the moment of crisis, is essential. There have been enough violent and obstructive incidents on enough campuses to permit institutions to assess alternative courses of action and to anticipate both the varieties of disorder which might occur and the most appropriate response.

Most importantly, university authorities should make known in advance that they will not hesitate to call on civil police when circumstances dictate, and should review in advance with police officials the degrees of force suitable for particular situations. It is a melancholy fact that even in cases where the need for calling the civil police has been generally recognized, the degree of force actually employed has frequently been perceived as excessive by the majority of the campus community, whose sympathies then turned against the university authorities. Indeed, there is reason to believe that a primary objective of campus revolutionaries is to provoke the calling of police and the kinds of police conduct that will bring the majority over to their side.

(3) Procedures for campus governance and constructive reform should be developed to permit more rapid and effective decision-making. There is great misunderstanding and confusion as to where ultimate authority for campus decision-making lies. The fact is that the authority is shared among several elements.

By law, trustees are granted full authority over colleges and universities. But trustees cannot supervise the day-to-day affairs of a university; hence they delegate power to the president. The president, however, in addition to being the agent of the trustees, is the leader of the faculty. His effectiveness derives as much from campus consensus of faculty and students as it does from the power delegated to him by the trustees.

In the American system of higher education, the faculty plays the primary role in determining the educational program and all issues directly relevant to education and faculty research. Unlike the systems of some other countries, educational control in the American system is faculty-oriented; anything else is a deviation from the norm.

Faculty control of education and research is the best guarantee we have of academic freedom. It is a precious asset that must not under any circumstances be sacrificed. Most student demands for change pertain to educational and research matters and too often their efforts have been directed toward administrative officers who usually do not have the power which students assume they possess. And often, too, some faculty members have mistakenly joined with students in using coercive force against administrative officers when it is the faculty itself that should deal appropriately and effectively with the issues in question.

Most other powers in the university are diffused. For most purposes, shared power is an asset. But to prevent disorders, universities must be able to respond quickly. Campus protests are sometimes escalated to the level of force because legitimate grievances, peacefully urged, have been referred to university committees which were slow to respond. Scholars have the habit of examining any hypothesis, debating it exhaustively, deferring decision to await more evidence, and when something must be decided, shunning a consensus in favor of subtle shades of disagreement and dissent. For the process of education, these are admirable qualities. But for dealing with naked force, they can be a prescription for disaster. Faculties therefore have a special obligation to organize themselves more effectively, to create representative groups with power to act, and to maintain constant and systematic lines of communication with students. They should be ready to meet every challenge to the educational integrity of the institution. If this integrity is compromised, it will be the faculty that suffers the most.

Students should, of course, have a meaningful role in the governance of all non-educational, non-research functions. They should serve, too, on committees dealing with educational and related questions, exercising their right to be heard on these subjects, so long as the faculty remains paramount.

(4) Faculty leaders and administrative officers need to make greater efforts to improve communications both on the campus and with alumni and the general public. Campus difficulties are constantly aggravated by misinformation and misunderstanding. On campus, large numbers of faculty and students often act on the basis of rumor or incomplete information. Alumni and the general public receive incomplete, often distorted, accounts of campus developments. The communications media, on and off the campus, concentrate on controversy. Much of the peaceful progress of our colleges and universities is never communicated to the outside world. Campus authorities have the responsibility to see to it that a balanced picture is portrayed.

IV.

To the larger society, we make these suggestions:

(1) The majority of the American people are justifiably angry at students who engage in violent and obstructive tactics. While the public varies widely in its desire for social change, it shares a common belief in the value of social order. It also regards university students as among the most privileged in society—among those who should understand best the importance of freedom and the dangers of anarchy. One outlet for this public resentment has been the support of legislation withholding financial aid both from students who engage in disruption and from colleges and universities that fail to control them.

There has also been a steady weakening of public sentiment in favor of the additional public funding that higher education so badly needs. Current appropriations for new facilities and for annual operating costs have been insufficient. Some private universities have faced a reduction in individual and corporate gifts.

Existing laws already withdraw financial aid from students who engage in disruptive acts. Additional laws along the same lines would not accomplish any useful purpose. Such efforts are likely to spread, not reduce the difficulty. More than seven million young Americans are enrolled in the nation's colleges and universities; the vast majority neither participate in nor sympathize with campus violence. If aid is withdrawn from even a few students in a manner that the campus views as unjust, the result may be to radicalize a much larger number by convincing them that existing governmental institutions are as inhumane as the revolutionaries claim. If the law unjustly forces the university to cut off financial aid or to expel a student, the university as well may come under widespread campus condemnation.

(2) We believe that the urge to enact additional legislation should be turned into a channel that could assist the universities themselves to deal more effectively with the tactics of obstruction. State and municipal laws against trespass and disorderly conduct may not be wholly effective means of dealing with some acts of physical obstruction. They were not written to deal with such conduct, and they do not cope with the central issue—forcible interference with the First Amendment rights of others. We are presently considering whether there is a need for statutes authorizing universities, along with other affected persons, to obtain court injunctions against willful private acts of physical obstruction that prevent other persons from exercising their First Amendment rights of speech, peaceable assembly, and petition for the redress of grievances. Such laws would not be aimed at students exclusively, but at any willful interference with First Amendment rights, on or off the campus, by students or by non-students. They would also be available to uphold the First Amendment rights of students as well as other citizens.

(3) Finally, we urge the American people to recognize that the campus mirrors both the yearnings and weaknesses of the wider society. Erik Erikson, a renowned student of youth, has noted that young and old achieve mutual respect when "society recognizes the young individual as a bearer of fresh energy, and he recognizes society as a living process which inspires loyalty as it receives it, maintains allegiance as it extracts it, honors confidence as it demands it."

One effective way for the rest of us to help reduce campus disorders is to focus on the unfinished task of striving toward the goals of human life that all of us share and that young people admire and respect.

Separate statement by Leon Jaworski, member of the National Commission, commenting on the main statement, June 9, 1969.

Separate Statement

With due deference to the majority of my fellow Commissioners, the statement on campus disruptions in my judgment does not go far enough. It not only fails to emphasize some of the more fundamental aspects of this problem that all good Americans must bear in mind, it also fails to make some specific recommendations in areas experience has taught are pertinent.

The Commission heard the testimony of a dozen university presidents and chancellors experienced in campus disorders. At the end of one of the sessions in which such testimony was heard, a university president summarized his recommendations in words that make sense to me. Other administrators present apparently agreed as none expressed a contrary word. What he underscored were the tactics which encourage disruption. He advised against any negotiation under duress and any discussion held under circumstances of coercion. He pointed to the mistake in any delay in calling outside enforcement authorities for assistance when disruptions occur. He strongly advised against the granting of any amnesty in instances of serious disruptions. He pointed to the encouragement in disorders resulting from confusion and indecision in disciplinary procedures, blaming both faculty and students. He deplored the delays that are occasioned in the prosecution of offenders—a problem lawyers, judges and all enforcement officers should take to heart and do something about.

These are the objective conclusions of those who have been subjected to the grueling experiences of insults, indignities, injustices, and deprivation of personal rights and liberties.

That the existence of the Vietnam War has contributed to student unrest is not to be doubted. To attribute the campus disruptions to this source alone ignores the facts. The university administrators who testified pointed time and again to numerous fantastic demands made by the disrupters, some of which were wholly inconsistent and some of which were completely nonsensical. These have not the slightest relation to the Vietnam War. Moreover, it is known that one of the greatest concerns of the campus militants today is what issue to seize upon once the Vietnam War has ended.

I recognize as do my fellow Commissioners that there have been shortcomings in some university administrations and that there are failures which need remedial action. No matter what these be, when violence is substituted for the processes that have served our nation so well for so long, our democratic institutions are sure to crumble. Violence in any form and at any place, whether in the alley or on the campus, must be condemned without extenuation.

The majority of the students on the campus do not believe in these disruptive tactics, although doubtless many of them have one or the other grievance regarding administrative matters. Their purpose is constructive and not destructive. They are not the troublemakers, and they believe in the processes of a democracy. Their opposites are those who label their demands as "non-negotiable."

The very concept of a non-negotiable demand connotes an unwillingness to listen and an unwillingness to live together, things which have thus far been essential to the survival of our nation. Whatever the cause, a non-negotiable demand reflects a destructive and irrational motivation.

If this were just an attack upon the university *qua* university, then we might expect university officials alone to be able to handle the situation. One president of a large university who testified before the Violence Commission admitted that things at his university were on the "edges of terror" and that the outcome depended on how the nation at large handles it and not merely the university officials. Chimed in another university president, "there is an attack upon democracy as well as an attack on the university." Finally, all the presidents agreed that this was not just a problem of the universities.

The time is at hand, overdue in fact, for all Americans who believe in our institutions to join in condemnation of violent practices on the campuses. My appeal in this separate statement is directed to the many fine young people on our campuses who are interested in an education and are law-abiding. Their voices have been all too silent in this setting. They need to speak up and oppose the destructive methods pursued by lawless minorities. To be sure, they should stand up for the right to be heard, but as well for orderly conduct as one is heard.

Conclusions of the Cox Commission, appointed as a Fact-Finding Commission to Investigate the Disturbances at Columbia University in April and May 1968.

Crisis at Columbia

General Observations

I

The April uprising started and grew haphazardly. As it developed to the final academic cataclysm, its entire character was altered.

The long series of turbulent demonstrations beginning in 1965, which were tolerated by most of the University community, leaves a tragic sense of the inevitability of the final escalation. Packing the lobby of Hamilton Hall—even the somewhat ambiguous obstruction of Dean Coleman's liberty—was scarcely different from the earlier confrontation in John Jay Hall or the sit-in following the CIA demonstration. SAS's decision to evict the whites and barricade the doors in a demonstration of black student power—one of the key turning points—was a response to an occasion thrust upon the black students. With each successive day the uprising gathered its own physical and emotional momentum.

We reject the view that ascribes the April and May disturbances primarily to a conspiracy of student revolutionaries. That demonology is no less false than the naive radical doctrine that attributes all wars, racial injustices, and poverty to the machinations of a capitalist and militarist "Establishment." Student revolutionists within SDS planned turbulent confrontations and revolutionary tactics. They manipulated facts in ways that created distrust and bred unwarranted antagonism. There apparently was occasional talk of wider revolution to overthrow the present political system. A very few revolutionists may have been in dead earnest. More, we suspect, were half in dreamland, feverishly discussing romantic tactics but hardly contemplating realistic execution. Part of the responsibility for the disturbances rests upon the revolutionaries consciously seeking to subvert and destroy the University but their total number was small—much less than the full SDS membership—and their activities were only the catalyst that precipitated a deeper movement.*

II

By its final days the revolt enjoyed both wide and deep support among the students and junior faculty and in lesser degree among the senior professors. The grievances of the rebels were felt equally by a still larger number, probably a majority, of the students. The trauma of the violence that followed police intervention intensified emotions but support for the demonstrators rested upon broad discontent and widespread sympathy for their position.

The record contains ample proof of this conclusion. The very number of students arrested in the buildings—524 Columbia students in the first police action—is convincing. Many more had been in the buildings earlier. Some of the latter were doubtless curiosity seekers. For others in both groups the affair probably had many of the elements of the once-traditional spring riots and subsequent "panty raids." But even after discount is made for those elements, the extent of active participation in violent and unlawful protest is significant.

The existence of broad underlying unrest is also shown by the progress of the seizures. The action of the black students in Hamilton Hall was entirely independent of SDS. The seizure of Avery Hall by architectural students was their own movement. The occupation of Fayerweather Hall, in which a large part of graduate study in the social sciences is centered, was apparently spontaneous; no evidence of an SDS connection has come to our attention.

Outside the buildings the militants enjoyed visible support in the form of the thousands who watched from various points on campus, most conspicuously at the Sundial. A campus poll reportedly boycotted by those in the buildings showed that 74 percent of the participants favored "end gym construction," 66 percent favored severing ties with IDA, and 37 percent even favored amnesty for all students involved in the demonstrations.

* By the same token our comments concerning the above group should not be applied to the much larger number who seek fundamental change in the established order without embracing doctrinaire revolutionary theory and tactics.

The events after the police "bust" point to the same conclusion. The emotions excited by the brutality must have polarized opinion. There would be a tendency to put unjust blame upon those who called for police intervention rather than those—chiefly from SDS—whose deliberate efforts to provoke disruptive turbulence made it almost inevitable that police action would be required. Despite these complex cross-currents, the extent and persistence of the ultimate reaction against the University Administration is adequately explained only by the presence of strong but latent dissatisfaction quickened by the violence of events.

For the future it is equally important to note that the support for the activists has come from the portions of the student body who are most energetically concerned with university and community affairs.

III

The avowed objectives of the April demonstrations, stripped of their context and symbolism, were inadequate causes for an uprising.

The University's IDA affiliation had little practical importance. It was being reviewed by the Henkin Committee as part of a larger study of Columbia's relations to outside agencies. There was not the slightest reason to doubt that the normal academic procedures could produce a reasoned and fair-minded decision upon the merits. The disruptive potential of the IDA affiliation at Columbia, as at other universities, was that it enabled the large part of the intellectual community, especially students, to transfer to the campus their intense moral indignation against the Vietnam war.

The gymnasium issue was more complex, but it too was a symbolic issue. At least some black students freely acknowledge not only that the issue was oversimplified but that the public gymnasium to be built by Columbia would be more beneficial to the community than the 2.1 acres of rocky parkland, *if* the project could be judged upon that aspect alone. But the project could not be judged out of the context of Columbia's relations with its poorer neighbors and society's treatment of racial ghettos.

The third issue, the discipline of the six IDA demonstrators, had somewhat greater substance. Although most students would probably have agreed that the disruptive manner of conducting

SDS demonstrations was becoming intolerable, many students were antagonized by the manner in which the "no indoor demonstration" rule was promulgated and the discipline was administered.

Since the rule came close to the area of free expression staunchly guarded by Columbia's liberal tradition, it was of intense concern to the entire University community. Nevertheless, the prohibition was promulgated by President Kirk without consultation with students, and apparently without prior discussion with faculty members. In fact, the rule ran contrary to the unanimous recommendation of a tripartite committee whose report the President withheld.

The rule, which was an obvious target for militants, was formulated in terms that hampered consistent administration and invited provocation.

Out of the 100 students who engaged in the March IDA demonstration, six SDS leaders were selected for punishment. It was difficult to persuade students that this was not a discriminatory selection even though the Dean's office explained that these six and no others were recognized.

The six IDA demonstrators were refused a public hearing and peremptorily punished. Although the older paternalistic procedures probably gave much greater protection to most student offenders, there is wide and justified campus support for the principles (1) that a student is no less entitled to due process of law than one charged with a public offense and (2) that students should share in disciplinary procedures as part of the right of participation in decisions affecting their interests.

IV

Three among the purely internal causes of unrest especially impressed us.

1. At a time when the spirit of self-determination is running strongly, the administration of Columbia's affairs too often conveyed an attitude of authoritarianism and invited distrust. In part, the appearance resulted from style: for example, it gave affront to read that an influential University official was no more interested in student opinion on matters of intense concern to students than he was in their taste for strawberries. In part, the appearance reflected the true state of affairs. The machinery of student gov-

ernment had been allowed to deteriorate to a point where Columbia College had no student government. The Report on Student Life was not released for seven months until CUSC * members threatened publication. The President was unwilling to surrender absolute disciplinary powers. In addition, government by improvisation seems to have been not an exception, but the rule.

2. The quality of student life was inferior in living conditions and personal association.

3. Columbia, like other universities, has scarcely faced the extraordinary difficulties that face black students in the transition from a society permeated by racial injustice to one of true equality of opportunity. We recognize, of course, the difficulty of immediately remedying such deficiencies as the paucity of black teaching and administrative personnel and of appropriate courses and counseling for all students, but the indisputable fact of alienation of our black students, with all that that fact entails, makes a more active and creative search for solutions particularly urgent.

V

The fabric of Columbia was twisted and torn by the forces of political and social revolution outside the University. Columbia's geographic situation symbolizes the relation between white and black, affluence and poverty, youthful reform and established order. The University's need for physical expansion in an urban center creates inescapable tensions but its relations with the community had further deteriorated because of its apparent indifference to the needs and aspirations of its poorer neighbors. The handling of the gymnasium controversy thus came, even somewhat unfairly, to epitomize the conflict between the spirit of the civil rights movement and the attack on poverty, on the one hand, and, on the other, the ways of an *ancien régime.* Energetic and idealistic students, alienated from the older generation by an extraordinarily wide gulf in manners and interests and offended by the plethora of human suffering, were drawn to the side of change. Where they were frustrated by the massive anonymity of the government and the unmanageability of the social system, they could strike out at the more vulnerable University.

In like fashion, the University became the surrogate for all the tensions and frustrations of United States policy in Vietnam.

* Columbia University Student Council.

The desire for student power, while scarcely articulated as a cause for seizing the campus buildings, was a powerful element of the explosion. Discussion since the uprising has focused upon the methods by which students may exert more influence upon the government of an institution of which they are vital and integral parts. Participation in self-government is a natural human desire that today's students feel with greater urgency, particularly at institutions with highly selective admissions policies because they are much better educated than their predecessors, more sophisticated, in many respects more mature, and more interested in social problems than seeking out conventional careers. (Unfortunately, they are also much less disciplined.)

VI

The hurricane of social unrest struck Columbia at a time when the University was deficient in the cement that binds an institution into a cohesive unit.

Again, geography is a factor. The competing attractions of the exciting metropolitan area, coupled with the housing problems that induce a majority of the faculty to live outside Manhattan, operate as centrifugal forces. Yet the dispirited quality of student life outside the classroom is not beyond the University's power of influence.

The formal organization of both the administrative offices and the faculties apparently tends to discourage the cohesiveness that comes from shared responsibility in matters of university concern. We were struck by the constant recital of an apposition between the Administration and the faculty as rival bodies with separate interests, for it would seem to us that on educational questions the two should be essentially one. The lack of a University Senate and the division of the professors and other teachers into three or four faculties—quite apart from the professional schools—where other universities have a single Faculty of Arts and Sciences, apparently discourages faculty participation in the formulation of University policy and the improvement of student life. The central Administration to which the full burden of the quality of student life is left is not equipped for the duty. Far too few members of the University family are closely involved, outside the classroom, in the constant informal enterprises and discussions by which the values of an academic community are constantly reexamined and those which stand the test are passed on to the next generation.

Institutional coherence is also affected by the presence or lack of a spirit of institutional self-confidence. Unhappily, despite her inherent strengths, the spring crisis struck Columbia when her self-confidence was shaken by the decline in relative position in AAUP rankings of graduate departments, the exclusion from a Ford Foundation grant for improvement of graduate studies, the resignations of a number of senior professors, and the Strickman filter incident.

VII

The scale of the disturbances was greatly enlarged in numbers, intensity and violence by the delay in calling the police—from Thursday night until Monday night—which the Ad Hoc Faculty Group forced upon the University officials. Although perhaps the effort had to be made, there was never a significant chance that the Group could negotiate a peaceful withdrawal from the buildings. Forcing the delay, by threats of physical interposition, increased the likelihood of violence and magnified the reaction by lending an air of legitimacy to use of the tactics of physical disruption as means of forcing one view of policy upon those who held another.

VIII

Our next five observations must be taken as a unit. Language requires stating them one at a time, but none can survive unless joined with the others.

A.

A university is essentially a free community of scholars dedicated to the pursuit of truth and knowledge solely through reason and civility.

A privately-endowed university depends upon the experienced guidance of wise counselors and managers both inside and outside academic ranks, and also upon the financial and moral support of a large, organized body of alumni and friends. But their vital contribution must never obscure the essential quality of the institution: the university is a community of scholars, both teachers and students. Any tendency to treat a university as business enterprise with faculty as employees and students as customers diminishes its vitality and communal cohesion.

B.

Resort to violence or physical harassment or obstruction is never an acceptable tactic for influencing decisions in a university. This principle does not require notions of property or legality to sustain it. It derives from three considerations.

First, force, harassment, and physical obstruction contradict the essential postulate that the university is dedicated to the search for truth by reason and civility.

Second, resort to such physical coercion tends to set in motion an uncontrollable escalation of violence. This is the plainest lesson of the rising cycle of violence that began at Columbia with the Naval ROTC demonstration in 1965 and culminated in the brutality of April 30 and May 22. The sequence of steps was not inevitable but each was the readily predictable consequence of those that went before.

Third, the survival—literally the survival—of the free university depends upon the entire community's active rejection of disruptive demonstrations. Any sizeable group, left to pursue such tactics, can destroy either the university by repeatedly disrupting its normal activities or the university's freedom by compelling the authorities to invoke overwhelming force in order that its activities may continue. The only alternative is for the entire community to reject the tactics of physical disruption with such overwhelming moral disapproval as to make them self-defeating.

This vital decision rests with the liberal and reform-minded students. They can save or destroy the institution.

C.

The acceptability of the foregoing principle depends upon organization of the scholarly community in ways that produce both loyalty and the relief of grievances. The government of a university depends, even more than that of a political community, upon the consent of all the governed to accept decisions reached by its constitutional processes. The consent of the dissenters depends partly upon their knowing that their views effectively entered into the process of consensus, even though they did not prevail. They must also be convinced that the opportunities for change are open and the goals and stance of the enterprise are sufficiently right for it to deserve their loyalty despite specific points of disagreement. Administrative intractability and resistance to change contribute to the breakdown of law and order.

D.

The student body is a mature and essential part of the community of scholars. This principle has more validity today than ever before in history. It is felt more keenly by a wider number of students, perhaps because of the increasing democratization of human institutions. As with all human activities, the wise division of functions and responsibilities must take into account the special skills or limitations of particular groups, as well as efficiency of operation. The process of drawing students into more vital participation in the governance of the university is infinitely complex. It cannot be resolved by either abstractions or tables of organization. It does not mean that issues must be settled by referenda. *We are convinced, however, that ways must be found, beginning now, by which students can meaningfully influence the education afforded them and other aspects of the university activities.*

The activist supporters of reform who voiced the grievances pressed by the rebels included many of the natural leaders among students—both political and intellectual leaders. They were deeply hurt by statements treating them merely as disloyal trouble-makers aligned with a small band of rebels. While their own releases, for reasons of student politics, contributed to the polarization of opinion by their lack of civility, we have not the slightest doubt that the survival of Columbia as a leading university depends upon finding ways of drawing this very large and constructive segment of the student body, which supported the strike, back into the stream of university life where it can share in the process of rebuilding.

With participation, students will surely acquire a more sophisticated understanding of the universities' difficulties and complexities and of the necessary functions of the faculty and administration, the alumni, and the governing body. In the same process, the latter would come to an understanding they cannot otherwise acquire of the true needs and aspirations of students and values and shortcomings of current educational measures.

E.

We add only that the success of those who must follow this difficult course will depend in no small measure upon the willingness of parents, alumni, and friends to recognize that the April crisis is thus being converted into a creative source of renewal.

CHAPTER 14

Hard-liners vs. Soft-liners

One of the most consistent exponents of a hard-line stance against SDS and other radical groups has been Sidney Hook, professor of philosophy at New York University. Hook stated that the "failure to act decisively" against illegal protests at Berkeley and Columbia encouraged subsequent disruption by making it appear that violence would "pay off." The source of this indecision he found to be in a "ritualistic liberalism" that overlooked the radicals' challenge to the social order. These liberals, not SDS, are the "Trojan horse in higher education," according to Hook.

On the other side, the President of Staten Island Community College, William Birenbaum, rejected the view that the maintenance of law and order was the paramount issue raised by campus protests. Birenbaum argued that the failure to realize due process in universities and to eliminate segregation by race, class, and status were more important problems.

The events at Cornell in the spring of 1969 precipitated one of the most dramatic splits in the establishment over the response to disruption. The dispute came to a head one Sunday in late April when Black students occupied Willard Straight Hall, the student union, and demanded that the university nullify disciplinary reprimands for earlier protests. That night, possibly in fear of an assault on the building by white groups, the Blacks armed themselves. They agreed to vacate the building when the administration promised to ask the faculty to nullify the discipline at a meeting the next day. On Monday, however, the faculty decided not to act on the administration request. This decision produced an outpouring of support for the Black students from the entire campus, and several thousand students began a round-the-clock sit-in in the Cornell gymnasium. The Blacks threatened further action, as did SDS, if the reprimands were not lifted. On Wednesday the faculty met and agreed to nullify the disciplinary measures. Several professors denounced the vote as a capitulation to force and resigned.

The Cornell debate begins with a statement against nullification issued before the Monday faculty meeting by thirty-one professors. They pledged to cease classroom instruction and to undertake a review of their relationship to the university if the discipline was abrogated. Next, Professor Milton Konvitz explained why he changed his vote at the second meeting. The faculty, he said, was not being threatened by armed Black students but pressured by the entire campus. While he conceded that the principles that impelled the Monday decision had lost none of their force two days later, Konvitz said he feared complete chaos on campus. It was this prospect which made him vote for nullification.

New York Times columnist Tom Wicker agreed that it was not the coercion of a small minority which forced concessions, but the demands of an aroused student body. He argued that the faculty correctly chose "humanity over principle" at its Wednesday meeting. In a reply to Wicker, Professor Allan Sindler, who resigned as the chairman of Cornell's government department in protest against the administration's soft line during the episode, insisted that the faculty had capitulated not to the demands of the students peacefully occupying the gymnasium but to the threats from Black students and SDS members.

From an article in the Educational Record, *Winter 1969, by Professor Sidney Hook, Department of Philosophy, New York University.*

The Trojan Horse in American Higher Education

Wherever American educators meet today, there is one overriding concern which shadows their deliberations even when it is not on the agenda. This is the mounting wave of lawlessness, often cresting into violence, that has swept so many campuses.

In an essay written shortly after the riotous events at the University of California at Berkeley in 1964, I predicted that American higher education would never be the same again, that a turning point had been reached in the pattern of its development.* I have been taken somewhat aback by the rapid change, if not by its direction, and by the escalation of the accompanying lawlessness. Equally significant in transforming the educational climate in the universities have been some of the secondary consequences of the accelerating disorders—fear among administrators lest their campuses erupt; confusion, bewilderment, and divided loyalties among faculty, together with some *Schadenfreude* at the humiliation of their administrations at the hands of arrogant and disrespectful student militants; sympathetic involvement in disruptive demonstrations by some of the junior faculty; sustained apathy among the majority of students whose education has been interrupted by radical activists; and the mixture of rage and disgust among the general public where political repercussions, already damaging to the cause of higher education, threaten to become stronger.

I propose to discuss some ideas and attitudes which have contributed to the encouragement of recent disorders on American campuses. In focusing on one aspect of the situation, I do not mean to imply that these ideas and attitudes explain the occurrence of student disorders. This is far from the case. The causes of student disorders are many and complex. But there are certain ideas and attitudes which tend to encourage rather than to check

* "Second Thoughts on Berkeley," *Teachers College Record,* October 1965, pp. 32–63.

the spread of disorder, to disorganize intelligent resistance to it, and sometimes to confirm the extremist view that force works best in making universities see reason.

Although comparatively few institutions have been the scene of violent demonstrations, I do not exaggerate when I say there is hardly a college or university in the country in which there is not some marked uneasiness, some movement toward direct action among students on the verge of exploding into sit-ins and other forms of mass violations of rules and regulations suddenly discovered to be silly, anachronistic, or authoritarian—as some of them undoubtedly are. But what has struck me about the mood of the students in scores of colleges I have visited is that even when these rules and regulations were *not* being enforced, and student conduct was as uninhibited as that on campuses not subject to these objectionable rules, there was an insistence on their abolition. This, despite the evidence that formal abolition would in all likelihood stir up a hornets' nest among alumni or townsfolk or state legislatures with the very real danger that attempts would have to be made to enforce these rules, or that university services required for the improvement of the students' educational experience would in consequence be severely restricted. Yet students often refused to let matters rest and enjoy the benefits of desuetude.

This testified partly to their impatience with the hypocrisy of tolerating laws that were not being enforced, but even more to a desire to precipitate a showdown with authority, to be where the action is, to have the nation's television cameras focused on the local scene and the local leaders of dissent. One of the undoubted effects of the coverage given campus disorders by the mass media, in the alleged desire merely to report their occurrence, is to encourage these disorders by exaggerating their scope and glorifying the "heroes" of the moment. Now that there are more than 300 chapters of the Students for a Democratic Society in universities across the country and more than 40,000 national and local SDS activists (there were only 60-odd at Port Huron in 1961) loose among student bodies, the prospects for a lively academic year are quite good. In traditional Chinese culture, one of the strongest curses that could be directed against a neighbor was: "May you live in interesting times!" American colleges and universities have been visited with the ancient Chinese curse.

Anyone familiar with its program and objectives with respect to American universities knows that the SDS is a formidable threat to peace and continued education, as hitherto understood, on American campuses. Its members constitute a hard, fanatical core of highly politicalized individuals among student bodies, extremely skillful at generating conflicts and disruption through agitation and manipulation of mass organizations. They and their congeners among the New Left, including their faculty allies, would be hard to contain even by wise and enlightened administrators and faculties. Unfortunately, wisdom and enlightenment have not been conspicuously evident even in places where one would expect them. This is suggested by the fact that the worst excesses have occurred at the most liberal institutions. The University of California, San Francisco State College, the University of Colorado, Roosevelt College, Columbia University, and New York University—these read like a roll call of the centers of intellectual dissent, experiment, and even educational permissiveness in American life. Why should this be so?

My thesis is that the explanation of the failure to meet the challenge of student disruption is a mistaken theory of liberalism, a reliance upon what I have called ritualistic rather than realistic liberalism, a doctrinaire view that does not recognize the difference between belief or doctrine and behavior, ignores the fact that in law and common sense incitement to violence is a form of behavior, and does not realize that although order is possible without justice, justice is impossible without order.

The realistic liberal outlook in education cannot be strictly identified with the liberal outlook in politics, because the academic community cannot be equated with the political community. Although we may recognize the autonomy of the academic community, that autonomy cannot be complete since the political community in many ways underwrites its operation. But what both communities have in common is the centrality of the notion of due process.

Due process in the political community is spelled out in terms of specific mechanisms through which, out of the clash of public opinion, public policy is forged. Where due process is violated, consent is coerced and cannot be freely given. The unlimited spectrum of ideas remains unabridged in the political community up to the point of advocacy but not to the point of violent action or the *incitement* of violence. The forces of the state, the whole apparatus of restraint and punishment, enter the scene where the citizens' freedom of choice is threatened by extra-legal activity.

Due process in the academic community is reliance upon the process of rationality. It cannot be the same as due process in the political community as far as the *mechanisms* of determining the outcome of rational activity are concerned. For what controls the nature and direction of due process in the academic community is derived from its educational goal—the effective pursuit, discovery, publication, and teaching of the truth. In the political community all men are equal as citizens not only as participants in, and contributors to, the political process, but as voters and decision-makers on the primary level. Not so in the academic community. What qualifies a man to enjoy equal human or political rights does not qualify him to teach equally with others or even to study equally on every level. There is an authoritative, *not* authoritarian, aspect of teaching and learning which depends not upon the person or power of the teacher, but upon the authority of his knowledge, the cogency of his method, the scope and depth of his experience.

But whatever the differences in the decision-making power flowing from legitimate differences in educational authority, there is an equality of learners, whether teachers or students, in the rational processes by which knowledge is won, methods developed, and experience enriched. In a liberal educational regimen, everything is subject to the rule of reason, and all are equals as questioners and participants. Whoever interferes with academic due process, either by violence or threat of violence, places himself outside the academic community, and incurs the sanctions appropriate to the gravity of his offense, from censure to suspension to expulsion. This is all the more true because the university is extremely vulnerable to violence and threats of violence. It has no physical means of its own to protect itself. It cannot even invoke, as the church does, the wrath of Heaven.

The peculiar deficiency of the ritualistic liberal educational establishment is the failure to meet violations of rational due process with appropriate sanctions or in a timely and intelligent manner. There is a tendency to close an eye to expressions of lawless behavior on the part of students who in the name of freedom deprive their fellow students of their freedom to pursue their studies. It is as if the liberal administration sought to appease the challenge to its continued existence by treating such incidents either as if they had never happened or, when the noise of shattered glass makes this impossible, as if the phases in the developing violence were stages, painful but progressive, in the transition to a better, restructured university. Here it is the first step which is not taken that costs so much. Both at Berkeley and Columbia failure to act decisively at the first disruption of university functions undoubtedly contributed to the students' expectation that they could escalate their lawlessness with impunity.

Sometimes the attempt to retrieve a failure to meet promptly and fairly student disruption results in a greater failure. When student defiance of reasonable rules and regulations is pointedly and continuously ignored, and then subsequently disciplined, the consequence may be worse than if the first infraction had been totally amnestied. Unnecessary delay in initiating the disciplinary measures, however mild, incurred by the infraction of rules can make it appear to large numbers of the uninformed that these students are the innocent victims of the vindictive punishment.

The occasion of the *fourth* and largest illegal trespass at Berkeley—the seizure of Sproul Hall—came as a consequence of the summons to four student leaders to appear before the Disciplinary Committee several weeks after they had committed violations. Similarly at Columbia. The first action which presaged the events of 1968 occurred in 1965 when students forcibly prevented the NROTC award ceremony. In 1967, according to the Cox Commission's report, "the administration cancelled the ceremony citing insufficient time to prepare against violence."

Violence seemed to pay off! A handful of students had forced their will on the university at the cost of seven letters of censure! After the ban on indoor demonstrations had been promulgated at Columbia—both because it interfered with teaching and because of the dangers of violence between opposing groups of demonstrating students—it was not enforced on three important occasions where it was clearly violated. When it was finally invoked, to many who were unaware of the past history of student provocation and university restraint, the disciplinary action, even if feeble, seemed arbitrary.

The irony of the situation is that despite the liberal character of these institutions, a false view of what it means to be liberal seems to provoke or to exacerbate disturbances on the campus. In certain faculty quarters it is believed that the very nature of a liberal educational community necessitates, independently of any student action, an absolute taboo against physical or police sanctions. At a large metropolitan university, during a student strike called by a small and fanatical minority to protest the dismissal of an administrator guilty of vicious anti-Semitic incitement, a faculty group tried to get a resolution adopted pledging the university "not to call upon the police *under any circumstances.*" Had such a resolution been adopted, it would have given those who made a cult of violence assurances in advance that they could carry on as they pleased no matter what the cost to life, limb, and university property. It would have sparked the very violence which those who favored the resolution professed to deplore. "What's so tragic about the destruction of a little property?" one professor inquired. He only shrugged when a colleague sardonically added, "Or a little fire?" In the academy, as elsewhere, there is no substitute for common sense! Actually, in the course of the strike, classes were disrupted, elevators were so jammed they had to be shut down, fire hoses were slashed, and the auditorium in the student center was set afire.

Some faculty members see truly, in the words of a perceptive member of the Columbia faculty, that "the authority of a university is not a civil authority, but a moral one." But this spokesman mistakenly concludes that the disruptive activities of students "can only be contained by a faculty and by other students, not by the police." This is a morality not of this world but of the tearful, hand-wringing, ineffectual spirit, which would leave this world and its universities in possession of those who use or threaten violence to impose their will on others.

"Confrontation politics" in the moral academic community "is inadmissible," we are assured by faculty members who love everybody and who want to be loved by everybody. Excellent! But what if some students do what is inadmissible? What if they resort to pillage, vandalism, personal assault? What if the torch of learning in some hands becomes a torch of arson? To say that only other students and not the police can contain them is to forget that once we leave the world of the spirit, this is an invitation to civil war. Wars of containment, as we know, can be quite bloody. The police may have to be called in to prevent students from containing (and maiming) each other. Fear of relying on the police in *any* circumstance to resist the militant politics of confrontation, which brutally scorns the rationalities of academic due process, is the politics of capitulation. It is administrative and/or faculty cowardice masquerading as educational statesmanship.

In the light of recent events on campuses and the reactions they have inspired, it should be obvious that the SDS is *not* the Trojan Horse in American higher education. It is today the armed warrior of anti-education. It makes no secret of its desire to destroy American democratic society and the universities which it considers a faithful replica of the iniquitous society. No, the Trojan Horse in American higher education is the rickety structure of doctrinaire thought that shelter the SDS, gives it a free field for operation retreats before the politics of confrontation and either shrinks from applying fairly and firmly the rules of reason that should bind the academic community or interprets them as if they had no more restraining force in times of crisis than ropes of sand.

Speech by Dr. William M. Birenbaum, President of Staten Island Community College of the City University of New York, to the 49th Annual Conference of the American Association of Junior Colleges, in Atlanta, March 5, 1969.

Segregation and the Abuse of Due Process on the American Campus: Whose Law and Order?

At every significant point in the history of American Education, the connection between the cultivation and use of intelligence has been a central theme. In behalf of this connection, Thomas Jefferson presented his case for the new university in Virginia, Horace Mann conducted his campaign for universal public education, and Congressman Morrill persuaded his colleagues to underwrite a whole new breed of people's colleges. From John Dewey's progressive left to Robert Hutchins' classical right, Education for Freedom in one form or another has been featured among the primary purposes of our educational systems.

The same issue is crucial today. What kind of a learning community do we need to carry out Education for Freedom in an America where adults over thirty are becoming a minority and losing touch with the younger majority, where Blacks at least are on the rise, where concepts of morality really are changing, where higher and higher levels of education are essential for economic survival and political power? This is the question that some of our best young people are putting to us today, and we are not responding. We are responding instead to another issue. A simpler one. One we know we can win. Law and order on the campus.

Clearly law and order is the issue of the day, and the hard line, not reform or even reconsideration, is what is being preached by liberal university professors, conservative governors and state legislators, and the President of the United States. Talk about power blocs. Can anyone really have any doubt who will "win" in law and order?

In my opinion the tides of reaction against the young, the Black, the poor, the powerless, the idealists, those searching for new commitments and for relevance, are in full flow and have yet to crest. Those in charge, armed with their formidable powers to suspend, to redistribute the credit hours without consultation, to withhold the loan or scholarship to regulate access to the lush middle-class job market, to influence the selective service status, to call police, will successfully put down the students, the few radical young faculty, the SDS crowd, and the militant Afro-Americans.

He who chooses reform will walk an increasingly lonely and dangerous road in the months ahead. He will be caught in a never-never land between the combatants in the law and order struggle that will continue to capture the headlines. Each side in that struggle will now retreat further from its own reality: The powerful, through brute force, from the reality of its own failure that caused the trouble in the first place, and the powerless, through more pot and even more outrageous disruptions, from the reality of a survival which depends upon getting an education they are not getting now.

In their zealous defense of our revered institutions, the power coalition has its own academic brand of sloganeering. The Berkeley students had their words, the Establishment has its own. Two of the most popular current slogans are due process and integration. Everyone is rushing in to defend due process and integration on the campus. The premise is that they exist. But what have due process and integration amounted to on the American campus?

A professor at the University of Chicago during that institution's most recent disorders said:

> A university is not a democracy, and never will be. Once we relinquish the power of choosing faculty to the students, the university will cease to be.

Is an undemocratic community the best environment in which to cultivate the intelligence required for effective participation in a free society? Is a consummate campus welfare state the best place in which to encourage self-discipline, individuality, the assumption of the responsibilities which are the burdens of free men, the experience of possessing and using decision-making power which is the essence of freedom education? Chancellor Hitler once told the German people: Give unto me your political and economic freedoms, and I promise you in return the greatest flowering of the sciences and the arts in German history. There were striking similarities between Hitler's Due Process in the Third Reich and the Due Process the German professors had built into their universities long before Hitler arrived on scene.

"Faculty democracy" on most of our campuses is, in fact, an oligarchy of the elite, in which elitism is defined mainly by the possession of tenure. The majority of those who teach full time on our campuses possess neither tenure nor the vote on those critical committees through which academic colleagues recommend the promotion of each other, award tenure, allocate the credit hour currency, and decide what shall be taught. Some due process.

The faculty committees now building Black subject matter in our educational program are almost exclusively white, they are also increasingly unionized, shored up by security-oriented civil service systems whose standards and values generally preclude the rapid engagement of specially qualified talent during this period of critical transition in American life. Some due process.

According to the recent report issued by the Educational Testing Service at Princeton, the Boards of Trustees who hold the ultimate power in our universities are overwhelmingly composed of adults over fifty-five, White Anglo-Saxon Protestants, representative mainly of the American industrial and banking corporate complex and Republicans. More than 80 percent of them now believe that disruptive students should be expelled; 70 percent believe that speakers on campuses should be screened by administrators; 53 percent believe that faculty members should sign loyalty oaths; 40 percent believe that student newspapers should be censored. If these are their beliefs, these governors are out of touch with the reality they are supposed to govern. Some due process.

In our universities the vital information required for academic government is generally monopolized by the administrative managers who, through the careful regulation of what is told and what is withheld, may frame policy decisions without being held accountable to those who are governed. Some due process.

Student lawlessness and disorder on the campus is a direct function of the authoritarian and oligarchical order imposed by those who now possess the law-making power in the University. Those who cry out most loudly now against the politicalization of the university are really making a last-ditch defense of the present political rigging of academic privilege and vested interest. Professor Sidney Hook says:

> We cannot believe that the mission of the university is to lead mankind to a New Jerusalem. Any attempt to do so would destroy . . . the university's role to serve as intellectual sanctuary when the winds of popular passion blow . . . The goal of the university is not the quest for power or virtue, but the quest for significant truths . . .

But the passion with which the winds of popular academic consensus now blow reveals how deeply committed the majority are to the present configuration of power in the university and to an elitist version of virtue. The significant truths may be absolute, but they are no longer absolutely Professor Hook's version of them. Indeed, Professor Hook's version of academic freedom, intellectual sanctuary and the quest for significant truths exists more in his mind than they exist or ever existed on the campuses of our universities. For those who rule her and enjoy her favors, the Old Jerusalem is not so bad.

At the core of the Old Jerusalem's political rigging is not that noble concept, integration, but segregation—by rank and by class, by the disciplines and the credit hours. In terms of prestige and rewards, the undergraduate is segregated from the graduate, the two year colleges from the four, the career programs from the liberal arts, research from teaching, learner from teacher, governed from governor. The admissions policies segregate the students into the segregated parts of the system by social class, cultural background, and race. Finally, as a consequence of this, the system tends to segregate the distribution of its ultimate rewards and thus of the opportunities those rewards make possible in the larger American society. The ultimate act of segregation is the wall around the campus which is meant to separate the university from the society which makes its existence possible. The wall fortifies the proclaimed "neutrality" and "objectivity" of an academic system which, inside the walls and in its implications beyond the walls, operates prejudicially and subjectively.

When the medieval scholars broke through the walls of the monastery to flee to the streets of the cities, the Church must have issued a press release warning against the New Jerusalem. Bologna, whose colors march first in our academic parades, was originally a storefront operation, housed in rented halls and cold lofts through which the winds of popular passion certainly blew. The retreat from the streets of the cities into the Oxonian superblock campus was no retreat from the politics of the time. The reconstruction of the monastery's wall around Oxford's superblock was an attempt at party discipline, a redevelopment act as politically charged as the Model Cities Program.

Today, from embattled parapets overlooking the plains of Harlem or the Southside neighborhoods of Chicago, modern knights in their new academic armor, cry out in behalf of their traditional rights and privileges, besieged by the motley hordes wanting in, searching for rights and privileges of their own. Other brave knights have stoutly defended their special privileges and vested interests before. But the walls did not keep the professions out. The walls did not keep the immigrant masses out. The walls did not keep the Manhattan Project out. The walls did not keep Hitler out. The walls did not keep the GI's or the Fulbright Program out. The walls did not keep the trade unions out, or the industrial recruiters or the ROTC credits. The walls *did* keep out the poor, the disenfranchised, the Blacks.

Perhaps, at an earlier time, the best defense of academic freedom required the organized centers of learning to build walls between themselves and the worldly arenas of action. But the modern city compels a new connection between thought and action. The new knowledge converts both the city and the urban center of learning into imperative action laboratories, without the use of which no significant learning can be produced. If we expect to reduce the academic crime rate and restore academic law and order, we must be prepared to share the process of academic law making with those we expect to govern. If we really mean an integrated America, we must invent fresh mechanisms for integrating the new knowledge into the curricula, and think afresh about the kinds of segregation we now enforce on the campuses. Finally, because we must live in the cities, because the cities are essential to our continued intellectual progress, we must restructure our institutions to honor and understand the mentality required for successful city life. To do this we must methodically break down our own walls, and launch vast new programs aimed at the disruption of our own un-American academic monopolies.

First, the old demarcation line separating the jurisdictions of the higher educational system from the lower makes less and less educational sense. It is no longer 17 or 18 that the demands of the post-school, adult world begin to take hold of urban youth. The process of education must correspond more realistically to the process of growing up in the city. Growing up in the city respects the reality of human biological development, the significant psychological and cultural events which begin to occur when a person crosses the line from childhood to adolescence. "College" and "high school" are no longer viable educational categories.

Second, the rejuvenation of the decaying urban communities requires a substantial transfer of power from white to black, from the more powerful to the less powerful. This transfer must engage and involve the deployment of our best and most sophisticated intellectual, technical, and administrative talents. The confrontation between the experts and the people in the context of a power transfer is the most important event in the life of both the campus and the city. This event must be enacted democratically, if education for freedom is really among our higher purposes.

Third, people work in places of learning, and learn in places of working. We must find new ways to honor the experience of those we seek to educate. The reorganization of our curricula around problems magnifies the importance of the student's experience in the educational process. As Aristotle said: "What we have to learn to do, we learn by doing." The city and the new knowledge invite doing as a part of learning, acting as a necessary part of thinking.

Fourth, the differences between the upper and lower ranges of performance on the tests we use to admit students, are far greater than the actual genetic and biological differences among the same sample of humans. We have not begun to educate people to the outer limits of their capacities. Educational systems, not human beings, are failing. We must confront this reality.

Fifth, the most squandered, underutilized, misused and abused educational resource in our colleges and universities is students.

We must ask ourselves: What setting, what network of relationships achieves the best environment for learning? The authoritarian, patriarchal response to this question is now untenable. Student freedom is an essential educational methodology.

Finally, the superblock campus—the monastic walls shutting out the neighborhoods of the contemporary American city—is a physical representation of monopoly—insular, monolithic, and exclusive. It centralizes buildings, activities, and power for the purpose of its own defense rather than disperses and diffuses its resources in order to equip the people with the power to defend themselves. The urban campus must be in the city. The city itself is the relevant place for learning, and the only campus which can really accommodate the implications flowing from the reforms necessary in the American university.

Cornell

Statement by 31 faculty members at Cornell University, April 21, 1969.

Pledge

We declare that the University cannot function when decisions are reached by negotiating with armed students.

Notwithstanding the President's statement this morning (April 21), belatedly forbidding the carrying of guns outside student rooms or the seizing of buildings, if Dean Miller's motion to declare the Conduct Board's judgment null and void is endorsed by the faculty, we pledge ourselves to cease classroom instruction and to undertake a review of our relationship to the University in the light of this intolerable and, one would have thought, unthinkable situation.

We are, of course, mindful of our obligations to our students and will do our best to carry out this policy without damage to their academic interests.

Article by Milton Konvitz, Professor of Law, Cornell University, in The New York Times Magazine, *May 18, 1969.*

Why One Professor Changed His Vote

This is being written the morning after. My estimate of what happened on the Cornell campus in the last few days takes its origin from "emotion recollected in tranquillity."

Yesterday, Wednesday, as I sat in Bailey Hall Auditorium, one of a thousand or more members of the university faculty, and listened—part of me intent and part of me numb—to the statements by Hans Bethe, Clinton Rossiter, Max Black and many other professors, in which they pleaded for the faculty to rescind the reprimand imposed on three black students for their conduct in demonstrations last December and January, my mind kept reverting to Hobbes's description of men in a state of nature—"a condition of war of everyone against everyone." For days now we have had "no arts; no letters; no society; and which is worst of all, continual fear and danger of violent death." And the end of that famous passage in *Leviathan*: ". . . and the life of man solitary, poor, nasty, brutish, and short."

For, tragically and unbelievably, the campus had suddenly, in a matter of hours, reverted to a state of nature. As we sat in the auditorium thinking, feeling, suffering and half-heartedly engaging in some sort of uninspired debate, we knew, from the expressed and implied threats, from the temper of thousands of our students and perhaps threescore members of the faculty, that in a matter of minutes the campus might become an armed camp.

We were asked by the Faculty Council to adopt a resolution nullifying the reprimands of the three blacks. Only two days before, on Monday, the faculty, in the same auditorium, had refused to accept such a resolution that was offered by the dean of the faculty, Robert D. Miller, who had negotiated the evacuation of Willard Straight Hall by members of the Afro-American Society. On the surface, it seemed as if we were being asked to declare on Wednesday that $1 + 1 = 3$, though on Monday we had said, firmly and decisively, that $1 + 1 = 2$. Were we wrong on Monday? What new facts had been presented to persuade us that we were wrong only two days before?

This is how things looked on the surface, and my impression was that the proponents of the resolution offered by the Faculty Council failed to dispel the apparent contradiction. Yet I had the feeling that most members of the faculty at the meeting sensed, though they could not express it, that the contradiction was only a verbal one. In fact, the issues on the two days were radically different, but this was difficult to express and communicate.

On Monday what the faculty saw as they voted was an agreement made while Willard Straight was still in a state of siege, held by students armed with weapons. The dean of the faculty explained that it was his belief that the black students sincerely believed that they needed the weapons for self-defense, for rumors had come to them of fraternity members preparing to attack and oust them. He said that the weapons were not a threat aimed at him. He did not, he said, capitulate under duress exerted by the blacks against himself, but under duress of the circumstances in their totality, for he was afraid that, if the building were not quickly evacuated, there was the great likelihood of danger to life and property.

At the meeting on Monday he tried several times to convey to the faculty the sense of urgency he had felt the previous day, and he wanted the faculty to place themselves in his position on Sunday, and to confirm as the principal what their agent, using his best judgment, had presumed to do.

But the faculty had a different picture before them. No one criticized Dean Miller. Perhaps each one individually might have done the same. No one said that he had acted hastily and without judgment or warrant. But collectively, they felt, they could not validate an agreement made under circumstances which imposed so heavy a burden on the mind and conscience of their representative. Even if the guns were not aimed at Dean Miller, the seizure and the weapons together meant force and violence aimed at the university and the faculty, and this could in no way be legitimated by expressly giving the blacks the fruit of their violence and threats of violence, even if the threats could be construed as meaning that they would use the weapons only if attacked. For they were the ones who had used violence by seizing the building, ousting, before 6 A.M., parents of students who were in the guest rooms, and ousting the employees, and guarding the doors to let no one into the student union. Violence breeds or invites violence, and when men start out to achieve what they want by strong-arm methods, they must be prepared to face the unforeseen consequences which may follow.

Some such line of thought, I think, must have run through the minds of the hundreds of faculty members as they voted to turn down Dean Miller's resolution. They did not then have their eye on the judicial system or on the penalties imposed on the three students. They thought only of refusing to hand to the Afro-American Society the fruit of its unlawful acts.

On Wednesday, as I sensed it, the faculty faced a radically different situation. Since Monday's faculty action, the two days and the hours and minutes had been used by leaders of the Afro-American Society and the leaders of S.D.S. to heat up the students, with the result that anywhere from 2,000 to 4,000 students (I think this is a fair estimate) were ready to throw the campus into utter turmoil if the faculty did not nullify the penalties against the three students. They, and some faculty members as well, stood ready to seize buildings, and after that there probably would have followed acts of harassment against many professors and administrators. For the spokesman of the Afro-Americans had, in an inflammatory interview on Tuesday, which was heard on the radio by thousands of the Cornell community, branded the faculty as "racist" and named some professors and administrators as "racists," and said they would be dealt with accordingly. He gave the faculty until 9 P.M. on Tuesday to act to nullify the penalties. The clear implication was that after that all hell would break loose. When informed that the faculty would meet on Wednesday at noon, he extended the deadline until after the meeting, to see what the faculty decided. He said that the Afro-American Society knew what its goals were, and that its members would seek to achieve them by whatever means. Thousands of students were waiting in Barton Hall to see what the faculty would do; several thousand of them had slept there through Tuesday night.

On Wednesday at 11 o'clock, an hour before the faculty meeting, more than 300 students of the School of Industrial and Labor Relations, where I have been teaching for 23 years, held a convocation to which the professors of the school were invited. Classes were suspended so that all students could come if they wished to do so. Some students wanted the meeting so that they could tell their professors how they felt before they went to the faculty meeting; some, perhaps only a minority, wanted the meeting in order to hear what their professors thought. In any case, as I sat through that session the message of the students came through to me very clearly: they were in no mood to listen to argument. With few exceptions they had made up their minds firmly and immovably: The faculty *must* nullify the reprimands or else. . . .

As the students gave thunderous applause to the student speakers who shared the Afro-American and S.D.S. position, I could not help but think of the philosopher Miguel de Unamuno. After Franco had taken possession of the universities, at a convocation at the University of Salamanca, where Unamuno was rector, he spoke out against the rule of force and violence, but he was shouted down with cries of: "Death to the intelligentsia!" I felt that I was hearing thousands of students cry out: "If you don't do as we want, death to the professors!" I had seldom in my years of life felt such deep bitterness of soul, as if all my thinking and working and teaching and writing had been nothing but vanity of vanities.

And then I went over to Bailey Hall and the faculty meeting. Little by little, as I sat and half listened and half mused, it came to me that in fact what the faculty was facing was not the Willard Straight situation. That was on Monday; but now, on Wednesday, the faculty was facing the wilderness, the state of nature as described by Hobbes. We are no longer a civil polity—or rather we stood on the brink. We could have a state of war. The president had asked for police to stand at the alert, and several hundred policemen and deputy sheriffs had come in from outside the city and county. But the arrival of police, as we know from events on other campuses, in itself contributes to a state of tension, and thousands of moderate students suddenly become militants as the police arrive. Possibly hundreds would be injured, many perhaps seriously, some might get killed, fires would be set, and worst of all it might take years, as at San Francisco State College or at Berkeley, to reinstitute peace and order and mutual trust and respect. A society can be destroyed in hours, but it takes years to build one.

This, it seems to me, was what the faculty faced on Wednesday. Unfortunately, the challenge came to the faculty in a verbal formula which made it seem that we were called upon to contradict ourselves. Actually, what we were voting on was whether to have a state of nature, with all that it implies for the present and future, or to try to renew the social contract. But the formula for this, forced upon us by the students, was one that called for a nullification of the penalties. To our students, and to the outside world, the faculty action must look like a faculty capitulation.

And this is how it looked, too, to the three professors who spoke against nullification. They had logical, orderly, principled arguments and statements. If it had been a debating contest they probably would have scored high on points. I listened to them with an open mind and was almost persuaded, but then I shook myself and said: "These men are right from the standpoint of an either/or logic. If we were right on Monday, then what was right then should be right on Wednesday. But this system of logic is not applicable. There is a both/and logic that is much more relevant."

We were right on Monday when the Cornell situation, as we then saw it, focused on Willard Straight Hall. We then were right in refusing to nullify. The Cornell situation on Wednesday, however, was the whole of Cornell University as a civilized, orderly community. The students were ready to nullify the social contract if we did not nullify the reprimands. Under these circumstances the majority voted to nullify—but, in fact, to refresh the social contract.

I voted for the resolution, but I could barely myself hear my "Aye." It was almost as if I would gag on the word. It was a very bitter pill to swallow. For I knew how eager students will be to interpret the vote of the faculty as an admission of weakness and cowardice, and how the world at large will construe the vote as a craven capitulation. And the Afro-American Society and the S.D.S. may in a short time (there are only a few weeks left to the current academic year, so perhaps there will be no further aggressive action now, when students need to finish up term papers and get ready for examinations) find new grievances—they are easy enough to uncover or create—and escalate their demands. There is no guarantee that what has happened once will not happen again and again, and next time what the faculty may be asked to agree to may be infinitely more important than the nullification of reprimands on three students.

But life today offers little stability in any respect. The quest for certainty ended some years ago. We live permanently in an encircling gloom, and the kindly light that we have is only a feeble candle of short-range vision.

Column by Tom Wicker in The New York Times, *April 27, 1969.*

Humanity vs. Principle at Cornell

Steven Muller, Cornell University's vice president for public affairs, came to New York this week for a television appearance, then flew right back to the troubled upstate campus. Tired from too little sleep, Mr. Muller yet managed in a brief conversation to put recent events at Cornell into a rather different perspective.

Muller was one of two university officials who went into Willard Straight Hall last Sunday and persuaded the armed young blacks to give it up; after that, he helped persuade the faculty to abandon its first position and uphold the agreement that had been made.

In Muller's view, the trouble really began much earlier, when as a result of demonstrations for a black studies program last December, university charges were brought against five blacks. The blacks responded that the demonstration had been by a group, not just by five members of it; that it had been directed at the university, which now sat in judgment; that there were no blacks on the judicial body; and that the proceeding was too long delayed to be just. Nevertheless, ten days ago, three blacks were reprimanded, while charges against two were dropped.

Whether, as the blacks contend, the whole proceeding was improper is a matter of judgment; Muller thinks it was unwise in such circumstances to press charges for what he calls relatively minor offenses.

The reprimands were issued on a Thursday; on Friday, a cross was burned in front of a black woman's residence at Cornell—an act which is not likely to be regarded lightly by blacks at any time or place. On Saturday, the black students seized Willard Straight Hall. They were not then armed; the building was not seized at gunpoint. The firearms were delivered later, in a car driven up to a doorway. No one, least of all Muller, suggests that the blacks were justified, by self-defense or any other motive, in arming themselves or even in seizing the building. Yet as one of those who talked to the blacks within their fortress, he paints a convincing picture of an almost paranoid sense of fear that hung about them.

The blacks had heard radio reports of carloads of armed whites moving toward the campus. A group of white students made one effort to enter the seized building and were beaten off. The burning cross was vividly on everyone's mind. And, as Muller described it, Straight Hall is a dark and gloomy old fortress of a building, in which a long night spent in darkness—so that they would not make targets against lighted windows—only increased the blacks' nervousness.

Muller believes it was a pervasive—even irrational—fear of white reprisal that led the blacks to arm themselves. He recalls that just as he and another university official had persuaded them to leave Straight Hall, Fred Whitfield, the Arkansan who leads the Afro-American Society asked:

"How can we be sure you're not taking us into an ambush?"

Muller replied that if it would make Whitfield feel better, he could have a university bus brought to the door to take the black students away.

"How do we know where the buses will take us?" Whitfield asked.

It was because of these fears that the blacks marched out of Straight carrying their weapons—although they had at least been persuaded to empty them of cartridges. The agreement to nullify the judicial proceedings, moreover, was not signed at gunpoint; it was not signed at all while the blacks occupied Straight Hall but later.

Muller, in fact, regards the evacuation of Straight not as a triumph of force but as a surrender by the blacks. And he insists that the agreement to urge the faculty to nullify the judicial proceedings was not wrested from reluctant officials by gun-pointing blacks; rather, it was the instrument by which the university itself sought to ease the situation before hysteria might bring on gunfire and bloodshed.

As for the faculty's reversal of its first decision not to accede to the agreement, Muller believes that the only real coercion involved was that of an aroused student body who came to favor the agreement in overwhelming numbers. Two thousand students —mostly liberals and moderates, by all accounts—sat through a night on a basketball court to show support for it; by the next afternoon that crowd had grown by some accounts to 9,000.

Muller cites one colleague who met a class of hundreds of biology students to find that not one of them wanted the agreement rejected. Muller quotes him as having then changed his vote to support the agreement because "I want to keep on teaching here and I won't have any students if I don't." That is hardly intimidation at gunpoint by a small minority.

Muller dares believe that Cornell ultimately will find itself the better for its week of upheaval—its students and faculty more nearly the free and open community that is the university ideal, and its blacks more fully a part of that community. And although he is saddened that a number of Cornell faculty members, including some with high standing, plan to resign in protest, Muller believes that they have the opportunity to stand on principle this week only because university officials were willing, last Sunday in Straight Hall, to put a real concern for humanity above abstract principle.

Letter to the editor of The New York Times, *dated April 28, 1969, by Professor Allan P. Sindler, Department of Government, Cornell University.*

Reply

With reference to Tom Wicker's Sunday column [April 27], may I reply to his endorsement of the "official" Cornell University explanation of the capitulation to the demands of black students. I would not have resigned my professorship and chairmanship had the issue been, as Wicker so simply poses, "humanity above principle."

President Perkins had viable options, also not leading to violence, other than complete capitulation. The official excuse for importation of firearms by black students in the seized buildings was their fear of an assault on them by white students. Any assault could have been rendered impossible by police cordoning off the building, leaving the black students in the building but requiring them to surrender their firearms.

The faculty reversal on Wednesday was not made in primary response to the peaceful sit-in of several thousands of students at Barton Hall, which would imply faculty willingness to go along with student opinion pure and simple. The real picture is rather different. The Afro-American Society leader had given the university "three hours to live," had threatened four administrators and three faculty by name over the radio, and clearly intended to have his group engage in aggressive action on the campus if the faculty did not reverse itself. The SDS left no doubt of its intention to occupy one or more buildings. More than a score of faculty had pledged themselves to occupy a building if the faculty vote did not nullify the judicial penalties.

Under these conditions, the presence of thousands of students in Barton Hall aggravated the coercion level decisively, since none could predict how many of them would join the other named groups in building seizures or worse. On Monday, recall, the faculty refused to nullify the penalties and called for a Friday meeting in a "free and nonpressurized context"; it was the above context of massed coercion and certain force that compelled the faculty to meet on Wednesday instead and to reverse its Monday vote.

The events of this past week are but one part of a pattern over the past eighteen months of the incapacity of the Perkins administration to contain and resist coercion-based demands. Militant student groups have rightly concluded that this is the sure way to extract concessions. Given the ideology of these groups, and their insistence on "cleansing" the campus of all vestiges of what they call "institutional racism" and the "military-industrial complex," no academic freedom is maintainable. These are the issues, Mr. Wicker, and not "humanity above principle."

PART V

THE COUNTERATTACK AGAINST THE STUDENT MOVEMENT

The preceding section dealt with the tactical disagreements within the establishment on the proper response to student protest. But the radical movement has not only produced a tactical response: it has also evoked an ideological counterattack from its adversaries. The following chapters deal with this counterattack and the response made to it.

Pervading the ideology of the anti-radicals is the charge that the student movement is part of a fundamental assault against reason, reality, and modernity. Sometimes this "irrationality" or "nihilism" is seen as immaturity, a result of a "generation gap" (Kirk, Chapter 15). Sometimes it is seen as part of a pathological cultural trend (Howe and Bettelheim, Chapter 16) or as the work of a few malcontents (Hayakawa, Chapter 16). But no matter what cause is cited, the charge remains essentially the same. The most elegant permutation of the argument comes in the final chapter, where Zbigniew Brzezinski describes the radicals as "historical irrelevants," romantics fighting pathetically against the rising "technetronic" order.

The counterattack takes other forms too: that the radicals are "today's fascists" or "left McCarthyites"; that they are acting out Oedipal rebellions in their attacks on university administrators; that they are the children of the rich, *jeunesse dorée,* disguising elitist sentiments in socialist garb, and so on. We have included only a small sampling of this literature.

CHAPTER 15

The Underpinnings of Protest: Generation Gap or Social Conflict?

One way to disparage the content and challenge of the radical movement is to suggest that it is the product merely of a "generation gap." Two weeks before the 1968 demonstrations at Columbia, President Grayson Kirk gave a speech entitled "The Umpirage of Reason" in which he asserted that there was indeed a gap between the generations and that it was socially divisive and potentially very dangerous. He suggested that U.S. withdrawal from Vietnam might do much to undercut and dissipate the student movement, which had elevated civil disobedience into a "civic virtue." The following week, a former president of Sarah Lawrence College, Harold Taylor, who was more sympathetic to the students, said he agreed with Kirk that there was a generation gap. But Taylor said it was caused by the unwillingness of the older generation to deal seriously with the issues the students were raising.

In a now-famous reply to President Kirk the day before the Columbia strike began, Mark Rudd denounced the "cry of 'nihilism' " and denied the existence of a generation gap. He claimed it was a "real conflict" between the oppressed and the oppressors. Strangely, a leading conservative thinker, M. Stanton Evans, agreed with Rudd that the generation gap was imaginary, the social conflict real. Evans, however, believed Rudd's radicalism was derived directly from the liberalism preached by his elders in the liberal university. Oddly, Evans came close to Harold Taylor's view that Kirk and the institutions he represented were responsible for the student movement's character. The difference was that Evans would include Taylor among the responsible, while Taylor would include Evans.

From an address by Grayson Kirk, President of Columbia University, at a Founder's Day celebration and the 225th birthday of Thomas Jefferson at the University of Virginia at Charlottesville, Va., April 12, 1968.

The Umpirage of Reason

. . . It is not too much to say that in many ways our society is in a more perilous condition than at any time since the convulsive conflict between the states a century ago. We seem to be in an era of transition from a past which we have abandoned to a future which we are unable as yet to comprehend but whose portents fill us with more dismay than anticipation. We have a multitude of contending counselors but we are unable to place our trust in any of them because we feel, almost viscerally, that they, too, are merely groping without great success to understand the new world about us, and still less do we feel that they have the wisdom to order its affairs to our satisfaction. Our nation is in trouble.

The enumeration of our present difficulties and dangers would ruffle even the calm temperament of a Jefferson. At home, disrespect for law and authority has reached such a level of acceptance that its natural concomitant, resort to violence, has almost achieved respectability. The old social sanctions of the church and family have lost much of their traditional force. Our young people, in disturbing numbers, appear to reject all forms of authority, from whatever source derived, and they have taken refuge in a turbulent and inchoate Nihilism whose sole objectives are destructive. I know of no time in our history when the gap between the generations has been wider or more potentially dangerous.

Honesty compels us to admit that we are threatened with a loss of our sense of national unity and with it our sense of direction. Our unity has been imperiled by our racial conflicts for which, despite good-will and honest effort, we can envisage no simple or easy solution available to us in time to avoid the danger of large-scale and continuing social disorder. Less imminently perilous but also damaging to our sense of unity is the generational gap to which I have just referred. Disunity is also being fostered by the growing incidence of friction in the attempted resolution of disputes between industrial management and organized labor. When even our teachers and our governmental employees feel free to strike in order to try to impose their collective will upon our people, I cannot but feel that all is not well with our society. . . .

Among all our grave national concerns, how shall we select those to which we would give first priority? The clamor of the present is so insistent that easy agreement on such a matter is perhaps impossible. Each person will make his own list; hopefully, he will do so with only one criterion, the national welfare. The lists will differ, for that is the way of democratic societies, but the exercise is important. Having said this, obviously I now have the obligation to indicate my own to you.

First on my list, in timing and importance, is the need for this country to extricate itself as quickly as possible from its current involvement in Vietnam. No other item on the national agenda can be dealt with effectively until this has been done. Not one of our great social, economic or political problems can be made manageable until this conflict can be brought to an end.

This is so because our present policy has produced among our people more bitter dissension than any issue since the tragic War Between the States. Abroad, it has given a valuable hostage to those who regard themselves as our enemies, and it has obliged us to sustain a serious loss of esteem among those who are our friends.

This is not a time for recrimination. Our policies have been made by sincere, honorable and patriotic men who do not deserve the calumny to which they have been subjected; they have been drawn almost inexorably into a tragic situation. Our national debate should not be based upon personalities but upon an assessment of the situation solely in terms of the present and future welfare and security of our country.

One developing by-product of our involvement is alarming but little-noticed. This is the evil effect which may come from the present tendency, born out of hostility to the war, to elevate civil disobedience into a civic virtue. It is difficult to disagree with the observation made recently by Judge Charles Wyzanski who wrote:

> "Every time a law is disobeyed by even a man whose motive is solely ethical, in the sense that it is responsive to a deep moral conviction, there are unfortunate consequences. He himself becomes more prone to disobey laws for which he has no profound repugnance. He sets an example for others who may not have his pure motives, he weakens the fabric of society."
>
> (*Atlantic Monthly,* February 1968)

The longer the present controversy continues, the greater will become this peril; it is one that could be around to haunt us long after the occasion which produced it has disappeared.

Nations as well as individuals can make mistakes. No matter how well intentioned an original course may have been, things do not at times turn out as planned. When this occurs, it is often wiser to face the changed situation squarely than to seek vindication through stubborn persistence in a course that appears to offer ever-fewer possibilities of final gains to match the costs involved. Given all the complexities of our present posture in Vietnam, it is my own unhappy conclusion that it is not possible for us to derive from this conflict, no matter how it is finally settled, enough long-range benefit to the security and welfare of our country to justify the effort we have made or may be called upon to make. Therefore, though sadly, because of the fiscal and human costs we have incurred, I am obliged to conclude that a first priority item on our national agenda ought to be an honorable and orderly disentanglement from this well-meant but essentially fruitless effort. The United States will be the greatest power in the world long after Vietnam has been forgotten; it will be a still greater power if it has not suffered the impairment of its own national unity and morale by undue persistence in a course which offers so many hazards and so few compensating rewards. . . .

The title for these comments this morning was taken from Jefferson's Third Annual Message to Congress. There he spoke eloquently "of cultivating general friendship, and of bringing collisions of interest to the umpirage of reason rather than of force." In the years ahead we shall have need to remember this counsel. If we fail to heed it and drift further into sterile and divisive conflict, we shall all be the poorer for it, and we shall not, in the end, be worthy of our heritage.

From a speech given by Harold Taylor, former president of Sarah Lawrence College, at the World Affairs Conference, University of Colorado, Boulder, April 16, 1968.

No Wonder the Gap Exists

A recent statement by President Kirk of Columbia University, a former professor of International Relations, is the first we have seen from a university president, even suggesting that there is anything wrong with United States war policy. But even this statement is flawed at the center where its moral impulse should be, when Dr. Kirk said that "It is not possible for us to derive from this conflict, no matter how it is finally settled, enough long-range benefit to the security and welfare of our country to justify the effort we have made or may be called upon to make."

What a specious argument. Apparently if we could gain more benefits by killing more people, devastating more villages and destroying more of Vietnam, we should go right ahead with the war. That is what I would infer from the statement. But then, Dr. Kirk's argument extends to the faults of the younger generation which is protesting against this kind of thinking. This is what he says about student protest. "Our young people, in disturbing numbers, appear to reject all forms of authority, from whatever source derived, and they have taken refuge in a turbulent and inchoate nihilism whose sole objectives are disruptive. I know of no time in our history when the gap between the generations has been wider or more potentially dangerous."

Of course the gap is wide, and no wonder it exists and is growing wider when the representatives of the older generation talk and think this way, and are so little in touch with the issues around which the student protests moves. If the university and its present leadership fails to act, either to stop the war, reform the archaic curriculum, grant legitimate student rights, take its students seriously, take a stand against racism and racial injustice, what else can serious people do, students or anyone else, than move beyond acquiescence into protest and resistance? . . .

Article by Mark Rudd in Up Against the Wall, *a Columbia SDS newspaper, April 22, 1968.*

Reply to Uncle Grayson

Dear Grayson,

Your charge of nihilism is indeed ominous; for if it were true, our nihilism would bring the whole civilized world, from Columbia to Rockefeller Center, crashing down upon all our heads. Though it is not true, your charge does represent something: you call it the generation gap. I see it as a real conflict between those who run things now—you, Grayson Kirk—and those who feel oppressed by and disgusted with the society you rule—we, the young people.

You might want to know what is wrong with this society, since, after all, you live in a very tight self-created dream world. We can point to the war in Vietnam as an example of the unimaginable wars of aggression you are prepared to fight to maintain your control over your empire (now you've been beaten by the Vietnamese, so you call for a tactical retreat). We can point to your using us as cannon fodder to fight your war. We can point out your mansion window to the ghetto below you've helped to create through your racist university expansion policies, through your unfair labor practices, through your city government and your police. We can point to this university, your university, which trains us to be lawyers and engineers, and managers for your IBM, your Socony Mobil, your IDA, your Con-Edison (or else to be scholars and teachers in more universities like this one). We can point, in short, to our own meaningless studies, our identity crises, and our repulsion with being cogs in your corporate machines as a product of and reaction to a basically sick society.

Your cry of "nihilism" represents your inability to understand our positive values. If you were ever to go into a freshman CC [Contemporary Civilization] class you would see that we are seeking a rational basis for society. We do have a vision of the way things could be: how the tremendous resources of our economy could be used to eliminate want, how people in other countries could be free from your domination, how a university could produce knowledge for progress, not waste consumption and destruction (IDA), how men could be free to keep what they produce, to enjoy peaceful lives, to create. These are positive values—but since they mean the destruction of your order, you call them "nihilism." In the movement we are beginning to call this vision "socialism." It is a fine and honorable name, one which implies absolute opposition to your corporate capitalism and your government; it will soon be caught up by other young people who want to exert control over their own lives and their society.

You are quite right in feeling that the situation is "potentially dangerous." For if we win, we will take control of your world, your corporation, your university and attempt to mold a world in which we and other people can live as human beings. Your power is directly threatened, since we will have to destroy that power before we take over. We begin by fighting you about your support of the war in Vietnam and American Imperialism—IDA and the School of International Affairs. We will fight you about your control of black people in Morningside Heights, Harlem and the campus itself. And we will fight you about the type of mis-education you are trying to channel us through. We will have to destroy at times, even violently, in order to end your power and your system—but that is a far cry from nihilism.

Grayson, I doubt if you will understand any of this, since your fantasies have shut out the world as it really is from your thinking. Vice President Truman says the society is basically sound; you say the war in Vietnam was a well-intentioned accident. We, the young people, whom you so rightly fear, say that the society is sick and you and your capitalism are the sickness.

You call for order and respect for authority; we call for justice, freedom, and socialism.

There is only one thing left to say. It may sound nihilistic to you, since it is the opening shot in a war of liberation. I'll use the words of Leroi Jones, whom I'm sure you don't like a whole lot: "Up against the wall, motherfucker, this is a stick-up."

Yours for freedom,
Mark

Article by M. Stanton Evans, editor, Indianapolis Star, *in a symposium in* The Antioch Review, *Summer 1969.*

Nihilism, a Product of the Liberal System

It is suggested that the new left stems from such inter-related causes as a rejection of "the system," a "generation gap" in which young people discard the values of their elders, the recoil of youthful idealism from a blemished society. On my observation, the truth of the matter can be more nearly approached if these and other such statements are reversed.

I think it can be argued, for example, that the difficulties we face are products of the system rather than reactions against it; that they derive from the things which unite the generations rather than the things that divide them; that they signify too little youthful idealism rather than too much. My rhetorical device, I am quick to add, overcompensates. Various qualifications and provisos need to be entered along the way. Yet in terms of general tendency and leading principles, I believe my version comes closer to the reality of the situation than does the original.

Let us consider the much-lamented "generation gap." A little reflection will suggest that the major conflict in our society derives not from age brackets, but from ideologies, and that the clearest demarcation line between the opposing sides is the boundary of the college campus. Leftward student opinion differs from adult opinion in the outside world, but it also differs from *youthful* opinion in the outside world. By the same token, adult opinion within the academy is markedly more liberal than either adult or youthful opinion elsewhere. It would be quite easy to demonstrate a "generation gap" in reverse by comparing the opinions of a 50-year-old professor with those of a 20-year-old pipefitter.

This ideological division between the campus and society at large is not, I grant, absolute. There are many overlaps and feedbacks as the colleges send their graduates into the outside world, and the mass culture in turn exerts its influence on the colleges. The communications media, in particular, have a powerful effect on collegiate and non-collegiate opinion alike. Still, the available data show the division is there, and that the split between those on campus and those outside it is more significant than the split between age groups. The distinguishing factor is not a matter of birth certificates so much as it is a matter of ideas.

What disturbs the more intellectual commentators, of course, is the difference which arises on the collegiate side of the line: The hostility of Students for Democratic Society toward a Grayson Kirk or Clark Kerr, the unremitting warfare the new left has waged against its liberal elders. Above all, there is despair and confusion over the readiness of the youthful leftists to tear everything down, to destroy without proposing anything "constructive," and to abandon the rules of fair discussion and orderly procedure in pursuit of their objectives.

Even taking the "generation gap" idea in this restricted sense, however, I think the argument is mistaken. I would suggest instead that the young people of SDS, and many of their less violent contemporaries, are faithful products of their academic experience. This is most obvious in terms of the issues the new left chooses to discuss. Whether the topic is Vietnam or the cold war generally, civil rights or egalitarian economics, the new left perceives events through the lenses provided by the ideology of liberalism, and responds with emotions liberalism has designated as appropriate.

This is not to say the substantive positions taken by either the senior liberals or the youthful leftists are necessarily incorrect—although I happen to think that in most cases they are. Nor is it to suggest that one is entitled to dismiss youthful complaints because they can be identified with the opinions of somebody else. The point is simply that, right or wrong, the new left is operating within a conceptual framework supplied by the professoriate. Its ideological position is an extension of the liberal view and not a repudiation of it.

The "generation gap" on campus, therefore, is a matter of procedural guidelines rather than of substance. The adult liberal is characteristically opposed to the war in Vietnam, but deplores the use of disruptive measures to express that opposition. The new leftist opposes the war also, but far from rejecting disruption seems to welcome the issue, or any other, as a pretext for kicking over the furniture. The difference in mind-set and tactics is acute. Yet even here, I think, the intellectual connection between the old left and the new is discernible.

The studies of Emile Durkheim and others of his school suggest that large-scale social disorders result from a loss of interior restraint on impulse. My own observations lead me to believe this is a powerful factor in the current upheaval on campus. The most common characteristic of students engaged in disruptive activity is, precisely, a rejection of the idea of limits—of the notion that their conduct should be subordinated to a system of higher values. The intensity of this feeling varies from case to case, but it obtrudes itself on nearly every campus with which I am familiar. The dominant urge is for impulse-release, for instant realization of emotional appetites and political passions.

To a certain extent this Faustian hunger is always prevalent among the young. Such attitudes are, in fact, the characteristic attitudes of the infant, and the process of maturation has traditionally been viewed as a laborious effort to get them under some kind of control. The remarkable thing about the present situation is that the rejection of limits is no longer viewed as childish or ignorant, but as a manifestation of a healthy zest for life. We have been hard at work in recent years exalting impulse and disparaging value, and nowhere more industriously than on the college campus.

At the theoretical level, the story is a familiar one. Although there has been some re-thinking of the matter in recent years, modern scholarship, particularly in the social sciences, has prided itself on being value-free. Nothing is conceived to be "true" except the findings of science. All else is opinion, relative to time and place. "Middle-class" values are looked upon as benighted ignorance, while religion is treated, at best, as a kind of useful mythology.

The impact of this doctrine has been considerable. It has affected our jurisprudence, our statecraft, and our popular culture. Most of all, it has affected the young. Studies of collegiate opinion show that belief in religious value and "old-fashioned" morality declines from the freshman to the senior year. I have interviewed numerous students who testify to this transformation in their views as a result of academic enlightenment. Such students, unfortunately, are given nothing very solid to replace the values they have lost. They are left hanging in a kind of ethical void.

Under the circumstances, it would be strange indeed if some of them did not pursue the line of least resistance and gratify their impulses as they arise. This likelihood is increased by the fact that, even as interior restraints are weakened, exterior ones are removed as well. Colleges have been systematically ridding themselves of parietal regulations, diluting disciplinary procedures, and in general abolishing the notion that life should be conducted according to rules. Add the widespread acclaim recently conferred on "civil disobedience," plus repeated amnestics for even the most violent and coercive behavior, and the recipe for disorder would seem to be complete.

A number of other factors on the campus and beyond it have obviously contributed to the present turmoil—including home life, earlier schooling, cultural pressures generally. The evidence suggests, however, that these tendencies are crystallized by the college experience, and that in themselves they are less decisive than the college experience in the transvaluation of youthful values. There is also reason to suppose the "permissive-expressive" home cited by Keniston, the lower schools, and the media—all staffed with previous generations of college graduates—are in some measure resultants of higher education.

It should be apparent, at all events, that the disorienting effect of the collegiate experience bears some relation to the nihilism of our youthful revolutionaries. Having programmed the young with a value-free mentality, we should hardly be astounded if some of them respond with a value-free political movement. Nor should we be astounded if this movement grows progressively more violent and insensitive to the rights of others, since these are characteristic features of nihilism. Those who start with unlimited freedom in the moral realm all too often arrive at unlimited despotism in the political.

The new left theology of "action" rather than ideas is an obvious product of nihilist beginnings. An uprising premised in the absence of value has no certain place to stand, no ready means of distinguishing itself from the surrounding society. Implicit acceptance of the political ideas of the adult community on campus both expresses the problem and intensifies it. Since there is nothing very unusual about his ideas, the new left revolutionary must set himself apart by idiosyncrasies of appearance and behavior. Thus the first step in the "rebellion" is generally a cultivated eccentricity of hair-style or clothing or language.

At most, however, these are feeble substitutes for the internalized value structure that gives significance and direction to life. There must be super-added the quest for sensation through such things as the drug-culture, political chiliasm, and—ultimately—violence. Efforts to escape from boredom and loss of purpose through violence are frequently noted in the behavior of juvenile delinquents, and I believe the same considerations hold, with different intellectual components, on the college campus. One proves himself and invests his life with meaning through constantly escalated challenges to authority. The experience of confrontation supplies "thrills" and makes society in general sit up and pay attention. Things happen, boredom is extinguished, one's importance in the world is duly certified.

It is in this respect, I believe, that the media have played their most important role in advancing the new left cause. The contributions of the media to the present crisis are many—including a constant hammering of materialist themes that feed the drive toward impulse-release. But they have most clearly helped create the new left phenomenon by playing it up to the exclusion of other developments on campus, by certifying its importance, by converting its leaders into powerful and glamorous figures. This treatment fulfils and emboldens those already in the movement and carries their message to potential new recruits.

The gathering together of the young in collectivities is a familiar behavior pattern which tends to become more frequent in periods of metaphysical uncertainty. The crowd serves to reinforce the individual's sense of his own power and worthiness. The psychologist Robert Lindner observed that juvenile pack-running was the natural correlate of an interior loss of value. Elias Canetti points out that the individual immersed in the crowd achieves a sense of mastery, feels capable of transcending all limits. Mass behavior of this sort is at once a compensation for the emptiness of nihilism and of fulfillment of the impulses that nihilism has released.

Compounding the problem is the fact that higher education itself seems these days to be without direction. The modern university has become a massive complex of activities which have no discernible focus, a situation which is harmful to the student in a number of different ways. The university's confusion accentuates the student's own. The diversion of energies to outside interests provides a whole clutch of issues—many of them, taken on their merits, quite legitimate—convenient for exploitation. And, most serious of all, the university's effort to be all things to all people means it has neglected its major purpose, that of teaching the student how to think. The result has been to produce large numbers of young people who are half-educated or not in any real sense educated at all, yet who are told they are the "best-educated" generation in history and sent forth into the world to change it.

The last is the unkindest cut of all. Constant repetition of the view that today's generation is the most knowledgeable ever has quite naturally led the students themselves to believe in it, even as the more vocal among them seem decreasingly capable of grappling with complex or unfamiliar ideas. Their education thus fails not only by leaving them ignorant, but—more tragic by far—by leaving them unaware of their ignorance. Thus we get the familiar syndrome of the new left activist: A sad poverty of ideas combined with a firm conviction of *gnosis,* a belief in the rightness of untutored emotions and half-digested gobbets of perception.

This is the rock on which the new leftist at last gains his footing, and on which he premises his much celebrated "idealism" and unwillingness to compromise. The certitude metaphysically lost is rediscovered in a millennial conception of the political order. Politics itself becomes a kind of religion, and those who stand in the way of the secular faith become heretics against whom any measures are justified. Thus, by a familiar conversion, does ethical relativism become political absolutism.

From where I sit, then, the new left movement appears both chaotic and coercive, and therefore dangerous. But it does not appear to be revolutionary in a philosophical sense, or even, in view of the total drift of our culture and the doctrines which prevail in the intellectual community, especially surprising. Indeed, it is hard to think of anything we might have done to create such a phenomenon which we have left undone. The only mystery in the case is whether, having conjured this spirit from the deep, we can eventually manage to control it.

CHAPTER 16

The Culture of Irrationality

Critics of student protest charged not merely that radicals were irrational in their behavior but that their movement was a *cult* of irrationality. Irving Howe, essayist and editor of *Dissent,* deplored the "growing current of irrationalism and anti-intellectualism," seeing it as part of a "world-wide cultural revolt against the modernist tradition, with its stress on complexity, irony, ambivalence and the problematical." Bruno Bettelheim, the orthopsychiatrist, denounced "the fascination in society at large with sex and violence, with drugs and insanity." Bettelheim did not view the "irrationality" of radicals as part of a revolt against modern culture, but as its direct product. Taking a slightly different position, S. I. Hayakawa derided the claims of alienation, suggesting that the students were "taught this alienation by professors." The left's irrationality, according to Hayakawa, was not the product of the entire culture, but the work of a few malcontents—"half-assed Platos," as he called them.

A few people sympathetic to the radical cause have accepted the accusation of irrationality, claiming that the negation of reason and technology is progressive. In a review of Theodore Roszak's *The Making of a Counter Culture,* Robert Paul Wolff took the more orthodox radical view, denying the established order's claim to rationality and criticizing those like Roszak who accept it. Wolff pleaded with the left not to abandon the defense of reason to conservatives, but to insist on a "renascence of true reason."

From an article by Irving Howe, in Dissent, *September–October 1969.*

The Agony of the Campus

. . . It would be foolish, at this point, to pretend that we have a unified explanation for the character and magnitude of student revolt. The two greatest mistakes are, taking at face value everything the students say about themselves and refusing to accept anything the students say about themselves. The familiar "sympathetic" explanations contain some truth: revolt against bureaucratism, revulsion against the Vietnam war, guilt over draft exemption, concern with poverty, etc. So do the "hostile" explanations: boredom among middle-class youth, purposelessness among those in "soft" disciplines like sociology and literature, delusions as to charismatic dictators in the Third World, abandonment of liberal norms, etc. But when you have so many explanations, then in truth you are still in a preliminary stage of analysis and are still sorting out the relative weights to assign to the various explanations.

Yet there is one aspect of student unrest that ought to be grasped more clearly than it has been by people outside the university. Together with the idealism and despair, there is a growing current of irrationalism and anti-intellectualism. There seems to be some line of continuity between the antihistoricism of the mindlessly contented students of the fifties and the antihistoricism of the passionately discontented students of the sixties. Since the phenomenon is worldwide (see, for a brilliant quasi-satirical portrait, Godard's *La Chinoise*), distinctively American factors of explanation cannot be sufficient. I think we are experiencing a worldwide cultural revolt against the modernist tradition, with its stress on complexity, irony, ambivalence and the problematical, to which is linked a worldwide revulsion not merely against the industrial-bureaucratic state but the idea of technique itself. The signs of a romantic primitivism are everywhere on the campus, and even those who cannot accept the deeper implications of this trend must admit that some of its external tokens are attractive. I think we are also witnessing, in some strange and inverted way, a quasi-religious impulse which through secular nihilism and alienated idealism seeks to break into a condition of religious transcendence. My own view is that the desire to achieve religious states of being through nonreligious, and especially political, agencies is full of serious dangers, both to religion and society; but let that rest for another occasion.

One immediate consequence on campus of this melange of styles and impulses is sometimes a revolt against knowledge as such. A few months ago I spoke at a university in California before an audience of graduate students, and for two hours I found myself arguing with them—graduate students, mind you—as to whether scholarship had a place in the university! . . .

From a statement by orthopsychiastrist Bruno Bettelheim to the House Special Subcommittee on Education, March 20, 1969.

Student Revolt

THE HARD CORE

. . . There is a fascination in society at large with sex and violence, with drugs and insanity which both influences the student militants and provides them with a noteworthiness which they exploit to the full. If students protest because of an idea or position and do so in orderly and rational form, they do not receive much public attention. But if they shed all their clothes and walk around naked, this makes news all over the nation, whatever the case they may or may not have had. It is part of a dangerous fascination with youth and its extreme positions. What passes for modern literature which these youngsters read already in junior high school intoxicates their minds with the appeal of drug induced madness, with sexual acting out and with violence.

The universities, because of their intellectual prestige, give the student activists a prestige for their revolutionary claims which they otherwise could never achieve. For example, for days not more than some 20 to 30 students occupied the administration building of the University of Chicago. They got headlines every day, and were prominently featured on radio and TV. If some 30 people would have demonstrated in any other place, they would have found no attention whatsoever. This the SDS knows, that is why it concentrates on the universities. The contrast between an institution devoted to the highest achievements of reason, and the obscenity and violence perpetrated there, makes it all the more fascinating. It is this fascination on which they try to build their revolutionary success. An idea in itself may be next to nothing, but it becomes news by interfering with something else which is considered, for one reason or another, to be of public importance. In themselves a couple of hundred demonstrators, somewhere in New York or Chicago would mean very little, but if some fifty students march into a large lecture hall, take control of the podium, and broadcast their ideas to people who came to hear something quite different, then they have made news.

Here, too, is where the function of political phraseology becomes operative. If someone advocates urinating on graves as the Fugs did, or if a few girls dress up as witches and put curses on professors, as they did in Chicago, if they would do so without reference to politics, people would rightly wonder about their sanity; but if they do so as a condemnation of the Viet Nam war, or take clothes off while claiming to be demonstrating for some good progressive cause, they have the support of many of the older liberals and enlightened radicals, who will inevitably consider it all to be very socially significant. If you are a teenager wrestling with the police and you say you are doing it because of the moral superiority of a future social order, you cannot fail to get the sympathetic attention of the editors of radio and TV stations rather than psychiatrists. The ritualistic invocation of ideology is thus both an alibi and a defense. . . .

Statement by S. I. Hayakawa, President of San Francisco State College, to task force of National Commission on the Causes and Prevention of Violence, in June 1969.

Alienation Is Being Taught by Professors

Central to the problem of violence on campus is the existence of a large number of alienated young men and women [who] practically take pride in being outside the main stream of the culture, of being against the establishment, against authority, against the administration of the college, the administration of the State of California, the administration in Washington, whether it's a Republican or Democratic administration.

How did they get alienated? Well, besides the usual psychologically neurotic reasons for this alienation there is something else that's going on.

I think they are taught this alienation by professors—especially in the liberal arts departments—the humanities, English, philosophy, sometimes in social sciences.

There's a kind of cult of alienation among intellectuals, among intellectuals in literary fashion such as you find in the *New York Review of Books* or the *Partisan Review*. They sneer at the world the way it's run by politicians, businessmen, and generals. Knowing that they themselves are so much smarter than politicians, businessmen, or generals, they feel there's a dreadful world which they themselves ought to be running instead.

The first great enunciator of this theory was Plato, who believed that philosophers should be kings, and notice that he himself was a philosopher. The contemporary literary critics and philosophers feel the same way.

Supposing you're an alienated intellectual. You're a professor of philosophy or something, you have no power, you have no influence in Sacramento or Washington. But you can influence your students. You use phrases like, well, a phrase I just picked up from a professor of English in San Diego the other day, "the illegitimacy of contemporary authority."

Now if contemporary authority, of the state government, the federal government, the San Francisco police, is illegitimate, then you are morally entitled to, in fact, it is your moral duty to oppose that force. It becomes moral duty to oppose that illegitimate authority.

The middle-aged professor passes this on to his young students. The young students are more likely to act upon this. The authority of the police is illegitimate, therefore it's proper and moral to throw bricks at them. It's proper and moral to resist the draft, to resist the authority of the government in any way.

And anyone who upholds civil authority or military authority is regarded as a tool of the interests, a tool of the military-industrial complex, etc., etc., and because the military-industrial complex is so powerful, so huge, it certainly looks huge if you lump everything together into one abstraction.

All means of bringing it down, fair or unfair, are justifiable. This is why you find among young people today, not simply violence, but completely outrageous forms of behavior.

You see, peaceful marchers protesting courageously racial injustice under the leadership of a Martin Luther King, never screamed obscenities. They held up for themselves very, very high and rigid moral standards. And by that they dignified their protest, they dignified their cause.

But our protests, especially from the white SDS, is full of obscenities, full of shocking behavior, full of absolute defiance of any values the civilized world insists upon.

This is what I find so terribly shocking, and I think it has its intellectual sources, in a kind of disaffection, among, shall I say, the frustrated intellectuals. To paraphrase a famous line, "Hell hath no fury like the intellectuals scorned."

Now, professors tend, therefore, to give A's in their courses to students that are alienated. And as the students get A's, they get appointed graduate assistants. Then they soon become professors themselves. And then they pass on this alienation to another generation of students, and college generations of students come fast, after all. And before you know it, you have whole departments which are basically sources of resistance to the culture as a whole.

All this upsets me very, very much. The universities and the colleges should be centers for the dissemination of the values of our culture, and the passing on of those values. But dammit, with enough half-assed Platos in our university departments, they are trying to make of them centers of sedition and destruction.

Review of The Making of a Counter Culture: Reflections on the Technocratic Society and Its Youthful Opposition *by Theodore Roszak, by Professor Robert Paul Wolff, Department of Philosophy, Columbia University in* The New York Times Book Review, *September 7, 1969.*

Reason and the Left

The fool who misplaces his trust becomes a misanthrope and hates mankind for betraying him instead of berating himself for his unwisdom. So too, Socrates tells us in the *Phaedo,* the novice philosopher who is taken in by a bad argument will often turn against logic, as though reason itself were to blame for his mistake. Misology, or the hatred of reason, is the greatest temptation of the fledgling intellect, and the only unforgiveable sin.

In recent years, many of our brightest and most gifted young men and women have been turning against reason. Horrified and revolted by the cruelties perpetrated by an established order which proclaims itself "reasonable," "pragmatic," "realistic" and "scientific," they conclude that a humane existence can be achieved only by a thoroughgoing rejection of the rational ideal which has dominated Western civilization since the time of the ancient Greeks. So they turn to drugs, to mystical experience, to Zen, and to such other bits and snatches of Eastern religious practices as have made their way to our shores. So too, more than half in earnest, they consult horoscopes and conduct bowdlerized versions of the Black Mass, hoping to liberate themselves from the evils of modern society by rejecting that "reason" in whose name the evils are committed.

Theodore Roszak, a history professor at California State College, applauds the "great negation" of the rebel young. In his new book, *The Making of a Counter Culture,* he argues that they are creating a new culture based upon a rejection of reason and the "objective consciousness" of science, and aiming at a liberation of the non-rational forces of the human personality. This new culture, as he sees it, is subjective rather than objective, tribal or communitarian rather than individualistic, transcendental rather than worldly. In a concluding chapter which we are apparently meant to take literally, Roszak calls for a renewal of the shamanistic world-view of our neolithic prehistory. Only through a release of the transcendent powers of the human spirit, he believes, can we break the all-encompassing, deadening, destructive domination of technocratic reason.

Roszak devotes almost half of his book to a discussion of the authors and practices to which dissident young people are drawn: Herbert Marcuse and Norman O. Brown, Allen Ginsberg and Alan Watts, Paul Goodman, LSD, marijuana, yoga, astrology, Zen, and so on. But these chapters, though well-written and insightful on a number of topics of contemporary dispute, are only ancillary to the main line of Roszak's argument, which can be summarized in four propositions: *First,* modern industrial society in general, and American society in particular, is ugly, repressive, destructive and subversive of much that is truly human; *Second,* the youthful outbursts of rebellion and dissent are amalgamating into a coherent, though as yet uncompleted, "counter culture"; *Third,* the root of our troubles is Western society's unquestioning acceptance of the "ideology of objective consciousness," the ideal and method of science; and *Fourth,* the anti-rationalist counter culture "that our alienated young are giving shape to . . . looks like the saving vision our endangered civilization requires."

The first of these propositions, I take it, is now acknowledged to be true by virtually every sensible man and woman. Anyone who still imagines that the United States is the land of opportunity and the bastion of democracy is a candidate either for a mental hospital or for Richard Nixon's Cabinet.

The second proposition is debatable, as Roszak himself says; but there is not much to be gained from disputing it. The crucial question is not whether a genuine counter culture is being born, but whether we wish to act as midwives or abortionists to it.

The fourth proposition depends for its plausibility on the third, and *that* is where the hard questions must be raised. Can we really trace the manifest evils of modern society to the methodology of science and a myth of objective consciousness? Roszak says yes. I say no.

First of all, Roszak is extremely ambiguous about the precise content of the "scientific world-view." His examples of repressive and inhuman social practices make it clear that his primary targets (and mine) are economic exploitation, political domination, and the depersonalization, which results from institutional bureaucratization. Hence his real villain is the social scientist, not the natural scientist.

Now, in a limited sense much explored by Max Weber, the bureaucratization of exploitation and domination can be traced to the functional principle of instrumental "reason." And it is certainly true that modern American political scientists, economists and sociologists are fatally prone to confuse functional rationality with reason itself. But one needn't take pot or study Zen to escape the grip of this fallacy. Countless rationalists, from Plato and Aristotle to Marx, Freud, Mannheim, and Weber himself have exposed the limitations of mere functional rationality and have recalled us to that substantive rationality on which a truly human existence is based.

The life of reason does not consist in planting symmetrical formal gardens, or in accumulating wealth out of all relation to one's desires, or in repressing spontaneous feelings, or in building weapons which no sane man could ever use. When twisted men offer for approval their efficient gas chambers and their utility-maximizing schemes of mutual annihilation, it is *they* who must be denied, not the ideal of reason which they falsely invoke.

Roszak reveals his confusion over the identity of his target in his quite insensitive discussion of the character of pure scientific investigation. He labors hard to persuade us that theoretical physicists and pure mathematicians are philistines whose work "depreciates our capacity for wonder" by reducing our majestic experience of the power of the universe "to manageable and repeatable terms, packaged up, mastered, brought under control." The beauties of creation, he says, can thus be "salted away in textbooks and passed onto posterity in summary form as established conclusions."

So it must seem to the humanistically inclined undergraduate laboring through a year of required science which he neither likes nor understands. But exactly the same soul-dampening tedium may be induced by reading half a dozen scholarly articles on the literary sources of William Blake's imagery. (Blake is one of Roszak's counter-cultural heroes.) If Newton and Einstein are to be believed, there is as much poetic wonder in the contemplation of the laws of the universe as in the worship of lightning or in reflection upon the sound of one hand clapping.

Despite the very great sophistication of his analysis, Roszak succumbs in the end to exactly the same sin of misology as the anti-rational students. When a farcical impostor like Herman Kahn hides his apologetics for Air Force policies behind a façade of "science" and "logic," Roszak is completely taken in. Instead of exposing the irrationalities in Kahn's sophistical arguments (not a very difficult task), Roszak retreats into oriental mysticism. One might as well forswear medicine because a quack once sold you snake oil!

For a variety of historical reasons the promising young radical intellectuals of the thirties betrayed their faith in the forties and retreated in the fifties to the ranks of establishment liberal ideologues. The men who should have leading voices on the left became instead apologetic for capitalism at home and anti-Communism abroad. This generational failure has imposed a heavy burden on America's postwar young, for they have had to search the past or other lands for the heroes and mentors who can give them guidance.

But time passes and a new generation of radical scholars is coming upon the scene. The convenient celebrations of American life are giving way to critical new appraisals of the injustices of our society. Roszak may be right that our young people are fleeing from the ideal of reason, but to encourage them in their flight is to play into the hands of reaction. The only hope for a just and humane America is a renascence of true reason, which can hold their allegiance and guide their energies in fruitful directions.

CHAPTER 17

The Student Revolt: Is It Historically Irrelevant?

The highest form of counterattack is to use the assumptions of the enemy to defeat him. Zbigniew Brzezinski charged the student movement with being "essentially counter-revolutionary," with being modern Luddites opposed to technological progress. Their slogans are "the death rattle of the historical irrelevants."

Not so, said Kenneth Keniston. Brzezinski's argument is an elaborate "put down," as is Lewis Feuer's theory of the Oedipal Rebellion. The student movement represents the confluence of two revolutions: the eighteenth-century revolution for egalitarian rights, and the new revolution of the post-industrial society, which is "against uniformity, equalization, standardization and homogenization—not against technology." *

* For a third view of the relationship of the radical movement to post-industrial society, see Mario Savio, Volume I, pp. 179–82.

Article by Professor Zbigniew Brzezinski, Department of Political Science, Columbia University, in The New Republic, *June 1, 1968.*

Revolution and Counterrevolution

(BUT NOT NECESSARILY ABOUT COLUMBIA!)

A revolutionary situation typically arises when values of a society are undergoing a profound change. The crisis in values in its turn is linked to profound socioeconomic changes, both accelerating them and reacting to them. For example, the transition from an agrarian to an industrial society produced very basic changes in outlook, both on the part of the elites ruling the changing societies and also of the social forces transformed by the changes and produced by them. Similarly, it can be argued that today in America the industrial era is coming to an end and America is becoming a technetronic society, that is a society in which technology, especially electronic communications and computers, is prompting basic social changes. . . . This automatically produces a profound shift in the prevailing values.

The crisis of values has several political consequences of relevance to revolutionary processes. First of all, it prompts ambivalent concessions by the authorities in power. The authorities do not fully comprehend the nature of the changes they are facing, but they are no longer sufficiently certain of their values to react in an assertive fashion—concessionism thus becomes the prevailing pattern of their behavior. Secondly, increasingly self-assertive revolutionary forces begin an intensive search for appealing issues. The purpose is to further radicalize and revolutionize the masses and to mobilize them against the status quo. Thirdly, limited claims begin to be translated into more fundamental claims. Expedient escalationism of demands is typically a revolutionary tactic, designed deliberately to aggravate the situation and to compensate for initial revolutionary weakness.

A revolutionary situation is thus a combination of objective and subjective forces. Revolutions do not come by themselves, they have to be made. On the other hand, unless a ripe revolutionary situation exists, revolutionary efforts can be abortive. Abortive efforts can contribute to the creation of a revolutionary situation, but a truly revolutionary situation arises only when a society is ill at ease with itself and when established values, legitimacy and authority are beginning to be seriously questioned.

In that setting, confrontations, the test of will and power, begin to be more and more frequent. Revolutionary forces engage in repeated probes to test the reactions of established authorities, while searching for appealing issues around which to rally. The initial phase of the revolutionary process thus involves a protracted game of hide-and-seek. The authorities try as skillfully as they can to avoid a head-on confrontation: they concede in a limited fashion while trying to avoid confronting fundamental issues. The revolutionary leaders, by their probes, seek to identify weak spots and to provoke a head-on, direct clash.

The critical phase occurs when a weak spot has been identified, appealing issues articulated, and the probe becomes a confrontation. At this stage the purpose of revolutionary activity is to legitimize violence. If the initial act of violence is suppressed quickly by established authorities, the chances are that the revolutionary act itself will gain social opprobrium; society generally tends to be conservative, even in a situation of crisis of values. Thus a revolutionary act is likely to be condemned by most, provided it is rapidly suppressed. If the revolutionary act endures, then automatically it gains legitimacy with the passage of time. Enduring violence thus becomes a symbol of the authorities' disintegration and collapse, and it prompts in turn further escalation of support for the revolutionary act.

Simply by enduring defiantly, the initial act of revolutionary self-assertion becomes legitimized and it contributes to further escalation of support as latent social grievances surface and are maximized. In every society latent grievances exist and a social crisis brings them to the forefront. Moreover, equally important is the manufacturing of grievances and demands to express unconscious resentment of authority. Most individuals and groups to some extent resent authority; a defiantly enduring revolutionary situation brings out this unconscious resentment and prompts the manufacturing of grievances and demands which are designed to define an anti-authority posture.

An important role in this revolutionary process is played by legitimist reformers and intellectuals. Intellectuals by their very nature are unwilling to pick sides, since they are better at identifying gray than siding with black and white. In a revolutionary situation, they are particularly concerned with not being stamped as counterrevolutionary conservatives. They are thus desirous of proving their reformist convictions, even at the cost of compromising their posture as reformers and becoming more closely identified with revolutionaries. Moreover, many intellectuals tend to be frustrated power-seekers, and a revolutionary situation creates a ready-made opportunity for the exercise of vicarious statesmanship.

In a revolutionary situation, their desire for power yet their inability to side with one or the other side prompts intellectuals to adopt a third posture, namely that of interposing themselves between the revolutionary and anti-revolutionary forces. In doing so, they often place their intellect in service of emotions rather than using emotions in the service of intellect. Many are highly excitable; their political weakness and lack of organization inclines them increasingly in a revolutionary situation to rely on demagogy. At the same time, accustomed generally to dealing with established authorities, they are more experienced in coping with the authorities than with the revolutionary forces. Thus, in the process of interposing themselves, they are inclined to apply most of their pressure against the established authority, with which they have many links, than equally against established authorities and the revolutionary forces on behalf of reformist appeals. In effect, irrespective of their subjective interests, the legitimist reformers and intellectuals in a revolutionary situation objectively become the tools of the revolutionary forces, thus contributing to further aggravation of the revolutionary situation and radicalizing the overall condition.

When faced with a revolutionary situation, the established authorities typically commit several errors. *First of all,* because they are status quo oriented, they display an incapacity for immediate effective response. Their traditional legalism works against them. Faced with a revolutionary situation, instead of striking immediately and effectively, they tend to procrastinate, seeking refuge in legalistic responses. *Second,* in so doing, they tend to opt for negotiating with the new interposing element, thus obscuring the clear-cut confrontation. An early confrontation would work to the advantage of the authorities, since mass support begins to shift to the revolutionaries only after the situation has been radicalized. *Third,* while negotiating with the interposing element, they tend to dribble out concessions rather than to make them in one dramatic swoop, thereby gaining broad support. *Fourth,* when finally force is employed, the authorities rarely think ahead to post-use-of-force consequences, concentrating instead on the application of force to the specific challenge at hand. They thus neglect the important consideration that the use of force must be designed not only to eliminate the surface revolutionary challenge, but to make certain that the revolutionary forces cannot later rally again under the same leadership. If that leadership cannot be physically liquidated, it can at least be expelled from the country (or area) in which the revolution is taking place. Emigrants rarely can maintain themselves as effective revolutionaries. The denial of the opportunity for the revolutionary leadership to re-rally should be an important ingredient of the strategy of force, even if it is belatedly used. *Fifth,* in the application of force, a sharp distinction should be made between the direct challenge and the masses which the challenge has tended to bring out. Thus, in the event of violence in a specific setting, the first objective of force ought to be the clearing of the area of those not directly committed and not involved in the revolutionary process. Only after the direct revolutionary participants have been fully isolated should force be directed directly against their strongholds. Moreover, if isolated for a period of time, the revolutionaries themselves may be more inclined to bargain. Finally, established authorities often fail to follow up effective violence with immediate reforms. Such reforms ought to be designed to absorb the energies of the more moderate revolutionaries, who can then claim that though their revolution had failed, their objectives were achieved. This is very important in attracting the more moderate elements to the side of the authorities.

For every revolution that succeeds, at least ten fail. It is not always a matter of abortive revolutionary situations. Frequently, the revolutionary leaders are themselves guilty of certain errors, typically tactical ones. Under the pressure of dramatic events, they tend to make more and more excessive demands, designed to radicalize and politicize specific grievances. In so doing, they often outrun their supporters and end up losing mass support. Moreover, they often engage in wrong symbolization, focusing on personalities rather than on basic issues. Such personal symbolization does not have staying power over the long haul, and it gives the other side the option to change or to keep the personalities involved, depending on the other side's judgment of the utility of one or the other tactic. Secondly, revolutionary leaders frequently overdo their reliance on emotionalizing appeals. For example, the condemnation of violence by revolutionaries is too transparent to be long effective. If sincerely meant, it stamps the revolutionaries as naïve, for violence necessarily accompanies a revolutionary process; if used as a tactic to mobilize support, it tends to backfire after a while because it eventually becomes evident that the revolutionaries themselves court violence in the hope of further radicalizing the situation. Finally, there is a tendency, and this is very important, of the revolutionaries to overestimate the revolutionary dynamic that they have set in motion. Revolutionaries tend to operate in a fishbowl atmosphere and to assume that their context and their appeals have universal validity. They thus underestimate the nonrevolutionary context of their own specific revolution. The French revolutionaries expected their revolution to sweep all over Europe; so did the Bolshevik revolutionaries. In most cases, this does not happen, and the revolutionaries, because they lose touch with reality, increasingly become separated from the reformers on whose support they desperately depend for their long-range success.

In that setting, the task of the reformers is to isolate both the revolutionaries and the reactionaries as extremists. This is a terribly difficult task, for in a revolutionary situation there is very little room for reformers. Accordingly, they must formulate tangible and attainable reforms, together with highly concrete action programs for their attainment. It is only through positive involvement that the reformers can begin to gain broader support. Moreover, they must not participate in activities designed to keep the pot boiling, for this, if successful, will benefit the extremist revolutionaries; if it fails, it benefits the reactionaries. Accordingly, if the revolutionary process is itself in motion, the reformers must decide whom to trust more. If they trust the promises of the authorities, they have little choice but to side with them until the revolution is crushed; if they do not trust them, they must side with the revolutionaries and eventually let the revolution consume them. In any case, they should not mislead themselves into thinking that by staying in the middle, they will impose a middle solution.

A crucial consideration in judging the validity and significance of the revolutionary process is to determine whether it is historically relevant. Some revolutions, by relating themselves to the future, clearly were. This was the case with the French Revoltuion, with the 1848 Spring of Nations, and the Bolshevik Revolution. They all were part of, as well as having ushered in, new historical eras. But very frequently revolutions are the last spasm of the past, and thus not really revolutions but counterrevolutions, operating in the name of revolutions. A revolution which really either is non-programmatic and has no content, or involves content which is based on the past but provides no guidance for the future, is essentially counterrevolutionary.

Indeed, most revolutionary outbreaks are of this character—they respond to the past, not to the future, and ultimately they fail. Examples are provided by the Luddites and the Chartists in England, who reflected the traumas of an agrarian society entering the Industrial Era; their response was spasmodic and irrelevant to the future. Peasant uprisings, whatever the merit of specific grievances, essentially fail for they do not provide a meaningful program for the future. Anarchist revolutions fall into this category. More recently, the Nationalist Socialists, the Fascists, and now the Red Guards in China are essentially counterrevolutionary: they do not provide meaningful programs and leadership for the coming age on the basis of an integrative analysis which makes meaningful the new era. Rather, they reflect concern that the past may be fading and a belated attempt to impose the values of the past on the present and on the future.

If it can be said that America today is ceasing to be an industrial society and is becoming a technetronic society, then it is important to decide whether some—though not all—of the crises and violence of today really add up to a meaningful revolution, or whether at least some manifestations are not counterrevolutionary in their essence. A revolution which has historically valid content for the future and which provides an integrated program for the future is historically relevant. In that sense, the civil rights revolution is a true and a positive revolution. Similarly, the important function of Marxism was that it made meaningful the revolutionary activities of communists by providing them with a sense of historical relevance and a pertinent program.

No such broad integrative ideology exists today in the United States, a country which confronts a future which no other society has yet experienced. On the contrary, it is revealing here to note that some of the recent upheavals have been led by people who increasingly will have no role to play in the new technetronic society. Their reaction reflects both a conscious and, even more important, an unconscious realization that they are themselves becoming historically obsolete. The movements they lead are more reminiscent of the Red Guards or the Nazis, than of the Bolsheviks or the French revolutionaries. Thus, rather than representing a true revolution, some recent outbursts are in fact a counterrevolution. Its violence and revolutionary slogans are merely—and sadly—the death rattle of the historical irrelevants.

Article by Professor Kenneth Keniston, Department of Psychology, Yale University, in The New York Times Magazine, *April 27, 1969.*

You Have to Grow Up in Scarsdale to Know How Bad Things Really Are

The recent events at Harvard are the culmination of a long year of unprecedented student unrest in the advanced nations of the world. We have learned to expect students in underdeveloped countries to lead unruly demonstrations against the status quo, but what is new, unexpected and upsetting to many is that an apparently similar mood is sweeping across America, France, Germany, Italy and even Eastern European nations like Czechoslovakia and Poland. Furthermore, the revolts occur, not at the most backward universities, but at the most distinguished, liberal and enlightened—Berkeley, the Sorbonne, Tokyo, Columbia, the Free University of Berlin, Rome and now Harvard.

This development has taken almost everyone by surprise. The American public is clearly puzzled, frightened and often outraged by the behavior of its most privileged youth. The scholarly world, including many who have devoted their lives to the study of student protest, has been caught off guard as well. For many years, American analysis of student movements have been busy demonstrating that "it can't happen here." Student political activity abroad has been seen as a reaction to modernization, industrialization and the demise of traditional or tribal societies. In an already modern, industrialized, detribalized and "stable" nation like America, it was argued, student protests are naturally absent.

Another explanation has tied student protests abroad to bad living conditions in some universities and to the unemployability of their graduates. Student revolts, it was argued, spring partly from the misery of student life in countries like India and Indonesia. Students who must live in penury and squalor naturally turn against their universities and societies. And if, as in many developing nations, hundreds of thousands of university graduates can find no work commensurate with their skills, the chances for student militancy are further increased.

These arguments helped explain the "silent generation" of the nineteen-fifties and the absence of protest, during that period in American universities, where students are often "indulged" with good living conditions, close student-faculty contact and considerable freedom of speech. And they helped explain why "super-employable" American college graduates, especially the much-sought-after ones from colleges like Columbia and Harvard, seemed so contented with their lot.

But such arguments do not help us understand today's noisy, angry and militant students in the advanced countries. Nor do they explain why students who enjoy the greatest advantages—those at the leading universities—are often found in the revolts. As a result, several new interpretations of student protest are currently being put forward, interpretations that ultimately form part of what Richard Poirier has termed "the war against the young."

Many reactions to student unrest, of course, spring primarily from fear, anger, confusion or envy, rather than from theoretical analysis. Governor Wallace's attacks on student "anarchists" and other "pin-headed intellectuals," for example, were hardly coherent explanations of protest. Many of the bills aimed at punishing student protesters being proposed in Congress and state legislatures reflect similar feelings of anger and outrage. Similarly, the presumption that student unrest *must* be part of an international conspiracy is based on emotion rather than fact. Even George F. Kennan's recent discussion of the American student left is essentially a moral condemnation of "revolting students," rather than an effort to explain their behavior.*

If we turn to more thoughtful analyses of the current student mood we find two general theories gaining widespread accept-

* For text, see pp. 12–23, Volume I.

ance. The first, articulately expressed by Lewis S. Feuer in his recent book on student movements, *The Conflict of Generations,* might be termed the "Oedipal Rebellion" interpretation. The second, cogently stated by Zbigniew Brzezinski and Daniel Bell, can be called the theory of "Historical Irrelevance."

The explanation of Oedipal Rebellion sees the underlying force in all student revolts as blind, unconscious Oedipal hatred of fathers and the older generation. Feuer, for example, finds in all student movements an inevitable tendency toward violence and a combination of "regicide, parricide and suicide." A decline in respect for the authority of the older generation is needed to trigger a student movement, but the force behind it comes from "obscure" and "unconscious" forces in the child's early life, including both intense death wishes against his father and the enormous guilt and self-hatred that such wishes inspire in the child.

The idealism of student movements is thus in many respects, only a "front" for the latent unconscious destructiveness and self-destructiveness of underlying motivations. Even the expressed desire of these movements to help the poor and exploited is explained psychoanalytically by Feuer: Empathy for the disadvantaged is traced to "traumatic" encounters with parental bigotry in the students' childhoods, when their parents forbade them to play with children of other races or lower social classes. The identification of today's new left with blacks is thus interpreted as an unconscious effort to "abreact and undo this original trauma."

There are two basic problems with the Oedipal Rebellion theory, however. First, although it uses psychoanalytic terms, it is bad psychoanalysis. The real psychoanalytic account insists that the Oedipus complex is universal in all normally developing children. To point to this complex in explaining student rebellion is, therefore, like pointing to the fact that all children learn to walk. Since both characteristics are said to be universal, neither helps us understand why, at some historical moments, students are restive and rebellious, while at others they are not. Second, the theory does not help us explain why some students (especially those from middle-class, affluent and idealistic families) are most inclined to rebel, while others (especially those from working-class and deprived familes) are less so.

In order really to explain anything, the Oedipal Rebellion hypothesis would have to be modified to point to an unusually *severe* Oedipus complex, involving especially *intense* and unresolved unconscious feelings of father-hatred in student rebels. But much is now known about the lives and backgrounds of these rebels—at least those in the United States—and this evidence does not support even the modified theory. On the contrary, it indicates that most student protesters are relatively *close* to their parents, that the values they profess are usually the ones they learned at the family dinner table, and that their parents tend to be highly educated, liberal or left-wing and politically active.

Furthermore, psychological studies of student radicals indicate that they are no more neurotic, suicidal, enraged or disturbed than are non-radicals. Indeed, most studies find them to be rather more integrated, self-accepting and "advanced," in a psychological sense, than their politically inactive contemporaries. In general, research on American student rebels supports a "Generational Solidarity" (or chip-off-the-old-block) theory, rather than one of Oedipal Rebellion.

The second theory of student revolts now being advanced asserts that they are a reaction against "historical irrelevance." Rebellion springs from the unconscious awareness of some students that society has left them and their values behind. According to this view, the ultimate causes of student dissent are sociological rather than psychological. They lie in fundamental changes in the nature of the advanced societies—especially, in the change from industrial to post-industrial society. The student revolution is seen not as a true revolution, but as a counterrevolution—what Daniel Bell has called "the guttering last gasp of a romanticism soured by rancor and impotence."

This theory assumes that we are moving rapidly into a new age in which technology will dominate, an age whose real rulers will be men like computer experts, systems analysts and techno-bureaucrats. Students who are attached to outmoded and obsolescent values like humanism and romanticism unconsciously feel they have no place in this post-industrial world. When they rebel they are like the Luddites of the past—workers who smashed machines to protest the inevitable industrial revolution. Today's student revolt reflects what Brzezinski terms "an unconscious realization that they [the rebels] are themselves becoming historically obsolete"; it is nothing but the "death rattle of the historical irrelevants."

This theory is also inadequate. It assumes that the shape of the future is already technologically determined, and that protesting students unconsciously "know" that it will offer them no real reward, honor or power. But the idea that the future can be accurately predicted is open to fundamental objection. Every past attempt at prophecy has turned out to be grievously incorrect. Extrapolations from the past, while sometimes useful in the short run, are usually fundamentally wrong in the long run, especially when they attempt to predict the quality of human life, the nature of political and social organization, international relations or the shape of future culture.

The future is, of course, made by men. Technology is not an inevitable master of man and history, but merely provides the possibility of applying scientific knowledge to specific problems. Men may identify with it or refuse to use it or be used by it for good or evil, apply it humanely or destructively. Thus, there is no real evidence that student protest will emerge as the "death rattle of the historical irrelevants." It could equally well be the "first spark of a new historical era." No one today can be sure of the outcome, and people who feel certain that the future will bring the obsolescence and death of those whom they dislike are often merely expressing their fond hope.

The fact that today's students invoke "old" humanistic and romantic ideas in no way proves that student protests are a "last gasp" of a dying order. Quite the contrary: *All* revolutions draw upon older values and visions. Many of the ideals of the French Revolution, for example, originated in Periclean Athens. Revolutions do not occur because new ideas suddenly develop, but because a new generation begins to take *old* ideas seriously—not merely as interesting theoretical views, but as the basis for political action and social change. Until recently, the humanistic vision of human fulfillment and the romantic vision of an expressive, imaginative and passionate life were taken seriously only by small aristocratic or Bohemian groups. The fact that they are today taken as real goals by millions of students in many nations does not mean that these students are "counterrevolutionaries," but merely that their ideas follow the pattern of every major revolution.

Indeed, today's student rebels are rarely opposed to technology *per se.* On the contrary, they take the high technology of their societies completely for granted, and concern themselves with it very little. What they *are* opposed to is, in essence, the worship of Technology, the tendency to treat people as "inputs" or "outputs" of a technological system, the subordination of human needs to technological programs. The essential conflict between the minority of students who make up the student revolt and the existing order is a conflict over the future direction of technological society, not a counter-revolutionary protest against technology.

In short, both the Oedipal Rebellion and the Historical Irrelevance theories are what students would call "put-downs." If we accept either, we are encouraged not to listen to protests, or to explain them away or reject them as either the "acting out" of destructive Oedipal feelings or the blind reaction of an obsolescent group to the awareness of its obsolescence. But if, as I have argued, neither of these theories is adequate to explain the current "wave" of student protest here and abroad, how can we understand it?

One factor often cited to explain student unrest is the large number of people in the world under 30—today the critical dividing line between generations. But this explanation alone, like the theories just discussed, is not adequate, for in all historical eras the vast portion of the population has always been under 30. Indeed, in primitive societies most people die before they reach that age. If chronological youth alone was enough to insure rebellion, the advanced societies—where a greater proportion of the population reaches old age than ever before in history—should be the *least* revolutionary, and primitive societies the *most*. This is not the case.

More relevant factors are the relationship of those under 30 to the established institutions of society (that is, whether they are engaged in them or not); and the opportunities that society provides for their continuing intellectual, ethical and emotional development. In both cases the present situation in the advanced nations is without precedent.

Philippe Aries, in his remarkable book, *Centuries of Childhood,* points out that, until the end of the Middle Ages, no separate stage of childhood was recognized in Western societies. Infancy ended at approximately 6 or 7, whereupon most children were integrated into adult life, treated as small men and women and expected to work as junior partners of the adult world. Only later was childhood recognized as a separate stage of life, and our own century is the first to "guarantee" it by requiring universal primary education.

The recognition of adolescence as a stage of life is of even more recent origin, the product of the 19th and 20th centuries. Only as industrial societies became prosperous enough to defer adult work until after puberty could they create institutions—like widespread secondary-school education—that would extend adolescence to virtually all young people. Recognition of adolescence also arose from the vocational and psychological requirements of these societies, which needed much higher levels of training and psychological development than could be guaranteed through primary education alone. There is, in general, an intimate relationship between the way a society defines the stages of life and its economic, political and social characteristics.

Today, in more developed nations, we are beginning to witness the recognition of still another stage of life. Like childhood and adolescence, it was initially granted only to a small minority, but is now being rapidly extended to an ever-larger group. I will call this the stage of "youth," and by that I mean both a further phase of disengagement from society and the period of psychological development that intervenes between adolescence and adulthood. This stage, which continues into the 20's and sometimes into the 30's, provides opportunities for intellectual, emotional and moral development that were never afforded to any other large group in history. In the student revolts we are seeing one result of this advance.

I call the extension of youth an advance advisedly. Attendance at a college or university is a major part of this extension, and there is growing evidence that this is, other things being equal, a good thing for the student. Put in an oversimplified phrase, it tends to free him—to free him from swallowing unexamined the assumptions of the past, to free him from the superstitions of his childhood, to free him to express his feelings more openly and to free him from irrational bondage to authority.

I do not mean to suggest, of course, that all college graduates are free and liberated spirits, unencumbered by irrationality, superstition, authoritarianism or blind adherence to tradition. But these findings do indicate that our colleges, far from cranking out only machinelike robots who will provide skilled manpower for the economy, are also producing an increasing number of highly critical citizens—young men and women who have the opportunity, the leisure, the affluence and the educational resources to continue their development beyond the point where most people in the past were required to stop it.

So, one part of what we are seeing on campuses throughout the world is not a reflection of how bad higher education is, but rather of its extraordinary accomplishments. Even the moral righteousness of the student rebels, a quality both endearing and infuriating to their elders, must be judged at least partially a consequence of the privilege of an extended youth; for a prolonged development, we know, encourages the individual to elaborate a more personal, less purely conventional sense of ethics.

What the advanced nations have done is to create their own critics on a mass basis—that is, to create an ever-larger group of young people who take the highest values of their societies as their own, who internalize these values and identify them with their own best selves, and who are willing to struggle to implement them. At the same time, the extension of youth has lessened the personal risks of dissent: These young people have been freed from the requirements of work, gainful employment and even marriage, which permits them to criticize their society from a protected position of disengagement.

But the mere prolongation of development need not automatically lead to unrest. To be sure, we have granted to millions the opportunity to examine their societies, to compare them with their values and to come to a reasoned judgment of the existing order. But why should their judgment today be so unenthusiastic?

What protesting students throughout the world share is a mood more than an ideology or a program, a mood that says the existing system—the power structure—is hypocritical, unworthy of respect, outmoded and in urgent need of reform. In addition, students everywhere speak of repression, manipulation and authoritarianism. (This is paradoxical, considering the apparently great freedoms given them in many nations. In America, for example, those who complain most loudly about being suffocated by the subtle tyranny of the Establishment usually attend the institutions where student freedom is greatest.) Around this general mood, specific complaints arrange themselves as symptoms of what students often call the "exhaustion of the existing society."

To understand this phenomenon we must recognize that, since the Second World War, some societies have indeed begun to move past the industrial era into a new world that is post-industrial, technological, post-modern, post-historic or, in Brzezinski's term, "technectronic." In Western Europe, the United States, Canada and Japan, the first contours of this new society are already apparent. And, in many other less-developed countries, middle-class professionals (whose children become activists) often live in post-industrial enclaves within pre-industrial societies. Whatever we call the post-industrial world, it has demonstrated that, for the first time, man can produce more than enough to meet his material needs.

This accomplishment is admittedly blemished by enormous problems of economic distribution in the advanced nations, and it is in terrifying contrast to the overwhelming poverty of the Third World. Nevertheless, it is clear that what might be called "the problem of production" *can,* in principle, be solved. If all members of American society, for example, do not have enough material goods, it is because the system of distribution is flawed. The same is true, or will soon be true, in many other nations that are approaching advanced states of industrialization. Characteristically, these nations, along with the most technological, are those where student unrest has recently been most prominent.

The transition from industrial to post-industrial society brings with it a major shift in social emphases and values. Industrializing and industrial societies tend to be oriented toward solving the problem of production. An industrial ethic—sometimes Protestant, sometimes Socialist, sometimes Communist—tends to emphasize psychological qualities like self-discipline, delay of gratification, achievement-orientation and a strong emphasis on economic success and productivity. The social, political and economic institutions of these societies tend to be organized in a way that is consistent with the goal of increasing production. And industrial societies tend to apply relatively uniform standards, to reward achievement rather than status acquired by birth, to emphasize emotional neutrality ("coolness") and rationality in work and public life.

The emergence of post-industrial societies, however, means that growing numbers of the young are brought up in family environments where abundance, relative economic security, political freedom and affluence are simply facts of life, not goals to be striven for. To such people the psychological imperatives, social institutions and cultural values of the industrial ethic seem largely outdated and irrelevant to their own lives.

Once it has been demonstrated that a society *can* produce enough for all its members, at least some of the young turn to other goals: for example, trying to make sure that society *does* produce enough and distributes it fairly, or searching for ways to live meaningfully with the goods and the leisure they *already* have. The problem is that our society has, in some realm, exceeded its earlier targets. Lacking new ones, it has become exhausted by its success.

When the values of industrial society become devitalized, the élite sectors of youth—the most affluent, intelligent, privileged and so on—come to feel that they live in institutions whose demands lack moral authority or, in the current jargon, "credibility." Today, the moral imperative and urgency behind production, acquisition, materialism and abundance has been lost.

Furthermore, with the lack of moral legitimacy felt in "the System," the least request for loyalty, restraint or conformity by its representatives—for example, by college presidents and deans—can easily be seen as a moral outrage, an authoritarian repression, a manipulative effort to "co-opt" students into joining the Establishment and an exercise in "illegitimate authority" that must be resisted. From this conception springs at least part of the students' vague sense of oppression. And, indeed, perhaps their peculiar feeling of suffocation arises ultimately from living in societies without vital ethical claims.

Given such a situation, it does not take a clear-cut issue to trigger a major protest. I doubt, for example, that college and university administrators are in fact *more* hypocritical and dishonest than they were in the past. American intervention in Vietnam, while many of us find it unjust and cruel, is not inherently *more* outrageous than other similar imperialistic interventions by America and other nations within the last century. And the position of blacks in this country, although disastrously and unjustifiably disadvantaged, is, in some economic and legal respects, better than ever before. Similarly, the conditions for students in America have never been as good, especially, as I have noted, at those élite colleges where student protests are most common.

But this is *precisely* the point: It is *because* so many of the *other* problems of American society seem to have been resolved, or to be resolvable in principle, that students now react with new indignation to old problems, turn to new goals and propose radical reforms.

So far I have emphasized the moral exhaustion of the old order and the fact that, for the children of post-industrial affluence, the once-revolutionary claims of the industrial society have lost much of their validity. I now want to argue that we are witnessing on the campuses of the world a fusion of *two revolutions* with distinct historical origins. One is a continuation of the old and familiar revolution of the industrial society, the liberal-democratic-egalitarian revolution that started in America and France at the turn of the 18th century and spread to virtually every nation in the world. (Not completed in any of them, its contemporary American form is, above all, to be found in the increased militancy of blacks.) The other is the new revolution, the post-industrial one, which seeks to define new goals relevant to the 20th and 21st centuries.

In its social and political aspects, the first revolution has been one of universalization, to use the sociologist's awkward term. It has involved the progressive extension to more and more people of economic, political and social rights, privileges and opportunities originally available only to the aristocracy, then to the middle class, and now in America to the relatively affluent white working class. It is, in many respects, a *quantitative* revolution. That is, it concerns itself less with the quality of life than with the amount of political freedom, the quantity and distribution of goods, or the amount and level of injustice.

As the United States approaches the targets of the first revolution, on which this society was built, to be poor shifts from being an unfortunate fact of life to being an outrage. And, for the many who have never experienced poverty, discrimination or oppression, even to *witness* the existence of these evils in the lives of others suddenly becomes intolerable. In our time the impatience to complete the first revolution has grown apace, and we find less willingness to compromise, wait and forgive among the young, especially among those who now take the values of the old revolution for granted—seeing them not as goals, but as *rights.*

A subtle change has thus occurred. What used to be utopian ideals—like equality, abundance and freedom from discrimination—have now become demands, inalienable rights upon which one can insist without brooking any compromise. It is noteworthy that, in today's student confrontations, no one requests anything. Students present their "demands."

So, on the one hand, we see a growing impatience to complete the first revolution. But, on the other, there is a newer revolution concerned with newer issues, a revolution that is less social, economic or political than psychological, historical and cultural. It is less concerned with the quantities of things than with their qualities, and it judges the virtually complete liberal revolution and finds it still wanting.

"You have to have grown up in Scarsdale to know how bad things really are," said one radical student. This comment would probably sound arrogant, heartless and insensitive to a poor black, much less to a citizen of the Third World. But he meant something important by it. He meant that *even* in the Scarsdales of America, with their affluence, their upper-middle-class security and abundance, their well-fed, well-heeled children and their excellent schools, something is wrong. Economic affluence does not guarantee a feeling of personal fulfillment; political freedom does not always yield an inner sense of liberation and cultural freedom; social justice and equality may leave one with a feeling that something else is missing in life. "No to the consumer society!" shouted the bourgeois students of the Sorbonne during May and June of 1968—a cry that understandably alienated French workers, for whom affluence and the consumer society are still central goals.

What then are the targets of the new revolution? As is often noted, students themselves don't know. They speak vaguely of "a society that has never existed," of "new values," of a "more humane world," of "liberation" in some psychological, cultural and historical sense. Their rhetoric is largely negative; they are stronger in opposition than in proposals for reform; their diagnoses often seem accurate, but their prescriptions are vague; and they are far more articulate in urging the immediate completion of the first revolution than in defining the goals of the second. Thus, we can only indirectly discern trends that point to the still-undefined targets of the new revolution.

What are these trends and targets?

First, there is a revulsion against the notion of quantity, particularly economic quantity and materialism, and a turn toward concepts of quality. One of the most delightful slogans of the French student revolt was, "Long live the passionate revolution of creative intelligence!" In a sense, the achievement of abundance may allow millions of contemporary men and women to examine, as only a few artists and madmen have examined in the past, the quality, joyfulness and zestfulness of experience. The "expansion of consciousness"; the stress on the expressive, the aesthetic and the creative; the emphasis on imagination, direct perception and fantasy—all are part of the effort to enhance the quality of this experience.

Another goal of the new revolution involves a revolt against uniformity, equalization, standardization and homogenization—not against technology itself, but against the "technologization of man." At times, this revolt approaches anarchic quaintness, but it has a positive core as well—the demand that individuals be appreciated, not because of their similarities or despite their differences, but because they *are* different, diverse, unique and noninterchangeable. This attitude is evident in many areas: for example, the insistence upon a cultivation of personal idiosyncrasy, mannerism and unique aptitude. Intellectually it is expressed in the rejection of the melting-pot and consensus-politics view of American life in favor of a post-homogeneous America in which cultural diversity and conflict are underlined rather than denied.

The new revolution also involves a continuing struggle against psychological or institutional closure or rigidity in any form, even the rigidity of a definite adult role. Positively, it extols the virtues of openness, motion and continuing human development. What Robert J. Lifton has termed the protean style is clearly in evidence. There is emerging a concept of a lifetime of personal change, of an adulthood of continuing self-transformation, of an adaptability and an openness to the revolutionary modern world that will enable the individual to remain "with it"—psychologically youthful and on top of the present.

Another characteristic is the revolt against centralized power and the complementary demand for participation. What is demanded is not merely the consent of the governed, but the involvement of the governed. "Participatory democracy" summarizes this aspiration, but it extends far beyond the phrase and the rudimentary social forms that have sprung up around it. It extends to the demand for relevance in education—that is, for a chance for the student to participate in his own educational experience in a way that involves all of his faculties, emotional and moral as well as intellectual. The demand for "student power" (or, in Europe, "co-determination") is an aspect of the same theme: At Nanterre, Columbia, Frankfurt and Harvard, students increasingly seek to participate in making the policies of their universities.

This demand for participation is also embodied in the new ethic of "meaningful human relationships," in which individuals confront each other without mask, pretenses and games. They "relate" to each other as unique and irreplaceable human beings, and develop new forms of relationship from which all participants will grow.

In distinguishing between the old and the new revolutions, and in attempting to define the targets of the new, I am, of course making distinctions that students themselves rarely make. In any one situation the two revolutions are joined and fused, if not confused. For example, the Harvard students' demand for "restructuring the university" is essentially the second revolution's demand for participation; but their demand for an end to university "exploitation" of the surrounding community is tied to the more traditional goals of the first revolution. In most radical groups there is a range of opinion that starts with the issues of the first (racism, imperialism, exploitation, war) and runs to the concerns of the second (experiential education, new life styles, meaningful participation, consciousness-expansion, relatedness, encounter and community). The first revolution is personified by Maoist-oriented Progressive Labor party factions within the student left, while the second is represented by hippies, the "acid left," and the Yippies. In any individual, and in all student movements, these revolutions coexist in uneasy and often abrasive tension.

Furthermore, one of the central problems for student movements today is the absence of any theory of society that does justice to the new world in which we of the most industrialized nations live. In their search for rational critiques of present societies, students turn to theories like Marxism that are intricately bound up with the old revolution.

Such theories make the ending of economic exploitation, the achievement of social justice, the abolition of racial discrimination and the development of political participation and freedom central, but they rarely deal adequately with the issues of the second revolution. Students inevitably try to adapt the rhetoric of the first to the problems of the second, using concepts that are often blatantly inadequate to today's world.

Even the concept of "revolution" itself is so heavily laden with images of political, economic and social upheaval that it hardly seems to characterize the equally radical but more social-psychological and cultural transformations involved in the new revolution. One student, recognizing this, called the changes occurring in his California student group, "too radical to be called a revolution." Students are thus often misled by their borrowed vocabulary, but most adults are even more confused, and many are quickly led to the mistaken conclusion that today's student revolt is nothing more than a repetition of Communism's in the past.

Failure to distinguish between the old and new revolutions also makes it impossible to consider the critical question of how compatible they are with each other. Does it make sense—or is it morally right—for today's affluent American students to seek imagination, self-actualization, individuality, openness and relevance when most of the world and many in America live in deprivation, oppression and misery?

The fact that the first revolution is "completed" in Scarsdale does not mean that it is (or soon will be) in Harlem or Appalachia—to say nothing of Bogotá or Calcutta. For many children of the second revolution, the meaning of life may be found in completing the first—that is, in extending to others the "rights" they have always taken for granted.

For others the second revolution will not wait; the question, "What lies beyond affluence?" demands an answer now. Thus, although we may deem it self-indulgent to pursue the goals of the new revolution in a world where so much misery exists, the fact is that in the advanced nations it is upon us, and we must at least learn to recognize it.

Finally, beneath my analysis lies an assumption I had best make explicit. Many student critics argue that their societies have failed miserably. My argument, a more historical one perhaps, suggests that our problem is not only that industrial societies have failed to keep all their promises, but that they have succeeded in some ways beyond all expectations. Abundance was once a distant dream, to be postponed to a hereafter of milk and honey; today, most Americans are affluent. Universal mass education was once a Utopian goal; today in America almost the entire population completes high school, and almost half enters college and universities.

The notion that individuals might be free, en masse, to continue their psychological, intellectual, moral and cognitive development through their teens and into their 20's would have been laughed out of court in any century other than our own; today, that opportunity is open to millions of young Americans. Student unrest is a reflection not only of the failures, but of the extraordinary successes of the liberal-industrial revolution. It therefore occurs in the nations and in the colleges where, according to traditional standards, conditions are best.

But for many of today's students who have never experienced anything but affluence, political freedom and social equality, the old vision is dead or dying. It may inspire bitterness and outrage when it is not achieved, but it no longer animates or guides. In place of it, students (and many who are not students) are searching for a new vision, a new set of values, a new set of targets appropriate to the post-industrial era—a myth, an ideology or a set of goals that will concern itself with the quality of life and answer the question, "Beyond freedom and affluence, what?"

What characterizes student unrest in the developed nations is this peculiar mixture of the old and the new, the urgent need to fulfill the promises of the past and, at the same time, to define the possibilities of the future.

PART VI

CONCLUDING ESSAYS

Radical Intellectuals in a Liberal Society

by IMMANUEL WALLERSTEIN

The student movement of the 1960s has revitalized the left in American life as a serious political force. Its success, however, has posed a serious dilemma for intellectuals on the left, one they did not have to face when the strength of the left was at a low point in the 1950s. It is the traditional moral dilemma of the radical intellectual in a liberal society: how does he reconcile participation in a movement for political change with an ongoing involvement in the occupational networks of the existing society, especially in a society that seeks to mute his radicalism with a carrot rather than a stick, or at least with the carrot first.

This revolt by young people has also been, in many ways, intellectually liberating for the entire American left. It liberated the left from the cramping fears instilled in them by the anti-Stalinism of the cold war period. Analyses bearing the terminology and methodology of leftist thought have become intellectually respectable once again, at least in the academy. The pieties of the cold war era have become points of view rather than unquestioned truths. Furthermore, not only has leftist ideology become respectable once again but leftist political action is now viewed as meaningful. During the cold war era, even those who remained leftist in thought tended to retreat into inactivity and a sense of hopelessness in the face of the seeming futility of leftist political action. Then young people came along who were not burdened with guilt for the errors of previous decades, who were not weary from battles fought and lost, who were naive still in their faith and optimism, and they breathed new life into the American left and even inspired those "over thirty."

Their revolt liberated the left from the cramping effects of the Stalinist style which had pervaded the remaining corners of the American left. The students denounced the bureaucratic ways of Soviet society as base imitations of American society. They reasserted earlier visions of democracy and socialism. By so doing, they made the American socialist movement, perhaps for the first time, an *indigenous* American political movement, a quality essential to longer-term political survival and eventual success, and one whose absence had been sorely felt in previous decades.

I say this despite the romanticizing of Mao and Ho and Che by student radicals, an activity which has more the flavor of *épater les bourgeois* than the sense of serious subordination to these foreign heroes. I say this, too, despite the putative steps toward re-Stalinization made by some segments of the New Left, which are noticeable in some of the recent writings included in this book. The indigenization of socialism will survive, while the restalinized groups will crumble. Destalinization has also been liberating for those over thirty because it has helped to restore their willingness to participate in a political movement and to reinfuse them with some political courage.

This revitalization of the American left by a spontaneous movement—largely of students raised in a "youth culture"—has created two dangers for the left. The first is that the left may tend to see the virtues but not the limitations of spontaneity. The second is that the left may tend to appreciate the need to differentiate itself from and struggle against the liberal center, and not the need to form alliances, when appropriate, with the liberal center in a struggle against the true right.

Spontaneity has had three guises in recent years in the United States: intellectual debunking, militant collective action, and personal liberation. The intellectual debunking may be found throughout this book. It essentially has two themes. One is the assertion that various concepts of liberalism—for example, "value-neutrality" or "access to education on the basis of performance"—are not self-evident truths. They are expressions of the ideology of particular groups in a particular system. They cannot be accepted, uncritically and at face value, by those of the left, but must be assessed in terms of their contemporary social function. The second theme of intellectual debunking is the demonstration that, even in terms of their own values, liberal institutions often *fail to play the game as they insist others should play it:* the universities' links to government intelligence, and their cooperation with the selective service system in ways that threaten the autonomy of the university. This has struck responsive chords in those of the liberal center as well as in those of the left. This is natural, as the former are merely honest liberals trying to preserve their system of values against the inroads of the right. It is probably true, nonetheless, that were it not for the intellectual challenges of the left, it would have been far less likely that liberals of the center would have raised these issues, and almost certain that had they done so anyway, they would not have succeeded. The reemergence of the American left made it possible to end, for example, classified defense research at American universities.

The second form of spontaneity has been militant collective action, the most important form of which has been confrontation tactics in the universities. This has been the least popular form of spontaneity with the liberal center. Yet there is no question that it has been an important factor in the relative successes of the left. The sit-ins, the obstructions, the disruptions have made the universities face the issues in ways that intellectual debunking alone could never achieve. And once the issues were forced on the universities in this way, they made significant concessions to the demands of the left. At the very least, the universities have been led to approximate more closely their own liberal ideology of autonomy from the state. They have also been led to reconsider their relationship with surrounding communities, especially in urban areas, to take seriously the charge of institutional racism, and to begin implementing some democratization of their internal governance structures. All these are serious gains that should not be underestimated; furthermore, it must be admitted that they were won largely as a result of confrontation tactics.

The third form of spontaneity has been personal liberation—

from personal appearance to music to sex to drugs. Albeit the least political of the forms of spontaneity, personal liberation in many ways created the atmosphere in which the other two could flourish. The movement for personal liberation has broken the cycle of socialization by which society prevented the growth of left ideology, and action among the young. Thus, those critics on the right, such as Stanton Evans, who claim that the permissiveness of the liberal center paved the way for the student movement, have an element of truth in their analyses.

If the three forms of spontaneity in the student movement have had positive effects, they also harbor the seeds of self-destruction. The student revolt can destroy the very American left they have rebuilt, and clearly some segments of it are moving in that direction.

Spontaneity is crucial in revolutionary action. But it also has pitfalls, as Frantz Fanon argued so cogently in *The Wretched of the Earth*. Let us look at the pitfalls of each form of spontaneity in the current situation. Each involved pushing a good thing too far for fear of backsliding.

Debunking is essential to clear away the cobwebs of deception. But if it is persisted in when there are few cobwebs left to clear, then it must invent them in order to have some to clear away. This is witch-hunting, and the most recent debates within the left show dangerous signs of this malady. Fear of success, and fear of cooptation, lead to a frenetic desire for purity, to a paranoiac fear of infiltration which becomes self-fulfilling, and to a casuistical concern with past peccadilloes and future dangers.

Militant collective action is necessary to counter the systematic violence of entrenched authority, and to shake up the timorous inertia of parlor pinks. But militant collective action is serious political activity and can only be undertaken when one has serious strength. While an element of political strength is self-reinforcing self-confidence, it is only one element. If one neglects to make sober calculations of one's real strength and moves too far in advance of it, repression and disaster are the result. Action then becomes adventurism, motivated by fear of collective and personal cowardice. This grievous tendency toward miscalculation is appearing again, as it so often has in the history of left movements, in the modern industrial world. The trouble with adventurist sects is that they not only destroy themselves—this would not be a trouble but a blessing—but that they bring others down in their wake.

Personal liberation is necessary to free the inner psyche from the social controls instilled in it by the dominant social system. It leads us back to using our primordial energies in the service of our values without fear of the frowns of those who are paid to frown. Here the danger is easy to see. Out of a fear of *embourgeoisement,* we can pursue the wisps of perpetual heterodoxy until we have in fact copped out of the central struggle.

Witch-hunting, adventurism, and the cop-out are the dangers. They are often seen clearly by one or another faction on the left. What is less often seen clearly is that they derive from one common cause: overreaction to disillusionment with the liberal center. The American left—having subordinated itself to an alliance with the liberal center since the New Deal era, and having been ill rewarded by the center when the center moved rightward during the cold war era—has been sorely tempted to turn against the liberal center and to see in it nothing but one face of the Janus of modern capitalism. This was the famous and ill-fated strategy of the German Communists in 1932 when they denounced the "social fascism" of the liberals and social democrats.

There is a third way, however, for the American left to relate to the liberal center. It does not need to subordinate itself as a junior partner to the liberal center, nor to fail to make meaningful distinctions among liberalism, conservatism, and fascism, different ideologies each, reflecting the needs and concerns of different social groups at particular moments of time.

The first need for the American left is intellectual clarification of the ways in which American and world society can and will transform itself into a socialist society. The left, no doubt, has a sociological perspective that is different from that of the liberal center. It also has the outlines of a theory of historical change that is distinct from that of liberalism, which explains why, even when their ultimate objectives seem to converge, radicals seldom agree with liberals on the efficacy of their methods for promoting change. The left is far from having a clearly developed social theory that can account for the continued resiliency of the existing world social system, and clearly indicate the modalities of transforming it.

There is much hard intellectual work to be done by the left. This intellectual work will never be done well if it is isolated from praxis, from involvement in a political movement and political action. But neither will it be done well if it is isolated from the pressures of competing intellectual ideas in the mainstream of intellectual debate, which in America is still located in the university. That the university should flourish is as crucial to the future prospects of the American left as the growth of a strong political movement.

It cannot, of course, be just any university, any more than it can be just any political movement. It cannot be a liberal university that refuses to admit its biases and continues to pretend that what is only its ideology should be considered to be universal truth. It can, however, indeed must be, a university that is open to many streams of thought, self-avowed, competing. It can, and must be, both politicized and open. I join Professor C. B. MacPherson, in his presidential address to the Canadian Association of University Teachers, in believing that our slogan must be "From the liberal to the critical university."

In such a university men of the left will have a place along with others. If such left intellectuals remain *engagé,* not only intellectually but within living political movements, they can draw sustenance from and give vitality to these political movements.

They can then operate, within a liberal society, in a way effectively to affect the liberal center, to push it leftward, to force it to be conscious of the real social choices, to appeal to its conscience and to its self-interest. The American left, under such circumstances, could ally itself with the liberal center when it was profitable, and combat it when it was necessary.

I have not spoken of the problem of the "third world" movements. But, *mutatis mutandis,* the problem the left faces concerning them is similar in many ways to those concerning the liberal center. These movements are left in orientation because they are emanations of oppressed ethnic groups. But they contain many conservative elements because of their need for group unity. The left must learn to support these movements and unite with them when appropriate, but also dissociate itself from them when their conservative elements gain control. This is a delicate and difficult task, and one which requires both knowledge and empathy to do well. But it can in fact be done.

Above all, the radical intellectual must operate with the passionate calm of one for whom the revolution is not a battle of a day, a year, or a decade, but one of centuries. And yet he must do this without fatalistic optimism. The revolution is only inevitable because people make it so. The student revolt has in many ways restored the possibilities for the radical intellectual to rise to his task and find his appropriate place in the movement. The dilemma of activism versus thought, of full-time revolutionary activity versus co-option is false. The radical must operate in both arenas at once. He must break down some, but not all, of the barriers between them. He must participate in the movement, yet also reflect upon it. He must defend the university, but also criticize it. He must encourage spontaneity and protect it, yet also save himself and others from being drowned in it.

Moving On

by PAUL STARR

The following is the text of a short speech I gave June 2, 1970 at Columbia University in St. Paul's Chapel, where about three hundred graduating students and five to six hundred parents and other students gathered after walking out of the regular commencement exercises on Low Plaza in protest against "graduation as usual." Other speakers at the counter-commencement, which did not disrupt the official ceremony, were Professor Howard Zinn of Boston University and two Black seniors from Barnard College, who read their own poetry. The reasons for the walk-out are explained below.

I had originally intended to use this space for an essay critical of some of the turns that part of the left has taken in the past two years. However, with the Cambodian invasion and other developments I decided it would be a mistake to spend energy in that direction. And in any case, most of the criticisms I wanted to raise—overconcern with the university, the reversion to a Marxist-Leninist framework, the left's alienation from the American people and the American past, "youth chauvinism," posturing about "armed struggle"—are implicit here.

We walked out of Low Plaza for a lot of different reasons.

There was the basic affront of conducting a regular commencement after this spring's strikes: after Nixon's strike into Cambodia, after Agnew's and Mitchell's strikes upon dissent and resistance at home, after our nationwide strike against government policy. To hold an unaltered commencement today was to disregard the almost universally supported protest on this campus a few short weeks ago.

There was also a more recent affront, just a few days ago. We made a simple request to President Cordier that Howard Zinn and a graduating student—a woman by the way—be added to the commencement program. We thought Cordier might want to bargain. After all, not every university excludes graduating students from its commencement program. But Cordier turned our request down flatly. After all the talk of restructuring and student participation and responsiveness, there was to be no student role in commencement. . . .

These things, however, were only the sparks that set off this protest. We walked out today as a climax of four years of learning about the university—a process that took us from the stage where we thought of the university as a purely benevolent institution to the point where we have begun to see how through the years it too has contributed to militarism and racism in our society. Let it be understood that we walked out on a university that performs war research and invites military recruiters each year, on a university that callously dispossessed hundreds of poor Black and Puerto Rican residents from Morningside Heights, on a university that has fought every attempt by its workers at unionization. You won't hear much about that aspect of the university out on Low Plaza. And if in the last few years, Columbia has made some concessions, we know and everyone else knows it has only been because of the pressure that students and faculty and campus workers and Morningside residents have brought to bear on this institution. Those concessions were not the fruits of benevolence, but of hard struggles that had to be fought again and again and still need to be fought.

We had a strike here this spring—an overwhelming strike—but what happened at Columbia was not an important development. After Nixon's announcement of the Cambodian invasion, everyone expected the Berkeleys and the Columbias and the Wisconsins to be shaken by protest. No, the real story was what happened at places like the University of New Mexico, the University of Kentucky, the University of Maryland, Ohio State, Kent State, the University of Virginia—those traditional hotbeds of campus radicalism. Take Virginia, for example—that's where rebellion originally had its start in America. Seven thousand students there, according to the *Washington Post,* showed up for a rally with a defendant from the Chicago "Conspiracy Trial." And a professor, standing next to an august statue of Thomas Jefferson, quoted Jefferson—oh, a hot-headed radical he was—as saying that twenty years was a decent interval between revolutions. Now there's a "southern strategy"!

Protest has moved beyond the Berkeley-Columbia circuit, and thank God for that. Because if the movement for change in America is to grow, Columbia must necessarily become more irrelevant and peripheral. Our movement will be strong when it has forgotten Columbia—in fact, when it has forgotten the campus altogether. Our movement will be strong when it is no longer a student movement or a movement of young people, but a movement of all people, young and old.

Unwittingly, by graduating us, the university is pushing us in the right direction. Now, many of us graduating today are completely at a loss about what we want to do. We're worried about taking jobs and ultimately being coopted. We're not sure what place we can take in a society we see as profoundly unjust. Many of us face the draft—some have a choice of exile, prison, or complicity in the war. At least one senior in the College I know will be leaving for Canada just next week.

We have a difficult situation before us. But the choice I think we have to make is to become involved in this society full-time—not to move into comfortable niches and forget our convictions, but to go back to our home towns, to take jobs and seek out roles in institutions of all kinds in our communities. We cannot think of organizing the grass-roots in America unless we sink our roots into it. Radicals have been too much on the outside of this country. In order to change it, we have to become part of it—not part of injustices, but part of their correction, not to enjoy privileges, but to eliminate privileges and replace them with rights.

We have been told that our radicalism is a youthful escapade. For some of us, that may turn out to be true, but not for all. I think the idea that our passion will subside with age will prove to be a delusion on the part of those who have underestimated the seriousness of the American crisis and our own seriousness. It is not that I place any special confidence in my generation; I just think we won't have much of an alternative. We are the Vietnam war generation, but Vietnam, I fear, is but the first step in our education.

It promises to be a long struggle ahead. We may never again know the quiet America in which we were born. I have no idea how it will all turn out, and I think it would be foolish for us to try to establish in advance that the means necessary for change will be either reformist or revolutionary. We will seek substantive changes—what roads we have to follow in pursuit of those changes we cannot now determine. If the government does not respond to legitimate demands peacefully raised, it will have to contend with demands violently made whether we want it or not. It was not Che or Malcolm X but John F. Kennedy who said, "Those who make peaceful revolution impossible make violent revolution inevitable." The situation will generate its own logic. Whether violence comes is not our decision; it is the decision of those who hold power and have a virtual monopoly on violence in the United States. We now offer them no serious competition. It is not within our power, nor should it now be our goal, to destroy the system; the system can only destroy itself—through the arrogance of power, through failure to deal with national problems.

We have no quarrel with those who ask for order in society and oppose disorder. But this society is now in disorder, through no initiative of ours, and stability will only be reestablished through radical change. They ask for security; so do we. But the United States will know no security if it seeks to suppress revolutions throughout the Third World and continues its mad expenditures on nuclear arms. What security do the mass of Americans have who know that with a serious illness, they will not be able to pay for hospital care, and that even without serious illness, old age spells poverty in an inflationary economy? They ask for respect for the law, but the leaders who shout the loudest about the law treat the Constitution with absolute contempt in the highest matters of war and peace. We cannot allow their pretense to go unchallenged. What passes for law, order, and security in this country is lawlessness in the affairs between nations, disorder at home, and insecurity for the vast numbers of Americans who must live with war, the continuing threat of nuclear extinction, unending inflation and increasing unemployment.

I have referred to things said by John Kennedy and Thomas Jefferson—intentionally. Let the people on Low Plaza who think they are upholding tradition with their commencement know that today we feel no distance from tradition. They are conforming to the formalities of tradition, having long forgotten their spirit. In protesting against the war, against racism, against repression, we are concerned not just with upholding, but with extending our traditions. And the traditions we have in mind are those of liberation and justice.

APPENDIX A: THE DEMANDS

We append the best-known sets of demands made by student rebels in 1968 and 1969. It should be noted that in the case of many institutions involved, further demands were made on other occasions. In addition, since confrontations often went on over extended periods of time, the demands were sometimes altered during the course of the conflicts. Also the wording sometimes changed from one mimeographed version to another. We present here what we believe are the most complete versions of each set of demands.

Howard University

FEBRUARY, 1968
"THE SPEAR AND SHIELD"

1. We demand the immediate resignation of the following Howard administrators on the grounds of their incompetence and obvious unwillingness to work toward a black Howard University:

a. President James Nabrit
b. Vice President Stanton Wormley
c. Liberal Arts Dean Frank Snowden

2. We demand the institution of the following curriculum changes by next semester:

a. We demand that Howard should be the center of Afro-American thought. We demand that the economic, government, literature and social science departments begin to place more emphasis on how these disciplines may be used to effect the liberation of black people in this country.

b. We demand the institution of non-prerequisite courses in Negro History.

c. We demand the immediate abolishment of Freshman Assembly. Black students are not culturally deprived.

3. We demand the immediate reinstatement of all Howard instructors who haved been unjustifiably dismissed for their political activism: [There followed a list of eight teachers, some of whom were not rehired when their terms expired the previous year, and others of whom received notice of non-reappointment when their current terms expired.] Measures must be instituted to insure that all instructors be given a fair hearing if considered for dismissal.

4. We demand the institution of a Black awareness Research Institute at Howard University.

5. Students are trained to be leaders only by learning to accept responsibility. We demand therefore that student autonomy—that is, student control in matters that concern only students. Therefore we demand:

a. The student judiciary and codification of rules presently submitted to the Faculty Senate Steering Committee should be immediately instituted.

b. That students must be authorized to control the budgeting and expenditure of the student activity fee.

6. Howard must be made relevant to the black community. The University campus must be made more available to all black people and programs must be instituted to aid the black community in the struggle against oppression.

7. We demand that Howard personnel begin to treat students like black people should treat black people, with respect and courtesy.

We allow you until February 29, exactly three weeks after the Orangeburg Massacre, to respond to our demands.

Columbia University

APRIL 23, 1968
STUDENTS FOR A DEMOCRATIC SOCIETY

1. All disciplinary probation against the six originally charged must be lifted, and no reprisals taken against anyone in this demonstration.
2. All construction of the Columbia gym must stop NOW.
3. The University must use its good offices to see that all charges against persons arrested at the gym site be dropped.
4. All relations with IDA must be severed, including President Kirk and Trustee William Burden's membership.
5. President Kirk's edict on indoor demonstrations must be dropped.
6. All judicial decisions should be made in an open hearing with due process judged by a tripartite committee of students, faculty, and administrators.

Northwestern University

MAY 2,1968
AFRO-AMERICAN STUDENT UNION

We demand positive responses from the Administration to the following demands:

POLICY STATEMENT

1) that the Administration accept and issue a policy statement [deploring "white racism."]

2) that the Administration restructure the University Disciplinary Commission or create a new judiciary to adequately and justly cope with racial problems and incidents.

3) that the Administration effect a new judiciary standard (as outlined) and apply this standard retroactively to the UDC decision of April 15th.

4) that the Administration allow the black community to a) approve all appointments to the Human Relations Committee and b) determine at least 50% of those appointments.

ADMISSION

5) that each forthcoming freshman class consist of 10% to 12% black students, half of whom are from the inner-city school system.

6) that the Administration institute a committee selected by the black community to aid the Admissions Office, especially in recruitment, which will have shared power with the Office of Admissions and Financial Aid in making decisions relevant to us.

7) that the members constituting this committee be in a salaried position.

8) that For Members Only be supplied with a) a list of all black students presently enrolled at Northwestern; b) a list including names, addresses, et cetera, of all accepted and incoming black freshmen; and c) a similar list of each forthcoming freshman class.

FINANCIAL AID

9) that the process of evaluating financial need and administering financial aid be restructured in conjunction with our Admissions and Financial Aid Committee.

10) that our scholarships be increased to cover what is now included in our "required" jobs and that funds be allocated for those who want or need to attend summer sessions.

HOUSING

11) that the University provide us with a black living unit or commit themselves to immediately getting rid of the present fraternity and sorority housing arrangement.

COUNSELING

12) that any hiring of personnel in the position of counseling the black community of NU be approved by the black community.

FACILITIES

13) that a committee of black students selected by us work with the Administration in meeting our needs for a Black Student Union.

OPEN OCCUPANCY

14) that we have access to the committee studying open occupancy and discrimination with review rights on the matters which they are discussing.

Stanford University

OCTOBER 8,1968
STUDENTS FOR A DEMOCRATIC SOCIETY

WE, the members of Stanford SDS and concerned members of the Stanford community, DEMAND that Stanford University, its wholly owned subsidiary, the Stanford Research Institute, and all members of the university community immediately halt all military and economic projects and operations concerned with Southeast Asia.

BECAUSE WE KNOW THAT:

a) SRI does chemical and biological warfare research (tear gas and crop defoliation).

b) SRI has had 55 staff members doing counter-insurgency work in Thailand since 1962.

c) SRI is performing cost analysis of alternative bombing sights over North Vietnam.

d) SRI is doing long-range surveys of investment opportunities in Southeast Asia for US corporations.

e) Many Stanford and SRI trustees are major executives of 1) war-based corporations such as McDonnell Douglas, Hewlett-Packard, and General Dynamics, and 2) corporations with heavy investments in Southeast Asia such as Tenneco, Utah Construction, and Kaiser.

f) Many Stanford faculty members consult for or serve as directors of nearby war-based companies, and serve on Defense Department subsidized advisory boards and committees.

FURTHERMORE, WE DEMAND THAT:

a) All contracts, both classified and unclassified, be made public, complete with information on the value of the contracts and the individuals performing the work.

b) Stanford and SRI trustees make public all their corporate and governmental connections.

c) Stanford faculty make public all their governmental and corporate contracts and connections.

BY MONDAY OCTOBER 14

San Francisco State College

NOVEMBER 6, 1968
BLACK STUDENTS UNION

1. That all Black Studies courses being taught through various other departments be immediately part of the Black Studies Department and that all the instructors in this department receive full-time pay.

2. That Dr. Hare, Chairman of the Black Studies Department, receive a full professorship and a comparable salary according to his qualifications.

3. That there be a Department of Black Studies which will grant a Bachelor's Degree in Black Studies; that the Black Studies Department, chairman, faculty, and staff have the sole power to hire faculty and control and determine the destiny of its department.

4. That all unused slots for Black students from Fall 1968 under the Special Admissions Program be filled in Spring 1969.

5. That all Black students wishing so be admitted in Fall 1969.

6. That twenty (20) full-time teaching positions be allocated to the Department of Black Studies.

7. That Dr. Helen Bedesem be replaced from the position of Financial Aid Officer and that a Black person be hired to direct it, that Third World people have the power to determine how it will be administered.

8. That no disciplinary action will be administered in any way to any students, workers, teachers, or administrators during and after the strike as a consequence of their participation in the strike.

9. That the California State College Trustees not be allowed to dissolve any Black programs on or off San Francisco State College campus.

10. That George Murray maintain his teaching position on campus for 1968–69 academic year.

THIRD WORLD LIBERATION FRONT

1. That a School of Ethnic Studies for the ethnic groups involved in the Third World be set up with the students in each particular ethnic organization having the authority and control of the hiring and retention of any faculty member, director, and administrator, as well as of the curriculum in a specific area of study.

2. That 50 faculty positions be appropriated to the School of Ethnic Studies, 20 of which would be for the Black Studies program.

3. That in the Spring semester the College fulfill its commitment to the non-white students in admitting those that apply.

4. That in the fall of 1969 all applications of non-white students be accepted.

5. That George Murray and any other faculty person chosen by non-white people as their teacher be retained in their positions.

University of California, Berkeley

JANUARY 21, 1969
THIRD WORLD LIBERATION FRONT

The Third World Liberation Front demands the following:

1. That funds be allocated for the implementation of the Third World College.

a. Department of Asian Studies: that positions and staff be set up to develop the Asian Studies Department controlled by Asian people.

b. Department of Black Studies as proposed by the AASU.

c. Department of Chicano Studies.

d. Department of Native American studies.

e. Any other third-world studies programs as they are developed and presented.

2. Third World People in Positions and Power:

Recruitment of more Third World faculty in every department and discipline and proportionate employment of Third World People at all levels, from Regents, Chancellors, Vice-Chancellors, faculty, administrative personnel, clerical, custodial, security, service personnel, and all other auxiliary positions and contractual vending services throughout the University system. Specifically and immediately:

1. Hiring of Third World Financial Counselors (Special Services).
2. Third World Chancellors in the University System.
3. Third World people put in the Placement Center as Counselors.
4. Third World Deans in the Letters and Science Departments.
5. Third World people in the Admissions Office.

3. Specific demands for immediate implementation:

a. Admission, financial aid, and academic assistance to all people in the Third World who apply to the University.

b. Thirty Work Study positions for the Chinatown and Manilatown projects, and 10 EOP counselors, including full-time Asian Coordinator.

c. Expansion of Work Study Program jobs to the AASU, East Campus Berkeley High School Tutorial Project (McKinley Project) to include at least 30 positions.

d. That the Center for Chicano Studies be given permanent status with funds to implement its projects.

4. Third World Control over Third World Programs:

That every University program financed federally or otherwise that involves the Third World communities (Chicano, Black, Asian, Native American) must have Third World people in control at the decision-making level, from funding to program implementation.

5. That no disciplinary action will be administered in any way to any students, workers, teachers, or administrators during and after the strike as a consequence of their participation in the strike.

6. These demands supersede any previous demands heretofore put forth by members of the Third World Liberation Front.

University of Chicago

JANUARY 23, 1969
COMMITTEE OF 85

There has been no positive response by the University to the demands of the open student meeting of Friday, January 15, that Professor Marlene Dixon be rehired and that students have equal control with faculty in all decisions on hiring and rehiring of faculty.

We regard the formation of the Gray Committee as an inadequate response to these demands. It is an excuse to waste time and to divert attention from the main issues. Further, it was improperly constituted.

We demand that 1) Marlene Dixon be rehired *jointly in Sociology and Human Development,* and 2) the principle of equal student control over hiring and rehiring of faculty, be accepted by the University no later than 9:00 A.M., Wednesday, January 29.

Unless these demands are accepted by this time, we will take militant action.

City College of New York

FEBRUARY 6, 1969
BLACK & PUERTO RICAN
STUDENT COMMUNITY

1. A separate School of Black and Puerto Rican Studies.
2. A separate freshman orientation for Black and Puerto Rican students.
3. That the SEEK students should have a determining voice in the setting of all guidelines for the SEEK program, including the hiring and firing of all SEEK personnel.
4. That the racial composition of the entering classes of City College reflect the racial composition of the City of New York public school system.
5. That Black and Puerto Rican history and the Spanish language be required of education majors.

Harvard University

APRIL 10, 1969
STUDENTS FOR A DEMOCRATIC SOCIETY
THE 8 DEMANDS

1. Abolish ROTC.
2. Replace ROTC scholarships with commensurate Harvard scholarships.
3. Restore scholarships of Payne Hall demonstrators.
4. Roll back rents in all Harvard-owned apartments to level of Jan. 1, 1968.
5. No evictions from Harvard's University Road apartments to make way for Kennedy Political Science Library facilities.
6. No eviction of black and white working people from the 182 units of Harvard housing to make way for affiliated hospital complex.
7. No punishment of any kind for anyone arrested at University Hall.
8. Black Studies as demanded by AFRO.

National Student Strike

MAY, 1970

We demand:

1) That the United States government end its systematic oppression of political dissidents, and release all political prisoners, such as Bobby Seale and other members of the Black Panther Party.

2) That the United States government cease its escalation of the Vietnam War into Cambodia and Laos, that it unilaterally and immediately withdraw all forces from Southeast Asia.

3) That the universities end their complicity with the United States war machine by an immediate end to defense research, ROTC, counterinsurgency research, and all other such programs.

APPENDIX B: REPORT OF THE PRESIDENT'S COMMISSION ON CAMPUS UNREST

Members of Campus Unrest Panel

Following is a list of the members of the President's Commission on Campus Unrest:

William W. Scranton, chairman, 52, former Governor of Pennsylvania.

James Ahern, 38, police chief of New Haven.

Erwin D. Canham, 66, editor in chief, The Christian Science Monitor.

Dr. James E. Cheek, 37, president of Howard University.

Benjamin O. Davis Jr., 57, Director of Civil Aviation Security, Department of Transportation.

Martha A. Derthick, associate professor of political science, Boston College.

Bayless Manning, 47, dean of the Stanford Law School.

Revius O. Ortique Jr., 46, a New Orleans lawyer.

Joseph Rhodes Jr., 22, a Junior Fellow at Harvard University.

The crisis on American campuses has no parallel in the history of the nation. This crisis has roots in divisions of American society as deep as any since the Civil War. The divisions are reflected in violent acts and harsh rhetoric, and in the enmity of those Americans who see themselves as occupying opposing camps. Campus unrest reflects and increases a more profound crisis in the nation as a whole.

This crisis has two components: A crisis of violence and a crisis of understanding. We fear new violence and growing enmity.

On the nation's campuses, and in their neighboring communities, the level of violence has been steadily rising. Students have been killed and injured; civil authorities have been killed and injured; bystanders have been killed and injured. Valuable public and private property, and scholarly products have been burned.

Too many Americans have begun to justify violence as a means of effecting change or safeguarding traditions. Too many have forgotten the values and sense of shared humanity that unite us. Campus violence reflects this national condition.

Much of the nation is so polarized that on many campuses a major domestic conflict or an unpopular initiative in foreign policy could trigger further violent protest and, in its wake, counter-violence and repression.

The Constitution protects the freedom of all citizens to dissent and to engage in nonviolent protest. Dissent is a healthy sign of freedom and a protection against stagnation. But the right to dissent is not the right to resort to violence.

Equally, to respond to peaceful protest with repression and brutal tactics is dangerously unwise. It makes extremists of moderates, deepens the divisions in the nation, and increases the chances that future protest will be violent.

We believe it urgent that Americans of all convictions draw back from the brink. We must recognize even our bitter opponents as fellow Americans with rights upon which we cannot morally or legally encroach and as fellow human beings whom we must not club, stone, shoot, or bomb.

We utterly condemn violence. Students who bomb and burn are criminals. Police and national guardsmen who needlessly shoot or assault students are criminals. All who applaud these criminal acts share in their evil. We must declare a national cease-fire.

There can be no more "trashing," no more rock throwing, no more arson, no more bombing by protesters. No grievance, philosophy, or political idea can justify the destruction and killing we have witnessed. There can be no sanctuary or immunity from prosecution on the campus. If our society is to survive, criminal acts by students must be treated as such wherever they occur and whatever their purpose.

Crimes committed by one do not justify crimes committed by another. We condemn brutality and excessive force by officers and troops called to maintain order. The use of force by police is sometimes necessary and legal, but every unnecessary resort to violence is wrong, criminal, and feeds the hostility of the disaffected.

Our universities as centers of free inquiry are particularly vulnerable to violence. We condemn those groups which are openly seeking to destroy them.

We especially condemn bombing and political terrorism. The full resources of society must be employed to bring to justice those who commit terroristic acts. Anyone who aids or protects terrorists, on or off campus, must share the moral and legal responsibilities for the crimes they commit.

We find ominous and shocking reports that students are laying in supplies of weapons and that others are preparing to take the law into their hands against protesters and minorities they dislike. There can be no place in our society for vigilantes, night-riders, or militants who would bring destruction and death upon their opponents. No one serves the law by breaking it.

Violence must stop because it is wrong. It destroys human effort. It undermines the foundations of a just social order. No progress is possible in a society where lawlessness prevails.

Violence must stop because the sounds of violence drown out all words of reason. When students and officials resort to force and violence, no one can hear. The nation is denied a vital call to conscience. It must stop because no nation will long tolerate violence without repression. History offers grim proof that repression once started is almost impossible to contain.

Campus protest has been focused on three major questions: war, racial injustice, and the university itself.

The first issue is the unfulfilled promise of full justice and dignity for blacks and other minorities.

Blacks, like many others of different races and ethnic origins, are demanding today that the pledges of the Declaration of Independence and the Emancipation Proclamation be fulfilled now. Full social justice and dignity—an end to racism, in all its human, social and cultural forms—is a central demand of today's students, black, brown and white.

A great majority of students and a majority of their elders oppose the Indochina war. Many believe it entirely immoral. And if the war is wrong, students insist, then so are all policies and practices that support it, from the draft to military research, from R.O.T.C. to recruiting for defense industry. This opposition has led to an ever-widening wave of student protests.

A third target of student protest is the shortcomings of the American university. The goals, values, administration and curriculum have been sharply criticized by many students. Students complain that their studies are irrelevant to the social problems that concern them.

They want to shape their own personal and common lives, but find the university restrictive. They seek a community of companions and scholars but find an impersonal multiversity. And they denounce the university's relationship to the war and to discriminatory racial practices.

Behind the student protest on these issues and the crises of violence to which they have contributed lies the more basic crisis of understanding.

Americans have never shared a single culture, a single philosophy or a single religion. But in most periods in our history, we have shared many common values, common sympathies and a common dedication to a system of government which protects our diversity.

We are now in grave danger of losing what is common among us through growing intolerance of opposing views on issues and of diversity itself.

A "new" culture is emerging primarily among students. Membership is often manifested by differences in dress and life style. Most of its members have high ideals and great fears. They stress the need for humanity, equality and the sacredness of life. They fear that nuclear war will make them the last generation in history.

They see their elders as entrapped by materialism and competition and prisoners of outdated social forms. They believe their own country has lost its sense of human purpose. They see the Indochina war as an onslaught by a technological giant upon the peasant people of a small, harmless and backward nation.

The war is seen as draining resources from the urgent needs of social and racial justice. They argue that we are the first nation with sufficient resources to create not only decent lives for some, but a decent society for all and that we are failing to do so. They feel they must remake America in its own image.

But among the members of this new student culture, there is a growing lack of tolerance, a growing insistence that their own views must govern, an impatience with the slow procedures of liberal democracy, a growing denial of the humanity and goodwill of those who urge patience and restraint, and particularly of those whose duty it is to enforce the law.

A small number of students have turned to violence; an increasing number, not terrorists themselves, would not turn even arsonists and bombers over to law enforcement officials.

At the same time, many Americans have reacted to this emerging culture with an intolerance of their own. They reject not only that which is impatient, unrestrained, and intolerant in the new culture of the young, but even that which is good. Worse, they reject the individual members of the student culture themselves.

Distinctive dress alone is enough to draw insult and abuse. Increasing numbers of citizens believe that students who dissent or protest, even those who protest peacefully deserve to be treated harshly. Some even say that when dissenters are killed, they have brought death upon themselves. Less and less do students and the larger community seek to understand or respect the viewpoint and motivations of the other.

If this trend continues, if this crisis of understanding endures, the very survival of the nation will be threatened. A nation driven to use the weapons of war upon its youth is a nation on the edge of chaos. A nation that has lost the allegiance of part of its youth is a nation that has lost part of its future. A nation whose young have become intolerant of diversity, intolerant of the rest of its citizenry, and intolerant of all traditional values simply because they are traditional, has no generation worthy or capable of assuming leadership in the years to come.

We urgently call for reconciliation. Tolerance and understanding on all sides must re-emerge from the fundamental decency of Americans, from our shared aspirations as Americans, from our traditional tolerance of diversity, and from our common humanity. We must regain our compassion for one another and our mutual respect.

There is a deep continuity between all Americans, young and old, a continuity that is being obscured in our growing polarization. Most dissenting youth are striving toward the ultimate values and dreams of their elders and their forefathers. In all Americans there has always been latent respect for the idealism of the young.

The whole object of a free government is to allow the nation to redefine its purposes in the light of new needs without sacrificing the accumulated wisdom of its living traditions. We cannot do this without each other.

Despite the differences among us, powerful values and sympathies unite us. The very motto of our nation calls for both unity and diversity: from many, one. Out of our divisions, we must now recreate understanding and respect for those different from ourselves.

Violence must end.

Understanding must be renewed.

All Americans must come to see each other not as symbols or stereotypes but as human beings.

Reconciliation must begin.

We share the impatience of those who call for change.

We believe there is still time and opportunity to achieve change. We believe we can still fulfill our shared national commitment to peace, justice, decency, equality and the celebration of human life.

We must start. All of us.

Our recommendations are directed toward this end.

Far more important than the particular recommendations of this commission are the underlying themes that are common to all:

¶Most student protesters are neither violent nor extremist. But a small minority of politically extreme students and faculty members and a small group of dedicated agitators are bent on destruction of the university through violence in order to gain their own political ends.

Perpetrators of violence must be identified, removed from the university as swiftly as possible, and prosecuted vigorously by the appropriate agencies of law enforcement.

¶Dissent and peaceful protest are a valued part of this nation's way of governing itself. Violence and disorder are the antithesis of democratic processes and cannot be tolerated either on the nation's campuses or anywhere else.

The roots of student activism lie in unresolved conflicts in our national life, but the many defects of the universities have also fueled campus unrest.

¶Universities have not adequately prepared themselves to respond to disruption. They have been without suitable plans, rules or sanctions. Some administrators and faculty members have responded irresolutely. Frequently, announced sanctions have not been applied. Even more frequently, the lack of appropriate organization within the university has rendered its response ineffective. The university's own house must be placed in order.

¶Too many students have acted irresponsibly and even dangerously in pursuing their stated goals and expressing their dissent. Too many law enforcement officers have responded with unwarranted harshness and force in seeking to control disorder.

Action—inactions—of government at all levels have contributed to campus unrest. The words of some political leaders have helped to inflame it. Law enforcement officers have too often reacted ineptly or overreacted. At times, their response has degenerated into uncontrolled violence.

¶The nation has been slow to resolve the issues of war and race, which exacerbate divisions within American society and which have contributed to the escalation of student protest and disorder.

¶All of us must act to prevent violence, to create understanding and to reduce the bitterness and hostility that divide both the campus and the country. We must establish respect for the processes of law and tolerance for the exercise of dissent on our campus and in the nation.

We advance our recommendations not as cure-alls but as rational and responsive steps that should be taken. We summarize here our major recommendations, addressed to those who have the power to carry them out.

Just as the President must offer reconciling leadership to reunite the nation, so all government officials—at all levels—must work to bring our hostile factions together.

Like the President, the Governors of the states should hold meetings and develop contacts throughout the school year to further the cause of reconciliation. Like the President, other Federal, state and local officials must be sensitive to the charge of repression and fashion their words and deeds in a manner designed to refute it.

We urge state and local officials to make plans for handling campus disorders in full cooperation with one another and with the universities. We urge the states to establish guidelines setting forth more precisely the circumstances that justify ordering the guard to intervene in a campus disorder.

We recommend that the Federal Government review all its current policies affecting students and universities to assure that neither the policies nor administration of them threatens the independence or quality of American higher education. At the same time Government should increase its financial support of higher education.

We urge public officials to reject demands that entire universities be punished because of the ideas or excesses of some members and to honor their responsibility to help preserve academic freedom.

We recommend that the Department of Defense establish alternatives to R.O.T.C. so that officer education is available to students whose universities choose to terminate on-campus R.O.T.C. programs.

We recommend greatly increased financial aid for black colleges and universities. All agencies of Government that support such institutions should massively increase their grants to enable these colleges to overcome past shortcomings.

We support the continuing efforts of formerly all-white universities to recruit black, Mexican-American, Puerto Rican, and other minority students, and we urge that adequate Government-sponsored student aid be made available to them. We recommend that in the process of becoming more representative of the society at large universities make the adjustments necessary to permit those from minority backgrounds to take maximum advantage of their university experience.

Bombing and arson pose an increasing threat to lives and property on campus. We urge prompt enactment of strict controls over the sale, transfer and possession of explosive materials. Such statutes are needed at both the Federal and state levels.

We have deep sympathy for peace officers—local and state police, national guardsmen and campus security officers—who must deal with all types of campus disorder. Much depends on their judgments, courage and professionalism.

We commend those thousands of law enforcement officers who have endured taunts and assaults without reacting violently and whose careful conduct has prevented violence and saved lives.

At the same time, we recognize that there have been dangerous and sometimes fatal instances of unnecessary harshness and illegal violence by law enforcement officers.

We therefore urge that peace officers be trained and equipped to deal with campus disorders, firmly, justly and humanely. They must avoid both uncontrolled and excessive response.

Too frequently, local police forces have been undermanned, improperly equipped, poorly trained and unprepared for campus disturbances. We therefore urge police forces, especially those in smaller communities, to improve their capacity to respond to civil disorders.

We recommend the development of joint contingency plans among law enforcement agencies. They should specify which law enforcement official is to be in command when several forces are operating together.

Sending civil authorities to a college campus armed as if for war—armed only to kill—has brought tragedy in the past. If this practice is not changed, tragedy will come again. Shoulder weapons (except for tear gas launchers) are very rarely needed on the college campus; they should not be used except as emergency equipment in the face of sniper fire or armed resistance justifying them.

We recommend that national guardsmen receive much more training in controlling civil disturbances. During the last three years, the guard has played almost no role in Southeast Asia but has been called to intervene in civil disorders at home more than 20 times.

We urge that the National Guard be issued special protection equipment appropriate for use in controlling civil disorders. We urge that it have sufficient tactical capability and nonlethal weaponry so that it will use deadly force only as the absolute last resort.

We urge that the President exercise his reconciling moral leadership as the first step to prevent violence and create understanding. It is imperative that the President bring us together before more lives are lost and more property destroyed and more universities disrupted.

We recommend that the President seek to convince public officials and protesters alike that divisive and insulting rhetoric is dangerous. In the current political campaign and throughout the years ahead, the President should insist that no one play irresponsible politics with the issue of "campus unrest."

We recommend that the President take the lead in explaining to the American people the underlying causes of campus unrest and the urgency of our present situation. We recommend that he articulate and emphasize those values all Americans hold in common. At the same time we urge him to point out the importance of diversity and co-existence to the nation's health.

To this end, nothing is more important than an end to the war in Indochina. Disaffected students see the war as a symbol of moral crisis in the nation which, in their eyes, deprives even law of its legitimacy. Their dramatic reaction to the Cambodian invasion was a measure of the intensity of their moral recoil.

We urge the President to renew the national commitment to full social justice and to be aware of increasing changes of repression. We recommend that he take steps to see to it that the words and deeds of Government do not encourage belief in those charges.

We recommend that the President lend his personal support and assistance to American universities to accomplish the changes and reforms suggested in this report.

We recommend that the President take steps to assure that he is continuously informed of the views of students and blacks, important constituencies in this nation.

We recommend that the President call a series of national meetings designed to foster understanding among those who are now divided. He should meet with the Governors of the states, with university leaders, with law enforcement officers and with black and student leaders. Each participant in these meetings should be urged to bring with him practical suggestions for restoring trust and responsibility among those whom he represents and commit himself to continue this process of national reconciliation in frequent meetings throughout the school year.

We strongly urge public officials at all levels of government to recognize that their public statements can either heal or divide. Harsh and bitter rhetoric can set citizen against citizen, exacerbate tension and encourage violence.

Every university must improve its capability for responding effectively to disorder. Students, faculty, and trustees must support these efforts. Universities must pull themselves together.

The university should be an open forum where speakers of every point of view can be heard. The area of permitted speech and conduct should be at least as broad as that protected by the First Amendment.

The university should promulgate a code making clear the limits of permissible conduct and announce in advance what measures it is willing to employ in response to impermissible conduct. It should strengthen its disciplinary process. It should assess the capabilities of its security force and determine what role, if any, that force should play in responding to disorder.

When criminal violence occurs on the campus, university officials should promptly call for the assistance of law enforcement agencies. When faced with disruptive but nonviolent conduct, the university should be prepared to respond initially with internal measures. It must clearly understand the options available to it and be prepared to move from one to another if it is reasonably obvious that an earlier tactic has failed.

Faculty members who engage in or lead disruptive conduct have no place in the university community.

The university, and particularly the faculty, must recognize that the expansion of higher education and the emergence of the new youth culture have changed the makeup and concerns of today's student population. The university should adapt itself to these new conditions. We urge that the university make its teaching programs, degree structure, and transfer and leave policies more flexible and more varied in order to enhance the quality and voluntariness of university study.

We call upon all members of the university to reaffirm that the proper functions of the university are teaching and learning, research and scholarship. An academic community best serves itself, the country, and every principle to which it is devoted by concentrating on these tasks.

Academic institutions must be free—from outside interference and free from internal intimidation. Far too many people who should know better—both within university communities and outside them—have forgotten this first principle of academic freedom. The pursuit of knowledge cannot continue without the free exchange of ideas.

Obviously, all members of the academic community, as individuals, should be free to participate actively in whatever campaigns or causes they choose. But universities as institutions must remain politically neutral, except in those rare cases in which their own integrity, educational purpose or preservation are at stake.

One of the most valid criticisms of many universities is that their faculties have become so involved in outside research that their commitment to teaching seems compromised. We urge universities and faculty members to reduce their outside service commitments. We recognize that alternative sources of university funding will have to be developed to take the place of the money attached to these outside commitments. Realistically, this will mean more unrestricted government aid to higher education.

Large universities should take steps to decentralize or reorganize to make possible a more human scale.

University governance systems should be reformed to increase participation of students and faculty in the formulation of university policies that affect them. But universities cannot be run on a one-man, one-vote basis with participation of all members on all issues.

Universities must become true communities whose members

share a sense of respect, tolerance, and responsibility for one another.

Students must accept the responsibility of presenting their ideas in a reasonable and persuasive manner. They must recognize that they are citizens of a nation which was founded on tolerance and diversity, and they must become more understanding of those with whom they differ.

Students must protect the right of all speakers to be heard even when they disagree with the point of view expressed. Heckling speakers is not only bad manners but is inimical to all the values that a university stands for.

Students must face the fact that giving moral support to those who are planning violent action is morally despicable.

Students should be reminded that language that offends will seldom persuade. Their words have sometimes been as offensive to many Americans as the words of some public officials have been to them.

Students should not expect their own views, even if held with great moral intensity, automatically and immediately to determine national policy. The rehetorical commitment to democracy by students must be matched by an awareness of the central role of majority rule in a democratic society and by an equal commitment to techniques of persuasion within the political process.

The commission has been impressed and moved by the idealism and commitment of American youth. But this extraordinary commitment brings with it extraordinary obligations: to learn from our nation's past experience, to recognize the humanity of those with whom they disagree and to maintain their respect for the rule of law.

The fight for change and justice is the good fight; to drop out or strike out at the first sign of failure is to insure that change will never come.

This commission is only too aware of America's shortcomings. Yet we are almost a nation of enduring strength. Millions of Americans—generations past and present—have given their vision, their energy, and their patient labor to make us a more just nation and a more humane people.

We who seek to change America today build on their accomplishments and enjoy the freedoms they won for us. It is a considerable inheritance, we must not squander or destroy it.

The text of the Conclusion of "The Killings at Jackson State," a special investigative report released by the President's Commission on Campus Unrest, October 1, 1970.

There must not be a repetition of the tragic incident at Jackson State.

We are heartened by the stated determination of Jackson city police and elected officials to take necessary steps to avoid the recurrence of tragedy at Jackson State College. It is imperative that this determination be reflected in action.

Chief Pierce has made it clear that the department policies with respect to the use of buckshot and birdshot will be re-examined. The chief testified that the police officers who lied to Sergeant Lee and the F.B.I. would be disciplined.

On the other hand, the reaction of the Mississippi Highway Safety Patrol to the deaths and injuries at Jackson State continues to be disturbing. Inspector Jones expressed the position of his patrol:

Q. Do you have any recommendations to make to the commission, particularly as it relates to command or control features for joint operation of law enforcement agencies, for this kind of thing if it should happen in the future?

A. No, sir; I don't.

Q. Does your department plan to take any corrective steps in view of what happened?

A. Not that I know of. . . . There was no doubt in my mind that some of us would have been killed down there if the volley of shots hadn't gone off, and I see no reason for disciplining a man for saving his own life.

Q. Does your department . . . plan to take any corrective steps in the future to prevent this?

A. Not that I know of.

We are also concerned with the escalation of rhetoric on the part of certain Jackson State students. While we understand the profound emotional impact of the deaths and injuries of fellow students, we condemn statements to the effect that the next time something happens "all the pigs" will not walk away from campus, or statements suggesting that students arm themselves because of anticipated future confrontations with police. We condemn any action on the basis of such statements even more strongly.

The commission has devoted a considerable portion of its efforts to the investigation at Jackson State and the parallel investigation of the May events at Kent State, which are the subject of a separate report. The lessons of Jackson State and Kent State are reflected in many of the recommendations the commission has made in the chapters of its report on campus unrest. The commission believes that if those recommendations are followed, the tragedy of Jackson State is far less likely to be repeated. Indeed, we believe that no one would have died at Alexander Hall if those recommendations had already been accepted and acted on by police and highway patrol units.

Even if there were snipers at Jackson State—a question on which we have found conflicting evidence—the 28-second barrage of lethal gunfire partly directed into crowded windows of Alexander Hall and into a crowd in front of Alexander Hall was completely unwarranted and unjustified.

The appropriate response to sniper fire is set out in Chapter 5 of our report. The guidelines stated there were violated in every respect at Jackson State. The police officers did not withdraw and seek cover even though they had an armored vehicle which would have provided ample cover.

The sniper team which was present at Jackson State did not fire single aimed shots at an identified sniper; instead a large number of peace officers fired shotguns loaded with buckshot or rifles loaded with armor-piercing ammunition into a crowded dormitory and into a crowd of protesters. Indeed, the police sniper team did not fire at all.

The peace officers did not have a mobilization plan, nor did they have a tactical plan directly agreed upon and understood by all the units involved. They had no formal chain of command and no clear notion of who was in command among the various police and military forces present.

They did not have a common radio channel for use during the disorder, nor did they have a central command post to provide liaison. The individual peace officers did not know, as they should, the destination and plan of their unit.

Furthermore, there had been no adequate consulation with college officials before the law enforcement officers were sent on the campus.

Jackson State officials must develop plans and procedures for dealing with campus disorders and for making prompt decisions if a disorder occurs. They should establish and maintain formal lines of communication with law enforcement agencies.

The authority and responsibility of campus security guards at Jackson must be clarified. A rumor center should be established during periods of campus disorder where students can obtain denial of rumored events.

All students, and particularly elected leaders, have a duty to condemn absolutely and unequivocally the use of force and violence. The aura of respectability that appears to surround violent protest when those protests are made in support of legitimate grievances must be eliminated. Possession or use of weapons on campus by students should be strongly condemned.

Students should recognize that the use of obscenities and derogatory terms such as "pigs" and "honkies" during a demonstration may trigger a violent if unjustifiable response by peace officers and that the use of such terms in every day speech in the presence of police officers escalates tension.

The Governor, the board of trustees of Mississippi's institutions of higher learning and the Mississippi Legislature should take whatever steps are necessary to insure that Jackson State College is developed rapidly to university status and that it becomes integrated.

The Federal and State Governments should provide long-term financial aid to Jackson State College—and to other predominantly black colleges—to insure that students attending these schools have opportunities equal to those available to students at predominantly white schools of comparable size.

The President should appoint a special adviser on black colleges. That adviser should prepare recommendations for specific Federal action in such areas as financial aid to black colleges.

The President and the Department of Defense must bring about integration of the National Guard at all ranks on more than a token basis. They should consider creation of additional positions to overcome the effects of past discrimination.

The President should direct the Department of Justice to review whether it would be appropriate for the United States to intervene in pending litigation to integrate the Mississippi Highway

Safety Patrol. In addition, the President should direct the preparation of any necessary legislation for authorizing action by the Federal Government to integrate police agencies.

The commission recommends that Federal, state and local officials take dramatic steps to reflect a commitment on the part of government to the protection of life and to the aggressive pursuit of equal justice—equal justice in the schools, in the courts, in jobs, and, most relevant of all to this investigation, equal treatment by policemen and just treatment of policemen.

By just treatment of policemen we mean that policemen receive recognition for the difficult job they have, particularly during times of civil disorders, and that unfair vilification of them be ended. We also mean that when policemen willfully violate the civil rights of black or white citizens, they should be prosecuted vigorously and fairly by the government.

The text of the Conclusion of "The Kent State Tragedy," a special investigative report released by the President's Commission on Campus Unrest, October 4, 1970.

Kent State was a national tragedy. It was not, however, a unique tragedy. Only the magnitude of the student disorder and the extent of student deaths and injuries set it apart from the occurrences on numerous other American campuses during the past few years. We must learn from the particular horror of Kent State and insure that it is never repeated.

The conduct of many students and nonstudent protesters at Kent State on the first four days of May, 1970, was plainly intolerable. We have said in our report, and we repeat: Violence by students on or off campus can never be justified by any grievance, philosophy, or political idea. There can be no sanctuary or immunity from prosecution on the campus. Criminal acts by students must be treated as such wherever they occur and whatever their purpose. Those who wreaked havoc on the town of Kent, those who burned the R.O.T.C. building, those who attacked and stoned National Guardsmen, and all those who urged them on and applauded their deeds share the responsibility for the deaths and injuries of May 4.

The widespread student opposition to the Cambodian action and the general resentment of the National Guardsmen's presence on the campus cannot justify the violent and irresponsible actions of many students during the long weekend.

The Cambodian invasion defined a watershed in the attitude of Kent students toward American policy in the Indochina war.

Kent State had experienced no major turmoil during the preceding year, and no disturbances comparable in scope to the events of May had ever occurred on the campus. Some students thought the Cambodian action was an unacceptable contradiction of the announced policy of gradual withdrawal from Vietnam, or that the action constituted invasion of a neutral country, or that it would prolong rather than shorten the war. Opposition to the war appears to have been the principal issue around which students rallied during the first two days of May.

Thereafter, the presence of the National Guard on campus was the focus of discontent. The Guard's presence appears to have been the main attraction and the main issue for most students who came to the May 4 rally. For students deeply opposed to the war, the Guard was a living symbol of the military system they distrusted. For other students, the Guard was an outsider on their campus prohibiting all their rallies, even peaceful ones, ordering them about and tear gassing them when they refused to obey.

The May 4 rally began as a peaceful assembly on the Commons—the traditional site of student assemblies. Even if the Guard had authority to prohibit a peaceful gathering—a question which is at least debatable—the decision to disperse the noon rally was a serious error. The timing and manner of the dispersal were disastrous. Many students were legitimately in the area as they went to and from class. The rally was held during the crowded noon-time luncheon period. The rally was peaceful, and there was no apparent impending violence. Only when the Guard attempted to disperse the rally did some students react violently.

Under these circumstances the Guard's decision to march through the crowd for hundreds of yards up and down a hill was highly questionable. In fact, the Guard never did disperse the crowd. The crowd simply swarmed around them and re-formed again after they had passed. The Guard found itself on a practice football field far removed from its supply base and running out of tear gas. Guardsmen had been subjected to harassment and assaults, were hot and tired, and felt dangerously vulnerable by the time they returned to the top of Blanket Hill.

When they confronted the students, it was only too easy for a single shot to trigger a general fusillade.

Many students considered the Guard's march from the R.O.T.C. ruins across the Commons up Blanket Hill, down to the practice football field, and back to Blanket Hill as a kind of charade. Tear gas canisters were tossed back and forth to the cheers of the crowd, many of whom acted as if they were watching a game.

Lieut. Alexander D. Stevenson, a platoon leader of Troop G., described the crowd in these words:

> At the time of the firing, the crowd was acting like this whole thing was a circus. The crowd must have thought that the National Guard was harmless. They were having fun with the Guard. The circus was in town.

The actions of some students were violent and criminal and those of some others were dangerous, reckless and irresponsible. The indiscriminate firing of rifles into a crowd of students and the deaths that followed were unnecessary, unwarranted and inexcusable.

The National Guardsmen on the Kent State Campus were armed with loaded M-1 rifles, high velocity weapons with a horizontal range of almost two miles. As they confronted the students, all that stood between a guardsman and firing was the flick of a thumb on the safety mechanism, and the pull of an index finger on the trigger. When firing began, the toll taken by these lethal weapons was disastrous.

The Guard fired amidst great turmoil and confusion, engendered in part by their own activities. But the guardsmen should not have been able to kill so easily in the first place. The general issuance of loaded weapons to law enforcement officers engaged in controlling disorders is never justified except in the case of armed resistance that trained sniper teams are unable to handle. This was not the case at Kent State, yet each guardsman carried a loaded M-1 rifle.

This lesson is not new. The National Advisory Commission on Civil Disorders and the guidelines of the Department of the Army set it out explicitly.

No one would have died at Kent State if this lesson had been learned by the Ohio National Guard.

Even if the guardsmen faced danger, it was not a danger which called for lethal force. The 61 shots by 28 guardsmen certainly cannot be justified. Apparently no order to fire was given, and there was inadequate fire control discipline on Blanket Hill. The Kent State tragedy must surely mark the last time that loaded rifles are issued as a matter of course to guardsmen confronting student demonstrators.

Our entire report attempts to define the lessons of Kent State, lessons that the Guard, police, students, faculty, university administrators, government at all levels, and the American people must learn—and begin, at once, to act upon. We commend it to their attention.

Note to the Reader

If you know of any good documents we've missed, please send them to us, care of Random House.

IMMANUEL WALLERSTEIN of the Department of Sociology at Columbia University was very active in the events leading up to, during, and after the Columbia revolt of 1968. He was chairman of the Faculty Civil Rights Group (1966–69), a member of the Steering Committee of the Ad Hoc Faculty Group (April 1968) and the first Executive Secretary of the Executive Committee of the Faculty formed on May 1, 1968. Author of *University in Turmoil: The Politics of Change* (1969), he has also written many books and articles on contemporary Africa.

PAUL STARR, twenty-one, was an undergraduate at Columbia during the 1968 revolt at that university. A co-author of *Up Against the Ivy Wall,* a narrative of the rebellion, he served as editor-in-chief of the *Columbia Daily Spectator* from March 1969 to March 1970. He is now a graduate student in sociology at Harvard.